BEAUTIFUL COUNTRY
Stories from Another India

SYEDA SAIYIDAIN HAMEED
GUNJAN VEDA

HarperCollins *Publishers* India
a joint venture with

New Delhi

First published in India in 2012 by
HarperCollins *Publishers* India
a joint venture with
The India Today Group

ISBN: 978-93-5029-130-6

2 4 6 8 10 9 7 5 3 1

Syeda Saiyidain Hameed and Gunjan Veda assert the moral right
to be identified as the authors of this work.

HarperCollins *Publishers*
A-53, Sector 57, Noida 201301, India
77-85 Fulham Palace Road, London W6 8JB, United Kingdom
Hazelton Lanes, 55 Avenue Road, Suite 2900, Toronto, Ontario M5R 3L2
and 1995 Markham Road, Scarborough, Ontario M1B 5M8, Canada
25 Ryde Road, Pymble, Sydney, NSW 2073, Australia
31 View Road, Glenfield, Auckland 10, New Zealand
10 East 53rd Street, New York NY 10022, USA

Typeset in 11/14 Arno Pro at
InoSoft Systems Noida

Printed and bound at
Thomson Press (India) Ltd.

Dedicated to the resilient and courageous women and men of India whose ordinary lives and extraordinary spirit inspired us to write this book.

Zard patton ka ban
Zard patton ka ban jo mera des hai
Dard ki anjuman jo mera des hai
Clerkon ki afsurda janon ke naam
Kirm khurda dilon aur zubanon ke naam
Post manon ke naam
Taange walon ke naam
Rail banon ke naam
Kaarkhanon ke bhooke jiyalon ke nuum

> – Faiz Ahmed Faiz: Dedication to his *Complete Works*

Wilderness of yellowing leaves
Wilderness of yellowing leaves, this my land
Assembly of pain, this my land
To the sad lives of clerks
To the deadened hearts and tongues
To postmen
To tongawallahs
To railway men
To hungry youth in factories.

Contents

Foreword by Montek Singh Ahluwalia   ix

Preface   xiii

1. Assam & Meghalaya   2

2. Manipur & Nagaland   25

3. West Bengal   58

4. Andaman & Nicobar Islands   84

5. Kerala & Tamil Nadu   131

6. Maharashtra   163

7. Gadchiroli & Ganiyari   185

8. Uttar Pradesh   209

9. Himachal Pradesh, Punjab & Haryana   237

10. Kashmir   263

11. Ladakh   279

12. Rajasthan   299

13. Madhya Pradesh   332

     Postscript   355

     Abbreviations   359

     Notes on Select Government Schemes   361

     Acknowledgements   367

Foreword

D r Syeda Hameed joined the Planning Commission in 2004 and it was shortly thereafter that she submitted her first report on a visit to an ICDS centre in one of the remoter parts of the country. I was struck by the quality of her writing. Syeda has the ability to make things come alive in a way that government reports festooned with official statistics can never do. I was reminded of the lines from *The Little Prince* by Antoine de Saint-Exupery, where he makes the telling point that adults think that only those things are true that can be described by numbers, whereas in fact it is much more interesting to describe things the way they really are.

Grown-ups love figures. When you tell them that you have made a new friend, they never ask you any questions about essential matters. They never say to you, 'What does his voice sound like? What games does he love best? Does he collect butterflies?' Instead, they demand: 'How old is he? How many brothers has he? How much does he weigh? How much money does his father make?' Only from these figures do they think they have learned anything about him. If you were to say to the grown-ups: 'I saw a beautiful house made of rosy brick, with geraniums in the windows and doves on the roof,' they would not be able to get an idea of that house at all. You have to say to them: 'I saw a house that cost $20,000.' Then they would exclaim: 'Oh, what a pretty house that is!'

How true.

This volume is a collection of Syeda and her young colleague Gunjan Veda's travel experiences, each one extraordinarily readable, evocative and provocative, even if not festooned with statistics. I recall acknowledging to them that though these reports were essentially anecdotal, they made dangerously powerful reading. They were somewhat disturbed by my use of the term 'anecdotal', as it seemed to be a criticism. I explained that what I meant was that any description of what went on in a particular school or ICDS centre or health clinic would always be subject to the charge that it is not a representative sample. With six lakh villages in the country, assessments of facilities at the village level based on a few, or even several dozen village centres, cannot be presented as a reliable description of the average. There is also the danger that we cannot be sure that the choice of villages is truly random and not influenced by the fact that these are the areas where the problems are more severe.

Syeda was gracious enough to recognize the statistical limitation I was concerned with, and since then she repeatedly qualified her findings with, 'Although they may be anecdotal but…' However, she remained an enthusiast for field visits and, with Gunjan, she produced numerous reports, all in her characteristically stylish prose. The reports provided graphic descriptions of the realities on the ground in the villages visited, with a mix of some heartening examples of initiatives that work but unfortunately also several heart-rending examples of those that don't!

Over time, I began to look forward to the reports as providing very useful feedback, and suggested to them that they should be published, with a suitable acknowledgement that they may not represent a scientifically random sample. I felt that these reports would bring to a wider audience a sense of the experience in different parts of the country based on personal observation, rather like Kusum Nair's *Blossoms in the Dust* which in the 1960s attracted a great deal of attention in the development community. This led to Syeda and Gunjan converting their five years of travel from Planning Commission into a thirteen-chapter book with the evocative title *Beautiful Country: Stories from Another India*. I am delighted that the reports have been turned into a volume which HarperCollins has decided to publish.

Knowing Syeda and Gunjan, I have no doubt that the reports collected here represent the truth, and nothing but the truth, about the places they visited. Of course, the essence of the problem of unrepresentative samples that I have mentioned is that they may not report the whole truth! For that we have to go to the numerous reports buttressed with statistical tables which are supposed to provide a balanced picture. However, I have no doubt that the reality reflected in this volume is all too true in a large number of cases. It represents a condition which we must acknowledge and also do something about. I do believe, and Syeda would not deny, that in many ways things are getting better than they used to be but indisputably they are not nearly as good as they should be while the expectations of our people are rightly rising and we cannot rest until they are met.

If this book persuades the reader that there is much that is being done but much more that needs to be done, it will have accomplished a useful purpose. Ideally Syeda and Gunjan should visit the same villages five years later and document whether they find them better and by how much. I look forward to that second volume.

New Delhi
26 January 2012

Montek Singh Ahluwalia
Deputy Chairman
Planning Commission
Government of India

Preface

Khol aankh zamin dekh falak dekh fiza dekh
Mashriq mein ubhar tey huey suraj ko zara dekh
Iss jalwa-e-be parda ko pardon mein chhupa dekh
Ayyam-e-judai ke sitam dekh jafa dekh

Open your eyes, look at the earth and the sky
Look at the sun rising gloriously in the east
Look at its unveiled glory hidden behind veils
Suffer the pain and torture of days of deprivation

These lines from Mohammad Iqbal's poem 'Rooh-e-arzi Adam ka istiqbal karti hai' (Spirit of the Earth welcomes Adam) from *Bal-e-Jibril* (Gabriel's Wing) reflect the five years we spent wandering across the country as part of our work in the Planning Commission. Five years of discovery and learning, of frustration and hope. Five years of coming to terms with the reality of India and of attempting to bring about some change.

Beautiful Country traces the journey of two women, one who has gone through life's countless by-lanes and served the country in both public and private capacities. The other, a young student of conflict studies, who brings to the book the perspective of 540 million Indian youth. Before we begin recounting our experiences, perhaps you, our reader, would like to know who we are and what made us write a narrative about our encounter with this country's gard aur gardish, dust and movement.

Syeda and Gunjan are the two people who make up the 'we' of this book. In five years, we travelled to different nooks and corners of the country, from the dhanis of Udaipur to the hamlets of Arunachal; from the scattered villages of Ladakh to the densely-populated bastis of Gaya; from the gallis of Varanasi to the forest dwellings of the indigenous tribal groups of the Andamans. These forays into the known, and often unknown, parts of the country, have revealed to us what we think is the 'real India'; an India which does not make it to the front page of newspapers, which has not been captured by the roving cameras of the 24x7 media channels, and which till today remains invisible to most Indians.

Syeda Hameed: I began my term as Member, Planning Commission, Government of India, on 1 July 2004. I came from an arts and humanities background, having studied in universities in India, the US and Canada. Over the years, my work came to be centred around the disciplines of gender and development but rather than being academic in nature, it became grounded in activism. I travelled extensively throughout the country to investigate and report on issues related to women, regardless of caste, creed or class. Holding investigations, public tribunals and jan sunwais (public hearings) were my forums. I also wrote articles and poems in journals and newspapers, wherever I could publish them.

One day, I got a phone call from the Prime Minister's Office. 'Mr Gujral would like to appoint you as Member of the National Commission for Women,' said the voice on the other end. It was fantastic news. Now I was to be part of the institutional mechanism created to stop injustices against women. For the next three years, I struggled to bring some justice to the few who crossed my path from among the 500 million women of my country. I learnt from my dear friend and firebrand activist, Mohini Giri, to jump into the fray without thinking of the consequences. My state of mind mirrored the philosophy of Iqbal for whom aql (reason) was always a poor second to the far superior ishq (love):

Be khatar kood pada aatish-e-Namrood mein Ishq
Aql hai mehv-e-tamasha-e-lab-e-baam abhi

Love jumped fearless in the fire of Nimrod
Reason stood at the edge watching the spectacle

It took me a year to understand that the mandate of the National Commission for Women (NCW) was not to firefight but to make systemic changes which would impact the lives of millions of women. The NCW term ended for me with some regret and some relief. I captured my experiences in a book of short stories about ten women whom I had met during my tenure. It was titled *They Hang: 12 Women in My Portrait Gallery*. The book sank without a trace; those who read it said they could not sleep until they had put it down. But no one marketed it, least of all me, since I have no skills in this direction.

When the government of Prime Minister Manmohan Singh nominated me as a Member of the Planning Commission, I found myself surrounded by economists, scientists, administrators, educationists and experts in several fields, all males, all of whom had been in the high echelons of academia and administration. My special quality, I think, was my unending interest in listening to people's voices and in recording what I had heard. So, for five years I travelled with my notebook to remote corners, sparsely inhabited places, crowded urban spaces and ghettos of India. My experiences were my 'chashm deed gawahi' (eyewitness accounts) of what I saw, especially what interested me the most, the social sectors. At the end of five years, I had prepared thirty-five reports, which I was told were unlike the reports normally submitted in government circles. My accounts centred on ordinary people, how they lived, what they felt, how they coped; they were not analysis of questionnaires. They did not involve data collection, sample surveys and random and control group samples. I used the existing data; but also my eyes, ears and heart, and asked many questions to understand and mentally process all that I witnessed. Within government circles, my work was appreciated, ignored, included and excluded. In one of my reports, which described a wonderful experiment in a remote corner of Maharashtra that helped reduce neonatal mortality, the prime minister wrote in his own hand: 'This should be upscaled all over the country.'

⌒

Gunjan Veda: I have been studying conflicts for most of my adult life. I began by analysing the 'low-intensity' armed conflict in the north-eastern state of Nagaland during my college days and went on to look at strife-torn Manipur and 'disturbed' Northern Ireland. I still remember the day I entered 'the corridors of power', not as a visitor, but as one of the many who were a part of it. It was in May 2005. I had been appointed as a consultant to the only woman member of the Planning Commission, one who was also perhaps the only activist in Yojana Bhawan. I had been to this building once before to make a presentation, but that had been different. Then I was on the other side, trying to convince the policy makers about what I believed in, what I was fighting for. Now I was going to be one of them. My emotions at this point were, at best, conflicting. I had always been on the side that criticized and evaluated the government, first as a journalist and then as a civil society activist. Now I was entering the very structure that I had questioned all these years. Most people who knew me were surprised at my decision: 'You and the government?' To some extent, so was I. But beneath the trepidation, there was excitement. As a journalist, I was often frustrated at not being able to bring about a change. I could see and show, hear and be heard. But that was it. I remember, after one such outburst my mentor warned me: 'You are a journalist, not an activist.' But even when I became an activist, I still had limitations. Now was my chance to make a difference.

I remember when I first met Syeda I told her why I wouldn't fit in. 'I'm a field person. I can't sit inside all day and study programmes. I need to be up and about, to see, hear and learn.'

'Well, then *don't* sit inside,' she said quite simply. 'In any case, it doesn't make sense to sit in air-conditioned rooms and make policies without knowing the people for whom these policies are being made.' I knew then that I had found a kindred spirit. She was voicing my own thoughts.

My first official visit, one that will forever be etched in my mind, was to the Andaman Islands. It had been a few months since the tsunami and we were going to take stock of the relief activities. It was a series of firsts for me. For the first time I stayed in a Raj Bhavan, debated with officials, flew in a chopper to remote islands and experienced the sheer devastation that nature could unleash. Perhaps this is why the Andamans have always held a special place in my heart. From then on, life was a whirlwind. My family had often joked that I was a nomad, someone who could never stay in one place. Now they were convinced. In five years, I visited every state of this country, looking into issues of health and nutrition, documenting the condition of artisans and their priceless arts, analysing the performance of flagship schemes and searching for innovations. In a desperate bid to record and capture everything, I took hundreds of pictures. My camera and my writing pad became extensions of my being.

No amount of reading or instruction could have taught me what I learnt in these five years. Henry Miller once said: 'One's destination is never a place, but a new way of seeing things'. As a twenty-four-year-old, I had been handed a rare opportunity to connect with my country and its people; to see and understand the everyday realities of life. The experiences humbled me. I learnt to be less judgemental. I saw first-hand the consequences of all that ails our system. Yet, for the first time, I realized how easy it was to blame the government for everything; stepping inside and instituting change was much more difficult. I recognized how isolated all of us are despite being connected through the news, media and the World Wide Web.

The first few visits gave me many sleepless nights. To see so much misery was unbearable. Gradually, I learnt to fight the distress. The resilience of the people I met in the flooded lands, crowded gallis and forgotten mohallas of our country taught me to hope, to believe. The sleepless nights continued, albeit for different reasons. It was no longer the haunting images of the day that kept me up but my resolve to find a way to change them. I discovered that the government and the bureaucracy are not one homogenous entity, as we often think of them. Just like this country, they are made up of different kinds of people. The most intelligent, compassionate and driven people share corridors and cubicles with some of the most corrupt and inefficient. Yes, there are problems. But there are also solutions. Finding these solutions and becoming a part of their implementation despite all the systemic obstacles became my quest.

In his book *The Prince of Tides*, Pat Conroy writes: 'Once you have traveled, the voyage never ends, but is played out over and over again in the quietest chambers. The mind can never break off from the journey'. It was six years ago, on an enervating summer afternoon that my journey began. It continues today.

∽

We were two witnesses to this vast country as it unfolded before our astonished eyes. We did not begin our course with a set agenda, set places to visit, set people to meet. Our journey just happened in a flow. At times, we were invited by ordinary people who hoped our visit would focus the government's attention on their area. We remember a few incidents which define our experiences. One such incident happened in Gyanpur village in Badohi District, Uttar Pradesh, where we were invited to a public hearing by activist couple Rajiv and Rolee Singh. Hearing about our arrival, a few Tehsil officers had also arrived. The issue was starvation deaths and about 2,000 people from nearby villages had collected. We sat on a rickety stage with intense sun beating at our backs, while women, men and children came up to tell their stories.

The face of Kanti Devi, with three small children clinging to her, became in our minds the face of poverty. Her complexion was blue-black; it blended with her blue sari, the end of which she had pulled over her head. Many months later, when photographs were being selected for this book, a dermatologist friend who happened to be looking at them pointed at Kanti Devi and said: 'A classic case of lead poisoning. The water around her village must be poison!'

Another such incident happened in Thane District, Maharashtra, in a tiny village in Jawahar Tehsil. We had been invited there by an organization, the Shetkari Sangathan. Almost 3,000 women had turned up from all over Thane for the public hearing. Most of them were single or widowed and all of them were destitute. Once again, the issue was hunger; they wanted Antyodaya cards, BPL cards, any piece of paper that could get them rice and wheat at Rs 3 a kg. 'They ask me for my address,' said a bent, wrinkled Kalavati Shinde. 'What can I say... I live under a tree?'

In Palamu District, Jharkhand, in 2009, this issue was once again before us. People on the edge of starvation had collected at a venue very close to the collectorate. The stories were the same as the ones we had heard in Badohi and Thane, but with their own singularities. 'What address can I give for my ration card' asked an old tribal man, looking straight into our eyes. 'When I build my house with leaves, the wind blows it off; when I build it with mitti (mud), the rain washes it away.'

On our return from such field visits, we called meetings, shared our findings, demanded explanations but also spent sleepless nights. The urgency to do more kept us awake. Over the months we realized the enormity of our task. The rot in the system had penetrated deep and was so well-rooted in tradition and norm that it was a Sisyphean task.

Our journeys, however, were not just about despair. Yes, we encountered misery. But we also found knowledge, wisdom and above all, hope. We discovered innovations, tales of great courage and resilience hidden away and invisible to many. These stories of hope were the adrenalin which gave us the impetus to carry on. We wanted to shout them out from the rooftops and carry them to the rest of India for in them we found the true beauty of our nation.

One story is that of Aamir Khan, who made films like *Taare Zameen Par* and placed dyslexia on the national agenda. He also stood up for handloom weavers whose skill is regarded by some people in government as a 'sunset industry'. Along with Kareena Kapoor, his co-star in *3 Idiots*, he went to the home of a weaver in Chanderi District, Madhya Pradesh, and announced to the youth of India: 'You think we are the kalakars! The real kalakars are these. Dress sharp, dress fashion, dress handloom!' Then there was Jalaja Chandran, president of a panchayat in Alleppey District, Kerala. She had turned to food processing to bring in an annual revenue of Rs 10 million for her panchayat. There were youth of the Matri Janshakti Sangathan in Jalpaiguri District, West Bengal, who decided to form bands and save villagers from being mauled by wild elephants. There were young girls in Kargil, with dupattas covering their heads, who aspired to become members of the Ladakh Development Council and the young blind boy in Vijaynagar District, Arunachal Pradesh, who sang 'Yeh Bharat desh hai mera', his sightless eyes shining with a strange light. And, finally, on Strait Island, Andaman and Nicobar, there was a small old woman with a head of close-cropped grey hair who told us softly of the extinction of her tribe of Great Andamanese people. She was the last living member of the Bo tribe. She died in 2010, ending one of the world's most ancient lineages.

Our book tries to capture this real, invisible India and to take it to the people, both in the country and around the world; to share with them the experiences, the knowledge, the wisdom, the despair and the hope this India has given us. It is a journey through a land which represents different things to different people. To some it is exotica, a land of mystery and romance, to others it is the country of mega malls, IT geniuses and a 10 per cent growth rate, and yet to others, it is a vibrant democracy embarrassed by the poverty, despair and illiteracy of its people. We found India to be all this and much more. It is a nation where ordinary village women have been trained to fight neonatal deaths, where children are willing to walk three hours every day to get an education, where bright, young doctors have given up big pay packets and the comforts of city life to provide health in tribal hinterlands. A country where thousands of skilled hands weave magical tales on their looms and yet waste away because of hunger; where sometimes young men are trampled by elephants in closed tea estates; where women of all ages still lift the solid waste of others; where people live on tiny riverine islands which are flooded every year. India is home to a helpless Maimun Nisa from Benaras, who has fed her two-and-half-year-old son nothing but sabudaane ka paani (tapioca water) since he was born. Yet it is also the birthplace of Rani Ahilyabai Holkar, who through her wisdom and foresight etched a design palette on the walls of the temples she built on the banks of River Narmada, a palette which till today provides livelihood to thousands of weavers. India can boast of a place called Malerkotla in the heart of Punjab which epitomizes tolerance and religious understanding. But it also has Khajrana, a slum in Indore, where innocent men, women and children were gunned down in a communal frenzy instigated by an event that occurred in far-off Jammu and Kashmir.

The perspective that we offer in this book is an inter-generational one. What emerges is a phad (folk) painting created by two pairs of hands – and hearts and minds – that come from divergent backgrounds. We have forged it with the fervour of youth, the mellowness of age, and the lens of different faiths, backgrounds, education and ethos. With these diverse perspectives, we worked as a team, moving over a terrain which was as variegated as us. What kept us together was the ability to see hope even in the bleakest of situations. We laughed and cried even as we tried to make course-corrections. We believed in people being the best agents of change. We also believed that, in the end, justice would prevail.

Beautiful Country is our story of five years as planners. It is the story of a nation whose beauty lies not just in its natural and cultural bounty, but in the resilience and the creativity of its people, in their ability to carry on despite all odds. It does not offer solutions or make predictions. It does not even attempt an in-depth analysis of pressing problems. It only shares. We leave it to you, our readers, to look at the composite picture and draw your own conclusions.

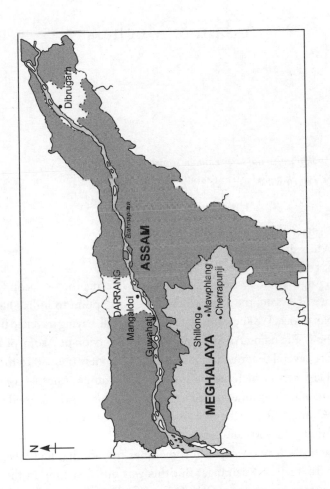

1

Assam & Meghalaya

Anokhi wa'za hai sarey zamane se nirale hain
Ye ashiq kaun si basti ke yaarab rehne waley hain

– IQBAL

Distinct in their style, unique in the world
Where do these lovers come from, Oh God!

In August 2007, we found ourselves in Dibrugarh, the second largest city of Assam, the state which is the entry point to India's beautiful North east. We knew this state relatively well, having travelled through much of it. The name 'Assam' is an anglicized version of 'Asom' or 'Axom'. There are several theories about its origin. One view traces it to the Bodo word 'Ha-Cham', which means 'low or level country'. Another ascribes it to 'Asama', meaning 'unequalled' or 'peerless'. This word was used to refer to the Ahom, a Shan tribe that ruled this land for six centuries from the thirteenth century AD onwards.[1]

Sometimes it was work and sometimes friends that had taken us to Guwahati, Tezpur, Kaziranga. But this was our first time in the state's north-eastern region and its hub Dibrugarh. Dibrugarh's name is derived from the nearby River Dibaru or Dibru, whose confluence with the mighty

---

[1] http://online.assam.gov.in/web/guest/historyofassam?webContentId=1093 44, accessed in Nov 2011.

Brahmaputra is about eighteen km east of the city. We had read that the city had been devastated by the great earthquake of 15 August 1950, with its epicentre in Rima on the border of China and Arunachal. The earthquake, measuring 8.6 on the Richter scale, raised the bed of the Brahmaputra, causing severe erosion on its south bank; as a result, the Dibru river got merged with its master stream in Rahmaria Mouza.

Dibrugarh has an interesting location. It is bounded by Dhemaji District, and a part of Lakhimpur District in the north, Sibsagar District and Arunachal Pradesh in the south, Tinsukia District in the east and another portion of Sibsagar in the west. All along the north-western boundary of the district flows the magnificent Brahmaputra, a wide and braided rope of water. Near the city it is ten km wide. It runs right up to the Patkai foothills in the south, with a total length of ninety-five km.

Our flight over the state followed the course of the great river. At first glance, it seemed as if the entire area was flooded; large chunks of barren brown land were surrounded by lazy stretches of equally brown water. Gradually we realized that what we saw below was no deluge but a slow devastation orchestrated by the leviathan as it chipped away at the armour of the surrounding land mass bit by bit. The steep slope, large volume of water of the river and its high-velocity flow together cause large-scale bank erosion – erosion that is constantly changing the boundaries of Assam's many towns and cities, all of which have thrived on the banks of the Brahmaputra for centuries. As it laps in circles around valiant sandbars of various sizes, some of them inhabited, the mighty river appears deceptively calm, almost sluggish. But we were not fooled – we had experienced its force in other parts of the state.

It was an hour's drive from Dibrugarh to the banks of the river from where we were to set off on our journey. Upon reaching the banks, we stood still for a moment to register the full force of the current.

We were hesitant to walk on the narrow plank placed between the shore and the large waiting boat. Too many eyes were watching our steps. The plank stretched some twenty feet from the bank across the slush to the deck. Our guides had told us that it had been raining non-stop for twenty days. Today, however, the sun was finally shining. The *Akha* (Assamese for 'asha' or 'hope'), the 'Ship of Hope' on which we were to ride that morning (beneath the ship's name on the mast were written these three simple words) was gleaming in the sunlight. This ship is the vehicle for the delivery of healthcare to tribes which live in some of the remotest human habitations of the state. To be honest, it was stories of the Akha that had drawn us to this historic town and its surrounding chars.

In preparation for our travels, we had read about the chars or the chaporis (pronounced 'saporis') of Assam. These riverine islands of varying sizes are formed out of the silt that comes along with the river currents. After some years, the silt collects and is covered by weeds and grasses. Gradually, humans and animals move to the larger and the more habitable of these sandbars. They are, however, subject to the constant mood swings of the great river that surrounds them. It is not an easy life, and yet, at 690 persons per square km, the density of population on these riverine islands is more than double that of the entire state.[2]

We knew of Majauli, the biggest char in the world, currently a UNESCO Heritage site. It was from this island that the young activist Sanjoy Ghosh was abducted and killed. We had read news clippings about the conditions of the char people but had never actually seen one until the day we crossed the immense Brahmaputra on the Akha. The ship was anchored in Maijan Ghat, an hour's drive from town. Our cars stopped at a tea garden from where we picked our way through the monsoon slush. The team was led by Sanjoy Hazarika, a former *New York Times* journalist who is managing trustee of the Centre for North-East Studies and Policy Research (C-NES). It was in the C-NES building in downtown Guwahati that the idea of *Akha* was first mooted. In his travels on the Tsangpo (the Chinese name for the Brahmaputra), one of the world's greatest rivers, spanning three nations, India, China and Bangladesh, Sanjoy realized the complete dependence of millions of people on the river for their livelihood, transport and communication. One of his conclusions was that the river itself could be used to respond to some of the problems and challenges people faced. Most

---

[2] http://www.hinduonnet.com/fline/fl2518/stories/20080912251803600.html, accessed in June 2009; http://newsblaze.com/story/20091130135508shan.nb/ topstory.html, accessed Nov 2011

of the chars lack basic services: health, schools, electricity, drinking water and sanitation. So why not use water transport to relieve this deprivation?

Some three million people or 12 per cent of the state's population live on 2,500 islands of the Brahmaputra. Most of these are poor migrants or tribals. At last count, there were 2,300 villages floating, on the river (many chars and, hence the villages on them, are semi-permanent). Country boats are the only means of connectivity, and these are usually dugouts pulled by oars. During floods, people's lives are shattered. Every year, lakhs of women, children and men become homeless and take shelter in temporary relief camps. Here, they huddle together for weeks, waiting for the water levels to recede.

The *Akha* was a small-size ship, twenty-two metres long and four metres wide. It had a beautiful deck on which we rode. It also had an OPD, cabins for medical staff, a small kitchen, toilets, crew quarters and a general store. Sitting on the deck, watching the magnificent river, we thought of the reach and grasp of the National Rural Health Mission that we had witnessed over the last four years. The NRHM is one of the government's flagship schemes, meant to deliver adequate and affordable healthcare to rural India. 'Have you ever thought about the chars?' Sanjoy had asked us in Delhi. 'Here, thousands of people live their lives in adverse conditions, cut off from mainland by a fast and furious river. The challenge is to give them access to basic health. How will they get sub-centres, leave alone Primary Health Centres? They don't even have drinking water.'

That morning, watching a mist rising on the Brahmaputra while the sun shone bright and harsh, we thought of the multiple complexities of our demography and terrain. The chars are flat lands, gently resting on the waters. Vulnerable to the undulation of the river, they have no protective mangroves and plants such as the ones we had seen all over the Andaman Islands (see Chapter 4), which had acted as a protective shield against the 2004 tsunami.

Our hour-long journey across the deceptively calm river was taking us to Dodhia Sapori. On the river we heard the rest of the *Akha*'s story. In 2004, when the concept of a boat health centre was showcased by C-NES, it won an award at the World Bank's India Development Marketplace Awards. With the award money, construction of the boat started. Carpenters from Dholla and Tinsukia worked tirelessly under the supervision of the engineer, Kamal Prasad Gurung. In June 2005, the ship that would bring hope to the lives of thousands of forgotten char dwellers was completed. Since then, the *Akha* has made regular trips to these small riverine islands, organizing medical camps, immunizing little children and providing basic medicines.

By now, we had almost reached our destination and we had our first real taste of the difficulties of living here. The ship could not get right up to the sapori. We had to drop anchor some distance away and climb into a 'phatphat boat', a noisy jugad (makeshift) boat-taxi to reach the island. The slush was almost knee-deep. We removed our shoes and walked through the tall khaironi (a type of grass used in building roofs), brushing against the sharp blades, dreading the insects and snakes lurking in the wetlands. The island was inhabited entirely by the Mishing, who are related to the Adi tribe of Arunachal Pradesh. They are also called the Miri. As we trudged on, it was evident that, until twenty-four hours ago, this land had been submerged in water.

We stopped at the first dwelling, a house built on stilts. On the verandah of the house, a stocky young man was sitting on his haunches along with his two sons. Bhaity Phaike was eight years old, and Lakhima Phaike was three. Their father was a schoolteacher but the school was flooded, and no children came. So he was at home, watching the flurry of activity that starts each time the *Akha* drops anchor. Waving goodbye to the Phaike family, we went deeper into the village called Kuligaon or Dodhiakule. Plodding through the khaironi we reached the building where the health camp was being run. This multi-purpose facility was also on stilts and served as a school, an anganwadi, and a sub-centre. It consisted of one large room fronted with a verandah. When we reached, a few patients were waiting outside. Two hours later the place was filled with people. Mishing women, in bright coloured shawls (which also served as baby slings) and sarongs which they had pulled up to mid-thigh were walking through the waist length khaironi grass. Babies were strapped to their backs as they stopped to wash their feet at a hand pump installed at the base of the centre. The doctors sat on the school benches, and consultation was going on across the school desks. Nurses examined women patients in a corner and referred them to the doctors in the room. Medical supplies, neatly arranged in one side of the room, were dispensed by a pharmacist. The place was buzzing with life; healthcare had been carefully extended to the most deprived of our people.

Dolly Champa Mishing was a cheerful young anganwadi worker. She had been called there to answer our questions. She said she had forty registered children 'as per the rules'. But there was nothing for them to eat. Her anganwadi had received no supplies. We asked about her qualifications. 'I have completed my matriculation. My salary is Rs 1,000, but I have not received it for the last three months,' she said.

Watching the doctors and nurses busy at work was elating, as C-NES, working in partnership with Government of Assam, the NRHM and UNICEF, had taken healthcare to forgotten people on the riverine islands of the Dibrugarh, Dhemaji and Tinsukia districts of Upper Assam. Healthcare had thus reached 10,000 people, including many children who would otherwise never have been immunized. But the challenge persisted because individual genius, which experiments and triumphs over adversities, is rarely used as a model for upscaling and replication. The government has the resources and the mandate to create a thousand 'Ships of Hope' which would bring health to people who are at the receiving end of a volatile and moody river. What we need is the humility and willingness to learn from those who have successfully experimented. With *Akha*, a beginning had been made; it is now up to us to follow it through.[3]

After Dibrugarh, our next destination was Darrang, the district neighbouring Guwahati. The name 'Darrang' originates from the Sanskrit word 'dwaram', which means a 'duar' (pass or gateway). In the past, there were some fixed duars on the northern side of the district through which the various hill tribes descended to the plains from the Himalayan ranges. Some of the areas still have the suffix 'duar' to their names. One of the six passes on the northern side of the present district is called Khaling Duar. In 1826, Darrang, like the rest of Assam, passed into the hands of the British after the Treaty of Yandabu. In 1933, it became a district with

---

[3] In 2008, the NRHM entered into partnership with C-NES to launch more boat clinics. By the end of 2010, fifteen boat clinics were operational in thirteen districts.

Mangaldoi as its headquarters. The current district of Darrang was created in July 1983, and at the time comprised only of the erstwhile sub-division of Mangaldoi.[4]

Today Darrang District has 653 villages and a population of 7.59 lakh people. It is a relatively poor district, with an average landholding of less than two bighas (a traditional measure of land, about one-third of an acre). More than 50 per cent of its population comprises Muslims, mostly Bangladeshi migrants. Less than five per cent of the population is SC (Scheduled Caste), and one per cent is tribal. In October 2008, this district witnessed violent communal clashes between the ethnic Bodo and the Bangladeshis. Thousands of families fled to shelter camps as their homes and hearths were reduced to rubble. However, when we visited the area in March 2008, the countryside appeared calm. Women and men were busy at work in their fields, in NREGS projects and in tea gardens. There were few brick houses in the area. Most homes were bamboo structures caked with mud. Amidst these indicators of poverty, however, stood the ubiquitous rooftop antennas, heralding Darrang as a new entrant to the country's infotainment fixation.

Having seen the condition of healthcare in the riverine islands of Dibrugarh, we wanted to see the condition of health centres in the interior of Assam. Darrang District is seventy km from the state capital. After about an hour's drive from Mangaldoi on broken country roads, our cars came to a halt in front of the Bajnapathar Community Health Centre. This CHC was five years old, with a thirty-bed capacity. At noon, when we reached, it was empty and locked. As we waited for some staff to turn up we met two brothers, Kushal and Milan Rajbanshi, who lived next door to the CHC.

'Where is everybody?' we asked.

'Didi, the Medical Officer (MO) was transferred six months ago. Since then, this hospital has been khallas (over). The last doctor they gave us was an ayurvaid (Ayurvedic practitioner), who was transferred along with the MO. Three months ago, the nurse, too, was transferred.'

---

[4] http://darrang.nic.in/; http://assamonline.in. Viewed in May 2009; Last accessed in Nov 2011

'What do you do when you fall ill?'

'Sometimes a nurse didi comes here from Guwahati but most of the time we have to go there. It's a one-hour journey by boat. Or we go to a pharmacy ten km away. When the doctor comes, he charges a Rs 20 flat fee for injections, fever, cuts and wounds.'

We turned back to the CHC. Unlike in other places where the CHCs we had seen were little more than a skeletal structures, Bajnapathar had a proper building. But the windows were boarded up and a lock hung on the front door. A windowpane was broken, so Milan thrust his hand in and opened the door. Inside, there were empty beds all around. Some equipment was visible among the piles of trash. We wondered if someone was using the place as a shelter at night. A woman walked up. 'I am Malati Rajbanshi,' she said. (The entire village was made up of the Rajbanshi tribe.) She told us that she had never heard of any deliveries taking place at this centre. Deliveries were conducted in the village by family dais (midwives). She had never heard of ASHAs or community health workers, and looked blank when we asked about the Janani Suraksha Yojana.

The Rajbanshi of the village knew nothing about the National Rural Health Mission. We compared this ground reality with the official version given to us at our meetings. Examples like Darrang were considered anecdotal evidence. When questioned by us the officials averred that this was a case of 'being at the wrong place at the wrong time'! Though we had been witness to too many such anecdotes, we were not able to stitch individual pieces into a compelling argument.

Having sampled the health infrastructure of Darrang, we moved to the village anganwadi centre. It was a small bamboo hut. There was a hand pump outside but we were told that the water was not potable because of its high iron content. A middle-aged woman, Nitimoni Devi, was the supervisor of twenty-eight different anganwadi centres. She said her biggest worry was the lack of rations with which she could feed the children 'Didi, at Bajnapathar AWC, they have received no food for one whole year, since February 2007. In fact, none of the centres I supervise have received rations since November 2007. It is heartbreaking to see the kids starving, and yet I can do no more than register a complaint at the district level.'

We had seen enough to realize that conditions in Assam (among other states) would ensure that we remain far from our own monitorable targets. Standing under the hot March sun, the road to rural health appeared long and ardous; nothing much might happen in the short term of our tenure unless we redoubled our efforts. Just as we were getting into the car with these thoughts, someone blocked our way. A slender, bespectacled young woman was standing in front of our sarkari Ambassador on the dusty road. She was out of breath. 'Miss Jili Das,' she said holding out her hand. 'I heard about your visit and have cycled three km from the Suktaguri Anganwadi No. 1. I had to meet you.'

Jili lived with her father, Binod Das, in the village of Khalikai Gandhiyapathar. She had studied in northern Guwahati, passed the higher secondary exam, and taught in a lower primary school for one year. Then she was appointed as an anganwadi worker and sent here. For one year she had received no food for the children. 'The village where I work is very poor, and a flood-prone area. Most of the 6,000 people there are migrant Muslims. Parents work as migrant labour and leave the children with me. Families are large as no sterilization can be carried out. People think they will incur Allah's wrath if they do so. We have only two AWCs. We need at least two more. We need toilets. There are a lot of skin diseases in our area. I have received no de-worming tablets for two years. I go from house to house and meet pregnant women but I have no rations to give them. I can only give them iron tablets which I get from the ANM. Even our village school has not received any food or books this year. It is so hard to watch the kids study on empty stomachs. Please help me.' The sweat from her forehead made tracks down her face as she looked at us with desperation in her eyes.

'What about you? Do you get your salary?'

She bowed her head. 'No, I haven't received anything for four months.' As we looked at this frail-looking girl standing before us, we realized that in her grit and humility there was still hope for this country. She was a living symbol of these lines of the poet Sahir Ludhianvi which were written to honour hope:

Jab ambar jhoom ke naache ga aur dharti naghme gaayegi
Voh subah kabhi toh aayegi

When the sky will break into a dance and the earth into song
That dawn will one day break

We wanted to write down Jili's contact details to ensure that her case was heard and the children of her village were taken care of. Jili looked at both of us with a shy smile. 'I can write,' she said.

We handed her a diary. In a beautiful neat hand she wrote:

Miss Jili Das 38 years

Centre – LNO Suktaguri

Kuruh Chapari

L.P. School

Our last stop was the CHC at Kharupetia. This large facility with thirty beds was empty despite the fact that it catered to a population of three lakh people (triple the norm) and was supposed to operate 24x7. As we went inside the CHC, we found most of the rooms locked. There was no sign of any patients. Suddenly there was a slight commotion. A burqa-clad woman walked in, supported by an older woman and a thin young man. She was barely able to stand.

'What has happened to her?' we asked.

The old woman answered, 'Asma, my daughter-in-law. She is eight months pregnant.'

We could see that the girl was in pain. We shouted for the doctor.

'We have come from Mandalpura village,' the husband, Ibrahim Shaikh said. 'But I will not allow a male doctor to attend to her. Let her follow her kismet (fate) and we will accept His will.'

We were angry and ready to scold him for his rigidity at a time when the girl was writhing in pain. But the MO, Dr Benoy Das, when he arrived, was calm. He simply said, 'I will refer her to the Mangaldoi Civil Hospital. As it is, only primary care is provided here. No surgery or operation has been performed for a long time.'

We looked at the MO in disbelief. After a quick tour of the hospital, we returned to look for Asma. She was gone. Whether to Mongaldoi or to serve His will, we will never know.

∽

A two-and-half-hour drive along meandering roads packed with smoke-spewing vehicles and trucks took us from the crowded streets of Guwahati to the picturesque hills of Meghalaya.[5] Literally 'the abode of clouds', this state is nestled amongst mountains which were once verdant and now bear the marks of human greed and callousness. In its better days, Meghalaya was called the 'Scotland of the East'. Formed in 1972 by grouping together the Khasi, Garo and Jaintia hills, Meghalaya is a relatively peaceful part of the north-east. It is also resource rich; there are large reserves of limestone, coal and uranium[6] in addition to good hydro-electric power potential. Its capital, Shillong, with the famous North-Eastern Hill University, has long been the hub of learning for the entire region. Formed in 1864 by the adventurous Commissioner of Assam,[7] Col. Henry Hopkinson, Shillong was for a very long time the capital of Assam (under the British). It was here that the British found refuge from the hot and humid climate of the Assam Valley. It was here that they established a military cantonment to keep an eye on the entire north-east region.

The word 'Shillong' comes from 'U Shylong', a supernatural half-deity of the hills born of a virgin, human mother.[8] With quaint little wooden houses dotting the hillside and lovely walks along the Ward's Lake located in the

---

[5] Meghalaya is a small state in north-east India, bounded by Assam in the north and Bangladesh in the south. It has a population of 2.3 million or twenty-three lakhs (2001 Census) and an area of 22,720 square km. Currently, it is divided into seven administrative districts: Ri-Bhoi, East Khasi Hills, West Khasi Hills , East Garo Hills, West Garo Hills, South Garo Hills, Jaintia Hills. Four tribal groups, the Khasi, Jaintia, Bhoi and War, inhabit east Meghalaya. They are said to belong to the Proto-Austroloid Monkhmer race, one of the earliest inhabitants of the Indian subcontinent. The Garo Hills are peopled by the Garo, who belong to the Bodo family of the Tibeto-Burman race said to have migrated from Tibet. The Garo prefer to call themselves Achik, and the land they inhabit as 'Achik Land'. See http:// meghalaya.nic.in; accessed on 9 December 2008.

[6] In fact, uranium mining in the state has been a very controversial issue.

[7] The Directorate of Information and Public Relations, Government of Meghalaya, *Meghalaya* (Calcutta, Government of Meghalaya, 1991) p.9.

[8] Ibid

centre of the city, Shillong could be any tourists' dream but for the never-ending line of honking vehicles and ever-present traffic jams. Despite the flashing red light and blaring sirens of our government cars, negotiating the town's traffic was not easy. Once outside Shillong, however, the beauty of the countryside left us wordless; only Li Po's words spoke to us:

> All the birds have flown up and gone
> A lonely cloud floats leisurely by.
> We never tire of looking at each other—
> Only the mountain and I.[9]

An hour later, the cars stopped at a place called Laitlum. In the Khasi language, 'lait' means 'peak' and 'lum' means 'hill'. Rolling green meadows were hiding behind playful clouds that seemed to bounce off the greens. We followed a narrow trail that led straight into the clouds. A few paces ahead of us the world ended. We felt as though we could stretch our hands and touch the rim of the horizon. Suddenly, as we reached what seemed the end of the world, a whole new vista opened up; a deep valley surrounded by tall peaks daintily dressed in bottle green and white. At a distance, we saw a small dab of colour. A few minutes later it turned into a young Khasi woman carrying a little child on her back. She was wearing a simple Khasi outfit – a blouse, a plaid blue-and-black body cloth (called the ka jympien), and a plum-coloured shawl which was thrown over her shoulders like a cloak and knotted in front (called ka jain kup). Panting, cheeks red from the effort of climbing, hazel eyes and betel-stained mouth, she was the picture-perfect Khasi woman. She gave us a quick smile as she perched herself on a rocky ledge. As early as 1914, P.R.T. Gordon, the then Commissioner of Assam, said of the Khasi:

> The people are cheerful in disposition, and are light-hearted by nature, and, unlike the plains people, seem to thoroughly appreciate a joke. It is pleasant to hear on the road down to Theriaghat from Cherrapunji, in the early morning, the whole hillside resounding with the scraps of song and peals of

---

[9] Li Po, *Alone Looking at The Mountain*; Cited in Jean Elizabeth Ward, *Li T'ai Po: Remembered*, Lulu.com, 2008, p 22-23. Available online at Google books.

laughter of the coolies, as they run nimbly down the short cuts on their way to market. The women are especially cheerful, and pass the time of day and bandy jokes with passers-by with quite an absence of reserve.[10] This cheerful woman fitted Gordon's description well.

The woman introduced herself as Annemaria; she had been trekking for the last five hours with her child to visit her sister in a nearby village. 'Look there,' she said, pointing towards the outstretched valley, 'My village, Mawphor, is hidden behind those clouds. We are around thirty families. There is no road, not even a kutchcha mountain tract. Actually, roads here are impossible. To go anywhere we have to climb. Whatever we need, we carry. Even little kids can walk long distances with head loads,' she explained. She patiently answered our questions in Khasi while an accompanying official translated. 'No, there is no anganwadi for the little ones. Who will bring the supplementary nutrition all the way to the village? We do have a school. It started recently.' After chatting with us, Annemaria straightened the cloth with which her tiny son was tied to her back, knotted her shawl loosely across her shoulders and set off once again. We watched her receding figure until she disappeared into the mist.

Our next destination was a quaint little hospital called John Herbal, located in a hamlet called Thangsning (literally meaning 'to burn a pig'). The village is about twenty km from Shillong. People from all over the north-east come to the hospital here, seeking treatment for ailments ranging from diabetes and arthritis to cancer and epilepsy. John Herbal is run by Dr John W. Khardiut, a lean, middle-aged Khasi man with salt-and-pepper hair and moustache. When we saw him, he was attending to his patients in a well-tailored grey suit.

Twenty-five years earlier, Dr John was just another semi-literate truck driver plying the roads of Meghalaya. One day, he decided to take another road. He remembered all that he had learnt watching his grandmother and uncles as they gathered and sorted the herbs from the mountain behind their village. He wrote down on a piece of paper the names of these herbs. Astonishingly, the list amounted to 112 different herbs. This was the first

---

[10] Lt General P.R.T Gordon, *The Khasis*, London: Macmillan, 1914, p 4

step towards what later developed into full-time work and a small hospital. Today, he owns seven hectares of land where he grows the herbs and is planning to start a research centre. Behind his neat little hospital in a small shed is stored his biggest treasure, herbs in neatly labelled containers. These are used for treating thirty out-patients and seven in-patients every day.

Punoti Phukan was one such patient. She had come to this clinic all the way from Digboi in Assam. We saw her walking slowly around the small hospital campus, each step taken with great difficulty, a wooden stick helping her to maintain balance. 'Due to a spinal injury, I was unable to walk, stand or sit. The first time I came here was on a stretcher. This is my third visit. Not only can I sit and stand now, with this stick, I can even walk,' she said, eyes sparkling with excitement. The recovery of Phukan and many others like her bring patients from afar to this little hospital hidden amongst the mountains. We met some others – a Khasi boy, no more than three years old, afflicted by epilepsy; an elderly Khasi woman with arthritis; a young Assamese woman diagnosed with stomach cancer. Such is his success that Dr John treats not just Indian patients, but visits the UK and the US at least thrice a year to provide treatment. His patients include the family of the Meghalaya governor, M.M. Jacob, Meghalaya's former chief secretary, D.K. Gangopadhyay and a host of the region's top army officers.

Barely five kilometres from Thangsning is the legendary village of Smit, an important Khasi landmark and a must visit for anthropologists and tourists. Every year, thousands of tourists come here to witness the traditional Nongkrem Festival where the Khasi thank the Almighty for a good harvest. In Meghalaya there are two main ethnic groups – the Garo, who inhabit the Garo Hills, and the Khasi, who inhabit the Khasi and Jaintia Hills. The Garo are of Tibeto–Burmese origin. It is believed that their ancestors were among the group of people who migrated to Myanmar from western China via Tibet and Assam. It was around 400 AD when they were driven out of the Irrawady and Chindwin valleys of Myanmar and found refuge in the Garo Hills.[11]

Khasi is the generic name for a number of communities like the Khyriam, the Pnar, the War, the Bhoi and the Lyngngam. It is believed that the Khasi

---

[11] DIPR, Government of Meghalaya, *Meghalaya*, p. 45-46.

are a mix of the Mongoloid (from west and south China) and the Proto-Australoid (or Austric) groups of people. The latter are believed to be among the first inhabitants of India, and include central Indian tribes like the Santhal, the Ho and the Munda.[12] The Khasi language is a part of the Mon Khmer group[13] (a branch of Austric languages), but there is no Khasi script. The story goes that once a Khasi and a Bengali were caught in a great flood and had to swim to save themselves. The Bengali tied his bundle of books on his head and started swimming. The Khasi held his books in his mouth by biting on them. Suddenly, a huge wave swept over them. Gasping for breath, the Khasi accidentally swallowed his books. His knowledge was safe but the script was lost![14] When the Welsh Calvinistic Methodist Mission came to Meghalaya in 1842, they studied the Khasi language and gave it a Roman script.[15]

Interestingly, the myths of origin of the Khasi bear many similarities with those of the Khmer of Cambodia.[16] According to Khasi legend, there was a huge tree called U Lum Sohpetbueng on top of a dome-shaped hill to the north of Shillong. This was used as a ladder by sixteen celestial families to travel between heaven and earth. One day, when seven of these families descended to earth, one among them cut the mighty tree with an axe, severing their connection with heaven. The Khasi believe that these seven families, known as Ki Hynniew Trep, were the first people on earth and it

---

[12] Ibid, p.41-43. In a book titled *The Khasis*, (London: Macmillan, 1914), Lt-Col. P. R. T. Gurdon, commissioner of the Assam Valley Districts and Honorary Director of Ethnography in Assam, extensively researched the affinity of the Khasi with the Naga, the Mon, the Khmer, the Dravidian, the Mongoloid and other ethnic groups. This is a thorough study of Khasi myths, traditions, costumes and cultural practices. The book is available online at http://www. archive.org/stream/khasis032728mbp/khasis032728mbp_djvu.txt.

[13] The name 'Mon Khmer' is derived from the Mon of south Burma and south-west Thailand and the Khmer of Cambodia.

[14] http://www.cherrapunjee.com, accessed on 26 November 2008.

[15] C. J. Lyall in *The Khasis*, op.cit. p xvii

[16] http://www.rupaliparda.com/khasi/introduction.htm, accessed on 1 December 2008; Last visit Nov 2011

is from them that all nations evolved.[17] The Khasi are divided into different clans which are headed by syiems or chiefs. All important decisions for the clan, administrative as well as judicial, are taken by the durbar (king's council) headed by the syiem and comprising myntries (ministers).

We stood before Balajied Sing, the syiem of the Khyriem clan. Behind him was his enormous house made of wood and bamboo in the midst of a large compound at the centre of the village of Smit. The syiem told us that his house was known as 'Ling Sad' meaning 'the House of the Holy and Supreme'. Traditionally Ka Siem Sad or the high priestess is the spiritual head of the Khyriem clan; she lives in the Ling Sad along with the syiem, who is usually her son, nephew or some distant male relative. Not a single piece of metal or nail is used to build this house. We looked at the Ling Sad very closely to see if we could find a stray metal rivet somewhere but none was to be found. Sing told us that earlier every village had a Ling Sad in accordance with the Niam Khasi religion, closely linked to nature worship. Now his house in Smit is the only Ling Sad left in the Khasi Hills.

The next day, we headed to Cherrapunji, which we knew from school days as the wettest place in the world. Nothing ever dries here; 'dampness,' to misquote Shakespeare, 'is all'. On the way, we stopped at an anganwadi in the village of Mylliem. The centre was built next to a school. It had a neat toilet and a few swings. As soon as we entered, to our great embarrassment, all the children started crying. We were shocked. 'What happened?' we asked the young ICDS worker who was trying very hard to quieten a three-year-old boy. She gave us an embarrassed smile, picked up the child whose nose had started running, and took him out. Meanwhile, her helper took a few other children outside but the collective crying only got louder and hoarser.

'Will someone tell us what is happening? What have they done to the kids?' we said to the accompanying officials in a whisper, afraid of scaring the children any further.

---

[17] The Directorate of Information and Public Relations, Government of Meghalaya, *Dwellers of the High Hills: The Khasis of Meghalaya* (Shillong, Government of Meghalaya, 2002), p.13-16; Soumen Sen, 'Belief, Legend, Religion and Identity: The Khasi Story Of Ki Hynniew-Trep', *Journal of the Folklore Research Department, Gauhati University,* Vol. 1, No. 1 (July 2008), pp. 27-31.

'They are afraid of strangers,' an official explained.

'We have visited anganwadi centres in every state. Never before did the kids start crying like this.'

By now, the young woman had come back after herding the kids outside. 'Just a couple of days ago, we had an immunization drive. When the children saw you come in, they were afraid of being poked,' she said simply. 'Just look outside.' We looked out of the window, the children were indeed laughing and playing on the swings. It was a happy sight.

Our next destination was the village of Nongkynrih. This place is known all over the state for its beautifully carved bows and arrows. We had heard that it wasn't football or cricket that caught the imagination of the Khasi; their favourite sport is still archery. In fact, Rong Biria, as the game is known, is also a religious tradition. When a person dies, arrows are shot in three directions. According to Khasi lore, Eve (Ka-mei-ka-nong hukum) gave birth to two sons. She taught them to shoot arrows but warned them against fighting over the game.[18] Since then, the hills and valleys of the area have echoed with the twang of bows. Between January and May, in many Khasi villages, weekly competitions are held where men – young and old – line up to display their shooting skills. The bows and arrows for this sport are made in this village – Nongkynrih – where we stood on a crisp August morning.

Climbing a rickety flight of wooden stairs, we entered a home where bows and arrows were being made. Feathers were scattered everywhere. An elderly man was busy slicing bamboo shafts. He got up to greet us and told us about his work. 'There are 200 families here that make bows and arrows. We buy vulture and eagle feathers from hunters, it costs as much as Rs 1,200 for a pair of wings from which we can get 200 arrows. The women make the arrows and the men, the bamboo shafts,' he said. His hands continued to slice the bamboo deftly. 'My family manages to make one hundred arrows and seven bows in a week. Each arrow sells for Rs 15 and a bow for Rs 60; our weekly income is Rs 1,400.' As he spoke and sliced, his wife cleaned the feathers and glued them onto the arrows. By the time we left the house, our hair and shawl had tiny black-and-white flecks of feather.

---

[18] Gordon, Op.cit, p.55.

At the village school, a dilapidated hut, there was no water supply. We saw a dozen pink-cheeked kids sitting on broken desks and chairs writing exams under the supervision of a teacher. This Khasi Mr Braithwaite (as in *To Sir, With Love*) had a betel-stained mouth with no front teeth. He spoke with some diffidence. 'There are ninety students, four teachers and four classes. There is a toilet but it is unusable as there is no water. Cooking is done in the open, so if it rains students have to go without food.'

As he spoke, we kept thinking about his lack of oral hygiene and what an example he must set for the young children! But then the deep red betel-stained mouth is a characteristic of the Khasi. In his study of the Khasi, anthropologist Gordon says, 'They are inveterate chewers of supari and the pan leaf (when they can get the latter), both [sic] men, women, and children; distances in the interior being often measured by the number of betel-nuts that are usually chewed on a journey.' Such is their devotion to the supari that the Khasi expression for the departed is 'ula lam kwai ha iing u Uei', meaning 'he who is eating betel nut in God's house'.[19]

The Khasi always greets visitors with a kwai (a combination of leaf of the betel vine, a piece of betel nut, and a smear of lime paste). The story goes that, long ago, there were two friends, one rich, the other extremely poor. One day, the rich man visited the home of his poor friend. The pauper entreated his wife to borrow food from the neighbours to welcome his friend. The wife went looking for food but no one was willing to trust the penniless couple. Humiliated and ashamed, she came home and killed herself. Soon, the man came to the kitchen and saw his dead wife. Distraught and embarrassed, he too, killed himself. The rich friend, who was wondering at the absence of his hosts, went inside and, on seeing their dead bodies, was filled with guilt and remorse and promptly took the kitchen knife and stabbed himself. Meanwhile, some villagers were chasing a thief who ran to hide in this very house. When the villagers came in and saw the three dead bodies, they realized what had happened. So it was announced that, henceforth, it would be sufficient to present a guest with a kwai to express hospitality. The Khasi believe that the betel leaf is symbolic of the wife and

---

[19] Ibid, p. 105. Full text available at http://www.archive.org/stream/ khasis032728mbp/khasis032728mbp_djvu.txt

the betel nut of the husband; the lime represents the friend who adds punch to life. Tobacco, which is usually hidden inside the mouth, is reminiscent of the thief who hid in the house of the poor couple.[20]

Leaving the betel-chewing teacher and his students, we got into our car and resumed our journey towards Cherra. Looking out of the window, we saw that parts of the mountains had been gouged out. The hills looked fragile in their tattered green cover. The officials accompanying us spoke of people using water pumps to bring down the sand and granite, thereby destroying much of the tree cover. Broom grass, a popular cash crop that saps the soil of all nutrients, was being planted everywhere. Illegal mining is widespread in the Khasi Hills. This uncontrolled, private and often amateur mining for coal and limestone is leading to the desertification of the landscape. Trees and forests have given way to grassy patches. Soon, these may also disappear. We learnt that, in Meghalaya, the coal seams are not deep; coal is hidden between the sandstone. The diggers just make holes, go in, extract coal with their shovels, and move on. This is known as rat-hole mining. They do not bother to refill the holes, and soon enough the hills crumble. The diggers take out the 'black diamond' at their peril. No safety measures are followed. They go inside the coal shafts which are full of methane gas with candles and without helmets. As we crossed Laitryngew, a hundred-year-old coal mine, we saw mounds of black coal along the road. The long-term consequences of this repeated abuse was written all over the scarred rocks.

Soon, however, we reached a spot which was yet to be soiled by human greed. It was pure magic; on one side of the road was lush green growth, on the other billowing powder-white clouds. The road ahead was invisible. This journey into the unknown was nothing short of mystical. As we turned back to look, we noticed that even our tyre marks had disappeared. We were moving from nothing to nothing.

Finally, we reached Cherrapunji or Sohra, as it is now called. Besides its rainfall, this town is famous for its limestone caves and orange honey. Here we learnt that though 90 per cent of the tourist traffic to Meghalaya visits Cherra, it hardly benefits the local economy. Most tourists come here on day trips from Assam or Shillong. They bring their own packed lunches so

---

[20] http://www.cherrapunjee.com, accessed on 28 November 2008.

the roadside dhabas (eateries) go empty. During peak season, a hundred taxis and fifty–sixty buses visit the area every day. Patiently the town receives them but gets nothing in return.

At Cherra, we met some villagers. Dainty, Moonlight, Rain, Fairly, Newton, Hardy – the Khasi names were unlike any other we had ever heard. 'The advent of the Welsh missionaries and the partial dissemination of English education have in some cases produced rather peculiar names,' writes Gordon. 'I quote some instances: U Water Kingdom, Ka Mediterranean Sea, Ka Red Sea; U Shakewell Bones, U Overland, Ka Brindisi, Ka Medina, Ka Mary Jones, U Mission, and Ka India.'

Moren Khonglam, a middle-aged man dressed in a white shirt, had come from Rymmai Khatarshnong, three-and-half hours from Laitryngew. The area is inaccessible and he had to walk over six hours to get to Cherra. The fatigue from the long journey was evident on his already wrinkled face. Hildamon Khonsit was a young man from the village of Dingsong. 'My village is located deep in the mountains. To get to the road there is a steep uphill climb for two km. Pregnant women, the sick and the elderly can never make it on their own. We tie them to chairs or put them in baskets and lift them up. But in case they are too heavy, they have to be left behind,' he explained. For residents of the village of Nonpriang, the situation is no better. It is a three-hour-long treacherous climb from their village to Cherra.

In 1914, Gurdon noted:

Khasis carry very heavy burdens, it being the custom for the coolie of the country to carry a maund or 82 lbs weight, even more occasionally, on his back, the load being fixed by means of a cane band which is worn across the forehead; women carry almost as heavy loads as the men. The coolies, both male and female, commonly do the journey between Cherrapunji and Shillong, or between Shillong and Jowai, in one day, carrying the heavy loads above mentioned. Each of the above journeys is some thirty miles. They carry their great loads of rice and salt from Therria to Cherrapunji, an ascent of about 4,000 feet in some three to four miles, in the day. The Khasis are probably the best porters in the north of India, and have frequently been requisitioned for transport purposes on military expeditions. [21]

---

[21] P.R.T. Gurdon, *The Khasis*, The Echo Library, 2006, p. 17

After seeing the terrain of the state it was easy to understand why. Traversing large distances on foot with heavy head loads is a necessity here and the Khasi have perfected the skill. The villagers told us that they do not enjoy living under such difficult circumstances but are unable to shift to more accessible places as local durbars do not give them land or allow them in. In Meghalaya, most property is community owned and so the writ of the durbar runs everywhere. Ironically, while the Khasi are matrilineal, their traditional institutions like the durbar still do not include women.

As we were getting back into the car, an elderly Khasi woman stopped us. 'The weather is clearing. Look there,' she pointed towards mountains in a distance. 'That is Bangladesh. Our limestone and boulders go there over a conveyor belt. They have set up a big cement factory that side, but what about us?' She was talking about the $255 million Lafarge Surma cement factory that had been started in Chattak in Bangladesh. At the time of our visit, large amounts of limestone were being transported to the plant from a mine near the village of Nongtrai in the Khasi Hills across a seventeen-km long conveyor belt. However, in early 2007, the Ministry of Environment & Forests put a ban on this in wake of the environmental degradation and damage to surrounding forests.[22] Later, the Supreme Court allowed operations by the company,[23] but NGOs and local bodies continue to demand the ban.[24] It is a tough decision to take, for the factory has provided livelihood to many in Bangladesh. For the people of Meghalaya, however, it has brought nothing.

Our last stop on the way back to Shillong was the Mawphlang Sacred Grove. Unbelievably, it is just twenty km from the capital. Despite human greed which indiscriminately destroys tree and plant life, Meghalaya still has

[22] http://www.minesandcommunities.org/article.php?a=1201, accessed on 1 December 2008.

[23] http://www.hindustantimes.com/StoryPage/StoryPage.aspx?sectionName=&id=19f89422-70a8-4187-89a7-bda1c899e5c4&&Headline=French+firm+allowed+mining+rights+in+Meghalaya, accessed on 1 December 2008.

[24] http://forests.org/shared/reader/welcome.aspx?linkid=105161&keybold=forest%20rights, accessed on 1 December 2008.

reasonable forest cover because of the sacred groves or holy forests. These forests are preserved by religious strictures. Nobody is permitted to remove anything, including lumps of soil, dead leaves or wayside rocks. These are the most verdant grounds in the world, and the impact it had on us is hard to describe. It was unspoilt nature at its mystical peak.

On the way to Mawphlang, we had noticed that the hills were covered with stone monoliths of various sizes, some horizontal, others vertical. They were reminiscent of the Stonehenge in England. 'Do these monoliths of Meghalaya have Celtic roots?' we asked our guide, Raj Turkem. 'No. These monoliths or kynmaw are part of the ancient Khasi tradition. Many of them, especially the horizontal table stones, are erected in honour of Ka Lawbei, the most important ancestress of the Khasi clan, the Tribal Mother. Others are erected as seats for the spirit of the departed, memorials for dead parents and relatives, and oath-taking stones.' One of the many trails that we followed inside the Mawphlang sacred grove took us to the other end of the forest. Here we came across a village picnic. Villagers were chatting, singing and cooking. A few young boys were washing their faces in a cool stream that ran into the forest. A bonfire had been lit just outside the perimeter of the grove. A few men were cleaning a pig that hung from a bamboo pole.

As our vehicle sped back towards Shillong on the winding roads, we wondered what other treasures and secrets lay hidden in the Purvanchal ranges of India's rich and diverse north-east. This we were soon to find out.

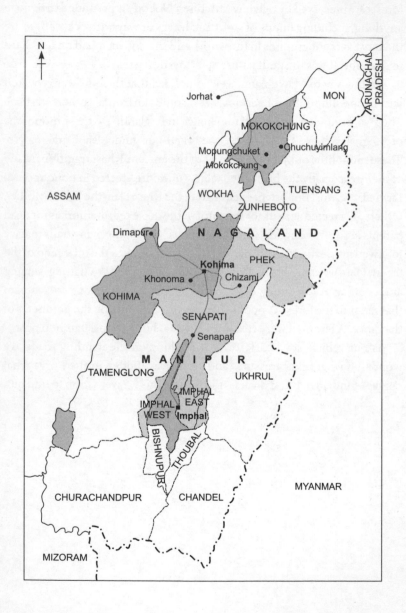

2

Manipur & Nagaland

Tere maathe pe yeh aanchal buhut hi khoob hai lekin
Tu iss aanchal se ek parcham bana leti to achcha tha

— MAJAAZ

How becoming is the veil draped round your face
Had you made it a banner what beauty would there be

unjan Veda: 15 July 2004. A group of phanek (sarong) clad Meitei women, in their thirties, forties, even sixties, marched up to the Assam Rifles headquarters in Imphal to protest against the alleged rape and killing of thirty-two-year-old Thangjam Manorama Devi.[1] Their anger was evident in the slogans they were shouting; these were soon picked up and repeated by people on the streets who had stopped to make way for them. Standing in front of the gates of the historic but hitherto unheard of Kangla Fort, these twenty-odd women did the unthinkable – they stripped naked in full public view before the sign which read 'The Assam Rifles'. Twenty-four hours later, when footage of this protest reached the television studios of New Delhi (even today, it takes a whole day for news from the

---

[1] Thangjam Manorama Devi, an alleged cadre of the proscribed PLA (People's Liberation Army) was picked up from her home by the 17th Assam Rifles at midnight on 10 July 2004. At 5.30 a.m. on 11 July, her tortured and sexually assaulted body was found.

north-east to reach Delhi), the nation watched in shock. Suddenly, the small state which appeared rarely even in the inside pages of dailies was making headlines. News channels went ballistic reporting this 'shocking' protest and its aftermath. The shock soon gave way to many different reactions. Some people, caught on camera, shook their heads in disapproval; others lowered their heads in shame. Some were curious; others angry. While these conflicting emotions flitting across the face of ordinary Indians were being flashed on television screens, I boarded an almost empty flight to Imphal.

It had been exactly one month since the killing of Manorama. The streets of Manipur's capital were deserted. 'It has been this way ever since her killing,' said Esther Chinnu Haokip, a Kuki woman of average build with short cropped hair. She had come to collect me from the Tulihal Airport and take me to my hotel in the main market area. 'Not that bandhs (strikes) or curfews are new here. We have one every few weeks. But this time it has been going on for too long. The people are really angry. They don't care if Manorama was an insurgent, she was a woman and no one had a right to violate or kill her,' she explained. As our auto rickshaw moved from one potholed back street to another – Esther warned me that the main roads were full of angry mobs throwing stones and jeeps of army and police personnel pelting rubber bullets – I caught my first glimpse of Imphal: desolate roads littered with remains of burnt tyres and charred wood, ramshackle houses, shuttered shops. There were very few people on the streets; those that were walked with a nervous jerkiness. The air was thick with tension and suspicion. Fear was palpable. It was difficult to imagine that this was the place which gave birth to the royal sport of polo[2]; where the dance drama *Ras Leela*[3] had originated. It was hard to believe that this place had over 2,000 years of history.[4]

---

[2] *Sagol Kangjei*, the Manipur form of polo, can be traced back to 1300 AD. It is played with seven players on each side. Writing in 1896, Major Gen. James Johnstone in his book *Manipur and Naga Hills* noted, 'In Manipur, every man who can muster a pony plays, and every boy who cannot, plays on foot.'

[3] The Manipuri *Ras Leela* depicts the eternal celestial love of Radha and Krishna. It was performed for the first time in 1779 in the reign of Maharaja Bhagya Chandra.

[4] R. K. Jhalajit Singh, *States of Indian Union: Manipur*, 1975, Publications Division, Ministry of Information & Broadcasting, p. 3.

As we braced ourselves for the uncomfortably long ride to the hotel, I recalled what I had read about this small north-eastern state and its people. Surrounded by Nagaland, Mizoram, Assam and Myanmar, Manipur with a population of 23.8 lakh people, acquired full statehood on 21 January 1972. The state has nine districts[5]. Almost 90 per cent of the terrain is hilly, inhabited by twenty-nine different tribes of Naga, Kuki-Chin and Mizo origin[6]. The bulk of the state's population, however, comprises the Meitei, who are concentrated in the four Imphal Valley districts of Imphal East, Imphal West, Thoubal and Bishnupur.

There is little consensus on the origin of the word 'Meitei' or of the people it represents. It is generally believed that 'Mei' means 'man' and 'tei' means 'separate', meaning the coming together of different people. Some sources trace the origin of the Meitei to the Tartars, the Shan, the Moi and the Mongolians. According to the historian Faubian Bowers, 'Racially, the Manipuri is a deeply mixed ethnic group. West was mixed with East and North with South. Chinese have blended with Aryans, Mongolians with Dravidians. This mixture creates the 'pure' Manipuri call(ed) Meitei, who lives in the Valley'[7].

The Meitei were originally divided into seven clans who fought with each other for supremacy. According to the Puwaris or the royal chronicles of the kings of Manipur, in 33 AD, the warrior king Nongda Lairen Pakhangba defeated all his rivals and established a Meitei kingdom under the Ningthouja dynasty. From then till the time of its merger with the Indian Union in October 1949, seventy-six kings have ascended the

---

[5] The nine districts are: Imphal East, Imphal West, Bishnupur, Thoubal, Churachandpur, Tamenglong, Senapati, Chandel and Ukhrul.

[6] The tribes of Manipur are: a) the Naga group: Kabui (Rongmei and Puimei), Kacha Naga (Laingmei and Zemei)called Zeliangrong, Mao, Maram, Tangkhul, Maring; b) Kuki-Chin-Mizo group: Gangte, Hmar, Lushai, Thadou, Vaiphei, Zou, Paite, Simte; c) Intermediary groups: Aimol, Chiru, Koireng, Kom, Anal, Chothe, Lamkang, Kairao/Thangal, Purum, Monsang, Moyon; d) Non-local groups: Angami, Ralte, Sema, Sukte. From Lucy Zehol, *Ethnicity in Manipur: Experiences, Issues and Perspectives*, 1998, Regency Publications, Delhi.

[7] Cited in Lucy Zehol, *Ethnicity in Manipur, Experiences, Issues & Perspectives*, Regecy Publications, 1998 p. 48.

throne of Manipur. The princely state first established contact with the British in 1762 and after the Anglo–Manipuri war of 1891, became a British protectorate.

My hotel was located in the heart of Imphal, in the Bazaar area. The front entrance was shuttered. Immediately, I panicked. 'Now where will I go?' I asked. Esther smiled. 'Don't worry.' She led me to a back door and I found myself in a lobby filled with journalists. 'This is a precautionary measure. Most hotels and shops here operate behind closed shutters on bandh days. After all, our guests are Mayangs (Meitei word for 'outsiders'). We don't want them to get into trouble with the local groups,' the receptionist checking me in explained.

By now, it was 4 p.m. The bandh was officially over. I decided to go out and speak to some people about what was happening. My first stop was the women's market, Ima Keithal. Located just behind my hotel, it is one of the biggest all-women markets of Asia. In the late nineteenth century, describing the market, Ethel St. Clair Grimwood said: 'No men were allowed to sell in this bazaar with the exception of a few Bengalee traders, who sat in a different part of the market and sold cloths. It was a pretty sight in the evening to see all the women hurrying along with their wares on their heads, and their little babies slung on their backs. They sat in long rows in the bazaar, and it was divided up in a most methodical way. Vegetables and fish occupied one end, and cloths and jewellery the other, and the whole of the female population turned out, and even the princesses occasionally sold in the bazaar'[8]. Over a hundred years later, the scene was much the same. Only now, there were no smiles, no laughter, no small talk. Everyone wanted to use the few hours of respite to sell their wares and stock provisions for their homes. The mood was grim and hurried. Every few minutes, buyer and seller alike would turn wary eyes towards the road, searching for the first signs of trouble.

I stopped in front of a young Meitei girl selling the best-looking pineapples I had ever seen. Her pink phanek with the traditional temple design on its border had been hitched to her knees. Over it she wore a simple

[8] Ethel St. Clair Grimwood, *My Three Years in Manipur* and *Escape from the Recent Mutiny*, Gyan Books, 2003.

white blouse and a loosely draped white shawl. Later, I learnt that pink and white are the colours of mourning in Manipur. Ever since the Kangla Gate protest began, women of all ages had been wearing them to express solidarity with the protesting masses.

'What's your name?'

'Binodini Devi.'

'Where do you stay?'

'Poana Bazaar. It's not very far from here.'

'You didn't join the protesters?'

'Oh, I do, off and on. Every locality has been carrying out protest marches. I join my neighbours when it's our turn.'

'But the bandh and the curfew, they have been going on for a month now.'

'Yes. They have become like a game. One follows the other. I am twenty-five years old. Yet I can't seem to remember a time when I wasn't caught in between the two.'

I detected signs of weariness and sadness in her voice.

'Why? How do people live like this?'

Binodini gave me a resigned smile. 'One gets used to it. You have to, else you can't survive. The last couple of weeks have been more difficult because of the bandhs in the hills. You see, our only road connection with the outside world is through the hills. Block it, and we are without essential supplies.'

'How long will this continue?'

'Who knows? But I know that this time we won't give up. I don't like the bandhs and I don't agree with the stone pelting but how long can we suffer? We are always caught between the security forces and the armed groups. Why can't the government just punish the killers?'

Sitting next to Binodini was an elderly woman with fine lines on her face. 'Your government does not want the Indian Army to get a bad name but what about us? What about our rights?' she asked.

I thought, '*Your* government?'

As I walked around the market, I was to hear the expression frequently. At one end of the market, a stout, middle-aged woman wearing a striped purple-and-black phanek was squatting next to her basket of water lilies. 'I don't want the army to go,' she whispered.

Startled, I listened.

'I know what happened was wrong and the killers of Manorama should be punished but if the army goes, the underground groups will become stronger than ever before. As it is, we have to pay them money. Then they will demand more and more.'

This fear I had encountered frequently, but more in the hills outside Imphal. Within the capital, the fury over the incident and the protest was so great that most people just wanted to see the army gone. Almost everybody, however, admitted that they paid taxes to the insurgent groups. 'Even bureaucrats, policemen and politicians are not spared,' a senior bureaucrat confessed. According to official records, there are some twenty-two active underground outfits in the state belonging to different ethnic groups and fighting for different causes. The Kuki groups are demanding a separate Kuki homeland, the Meitei groups, an independent Meitei Leipak (the original name of Manipur), the Naga groups the integration of Naga-inhabited areas. Other ethnic groups have formed militias just to protect their own interests. The differential aspirations of such diverse groups of people often led to violence and yet more bandhs.

I had witnessed a similar scene during my first visit to the Manipur hills. It was October 2001, and I was a college student studying the Naga conflict. I had travelled on a local bus from Kohima to Senapati, on the very highway that Binodini had called the lifeline of the Valley. At the time, I had met the Naga tribes of Manipur. When the Government of India accepted the demand of the Naga armed groups to extend their ceasefire to the Naga-inhabited areas of Manipur, the Meitei of the Valley rose in protest. They saw this as the first step towards the disintegration of their homeland and in the ensuing violence most Naga families fled the Valley. I met them in Senapati, living in empty classrooms and badminton courts with nothing but their coarse handwoven shawls and phaneks for warmth. Even at the time, the problem had seemed intractable. The more I travelled around Manipur, the more I realized that life here had indeed become a zero-sum game – the aspirations of the different ethnic groups inhabiting this state were not just different, they were often deeply conflicting.

By the time I left the Ima Market, I still had an hour to spare before the evening curfew would be imposed. I decided to visit the office of the Apunba

Lup, the apex body of thirty-two organizations that was spearheading the protests in Manipur. The government and the mainstream media often questioned their motives and their affiliations. More than once it was suggested that they were orchestrating the protest on behalf of the insurgent groups who wanted the army to leave the state. Yet the group of people I met did not make up a hardened militia nor were they scheming activists. They were a collection of young men, mostly in their twenties. Their anguish was clearly evident in their tone and their body language. 'The women who are raped are our mothers, sisters, wives and daughters and yet we can do nothing. We are forced to be mute spectators lest we be arrested on charges of sedition or some such thing. The women who disrobed, we call them "imas". You know what the term "ima" means? Mother. Can you imagine what we are going through?' The speaker was a young college student. Among his colleagues were lawyers, journalists, activists and lecturers. 'Before the agitation most of us didn't even know each other. But we have all banded together because this injustice has to stop. And we will do whatever it takes to ensure justice for Manorama and for all the others whose lives have been ruined or taken,' they said.

By now, it was just fifteen minutes before curfew. I quickly found a cycle rickshaw to take me to my hotel. I had noticed a strange thing about rickshaw drivers in Imphal. Most of them had handkerchiefs tied over their faces that hid everything but their eyes and the tip of their noses was hidden behind the mask. I was curious. Maybe they wanted to keep out the dust – there was construction work going on everywhere. Or maybe they had some disease; drug abuse and gutka (stimulant made of areca nut, tobacco, etc.) are ubiquitous in these parts. Or was it because they were insurgents concealing their identities? Assailed by doubt, I was relieved to enter my hotel, this time through the front gates. When I shared my apprehensions with a group of local journalists, they smiled. 'Oh, Lord! Insurgents, indeed!' said a middle-aged reporter who worked with the local ISTV. 'No. These youth that you see driving the rickshaws are people who have graduate and postgraduate degrees and are unable to find jobs. Government jobs are scarce and private companies just don't exist here. So these qualified youth who are forced to drive rickshaws cover their faces in shame.' I realized how vulnerable these youth were to joining the underground movements. As if reading my thoughts, a journalist from New Delhi said, 'As it is, many of the insurgent groups in the state are extremely volatile. They band and disband quickly because they are just groups of unemployed youth who see it as a quick way of making money in an economy that does not offer them jobs despite college degrees.' This view was echoed by the head of police who I met the following day.

The next morning, there was another bandh called and I waited in the hotel lobby trying to figure out how serious it was. 'Don't go outside right now. The protestors are in the Bazaar area,' the receptionist warned. I noticed that the shutters of the hotel were once again down. So I called Esther and asked if I could meet a few people. 'You are too new to venture out on your own. Let me figure something out,' she said.

A few hours later, there was a knock on my door. A slim, middle-aged woman dressed in a pink phanek and shawl, her lips red from chewing betel nut, was standing outside. 'Sitara Begum. I am President of the All-Manipur Muslim Women's Organization,' she said. A few months earlier, I would have been surprised to hear about Muslims in Manipur. But the bandh had given me a chance to read more about the state. Approximately seven per cent of Imphal's population comprises Muslims who are called Meitei Pangal. The word 'Pangal' is a corruption of Bengal. In 1606, the Prince Sanongba raised an army in Cachar to fight against his brother, King Khagemba of Manipur. He was defeated and many Muslims from his army were taken prisoners. Realizing that these Muslims were skilled weavers, blacksmiths, carpenters and tailors, King Khagemba allowed them to mingle with the local population. Since they were from Bengal, they were called Bangal, which was later corrupted to Pangal. The Pangal are regarded as Meitei and inhabit the Valley areas. I was surprised to learn that Sitara Begum had walked seven kilometres to meet me. 'Because of the bandh, no autos are plying,' she explained. She then went on to enumerate the problems of the state. 'Drug abuse is rampant. We are losing our youth. Prevalence of HIV is high. All of this is in some way linked to economic deprivation and the fact that we lie on the major drug smuggling route. Drugs enter the country from Moreh, on the Myanmar border.'

Talking about the recent agitation, she expressed anguish at government apathy. 'It is so infuriating. Over the last few months, there has been a lot of anger building up among the people. We are fed up of always living in fear. If the security forces had done their job properly, this anger would have been unleashed against the underground groups. But instead, the impunity with which the security forces operate has been increasing progressively.'

'Have you met Irom Sharmila?' she asked.

'No.'

'You should, if you get the permit. They keep her under arrest at the government hospital.'

I had been hearing about the 'Iron Lady of Manipur' and her non-violent and relentless struggle to ensure justice for the people of the state for some time now. After the Malom massacre in 2000, a twenty-eight-year-old Sharmila had started a fast unto death demanding the repeal of the Armed Forces Special Powers Act (AFSPA), 1958, which gave army officials the right to search, arrest and even kill locals on mere suspicion. That was in November 2000. The government responded to her protest by force-feeding her through nasal tubes and keeping her under arrest. At the time of my first visit to Imphal, Sharmila's fast was in its fourth year. Today, it is in its twelfth year. Since then, I have met her on one occasion, at a dharna (peaceful protest) outside the Jantar Mantar in New Delhi. I can never forget this feeble-looking woman, lying crumpled up under a tent, unable to speak or move. Irom Sharmila had smuggled herself out of Imphal to the capital, to make the world listen to her frail voice.

Over the next week, my days fell into a pattern. Every morning, I would wait at the hotel reception with media persons for some indication about the situation. At times I would get visitors, people from different backgrounds and ethnic groups, each of whom wanted to ensure a better future for their state and its people. Their names and faces will forever be etched in my memory: Hanjabam Shubhra Devi, the beautiful Meitei activist who is a health trainer; Ch. Sarat Kumar Singh, a strapping young advocate from the Guwahati High Court Bench in Imphal; Jiten Yumnam, a freelance journalist; Rose Mangshi Haokip, a lecturer at G.P. Women's College; Valleyrose Hungyo, editor of a Tangkhul (a Naga tribe) newspaper. In those few days, I closely observed the ethnic differences and tensions at play. At the same time, I also saw a bonding born of adverse circumstances and a determination to bring peace and prosperity to the state. It is with these people that I travelled around the Imphal Valley, meeting lawyers, college lecturers, social activists, politicians, doctors, army personnel and even bureaucrats. It is with their help that I communicated with the Meitei-speaking rickshaw drivers and the shopkeepers. Through them I learnt a lot more about the state and its problems.

For instance, I found out that the Meitei, most of whom are presently Hindus, were till a few centuries ago animists who followed the Sanamahi faith. They believed that Sanamahi or the Sun God created all living beings and sent his son, the illustrious King Pakhangba to earth to protect the people. However, in the early eighteenth century, King Pamheiba, better known as Garib Niwas, came under the influence of Shantidas Gosain, a preacher from Sylhet (now in Bangladesh). The king declared Hinduism the state religion, and people converted out of fear. In 1729, he burnt all the holy books or Puyas of the Sanamahi faith. The Meitei Mayek, the original script of the Meitei, was replaced with Bengali. It was during this period that the name Manipur, literally the 'Land of Jewels', was coined and myths tracing the ancestry of the Meitei to the Puranas, and Shiva and Parvati were cultivated. Between 1890 and 1930, Hindu Vaishnavism was firmly established.[9] The last few decades have, however, seen a revivalist movement in the state. In 1930, it was Laininghan Naoria Phullo who initiated the movement and by 1976 scholars had agreed upon a new version of the Meitei Mayek script. This ongoing agitation to replace the Bengali script with the Meitei Mayek has led to violent agitations in Manipur.[10]

By my third day in Imphal, I began to feel the pulse of Manipur. Like the locals, I would consult the local papers in the morning to find the likely trouble spots. Then I would venture out but take circuitous routes to avoid the protest areas. I had learnt that in Manipur people avoided fixing meetings. 'We never know if another bandh or curfew will come up,' a lecturer explained. 'So we just play it by the ear.' In a society that had been

---

[9] Gunjan Veda, *Tailoring Peace*, North-East Network, New Delhi, 2005, p. 5.

[10] On 13 April 2005, the Central Library at Imphal was set ablaze as part of this agitation. Thousands of rare books were lost. Instructions were also issued to schools to burn textbooks, and to newspapers to print their front page in the Meitei Mayek script.

living under the shadow of violence and constant tensions for the last four decades, suspicion was like breathing. A shopkeeper explained: 'We can't even trust our own neighbours. We don't know if they have affiliations with the underground groups. After all, the insurgents here are not outsiders but our own friends, acquaintances and even our children.'

On one such morning, I wandered to the Beganchandra Open Air Theatre. This was where the Meira Paibis or the torch-bearers of Manipur lived. Manipur has long been known for its strong women. As early as in 1904, the women of Manipur had got together and successfully protested against the British policy of sending their men to Kabaw Valley in Myanmar to collect wood to build the house of the assistant superintendent. This was known as the first Nupi Lan. Their second victory came in 1939, when they forced the British government to stop the export of rice when the rest of the state was facing food scarcity. I had often heard of how the Manipuri women had participated in the freedom struggle and had successfully launched prohibition in their state. It was these women who had once again taken up the demand for justice for Manorama. It was they who had stripped at the Kangla Fort. That day, 15 August, the Indian Independence Day, seemed perfect to meet these women.

Ramani Devi, an elderly Meitei woman with a grandmotherly face, did not speak a word of Hindi. She was the secretary of the All-Manipur Women's Social Reformation and Development Samaj. Through Shubhra who acted as my translator, she told me about the Meira Paibi movement. 'In the 1970s, consumption of alcohol was at an all-time high resulting in serious violence against women. So the imas came together under Mamon Devi and, in April 1975, the Nishabandi Movement was launched. After a day of back-breaking work, the women would take turns to stay up all night and keep vigil. The movement was successful.'

Taruni Devi, another Meira Paibi with a smiling, finely-lined face, continued the tale. 'Then, in the late 1970s, atrocities by the security forces escalated. Young boys would be picked up at night and beaten mercilessly. It was 29 December 1980. After a blast, the police came to pick up a boy named Ibomcha. We got together and stopped the arrest. That day, the Meira Paibi Movement was born. It has not been easy but today we have 2,500 clubs and associations across Manipur.'

The women told me that much has changed since the early days. Now the people respected them and came to them for solving social disputes. Every married woman automatically became a member of the Meira Paibi Association of her area. 'And we no longer have to stay up all night. If there is a problem, a woman has only to ring the lamp post of her locality and every Meira Paibi will come out,' said Taruni, who had left her home many years ago to strengthen this movement.

While the history of the movement helped me understand the women of Manipur better, I still wanted to discuss the events of 15 July.

'Ima, it is about 15 July. What happened that day?' Shubra asked Ima Taruni on my behalf.

'It was not an easy decision. In Manipur, a married woman does not even take off her shawl in front of others. But our hearts were bleeding. We had suffered enough. On the night of 14 July, we met and decided to do something drastic to make the authorities take notice. The next morning, two hundred women were to meet at Sinjamai but when I went there, not a soul was present. They had been dispersed by the army. That was the final straw. I began marching to Kangla along with a group of Meira Paibis. The men and some journalists asked us what we wanted to do but we just told them to follow at a distance and not get in our way. You have already seen the rest of the story,' she said with tears in her eyes.

'Since that day, we have been called many names. People have called us shameless and our men folk were furious, but tell me, what choice did we have? Here we are stripped of our dignity every day,' Ima Ramani added, putting a comforting hand on her colleague's shoulder. Suddenly, there was a commotion outside. A young boy in his twenties came running in and screamed something in Meiteilon (the Meitei language). The expression of the Meira Paibis changed. A few shrieked. Ima Taruni and Ima Ramani scrambled to their feet, anger evident on their faces.

'What has happened?' I asked a visibly shocked Shubhra.

'A young boy has committed self-immolation in protest against the AFSPA. They have taken him to the hospital but his condition is very critical. He was just twenty-eight,' she explained and broke down. Ima Ramani spoke to Shubhra. Nodding her head, Shubhra turned to me. 'We should leave now. The police have imposed curfew and the protestors are defying it in anger. Things can turn very violent.' So we hurried to my hotel and switched on the television set. I watched in shock as the news channels relayed the entire immolation attempt of Pebam Chittranjan. And suddenly, I was very angry, angry at the state for allowing this to happen; angry at the security forces for driving youth to such extremes and most importantly, angry at the policemen and the cameramen who watched in silence as a youth was burning. They had done nothing to save him.

I left Imphal the next morning through back lanes with a placard on the taxi; 'Sick', it said. It happened to be the truth. I was sick ... at heart.

Over the next few months, I visited Manipur a few times. Each time, the story was the same. Bandh. Curfew. Protest. Anger. Despair. A rickshaw-driver told me: 'I know that if the police catch me during curfew hours I will be arrested. And if the protestors find me, I will be hurt but do I have a choice? Didi, these protests have been going on for months now. There is no food at home. I can't watch my children starve any longer.' A shopkeeper confided: 'We are out of essential supplies. I have to walk to and from my shop because there is no petrol at the pumps. You can find people selling some on the roadside at Rs 100 or Rs 120 per litre.' An angry school principal said, 'In the last seventy-five days, we have had classes for just ten days. The other day, the protestors demanded that our children join their rally.' With each visit, the murmurs became stronger, the voices angrier.

Then, just as I thought the dam would not hold, the central government made an announcement – the prime minister would visit Imphal on 20 November 2004, and return Kangla Fort to the people of Manipur. All at once, the mood changed. Kangla Fort, the site before which the Meira Paibis had disrobed, is a place of great cultural, historical and emotional significance for the Meitei. For many centuries, it was the seat of the Manipur kings. Inside its perimeter are 360 places sacred to the Manipuris. The locals lost access to the Fort when the British captured it during the Anglo-Manipuri war. After Independence, it continued to be used by the army and the Assam Rifles. The return of Kangla had been a long-standing demand of the people and finally, it was to be fulfilled.

∽

The flight that we took to Imphal was not empty this time. It was filled with bureaucrats and media persons.

From the airport we went straight to Hotel Nirmala where different stakeholders of Manipur had come together at one table to find a solution to the problems of the state. A round-table conference was organized by North-East Network, a Guwahati-based NGO. All the faces that we had come to know over the last few months were there, discussing plans with media persons, activists and even government representatives from across the country. As they debated the need for the repeal of the AFSPA, as they talked of economic opportunities for the youth of the state, they did not forget to recognize the role of the Meira Paibis in the return of Kangla. They acknowledged that it was their unique protest that had taken Manipur to the mainstream media; it was their persistent effort that had kept the agitation alive without turning too violent.

That evening, we took a small delegation of Meira Paibis to meet Prime Minister Manmohan Singh. There were six women, some of of them with shawls draped over their heads, who spoke softly to a sensitive and attentive prime minister. We felt a sense of relief even as they spoke.

The next day was 20 November. The air was rife with excitement. In the afternoon we went to the Fort with the rest of the round-table delegates. The streets were flowing with an endless mass of people, all heading in a single direction. Young and old, men and women, Meitei and Pangal, Naga and Kuki, they all entered Kangla as one people. In the huge crowd inside the Fort walls, we saw many familiar faces. A few of them, including some members of the Apunba Lup (the apex body of the different groups fighting against the AFSPA), were busy waving the Indian tricolour being distributed by some enthusiasts. It was a sight we had never expected to witness. Gone was the fear, the suspicion, the wariness that had become a trademark of Manipur. There was just one overriding emotion – expectation. Finally, the prime minister handed over a huge key encased in a glass box to Ikram Ibobi Singh, chief minister of Manipur, and the crowd turned hysterical. We watched in amazement as young people started cheering; elderly men and women had tears in their eyes. Many were jumping and laughing like children. Next to us, a woman was softly offering a prayer of gratitude. Her five-year-old daughter was singing with her friends. We had grown used to seeing a desperate Manipur, an angry Manipur, a struggling Manipur. That winter evening, for the first time, we saw a smiling Manipur, a joyous Manipur. As the ecstatic crowds swept us out of the Kangla premises, we realized that we had just witnessed history in the making. Lines of the poet Faiz Ahmed Faiz came to mind:

Jab dukh ki nadia mein humne jeewan ki naao dali thi
Kitna kas bal tha bahon mein lahu mein kitni laali thi…
Kuch manjhi the unjaan bahut
Kuch undekhi manjdharein thein
Ab tumhi kaho kya karna hai
Ab kaisey paar utarna hai?

When we lowered our life's boat into the waters of pain
We had strength in our arms and redness throbbed in our blood …
Some boatmen were novices some rip tides were unknown
Now tell us what needs doing and how to go across?

ᐩ

Syeda: The chopper flew over the lush green foliage clothing the hills and valleys of India's least explored frontier. We were flying to Nagaland, a small state tucked away in the north-east corner of the country; a state very remote and unconnected from the chaos and bustle of mainland India.

To most Indians, the name Nagaland means little. Ask your neighbourhood chemist or mechanic, your colleague at work. Chances are that you will encounter ignorance or indifference. A few assiduous newspaper readers, recalling the occasional snippet about the NSCN (National Socialist Council of Nagaland) ceasefire or protests, will tell you that it is 'a disturbed state'. Some traveller will describe it as a place of pristine beauty, shrouded in mystery, and home to a people who wear colourful costumes, do the bamboo dance (which incidentally is a Mizo dance form, taught as 'Naga dance' in schools across the mainland) and jump up shouting war whoops. This is what most of urban India knows of Nagaland; till a few years earlier, Gunjan realized she had been no different.

ᐩ

Gunjan: Sometimes a small event can change your life. In my case it was a college lecture that I missed. I ended up being assigned a paper on the only state no one had chosen: Nagaland. And thus began my love affair with the state. The more I read, the more it grew on me. In October 2001, I found myself in Dimapur. At the time I was a college student with little money or information, and no contacts. As early as 1921, James H. Hutton said[11]:

> One of the first characteristics that strike a visitor to the Angami's country is his hospitality, a hospitality which is always ready to entertain a visitor and which forms a curious contrast to the very canny frugality of his domestic economy… Another very striking trait of the Angami is his geniality. Both men and women are exceedingly good-humoured and always ready for a joke. They will, moreover, break into merriment under the most adverse circumstances and on the slightest provocation.

As I stood on the same ground almost a century later, I found that not much had changed. The ravages of time and the persistent low-intensity conflict notwithstanding, the Naga have retained their cheerful disposition.

Yet there was a feeling of distrust, especially of 'Indians'. My days in Nagaland and interactions with the villagers, students, politicians and townspeople, made me understand this. Innocuous statements like – 'Unlike Indians, we Naga treat our men and women, children and adults alike,' – took on a new meaning. I realized that the distance between mainstream India and the warm but fiercely independent Naga is not just physical, but psychological and emotional. It is a distance born out of a series of political mishaps and policy failures, of atrocities committed by armed personnel, of the uncaring and callous attitude of the rest of India. A distance reflected in our lack of knowledge about a state which is a part of the Indian Union but somehow does not feature in the public's 'idea of India'; a distance that becomes defined every time a Naga in New Delhi or Bangalore is asked for their passport. It was in the tiny Naga villages surrounding Kohima that I understood this distance for the first time. That was four years ago. Now,

---

[11] John Henry Hutton, *The Angami Nagas: With some notes on neighboring tribes*, OUP, 1969, p. 39.

once again, I was heading back to the state that I had come to understand and love. Only this time, I wasn't on a local bus filled with Naga and their livestock but in a government chopper.

⟳

As the chopper landed on the tiny airstrip in Kohima, we could see half a dozen people on the tarmac. Though a state capital, this hill town of 79,000 people[12] does not have rail or air connectivity. The nearest and, in fact, the only railway station and airport in the state is located seventy-four kilometres away at Dimapur. From there it is a two-hour road journey on a local bus or shared taxi. We had got a government helicopter to fly us straight to Kohima from Guwahati.

When we got off the chopper, our eyes were drawn to the bright wrap-arounds and stylish blouses worn by the women in the welcome party. Rich, handwoven Naga shawls held their shoulders in a lazy embrace and in their hands were flowers so well crafted that it took us a while to realize they weren't real.

The Naga are skilled craftsmen. Their talent is reflected in their weaves, in their bamboo and cane furniture, in their intricately beaded jewellery and in the finely-carved totem poles that at one time stood outside their homes. In fact, like in other states across the north-east, most women here are adept at weaving on the traditional loin loom. The cloth that they produce is thicker; the colours brighter and the patterns bigger and much less detailed than we see in other states. The weave has a meaning; each tribe has its own colours and patterns and just by looking at a shawl or a wrap-around, most Naga can identify the weaver's tribe.

Contrary to popular belief, the term Naga does not refer to a homogenous group of people. It encompasses sixteen major tribes[13] who

---

[12] 2001 Census.

[13] Though there are many Naga tribes and sub-tribes spread across Myanmar, Manipur, Arunachal Pradesh and Assam, there are fourteen main tribes in the present state of Nagaland. They are the: Angami, Ao, Chakhesang, Chang, Khemungan, Konyak, Lotha, Phom, Pochury, Rengma, Sangtam, Sema, Yimchunger and Zeliang.

share certain characteristics and aspirations[14] but have their own dialect, dress code, cultural practices and myths of origin. The genesis of the term itself remains unclear. Often, it has been traced to the Sanskrit 'nagna', the Hindustani 'nanga', the Bengali 'nangta' and the Assamese 'noga', all of which mean 'naked'. While it is true that the Naga were more scantily clad than the people from the plains, this was the case with many other tribes. Some anthropologists therefore feel that the term was born out of the Sanskrit 'nag', meaning 'mountain' or the Burmese 'naka' meaning 'earring'. Scholars like S.E. Peal, E.A. Gait and Holcombe link it to the Konyak word 'nok' or 'noka', which means 'people'.[15] This we had learnt over the last few years.

The next morning, we set off for Chizami, a small village in the neighbouring district of Phek. As the car moved over winding mountain roads, we drank in the freshness of the Naga country. Every turn of the road revealed land, greenest of green, and sky, bluest of blue. Slender bamboos rose through dense forest cover and a riot of colours was splashed on the green foliage in the form of poinsettias, hibiscus, bougainvilleas, and scores of varieties of orchids. Was this what the ancestors of the Naga tribes saw when they first got here?

The origin of the Naga tribes is still shrouded in mystery, partly because they have no script and hence no written records. According to Naga lore, their script was written on an animal skin and lost when it was devoured by a dog. The myth of the origin of the four major Naga tribes – the Lotha, the Sema, the Rengma and the Angami – is related to a place called Khezakenoma in Phek District. It is close to the border of Manipur. The traditional belief is that a couple in this village owned a large stone slab that could double the quantity of paddy spread on it. Their three sons used it by rotation. One day, there was a quarrel between the sons and fearing bloodshed, the parents destroyed the stone. The sons then left

---

[14] Also, according to Naga mythology, a common ancestor.

[15] Reisang Vashum, *Nagas' rights to self determination: An anthropological-historical perspective*, Mittal Publications, 2005; pp 11-12; Renu Suri, *The Angami Nagas*, Mittal Publications, 2006, pp 4-5; Frans Welman, *Out of Isolation: Exploring a Forgotten World*, HPC Imprints, 2007, p. 27; Plus descriptions and text by British agents who visited the area in the 19th century.

Khezakenoma and became the forefathers of the Angami, Sema and Lotha tribes. The Rengma believe they are a subgroup of the Lotha.[16]

Anthropologists believe that the roots of the Naga lie much farther away as these tribes have strong cultural affinities with the people of Borneo, Philippines, Indonesia and Malaysia. It is believed that they migrated to their present abode from south-east Asia many hundreds of years ago. This is perhaps why a mountain people, far from the sea, extensively use ornaments made of cowries and other seashells. All along the way, we saw women wearing such necklaces made of seashells. Traditionally, cowries signified martial achievements and were used by the male only, especially among the Angami.[17]

The ninety-kilometre-long car ride to Chizami gave us a glimpse of the Naga way of life. There were few shops or vendors along the road; just trees and the occasional habitation. The houses were simple and neat; rows of beautiful flowers lined the courtyards. Women sat behind the counters in the tiny village shops; everyone's mouths were incessantly at work – chewing betel nut is a common habit. Every village had a church. Christianity was brought to Nagaland by Edward Winter Clark, an American missionary, and his Assamese evangelist friend, Godhula. While the first conversions of the animist Naga took place in Sibsagar District in Assam as early as 1847, it was only in the 1870s that Clark entered the Naga Hills[18]. He began his work in Mokukchung District, preaching the message of Christ, opening schools and exhorting the tribals to give up religious and cultural practices like head-hunting and drinking zutho, the traditional Naga rice beer. Gradually, more and more people accepted the faith. Today, over 90 per cent of the state's population is Christian, and English is the official language. Yet most Naga use Nagamese (a mix of Naga and Assamese) or Hindi.

After about two-and-a-half hours on winding roads we reached Chizami. Our friend Monisha Behal, a tireless worker and respected leader of the

[16] J.H. Hutton, *The Angami Nagas with some notes on Neighbouring Tribes*, Macmillan and Co., 1921

[17] Ibid, Hutton; p 27

[18] Inato Yekheto Shikhu, *A Re-discovery and Re-building of Naga Cultural Values*, Regency Publications, New Delhi, 2007, pp. 69-72

north-east in the best intellectual tradition of Assam, had been telling us about this tiny village for two years. She had started working in Nagaland with women and youth on issues of health. A small core group of women who were determined to better the lot of their people had come together with her to form the Chizami Women's Society. For the first few years they worked from their homes. Then a local man N. Lohe, who had for two years observed their dedicated work, gave them a gift, a piece of land on the hillside. Thus the North-East Network Resource Centre, Chizami, was born. The villagers of Chizami donated materials and labour. Seno Tsuhah, a woman from the village, became the moving spirit of the Centre. The building came up like a crest placed over the mountains. On that nippy October morning, we were in Chizami, having come a long way to see how a band of women could transform a whole society.

The very sight of the Centre was intensely pleasing. With a sloping roof and a cheerful façade, it was an example of 'communitization', the Naga concept of community ownership. The carefully planted rows of marigolds lining the various sloping paths which led up to the main building were a visual feast. The place was buzzing with activity. Everyone was chipping in to ensure that the inauguration of the Resource Centre went smoothly. We saw many twelve- to fourteen-year-old village kids rushing around, dressed as 'green volunteers'. Athsole, a bright Naga girl with thick black hair flowing to her waist, was our guide. 'We had to cut 139 trees to construct the centre. But we have started replanting tree for tree. Forty-nine have already been planted, all of them fruit trees,' she said with a shy smile.

Chizami is all about the former President A.P.J. Abdul Kalam's theory of PURA (Provision of Urban facilities in Rural Areas). Bringing urban facilities to rural hinterlands is to give youth a level playing field, and an incentive to stay on instead of flocking to cities like Kohima, Dimapur or even Delhi. Chizami is a centre for village youth where they can work and play; where they can get involved with village development – from health and education to handlooms and handicrafts. No magic mantra, just common sense to engage young men and women in development, giving them a sense of ownership and responsibility. This is the spirit of Chizami, Monisha explained.

Soon, the governor of Nagaland, Shri Shyamal Dutta, whose cavalcade of cars we had passed on the way, arrived to inaugurate the centre. We sat on a platform built entirely of green bamboo. Our audience, the villagers of Chizami, sat on the mountain slopes; it was a unique natural amphitheatre. Boys and girls appeared in their traditional regalia. The boys wore a short black kilt. Around their waist was a belt with long white tassels which swung vigorously at the slightest leg movement. Their upper torso was bare except for two thin criss-crossing strips of white cloth with red tassels. On their heads they wore black caps, each with a single white feather. Thick wooden armlets, red woven wristbands and red-and-white leg ornaments completed their costume. The women were dressed in white blouses and ankle-length wrap-arounds of the same colour. A short black shawl edged with red was draped across the upper torso and knotted over one shoulder. Their hair was held in a bun with a finely-crafted wooden pin; several strings of coloured beads (primarily yellow) adorned their neck, and two thick silver armlets encased each arm. The wraps of the young girls were of knee length, and their blouses sleeveless. This was the attire of the Chakhesang tribe, now worn only at festivals.

Phek District, which was carved out of Kohima in 1973, is inhabited primarily by the Chakhesang, who were known to the British as the Eastern Angami. The term 'Chakhesang', we learnt, is an acronym made up of the first few letters of the three tribes that came together under this name – Chakhru, Khezha and Sangtam.

All through the day, there was music and dancing on the mountain slopes. A Naga skit told the story of a dying mother with three sons, each wanting to be her heir. The dying woman was Earth and her three sons were Tiger, Devil and Man. She did not want her inheritance to go to her Tiger son, who would eat up everything in sight, or her devil son who would trick, mislead and spread canards. It was only her Man son who could preserve the heritage and save the earth. So Man inherited the earth. What he did with it was another story. The message was however clear: it is the responsibility of humans to protect the environment and preserve the ecology. The play was a contemporary comment on human culpability for environmental degradation.

The cultural extravaganza ended and we were pulled away to a review of the affairs of the Village Development Board. Naga tribes are famous for their democratic functioning and Nagaland has had village development boards, similar to the panchayat, for a long time. 'In November we are going to commission our very own hydro-electric project. After our needs are met, there will be a surplus. Will you help us to set up a mini industrial park for the youth of Chizami? It will give them skills. We can teach them woodwork, food processing, granite, even gems ...' Big plans were unfolding before us. We looked at the young girls and boys rushing around the campus, bright faces full of laughter. Just the right age to learn from the work of their elders while continuing to have fun.

At lunch, we were served the best Black Forest cake we had tasted anywhere in the world. We asked for the recipe. 'There was no oven. So we used hot sand to bake,' said Athsole softly, speaking about her wonderful innovation.

We left the resource centre laden with jams, preserves, juices made by young women and men from the local produce – pineapples, guavas, passion fruit, amlas. At 4 p.m. it was already getting dark. In the east the sun sets early, and the mountains wore a different look. Happy faces lined the hillside to wave goodbye. We left with regret; we felt we were being wrenched away just when we were having such a good time!

The next morning, we set off for the Naga Heritage Complex at Kisama, fifteen kilometres from Kohima. Inaugurated in 2003, this complex offers tourists a slice of Naga life. It is here that the famous Hornbill Festival is held in December every year. At that time, the place is packed with people but when we saw it, there were just a few local tourists who had come to picnic with their families. All around us were huts of different shapes and sizes. 'The traditional houses and morungs of each of the sixteen principal tribes have been reconstructed here,' our guide, a young Naga named Neizokhotuo explained.

'Morung?'

'Oh, they are the youth dormitories, though normally it is used to signify the male dormitory. Traditionally, every Naga village had one morung for the men and one for the young women where they stayed together and participated in social, educational, religious and social activities. They learnt about their ancestors, myths, legends and war tactics there. No woman could enter a male morung and no man could enter the women's dormitory.'

'Do they still exist?'

'No, in most villages, they vanished long ago. A few have been retained for tourist or cultural reasons.'

By now, we had reached the Rengma hut. It was a circular wooden structure with a three-tiered thatch roof. The front of the hut was finely carved with bull heads and other traditional designs. Inside, the utensils and furnishings were typical of a Rengma home and morung. As we went from hut to hut, our guide told us more about the tribes inhabiting the state. Each tribe was generally concentrated in a geographic location. 'Mokokchung District is the abode of the Ao, Mon District of the Konyak, ruled by powerful chiefs called Anghs, Wokha District of the Lotha, Peren District of the Zeliang (or Kacha Naga), Kohima of the Angami and the Rengma and Zunheboto districts of the Sumi. The Chang, Sangtam, Khiamniungan, Yimchunger tribes inhabit Tuensang, the easternmost district of the state, while the Phom are found in the newly-carved district of Longleng. You already know about the Chakhesang,' he explained. Naga tribes, we learnt, are also found in parts of Myanmar, Manipur, Arunachal Pradesh and Assam. The Tangsa, Wancho and Nocte Naga are found in Tirap and Changlang districts of Arunachal. Myanmar is home to the western Konyak, Khamingan, Thikir and Chir, and Manipur to the Tangkhul, Mao, Maram and Kabui tribes. Zemei, Kabui, Rengma, Sema and Konyak Naga live in Karbi Anglong and North Cachar districts of Assam[19]. In fact, integration of all these Naga-inhabited areas to form Nagalim or Greater Nagaland has been a longstanding demand of the Naga insurgent groups.[20]

During Gunjan's college years and her previous visit to Nagaland, she had closely followed this demand and tried to trace its history. Till 1832,

---

[19] Inato Yekheto Shikhu, *A Re-discovery and Re-building of Naga Cultural Values*, Regency Publications, New Delhi, 2007, p. 10; Ramamoorthy Gopalakrishnan, *Political Geography of India's North East*, Har-Anand Publications, 1991, p 140

[20] The demand for Greater Nagaland is to integrate 3.5 million Nagas spread across an area of 120,000 square km.

the Naga lived in their own villages and their interaction with the outside world was limited to the kingdoms of Ahom and Manipur. Then the British entered Naga territory to secure their own commercial interests in Upper Cachar, Myanmar and North Assam and find easy access to Manipur. Though the Naga put up a fierce resistance, they were finally subjugated and their territory became the Naga Hills District of Assam. The British, however, did not interfere with their internal affairs. In 1946, Angami Zaphu Phizo, a young Naga who had served with the Japanese in World War II, set up the Naga National Council (NNC) and put forward a demand for Naga independence. His reason was simple and straightforward: the Naga did not have any historical or cultural affinities with the rest of India and hence should be left independent. This demand went unheeded, and eventually in 1956, the NNC formed a parallel Federal Government of Nagaland and began collecting taxes. The Indian government retaliated by increasing troops in the state, carrying out aerial bombings and introducing the AFSPA, 1958, which, as mentioned before, gave security personnel extensive powers to question, search, arrest and even kill a person just on suspicion. During the years of active armed conflict that followed, atrocities were carried out by both sides, and hundreds of innocent lives were lost. Yet little information trickled out to the mainland. The NNC later entered into a ceasefire with the government and a splinter group led by Thuingaleng Muivah, Isaac Swu and S. S. Khaplang formed the National Socialist Council of Nagalim (NSCN). This group again split up into the NSCN (Isaac–Muivah) and NSCN (Khaplang) factions, both of which are actively at war against each other. Since 1997, there has been a ceasefire between the Government of India and the different Naga groups. The bloodshed has stopped, but the battle continues.

Till date, armed security personnel can be seen in every street and corner of the state, especially in Kohima. Like in Kashmir, here too, locals fear coming out of their houses after dark, lest they be taken for questioning. Gunjan had experienced this firsthand during her visit in 2001. The Naga students who accompanied her all over the state were often stopped by security personnel when they returned home after dropping her at her hotel. At one time, she had to come out of her room and assure two suspicious security men that the boys were not lying when they said that they had been out to drop her. Such instances have fuelled resentment against the security forces and have strengthened the demand for the repeal of the AFSPA.

Meanwhile, the Naga groups haven't given up their demand for Nagalim. While studying the history of Nagaland, one name crops up frequently – Khonoma. This legendary warrior village is believed to be the birthplace of Phizo. It was our next destination.

Located twenty kilometres west of Kohima, this picturesque village atop a hill draws many tourists. It is surrounded by terraced paddy fields and thickly forested slopes. In 1914, L.W. Shakespeare described Khonoma and its surroundings in his *History of Upper Assam, Upper Burmah and North Eastern Frontier*[21] thus:

> To a stranger suddenly arriving in the Angami country nothing strikes him with greater surprise and admiration than the beautifully terraced cultivation that meets the eye everywhere, on gentle slopes, sides and bottom of the valleys, in fact, wherever the land can be utilized in this way...To pass through the valley where stand the two powerful villages of Khonoma and Mezoma during late October when the grains are ripe is indeed a delight for the eye—[a] veritable golden valley.

On entering the village, the first thing a visitor encounters is a huge rock pillar inscribed with the words of Khrisanisa Seyie, the first president of the Federal Government of Nagaland.[22] The inscription reads: 'Nagas are not Indians, their territory is not part of the Indian Union. We shall uphold and defend this unique truth at all costs'.

Most of the six hundred households here rely on tourists for survival. Going around the village, we noticed the rampant commercialization. Locals often sport the traditional Angami regalia and let out rooms to visitors anxious for a taste of Naga life. Our guide took us to an open area

---

[21] Spectrum Publication, 2004, p. 206.

[22] It is also the village that has produced the first Naga graduate, half a dozen Indian Administrative Service (IAS) officers, a hundred state gazetted officers, thirty doctors, twenty engineers and more than one hundred lecturers. http://www.indianexpress.com/news/naga-movement-founders-village-to-vote-for/279787/

with many stone slabs arranged in a circle. This was the khel, the place where the elders sat together. Traditional Naga society (in most but not all tribes) is a democracy in which the village elders take collective decisions, their decree being followed unquestioningly by everyone.

By the time we left Khonoma, it was evening. We immediately set off for Dimapur to be able to take the flight to Delhi the following morning. On reaching the city, we were told that a fashion show was being held in an open ground nearby. We saw hundreds of youth, boys and girls, among the audience. They sang full throated, along with the a young band playing music on the stage. Soon, the music changed tenor and elegant high fashion models, both male and female appeared on the ramp. They displayed Naga weaves that had been fashioned into skirts, dresses, bags and trousers. The designs were beautifully cut and styled. If only they were shown in big cities they would blaze a new fashion line. We turned to Monalisa Changkija, a poet, journalist and women's rights activist to ask her opinion about this. She agreed. 'It would be wonderful if our weaves could be marketed the world over but for one consideration. Most of our weaves have some cultural significance and some of us are still not comfortable with using them as throws to sit on. Perhaps there could be design interventions to take care of that,' she suggested. 'But meeting bulk orders would be a problem as the industry here is unorganized and home-based.'

A year and a half later, we returned to Nagaland, entering through the winding road which goes from Jorhat in Assam to Mokokchung District. This picturesque district with resplendent blue-green mountains is home to the Ao Naga. It is said that the term 'Ao' means 'going' or 'gone' and refers to the group of Naga migrants who left their original settlement and crossed the river Dikhu.[23]

Mokokchung was the first district in Nagaland to embrace Christianity. Education was introduced early, and hence it has high literacy rates. The district has yet another distinguishing feature. In a country where the female foetus is increasingly being destroyed in the womb, it has the distinction of having the highest sex ratio. The Ao Naga love and nurture their girl children.

---

[23] B.B. Ghosh, *Mokokchung District Gazetteer*, Government of Nagaland, Kohima, 1979, p. 3.

As we entered the district headquarters of the town Mokokchung, we were greeted by hundreds of cheerful women sporting the Ao colours – red sarongs and deep blue shawls. Their hair was knotted with black-and-white tassels. Necklaces of ochre and aquamarine beads with silver spikes were strung around their necks. They were members of the Watsu Mundang, the apex organization of Ao women. It was on their invitation that we had returned to Nagaland.

It was 20 April 2007, a day to celebrate. The Watsu Mungdang had completed twenty-five years. 'What is the Watsu?' we asked Dr Chubatola Aier, a slim, middle-aged Ao woman with a ready smile. She was the president of the Watsu. 'It is a woman's organization. All Ao women are members of the Watsu; a membership fee is collected from girls who cross the age of eighteen,' she explained. 'We work on issues which concern us, such as the Total Prohibition Campaign in Nagaland.' We had long heard and read about the strength of the Naga woman, and today we were to take part in an event that celebrated this strength.

The community hall was filled with people: 2,000 women and 1,000 men. We marvelled at the discipline with which they sat for the entire three-hour-long inaugural ceremony. A small choir sang hymns in the most mellifluous tones. Throughout the morning, not a single cell phone rang. No one moved, no one talked or walked out of the hall. This gracious discipline is unheard of in most other parts of the country. One by one, the women pioneers of the Ao tribe were commemorated: the first woman graduate, teacher, dentist and doctor.

That afternoon, we once again basked in the warmth of Naga hospitality. They were meticulous in their care of every detail – from the beautiful bed linen and towels that they had brought from their homes to the meals that were carefully served by the Watsu members. Given the fact that their staple is rice and pork, in deference to us (some vegetarians and some non-pork eaters), they served meal after meal of delicious chicken and fish preparations, paneer and even aloo parantha. The state guest house had a tiny kitchen, so individual members were assigned the responsibility for our breakfast, lunch and dinner. Carrying casseroles and plastic containers in their hands, they trudged up the hill to serve us pineapple cakes, scones, muffins and sandwiches in addition to our regular meals. Young girls would stand and serve, and when we asked in amazement, 'Who has made this?', someone would quietly answer, 'I did'. Nanu was one such girl. At one time, she worked for Hindustan Computers Ltd (now HCL Technologies) in Delhi but came back to her village to look after her mother. 'Now I run a restaurant in Mokokchung town called Dolphin. We serve Chinese cuisine,' she told us. Sampling her cooking, we could imagine how well her restaurant would be doing.

The Ao women are among the most talented in the country. Interior decoration, cooking and flower arrangements are their forte. They prepare the most delectable confectioneries and are experts in many cuisines. Unfortunately, when in search of employment, they move out to Kohima and big cities like Mumbai, Delhi, Kolkata and Bangalore where they end up waiting tables or making beds at five-star hotels. This is a sad waste of their talent when they can add immensely to the aesthetics of any public place: hotels, guest houses, airport, lounges, etc.

The next day, a few village visits had been planned. On the way we once again saw flowering shrubs dotting the hills and lining the streets. Everywhere, even in humble homes, there were red Easter lilies, lilium, single carnations and anthuriums. Mokokchung can be called the garden of India, the land of passion fruit, oranges, papaya and ginger. Houses on either side of roads that connect one village to another have window-boxes with multicoloured flowers. Even the 150-bed Dr Imkongliba Memorial Hospital located in the centre of the town has a beautiful garden. Unlike many health centres in the country, this hospital, the second to be constructed in the state, was well kept and friendly. This is because the community has been actively involved in its functioning. Some time earlier, the community had collected Rs 25 lakh for the Oncology Department here. Currently, there is a community kitchen where the families of patients can cook and eat their meals. Next, we saw the Telemedicine Unit where the resident paediatrician was discussing reports with specialists at RIMS, Imphal. 'We do not have any telemedicine co-ordinator or technical assistance to run this unit. So whenever I get time I look after this unit. Of course this means sub-optimal utilization, we can only do one or two weekly referrals,' the doctor confided. 'How much population do you cover?' we asked. 'Five lakhs. We get patients from four districts: Tuensang, Longlei, Zunheboto and Mokokchung. Actually we are connected to over 300 hospitals through telemedicine but we need staff.'

Doctors at the hospital told us about the high incidence of HIV in the area. There had been 3,300 HIV-positive cases detected at the hospital until 2006. The state government was now planning to start an ART (Antiretroviral Therapy) centre for HIV patients. Counselling and testing had also been started.

As we were leaving, we saw there was an exhibition of herbs in the premises. 'We have identified 2,500 plants that can be used for making herbal medicines,' Imchawabang, who has been practising herbal medicine since 1954, informed us. He showed us each exhibit and explained the uses of various plants. 'Umrem, a local vegetable is good for high blood pressure, nokua, a popular local salad, helps purify blood, Tinospora cordifolia is an aphrodisiac.' The list went on. We had also been advocating alternative medicine in all our travels across the country. In fact, from the Amchi medicine of Ladakh to the Ayurvedic treatment of Kerala, we had ourselves experimented with different types of medical systems before advising other people to try them out. It was pleasing that the government of Nagaland was planning to develop a pharmacopoeia and establish the medicinal value of the various traditional herbal remedies.

Our next stop was at the village of Mopungchuket. Here, we finally saw the famous communitization initiative which was integrated into district planning by the then chief secretary of Nagaland, A.M. Gokhale, in Phek District. The sub-centre is situated in this village of 6,000 people, mostly retired army men. It is one of the few neat and aesthetic health centres we have seen in India, a tiny two-room wooden structure on the hillside. In one room were two neatly made beds, one of which was occupied by an elderly woman. Cheerful curtains hung at the windows, and flowers were laid on the stools next to the beds. Clean chairs lined the waiting area along with a few bowls of flowers. In the examination room sat a nurse who showed us her well-organized registers. Particulars of every patient who visited the centre had been recorded: name, age, ailment, treatment suggested, and medicine given, all put down in a clear hand. Most of the patients we noticed were eighty-five years of age or more.

'What medicines do you give?' we asked the ANM.

'We try to provide the basics. The villagers all chip in with money to ensure that the centre is always well stocked and that no one in need is denied help,' she explained. We thought of the unhygenic and often closed one-room sub-centres we had seen in states like Maharashtra, Uttar Pradesh, Rajasthan, Madhya Pradesh and Orissa. Those centres would never have been in such decrepit state had the local community participated in making them work.

Next, we visited one of the eight anganwadi centres in the village. The tiny hut was full of happy, chirpy kids. The children were neatly scrubbed and looked well cared for. They were provided two mathris (biscuit like savouries) made out of ready-to-eat powder, micronutrient candies, glucose biscuits and milk. Boiled water was brought from the nearby houses and stored in neat containers. This was in sharp contrast to the anganwadi centre we had seen in Chizami, a dark, dingy room stuffed with forty grubby kids who received just two glucose biscuits a day. Here, the community had come together to ensure that their children stayed healthy and happy. As we got into our cars to leave Mopungchuket, the children waved cheerily.

At a clearing just outside the village, our cars stopped again. 'Why are we stopping here?' we asked our driver.

'Madam, if you want to see the skill of our people, you should see the wood sculptures here,' he said.

We got out and saw huge sculptures with intricate carvings standing in a clearing. They had been made by a local artist, R. Libden. A few depicted the love story of Idiben and Ginasangba. There were others based on traditional Ao beliefs like the 'Eye of the Universe' and the 'Pillar of Time'.

We then resumed our journey. At the village of Yisenyou a few kilometres away, we stopped at a project being undertaken in Public-Private Partnership (PPP) mode under the National Horticulture Mission. Here we saw an amazing collection of anthuriums, roses and liliums. Farmers were coming in with their produce. 'They get Rs 15 or 20 for one stem of lilium, depending on the quality. So a farmer easily makes Rs 4,000 a month even if he does this as a part-time activity,' an accompanying official explained. Fascinated, we watched as young Naga boys sorted and graded the flowers before putting them in cold storage. 'These flowers will go to Jorhat and from there to Kolkata, Delhi and other big cities.'

Our final stop for the day was at the village of Chuchuyimlang, with a population of ten thousand. By the time we reached it was raining. Yet a small crowd of men and women had gathered to meet us. After a traditional Naga welcome – the village elder draped a beautiful shawl around our shoulders – we were taken inside the PHC. The centre was running out of an old school building constructed in 1963. Of the twelve beds, only one was occupied. This PHC, which catered to 36,000 people across nine villages, had not had a doctor for over three weeks now. 'The resident doctor married and settled in Delhi,' a villager explained. No power back-up was available. Inside the centre a small crowd was waiting to greet us and apprise us of their situation. Surprisingly, no women were present. Even the ones who had come to meet us outside had disappeared. Puzzled, we asked the village development board members. 'Don't you have female members?'

'The women are busy at home,' one man said.

'We didn't inform them,' said another.

Suddenly, we recalled a meeting we had had with some women's groups in our hotel in Kohima during our previous visit. They had complained about the denial of rights to Naga women. At the time, we had been surprised, almost disbelieving. We had heard of the Naga Mothers' Association and their work. Now, sitting in a dilapidated old building with the rain coming down outside, we could clearly see what our Naga friends had been talking about. The Naga do not kill their girls but they are yet to give them their rights. With the Watsu's effort, women are beginning to be elected to the village development board – there were eight women members in Chuchuyimlang – but they are yet to get any powers.

As in other villages here, what clearly emerged was the need for geriatric care. The oldest man in Chuchuyimlang was over a hundred years old; the oldest woman was 105. Many villagers were hovering between eighty and hundred years of age, and they were still actively involved in community life. We were happy to see that unlike in mainland India, in Nagaland, the elderly were not being abandoned, but provisions for their medical care need to be improved. The needs here were very different from other parts of the country. But sitting in Delhi and making uniform policies for the country, we could not see this. It is only travel to the hinterlands that brings out the discrepancies and loopholes in our planning. Mark Twain once said: 'Twenty years from now you will be more disappointed by the things you didn't do than by the ones you did. So throw off the bowlines. Sail away from the safe harbor. Catch the trade winds in your sails. Explore. Dream. Discover'.

In this verdant periphery of the Indian republic, the wisdom of his words struck us. And we made a quick promise to ourselves to never stop exploring.

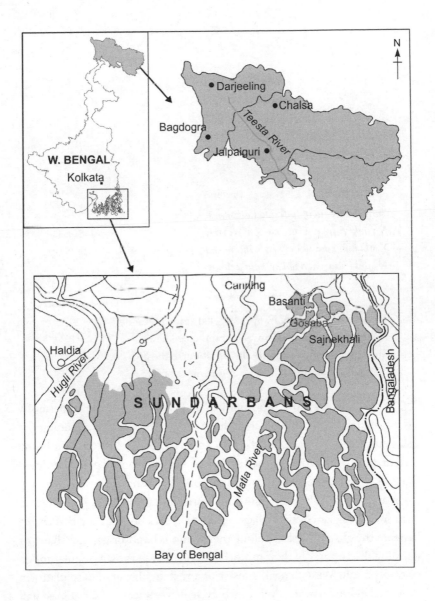

3

West Bengal

Yunhi hamesha uljhati rahi hai zulm se khalq
Na unki rasm nayi hai na apni reet nayi
Yunhi hamesha khilaye hain humne aag mein phool
Na unki haar nayi hai na apni jeet nayi.

— FAIZ

Thus have the masses always struggled against tyranny
Neither is their custom novel, nor our creed new
Thus have we made flowers always bloom in the fire
Neither is their defeat novel, nor our victory new.

It was a sultry June morning in 2008. We had left the impatiently honking traffic of Kolkata behind and were now driving along the vibrant Bengali countryside – scrawny, bare-chested kids being splashed with dirt as they pushed and shoved to gain control of the muddied football, a constant cascade of sweat running down their grimy faces giving them a mottled look; women in soft, worn-out cotton saris, washing and swimming in algae-covered village ponds; thin dark bodies, their ribs visible beneath the glistening skin pulling the infamous hand-drawn rickshaws or gunning the engines of their motorbike vans. These vans, a popular mode of transport in West Bengal, consist of a rectangular or square platform mounted behind a motorcycle or a bicycle driver's seat. To see at least half a dozen passengers clutching their luggage and precariously balancing themselves on these platforms is common.

These now familiar glimpses of rural Bengal flitted by as our car sped towards Sonakhali – one of the two entry points into the world's largest delta, the Sundarbans. We had brought along a copy of *The Hungry Tide*, Amitav Ghosh's book that blends history and legend with fictional characters to make readers experience life in these swampy wetlands, a life lived under the shadow of the Royal Bengal Tiger.

As a child, Gunjan had faithfully visited the country's culture capital during every summer vacation. She had experienced many of Kolkata's innumerable delights from the rich history resonating through the marbled hallways of the Victoria Memorial to the spicy punch packed into what definitely qualify as the country's best golgappas (hollow wheat balls filled with mashed potatoes, tamarind paste and mint-flavoured water). Yet, she had never visited these riverine islands located just a hundred kilometres from Dominique Lapierre's 'City of Joy'. She had read in school that they had been formed by alluvial deposits from the Himalayas brought in by the rivers Ganges, Brahmaputra and Meghna. Covering an area of approximately 10,000 square kilometres across India and Bangladesh, they have the largest tiger population in any given place – tigers which unlike those elsewhere are known to attack humans.

A few months earlier we had three glorious sightings of tigers at the Bandhavgarh National Park in Madhya Pradesh; but the man-eaters of the mangrove country evoked different feelings. They had a mysterious air to them, just like their mysterious habitat. This for us was the allure of the Sundarbans. It was almost as if these estuarine forests and their inhabitants were beckoning us to experience their world, a world so very different from our own, though right next door.

As we neared Sonakhali, the green fields running on either side of the road became pisciculture tracts – small plots of land covered in water; each had a series of blue nets spread across the water and an occasional hut on stilts. At Sonakhali, we got out of the cars to begin our experience of the tide country. Henceforth, boats would be our only mode of transport.

The small jetty was bustling with locals and tourists. Across the stretch of water on the other bank of the river Hoogal, we could see the town of

Basanti with its array of shops. Small country boats filled with villagers were going back and forth between the two banks. Standing next to the jetty was a small purple-coloured launch (a steamer-like boat) with the words 'DM's Boat' (DM stands for District Magistrate) written across it in bold letters. This was our boat. To get to it we had to walk across a narrow plank of wood which was precariously balanced between the edge of the jetty and the rim of the boat. Over the next two days, 'walking the plank' became a common occurrence and by the end of our visit we had become quite proficient at it. Quick, confident steps were the key. The first time, however, was not easy, and taking deep breaths, we placed our feet gingerly on the plank. Once safely on board, we looked over the covered deck. Under the large hood there was a small davenport with a bright red cotton bedspread. On both sides of the bed there were cheap-looking plastic chairs covered with colourful sarkari (government) towels. Two of them were occupied by officers in khaki uniform – the forest rangers who would be our guides during the tour. Next to the bed, a narrow flight of steps led to the belly of the boat. This was where the kitchens and the toilets were. It was simple, even shabby, but compared to the other engine-powered tourist boats, it looked clean. Moving at the speed of six kilometres per hour, this boat consumed fourteen litres of diesel every hour, i.e., almost two-and-a-half litres of diesel for every kilometre travelled. An ordinary diesel-fuelled car like Indica covers thirteen–fifteen kilometres per litre of diesel while the fuel efficiency of a nine-ton truck is still four–five kilometre per litre.

Soon, our launch started to move and we got our cameras to capture images of the tide country – narrow mud tracks on both sides of the river, kutchcha houses, country dinghies (small, narrow fishing boats) bobbing in the calm waters, people standing in waist-deep waters, trying to catch prawn seeds with coloured nets. The stormy skies traced patterns on the muddy green waters which we captured on film. We saw the white dome of a mosque and the yellow spires of temples standing amidst a row of pukka houses. 'What's that?' we asked Pahari Babu, an officer with the Planning Department of the West Bengal government. In the last three years, this tall, bespectacled Bengali man in slightly rumpled clothes and worn-out chappals, had been the one permanent fixture of all our official visits to Kolkata. He would receive us at the airport each time as the protocol officer and remain with us throughout. He had often offered to take us to the Sundarbans but we discovered that his knowledge of the tide country was limited to tiger tales: 'the dangerous man-eaters come out at night, swim to the boats and take away unsuspecting victims'. So we decided to repeat our question to the two range officers.

'That's Gosaba. Surrounded by the Matla and Zilli rivers, it is one of the bigger villages here; in fact, the last inhabited village before the Tiger Reserve starts,' Abdul Mannan, the older ranger said.

Gosaba. The name was familiar, just like Basanti and Sonakhali. We had come across them in Ghosh's novel. We could see the township which seemed to be the centre of much activity. Tiny boats were unloading passengers on the banks. A bigger boat with the sign 'SHIS Medical Dispensary' was anchored close by. We passed many fishermen in their twelve feet by five feet dinghies. Across the middle of the boat was a small covered area where the clothes and food was stored. Despite the constant movement of people and goods, there was a measured tranquillity about the place. Having read about the hardships faced by fish workers in these parts, we knew that this idyllic setting that we now saw hid behind it a never-ending saga of struggle. Yet, at that moment, from the sanctuary of a high-powered government boat, we were slightly removed from their reality. Life in the tide country seemed to move at its own pace – it was neither fast nor slow, just mann mauji (happy-go-lucky).

After about two hours on the boat, a signboard on a tiny patch of green informed us that we were entering the 2,585 square kilometre Tiger Reserve.[1] An eerie silence descended on the boat. Suddenly all of us sat up, craning our necks in every possible direction, anxiously trying to locate the man-eater. It is said that every person living on the fifty-four inhabited islands of the Sundarbans knows someone who has fallen prey to the yellow-and-black-striped cat. Unofficial statistics say that between eighty to

---

[1] As early as 1875, the Sundarbans were declared a Reserve Forest. Then, in 1973, about 258,000 hectares of land were declared as the Sundarbans Tiger Reserve. In 1976, the Sajnakhali Wildlife Sanctuary was established, and in 1984, the Tiger Reserve established as a National Park. Source: http://www.unep-wcmc. org/sites/wh/pdf/Sundarbans%20[both].pdf Accessed 24 March 2009.

hundred deaths take place each year, most of them of men who venture into the deep mangrove swamps to fish or to collect honey, venison and other forest produce.[2] Nobody knows why there is this fondness for human flesh on the part of the tigers here but theories abound. Some blame it on the salt water and harsh ecosystem. Others cite a scarcity of food resources. A few wildlife experts theorize that tigers are territorial animals. In the tide country, however, the scent and territorial markings of these big cats are washed away, making them aggressive. Whatever the reason, the battle lines between humans and nature are clearly drawn in these marshy forestlands; no one knows in whose favour the scale will tip.

We spent the next forty-five minutes in a vain attempt to spot at least one of the Reserve's 250-plus tigers. Before we knew it, we had arrived at our first stop, Sudhanyakhali, marked by little more than a makeshift wooden jetty and a green signboard. Next to the jetty, an engine-powered boat almost the same size as our launch was anchored. These boats, known as photphoties, are used by tourists to traverse the tiger territory. We disembarked. A narrow mud track led us from the jetty. On either side, there was barbed wire fencing. A large doll's house stood next to the jetty with three clay dolls inside. However, from the reactions of our escorts, it was obvious that this was no doll's house but a mandir (temple) with three idols. In the centre sat a black-haired, sari-clad goddess, one hand raised in blessing, the other placed on her lap. She was Bon Bibi, the 'lady of the forest' and protector of the people of the Sundarbans. According to lore, Bon Bibi was chosen by Allah to protect the people working in the mangrove forests from a greedy man-eating half-tiger demon called Dokkhin Rai. Bon Bibi is the deity of all those who live in the area, both Hindus and Muslims. Next to her, carrying a staff was the bearded idol of her brother, Shah Jongli. On her other side, sitting with folded hands was a tiny boy called Dukhey.

After bowing to the idols, we followed the barricaded path. On the left was a mangrove park; on the right a rusty catamaran on which a board was pinned announcing that a tiger had been sighted in this area just three days earlier. Hafizullah, a middle-aged guard with white streaks in his hair and

2 http://search.japantimes.co.jp/cgi-bin/fv20020409a1.html, accessed 2 April 2009

a black mole sitting prominently on his nose, told us the story. 'I saw the tiger that day. It was around 5 p.m. He was huge,' he explained excitedly as we walked towards the green watchtower. From the height of the tower, we could see large tracts of swamps that had been cleared 'for sightings'. We sat in silence on the platform of the tower. While we waited for a sighting, one of the guards whispered the story of Bon Bibi to us.

The story began in the plains of Arabia. Ibrahim, a childless fakir, was blessed with twins – Bon Bibi and Shah Jongli.[3] When the twins grew up, the angel Gabriel asked them to go to 'the country of eighteen tides' to make it fit for human habitation. At that time, the Sundarbans were the realm of the demon king Dokkhin Rai who hated humans; under his rule, the tigers and evil spirits killed men, women and children. Bon Bibi fought Dokkhin Rai and his mother, Narayani, and defeated them. But she was merciful to her enemy and decided that one half of the tide country would remain the realm of Dokkhin Rai and his subjects, the tigers. The other would be inhabited by humans. Thus peace was restored. Then, one day, a man called Dhona,[4] who lived at the edge of the tide country, decided to make a fortune from the jungle. Among his crew was a young boy named Dukhey. Dhona's boats landed at a place inside the realm of Dokkhin Rai. The demon king struck a bargain with Dhona, promising him riches and wealth in exchange for Dukhey. Overcome by greed, Dhona agreed, and set sail leaving the poor boy behind. Just as Dokkhin Rai, disguised as a huge tiger, was ready to pounce on Dukhey, the boy called upon Bon Bibi to protect him. She, along with her brother Shah Jongli, immediately came to his rescue. They then told Dukhey, Dokkhin Rai and Ghazi, a pir who was a friend of Dokkhin Rai's, to make a pact that henceforth both humans and animals would respect each others' needs. Just as the story ended, Hafizullah produced a worn copy of *Bon Bibi Zahurnama* (The Prayer of Bon Bibi) and started reciting:

---

[3]   Some versions of the story say that Ibrahim had left his first wife. She gave birth to the twins but could only nurture one of them – Shah Jongli. Bon Bibi was left in the forest and suckled by a deer. When the twins grew up, they were united and sent on the mission to the Sundarbans.

[4]   Some versions of the tale say that Dhona was Dukhey's uncle.

Allah Pak Parvar
Srijan Pallanjhar
Kripataa Aseem Sagor
Tar Taripe Bani
Aami ki kohite jani
Pehla Apon noore kotha mor
Noor nabi paida kare...

We were delighted at the mixed use of Bangla–Urdu–Arabic in the poem. We noticed that the book was written from right to left as in an Urdu text. The Bengali verses were, however, written from left to right like in English. It was the strangest and most eclectic text we had ever seen. In her photographs, the goddess with a Muslim name looks every bit a Hindu deity; her brother looks like an Arab sultan. The universal acceptance of her power creates a bond among the people, a bond forged on the basis of a common fear, one that stretches beyond the realm of any single religion.

We spent about half an hour at the watchtower but neither Dokkhin Rai nor any of his subjects appeared. Suddenly it started raining and we rushed to our boat. Our next stop was at the Sajnekhali Visitor Centre. On the way, we saw the brown and, at times, sun-bleached roots of the mangroves lining every visible stretch of land along both banks. At Sajnekhali we were once again greeted by a Bon Bibi shrine (here spelt Banabibi). Inside the fenced-off compound of the Visitor Centre was a model of the entire Reserve, including the 1,330 square kilometre core area which had been declared as a World Heritage Site and was out of bounds for both locals and tourists. The museum had information about the legends, fauna and flora of the region. There were exhibits were about the different kinds of mangroves and the sundari trees after which the delta is named. After strolling around the centre, we moved to the village of Dayapur located just across the water from Sajnekhali. Here, a new hotel, Suranjana Tourist Lodge, with a beautiful garden and a breathtaking view of the river, was to be our night halt.

At 6.30 a.m. the next morning, we were on our boat and heading towards the Dobanki Cheetal Research Centre more than three hours away. By now, we had given up hope of sighting a tiger. In fact, the only animal or bird we saw was an egret perched on one leg. Abdul Mannan, the ranger, explained why sighting a tiger in the Sundarbans was difficult despite its huge tiger population. 'In other areas, you go into the forest where the animals roam. Here, you are always on the water or in watchtowers. You never get a chance to go inside the forests. Besides, during the day it is too hot for the animals to come out.' It was high tide now, and the mangrove country seemed to have taken on a whole new persona. The exposed roots of the mangroves, the glittering silver sands and the thousands of red crabs we had seen the previous afternoon were no longer visible. The mustard-and-brown country of yesterday had donned blue-and-green robes. In this part of the Reserve the country dinghies of the fisher folk were not visible. As our boat moved between rain and sunshine on the sometimes narrow, sometimes wide straits, we seldom saw or heard any sound. Like the Jarawa Reserve of the Andaman Islands,[5] here too, the silence stretched for miles. The only sound was the click of our cameras as we tried to capture every mood, every expression of this tide country.

Finally, we reached Dobanki. Suddenly there was a commotion. It was a photphoti full of tourists from Kalimpong. They were singing at the top of their voices; we fought the urge to shout at them for their crude intrusion into the silence of the groves. At Dobanki we saw no animals, just a few deer inside the compound. By the time we left, it was 11.30 a.m.

Soon we came upon a huge stretch of calm blue waters. 'This is the place where the Vidyadhari and Sonakhali rivers fall into the Bay of Bengal,' our ranger informed us. We could see many small boats filled with fishermen busy at work. After a typical Bengali meal of dal, rice, aloo bhujjia, aloo patol and fish, we decided to stop at one of the riverside villages. We wanted to see what these surroundings (which people came to see from the farthest reaches of the globe) meant to the people who inhabited them; people who had to brave the cyclonic storms of the Bay of Bengal and fend off animal attacks.

Pahari Babu was reluctant to stop. 'We are getting late. It's time to head back,' he urged but gave in at our insistence. At 1.30 p.m. we reached the village of Dakhin Bartola, which was close to Gosaba. As we prepared to step on the jetty we saw dung cakes drying on it. Next to it, a number of young girls were prawn fishing. We had learnt that collecting the eggs of

5 See Chapter 4.

tiger prawns was a relatively new activity in this area. It had started in the eighties and became popular because of the high financial returns.[6] On an average, an adult collected 1,000 eggs a day for which the payment was Rs 135. The girls at the jetty happily told us their names, Shuma, Abida, Mungli, Anamika Sinha. They were all students of Class 4 at the Government Primary School, Bartola. After classes finished, they would run here, cast their nets and do their bit to supplement the family income. Dipti Haldar, a six-year-old wearing a red-and-black frock with a white necklace, was in Class 2. 'There are twenty-five to twenty-six students in my class. We have three teachers but only one comes to my class.'

'Do you get anything to eat at school?'

'Yes, didi – eggs and khichdi.'

By now, we had attracted a group of villagers. From them we learnt that there were a hundred houses in this village. Almost three-quarters of the 2,000 people here were Hindus; the rest were Muslims. Prashant was a young man dressed in well-pressed trousers and shirt. He had passed Class 10 from the village high school, where he was now a 'tuition teacher'. He told us about life in this riverine village. 'Fishing is the main occupation but we also cultivate paddy. Our agriculture is rain fed and we have one crop a year. Drinking water is a major problem and we have to rely on tubewells. Earlier, we had a higher secondary school in the village, but now we only have till Class 10.'

'What about NREGA?' we were curious to see if the rural employment scheme had reached these remote islands.

A young man in a light-blue shirt and dhoti spoke up. 'I am Nazrul Islam. So far, I have got ten days' work this year at a daily wage of Rs 75. We were making side embankments and check-dams. There are six people in my family. I have no boat or land, just one fishing net. NREGA would have solved my problems but finding work in spite of the job card is difficult,' he complained.

Walking with us on a brick-lined pathway into the village were a few women. We asked them about anganwadi and health facilities. 'There are

---

[6] http://whc.unesco.org/archive/periodicreporting/APA/cycle01/section2/452.pdf, accessed 11 April 2009.

two anganwadis in this village. The children get some khichdi and a doctor visits to check on pregnant women. The nearest hospital is at Basanti, one hour by boat and eight kilometres by road. Recently, an ASHA (Accredited Social Health Activist) worker has been appointed,' explained Chopala Haldar, in her early forties, dressed in a simple taat sari hitched to her knees.

By now, we had reached a cluster of huts. In the middle of the muddle sat a large house. It belonged to Ruby Naiyya, a member of the local panchayat samiti and a Communist Party of India (CPI) cadre. Dressed in a green tangail sari with a prominent line of sindoor and a bindi, Ruby told us that this was her second term as panchayat member. 'And in between my two terms, my son Ashok was also elected. We represent the three villages of Dakhin Bartola, Ramkrishnapur and Masjidbatti,' she informed us with pride. Then in a more subdued voice she continued, 'But we have so little government suvidha (amenities) – 7,000 people in my three villages, and only one dawakhana (dispensary) in Ramkrishnapur, with a male health worker. Sister (the Auxiliary Nurse Midwife) visits twice a month. Almost all deliveries take place at home with the help of our local dai (mid-wife). There is a hospital at Basanti, but no doctor. Shishu mrityu (Infant Mortality Rate) and mata mrityu (Maternal Mortality Rate) is too much, didi. Fifteen out of hundred of our women die during child birth.'

'You mean 15 per cent?' we asked incredulously.

'Yes, didi. In the last one year, eight women and thirty newborns died in our three villages alone. And look at the children, how thin they are.' She pushed a few young boys and girls forward. 'Garibi, didi, ghor garibi (poverty, acute poverty).'

'And tiger attacks?' we questioned.

'Not here. In these villages there have been none though a few instances were reported earlier from Gosaba. But when our men go into the Reserve Forests, we are very afraid.'

We looked at the people around us. All of them were silent. Some heads were bowed. Some eyes were looking straight ahead at us with curiosity and small hope. Some looked angry. Their expressions mirrored their hardships. Even as India has entered the twenty-first century, here on the riverine islands, not much has changed.

It has often been said that the Sundarbans represent one of the final frontiers between humans and nature. This is a story of the constant tussle between people and animals, a story of human tenacity in the face of great adversity and of human greed and its consequences; a story that is often lost in the silence of the winding creeks and marshy forests that unite the two.

The quiet undulating terrain of north Bengal where we went next is a stark contrast to the swampy forestlands of the Sundarbans. Gone are the brown dhoti-clad boatmen with sweat on their emaciated bodies, women with threadbare saris on their thin frames catching prawns in waist-deep waters, the coloured idols of Bon Bibi and Shah Jongli. This is tea country. Here, the countryside resonates with the soft chuckle of River Teesta as it happily skips around its home territory. Narrow, often circuitous, roads yield to criss-crossing rivulets. Hills are carpeted with tea bushes and lush forests. The all-pervasive sultry mugginess of Kolkata and the wetlands gives way to much cooler climes. By evening, there is a nip in the air. Even the people here look different. The singularity of appearance that marks the inhabitants of the tide country is no longer evident. Here, there is an intermingling of features and complexions – from the sharp, well-defined Bengali faces to the Indo-Mongoloid features and paler skin tones of the Rajbanshi to the flatter noses and narrow foreheads of the Oraon.[7] So palpable is the difference between the tide and the tea countries that at first glance it is difficult to believe that these two extremes are part of a single state. And yet, as we discovered in June 2007, these visible distinctions are just skin-deep. There is a much stronger, albeit less evident thread of commonality that binds these two topographically diametrically opposite biospheres.

---

[7] The Oraon are an agricultural tribe found mainly in Orissa, Bihar, Jharkhand and West Bengal. It is believed that the British brought the Oraon to West Bengal from Bihar and Orissa to work in the tea gardens. They are the most prominent tribe of New Mal, which comes under the Jalpaiguri district of West Bengal, where they still work in the tea gardens. Source: http://www.rrh.org.au/articles/subviewnew.asp?ArticleID=385, accessed 10 April 2009.

We got off at Bagdogra airport in Darjeeling District and climbed into the white sarkari Ambassador which would take us in and around the tea country for the next two days. From here, it was a fifty-seven kilometre drive to the adjoining district of Jalpaiguri and its headquarters of the same name. According to some, Jalpaiguri gets its name from the Bengali 'jolpai' or olive. Others trace its origin to the Bhutanese term je-le-pe-go-ri, meaning 'a place where warm clothes are bought and sold'. A few devout Hindus believe that it is named after 'Jalpesh' or Shiva, who is the presiding deity of the region. But for most tourists who have experienced the cultural extravaganza of Bhutan, Sikkim or India's north-east, New Jalpaiguri is no more than a gateway to the exotic, the nearest railhead.

Located across the narrow chicken neck that connects the Indian mainland to its north-eastern states, Jalpaiguri District shares its borders with Bhutan, Bangladesh, Assam, Cooch Behar and Darjeeling. It is located in the fertile flood plains known as the Dooars,[8] literally meaning 'doors' or 'passageways'. It is believed that there were eighteen such passageways in the area that were used for travel and trade with Bhutan. Historically, the area was part of many kingdoms of Assam, Bengal and Bhutan including the Kamarupa, Koch and Bhotia empires. Then, in 1869, the British created a new district – Jalpaiguri.

We were heading towards the small town of Chalsa located about fifty-five kilometres from the district headquarters. Soon the tea gardens began to appear. The Dooars account for 15 per cent of the country's tea production. Tea plantations here are a legacy of the British. *The Imperial Gazetteer of India* published in 1908 noted that in Jalpaiguri District, 'Tea is cultivated on 121 square miles or 9% of the area under cultivation. This industry was introduced in 1874, and is carried out mainly by European enterprise and with European capital. In 1876 there were 13 gardens with an area of 818 acres, yielding 29,520 lb of tea. The cultivation was rapidly extended during the last decade of the nineteenth century; and by 1901 the number

---

[8] Stretching from River Teesta on the west to River Sankosh on the east, over a span of 130 km by 48 km along the foothills of the Himalayas, the Dooars occupy a major part of the Jalpaiguri and Cooch Behar districts of West Bengal. These are highly fertile flood plains known for their wildlife and lush forests.

of gardens had increased to 235, with a planted area of 109 square miles, and an outturn of over 31,000,000 lb'.[9] According to recent estimates, 32 per cent of the area of the district or 1,987 square km is under 284 tea plantations.[10] The last few years have, however, seen a crisis in the tea industry here. At the time of our visit in June 2007, fourteen estates were closed.

By the time our car drove into Sinclair Retreat Dooars, our hotel in Chalsa, it was late afternoon. It was a simple yet tastefully done hotel. Every room was furnished based on a regional theme which was displayed in the handlooms and handicrafts used in the decor. The lobby, the restaurant and even the bar used furniture and window-screens made of cane and bamboo. For the last three years, we had been advocating the use of local handlooms and handicrafts to promote culture tourism and support livelihoods. Finally, in the tea country, we had found a hotel doing exactly this.

At the hotel we met with the rest of our team: Mohini Giri (Guild of Service), Malini Bhattacharya (National Commission for Women), Krishna Tirath (Member of Parliament), Usha Rai (senior media and communication expert), Sreerupa Mitra Chaudhury (National Legal Services Authority), Sandhya Bajaj (National Commission for Protection of Child Rights), Pam Rajput (Women's Resource and Advocacy Centre), Gangotri Dutta (senior advocate) and Rupali Moulik (Save the Garden campaign). We were eleven women from different walks of life and age groups, the youngest among us being twenty-six years old, the oldest, over seventy. What had brought us together was our growing concern for the tea plantation workers. By the time we had all collected to go to the estates, it was getting dark. We reached our first stop, Ranicherra Tea Estate after 7 p.m.

It was pitch-dark but we could sense the large crowd which had gathered to meet us. Torches flashed, showing the way to a small hut. By the light

---

[9] *Imperial Gazetteer of India*, vol. 14, Oxford, Clarendon Press, 1908-1931. Accessed online at http://dsal.uchicago.edu/reference/gazetteer/pager. html?objectid=DS405.1.I34_V14_042.gif on 9 April 2009.

[10] http://jalpaiguri.gov.in/MAP1.html Website of the District administration accessed on 5 April 2009 and http://www.rrh.org.au/articles/subviewnew. asp?ArticleID=385, accessed 10 April 2009.

of a battery-powered bulb, we saw a young girl no more than nineteen or twenty years old. Her face was blank; her eyes had a terrified expression. She clutched a small child in her arms. An older one clung to her sari. 'This is Lakshmi,' said a voice out of the dark.

In her silent presence, the same voice recounted her story. Ten days earlier, Lakshmi had been sitting outside her hut with her husband, Sanyasi Mungeri. Their two sons aged one and four were asleep inside. Suddenly they heard a crash. 'The elephants ... Run!' shouted Sanyasi. Lakshmi grabbed her sons and ran without looking back. She managed to drag her children to safety. Breathing a sigh of relief she turned towards her husband only to realize that he was not there. The elephants had taken him away.

'Mauled to death,' said the voice. In the flickering light we saw Lakshmi's tear-stained face. 'Do things like this still happen?' we asked the disembodied voice. There was no response. What could these unfortunate victims say to us? They were sitting in the dark, unaffected by the new highs of development and double-digit growth. We remembered the grisly tales of tiger attacks we had heard in some villages of the Sundarbans.

'What now? How will you take care of yourself and your sons?' one of our companions asked gently. Lakshmi remained silent; we could sense she was crying again. Then a woman's voice answered. 'Madam, as always the owners simply washed their hands of the incident. Since her husband was not a registered employee, just a bigha mazdoor.'

'Bigha mazdoor?' we asked.

'Yes. Normally, if an estate needs 1,000 workers during the peak season, only 300 are employed as registered workers. The rest are hired on a daily basis as bigha mazdoors. They find work for three-four days in a week. While a registered worker gets between Rs 50 and 60 a day, bighas earn that much in one week. They are only paid Rs 3 per hour.'

'Rs 3 an hour?'

'Yes. Madamji, even when Sanyasi was alive, this family lived on Rs 12 a day. Now Lakshmi will have to find work as a bigha mazdoor. But she is scared to leave her children alone.'

'What about compensation?'

'The Forest Department gave a compensation of Rs 25,000. But no bank account was opened. The money is lying with a local shop-owner.'

We turned to Lakshmi. 'Do you have an Antyodaya card? The one on which you can get rations at Rs 2 per kg?' Almost imperceptibly, she shook her head. We learnt that Lakshmi did not even have a ration card. Her only asset was her 'house', plastic sheets strung on bamboo poles. We could find no words of consolation to offer the young girl who sat with her head bowed. As our cars began to drive out of the area, we turned around to take a last look. And there, in the dim light of the lone bulb, was a faint silhouette, the anxious figure of a frightened mother who watched over her babies night after night, straining for the first sounds of another elephant attack.

After a bumpy half-hour ride, our cars came to the hundred-year-old Nagaisuree Tea Estate, owned by the Goenkas. In the terrifying darkness, we picked our way with great care; someone spoke about snakes and leopards freely wandering around. 'Leopards always attack the necks of young girls,' someone said and all of us hurriedly wrapped sari pallus and dupattas around our necks and quickened our pace. 'Stamp your feet. It'll keep the snakes away,' another advised. In the pitch-black we used cell phones to light our path. The people here had never seen electricity. Not once in the last seventy-five years did the tea estate owners think of bringing light into the lives of their plantation workers, we were told. Darkness makes workers easy prey. Four wildlife sanctuaries: Buxar, Mahananda, Godumara and Jaldapara, surround these estates. Animals often wander through the estates; there is no light, no security, no fencing.

We reached a cluster of huts. 'This is Sujtao Oraon,' someone told us as another woman came out of the dark. By the light of our cell phones, we saw her face; she must have been in her late forties. 'It was 3 a.m.,' she spoke softly. 'I was sleeping inside my house when they (the elephants) came. See here … they broke the wall, then dragged him.' It was from his own home that her husband Ram Oraon had been taken away and mauled. 'Didi, I could do nothing. I hid my five children in the farthest corner of the hut and waited. The elephants must have had their fill, they never came back. Some villagers searched all night.' She broke down. Someone moved to place an arm around her. 'His body was found the next day', she said, her voice choked with tears.

Sujtao, we learnt, was luckier than most widows in the area; and there were many of them. She was a registered worker, so Rs 60 per day was confirmed. By now, other shadowy figures had surrounded us. The atmosphere was eerie and, ever so often, we found ourselves straining for the sounds of some animal on the prowl. One by one, the shadowy figures (nameless, faceless workers) told us about their life in the gardens without bijli (electricity), paani (water) and sometimes even sadak (road). There was no drinking water in this particular labour line. The garden school was up to Class 4. To study further, children had to go to Malbazaar; it took at least one hour by bus. Many had dropped out. The stories of despair and distress seemed unending. By the time we left the estate we were simmering with rage. As we prepared ourselves for another sleepless night, we asked each other where the estate owners were. In their comfortable homes in big cities, where the tragedy of tea workers was too far away to cause discomfort. Someone recited lines from a poem by Faiz Ahmed Faiz:

> Un dukhi maaon ke naam
> Raat mein jin ke bachche bilaktey hain aur
> Neend ki maar khaaye huey baazuon se sambhaltey nahin
> Dukh batatey nahin
> Minnaton zaariyon se baheltey nahin

> Lines to mothers whose
> Children wail all night
> Whose arms heavy with sleep can't hold them
> Children who don't tell their pain, who
> Refuse to be calmed by mothers' entreaties.

The next morning we woke up with a sense of foreboding. The estates we had visited last night were the ones that were still running. That day, we had planned to see labour lines in the estates that had closed down. We would be meeting people who had been without jobs for almost five years now. What does one say to people who have known persistent hunger for five years?

Our first stop was Kathalgudi Tea Estate. This was among the first estates to close, in June 2002; the 1,479 registered workers and 1,500 bigha workers employed here have been unemployed since then. A few months earlier, the government had announced a welfare package of Rs 500 per month and subsidized rations for people who had been employed on closed tea estates.

But this was only for the registered workers. Meanwhile, in 2004, the lease of Kathalgudi was cancelled and, at the time of our visit, the government was planning to auction it off. The explanation of why so many estates had closed came from a young man in a checked shirt whom we met at the entrance to the estate. When tea plantations were introduced in the area, land was given on lease for ninety-nine years. But the leaseholders or plantation owners (as they were called) assumed ownership rights over the land and sold it many times over. This resulted in legal battles. The present owners are no longer content with a renewal of the lease. They want a transfer of the land in their name and consequently the deadlock. They abandoned the plantations, leaving thousands of families who had been working here for generations stranded. Suddenly the workers had nowhere to go. As if this was not enough of a blow, tea-processing factories also began to shut down. This happened because the estates had been demanding the same subsidies as agriculture. But, so long as the factories ran, they could not claim the same status. So, factories were shown as sick, and closed. Overnight, hundreds of factory workers lost their jobs. In the last few years, in Jalpaiguri alone, fourteen tea estates have shut down, affecting over 3.5 lakh people.

As we entered Kathalgudi, it was evident that this estate was different from many of the operational ones which we had seen on our way. Due to disease and lack of maintenance, tea bushes were turning from lush green to a sickly brown. Soon there would be no leaves left.

There were twelve labour lines or 'workers' colonies' at this estate. By the time we reached the Hudkola Labour Line, it was 10.30 a.m. Fifteen hundred people from 131 households lived here. A public hearing had been arranged. Hundreds of people had gathered inside a makeshift plastic tent. Most of them were tribals – Gond, Oraon, Santhal – or Nepali. Jalpaiguri District has a rich ethnic mix. While the Bengali and the Rajbanshi (people of Indo-Mongoloid origin, who are found in Nepal in large numbers) are the dominant groups, the tea estate labourers are mostly tribals from Bihar and Jharkhand. This has been the trend ever since the first estates were set up in the late nineteenth century. *The Imperial Gazetteer* took cognizance of this: 'There is also an enormous immigration of tea garden coolies from Chhota Nagpur and the Santhal Paraganas; Ranchi alone supplies more than 80,000 Oraons and Mundas, and the Santhal Paraganas 11,000.

Many of these coolies are settling down permanently, either in the gardens or as cultivators and cart owners, but many return at intervals. In the tea gardens on the higher slopes at the foot of the hills, Nepalese replace men from Chhota Nagpur, and many of these also find a permanent home in the district.'[11]

One by one, people spoke. Kalpana Kami, Maya Devi, Fulsari Kami, Basanti, Navin Chhetri, all had similar stories. They had worked here for years. Then, suddenly, one day, they found themselves without work. Their electricity was cut off immediately after closure as the estate owners had not settled the bills for a long time. They had to fight the animal menace in darkness. No electricity also meant that the four tube wells on the estate stopped functioning. So, for drinking water, they were forced to go to the neighbouring Dooars Tea Estate (two km away) or drink from streams, which have high dolomite content. This has resulted in various disabilities caused by dolomite poisoning. According to hospital records, in the fifteen months immediately after the estates closed, there were 378 deaths. The people quote a higher figure, 531. The cause: malnutrition.

'What about your anganwadi centre?' we asked.

'There is none here.'

'The children must be going somewhere?' we persisted.

'There is an anganwadi outside the estate, more than one kilometre away. But we can't send the children there by themselves. With the animals prowling around the estates, it's not safe.'

'Health facilities?'

Silence.

Then a middle-aged man dressed in a shirt and shorts got up to answer. 'Along with the estate, the hospital also closed. For a long time we had no help. Then the Supreme Court intervened, saying that all workers on closed tea estates should be declared BPL (Below the Poverty Line) and get health facilities, water and work for fifteen days every month. Now a mobile clinic is held twice every week. It dispenses medicines for fever, diarrhoea and does immunization. For everything else, people have to travel eight kilometres to

---

[11] *Imperial Gazetteer of India*: Provincial Series - Eastern Bengal and Assam; Superintendent of Government Printing; Calcutta; 1909

the PHC (Primary Health Centre) or thirty-three kilometres to the CHC (Community Health Centre),' explained Kaulan Rai. Suddenly a number of voices spoke up.

'As if the PHC is any help!'

'The CHC covers 4.35 lakh people but they have neither adequate staff nor medicine.'

'There is no place to set foot in the sarkari hospital.'

'What about work?' we asked.

A thin woman in her late twenties with a mix of Nepali and tribal facial features got up to speak. She was dressed in a bright salwar suit and a thick red line of sindoor filled the parting in her oiled hair. 'There is no work. Many of our men go across the border to Bhutan to break stones or work in the dolomite mines. The border is just half a kilometre from here. The OMC occasionally gives work but only to some registered workers.'

The OMC (Operating Management Committee) was a local body which had emerged after the closure of the estates. It had taken charge of the gardens and gave sporadic employment to registered workers for the collection of residue leaves from the bushes. These were then sold as CTC (black tea). Durga Prasad Oraon was a representative of the ten-member OMC. He told us that they had provided 111 days of work at Rs 45 per day. They had managed to collect kachcha patti (loose leaves) and sell it as CTC, making Rs 98 lakh in one year. This source of income would, however, dry up very soon, Rajat Kanti Rai who had earlier worked as a store supervisor in the estate warned. 'Closure of estates has meant no maintenance, no manure for the plants. People simply collect whatever little grows. Moreover, the life of a tea plantation is no more than sixty years. Most have gone well past this age and need replanting. But that would mean a cost of Rs 10 crore for an estate like this one with 1,200 acres of land,' he explained.

A man in his mid-thirties holding a tiny girl in his arms approached us. The child barely looked nine months old and showed signs of physical and mental disability.

'What's her name?' we asked.

'Sanjana. She is two-and-half-years old,' the father, Sumesh Oraon, answered.

'She is very thin,' we said. What we meant to say was that she was horribly malnourished and probably would not live even a year. 'What do you do for work?'

He told us that he was once a registered worker on the estate. Now the OMC gave him work three days a week. For the remaining days, he went to Bhutan. 'My other daughter was four. She died,' he said. The symptoms he described – fever and vomiting – indicated severe malnutrition. By his side, with her head lowered, stood his twenty-seven-year-old wife, Vyjayanthi. Dressed in a light pink nightie, she was mere skin and bones.

We looked for immediate help for this unfortunate family. A group of young girls between the ages of seven and seventeen came up to where we were standing. Sanjana reached out to a small girl in a green frock. The girl smiled and held the child's hand. She told us her name was Hema Chettri. A few other younger ones wore thin cotton frocks or skirts. The elder ones were in saris. Hema said she walked four kilometres every day to get to school. 'We had a school in our bagan (garden) earlier but it shut down. Now two didis (older sisters) hold classes in the closed staff quarters. They charge Rs 50 as fee. Since we can't afford it, most of the children have to walk long distances to government schools,' someone explained.

'For the midday meal, there is patli (thin) khichdi,' fifteen-year-old Anju, a Nepali girl wearing a sari, said with a grimace, 'We hate it.' Anita, Champa and Saraswati, all students of Classes 8 and 9, wanted transport for the eight kilometre travel to the government-aided school at Banarhat.

As we got up to leave the estate, a few elderly women surrounded us. Twenty-five per cent of women workers on the estate were well past their sixties. They did not receive any old age pension and were incapable of going across the border to Bhutan to break stones. When the estates were running, a portion of their wage was put aside each month as Provident Fund. But here again they were duped. This money was not deposited in the bank. When the factories and the estates were abandoned, the PF money disappeared. The workers lost jobs, and along with them all their accrued savings.

Dilmaya was a frail, elderly widow. White hair pulled back in a severe bun, she wore a gamcha (coarse cotton cloth) over her white blouse. She clutched a photograph tightly in her calloused hands. 'My twenty-year-old grandson, Manoj Chhetri,' she cried. 'All my children are dead. He is all I have, my only family. In June 2005, an agent promised him a job and took him away. Ever since then, I have no news. Where do I go?' Crying helplessly she clutched our hands. 'Please, didi, you help me.' We looked for a response from the district collector, who had joined us a few minutes ago. He promised to have the matter investigated. Anju, who had earlier asked for school transportation, shyly came forward. 'Sir, maybe you can help the rest of us as well. Girls and boys from our area are lured by agents and sold into prostitution, manual labour or domestic labour. Some of my friends were taken to Sikkim and Kerala as domestic workers. We never heard from them again.' Indrajeet, a young worker from a local NGO, Birpara Welfare Organization, told us that forty-two children had been trafficked from Kathalgudi Tea Estate alone. 'These cases, like Dilmaya's, are hopeless because the police refuse to register them.' The assurances from the district collector were all we could get on the spot; there were no instant executive powers we could command. Saddened, we headed towards our next destination: the Neponia division of the Dheklapara Tea Estate.

Our vehicles were travelling through a riverbed; rivers surround Dheklapara on two sides. When it rains, people are cut off from schools, health, rations and all outside contact. Every year, the waters gobble up one or two bighas of land. In this particular subdivision of the estate, which closed seven years ago, there are 250 registered labourers and a population of thirty-five hundred. In the case of Neponia too, with closure went electricity and drinking water. An OMC was formed and they managed to get an annual turnover of Rs 2.5 lakh from the residue leaves. People spoke of trafficking, malnutrition, absence of health facilities, closing of garden schools and mauling by animals. Putul Oraon, a twenty-year-old disabled girl, was brought to us. 'Her mother died of starvation and her father is mentally unstable. Didi, there are many such Putuls in these gardens who become victims of trafficking. Disappearance stories are too many to recount,' a woman holding Putul's hand said. We noticed her blank eyes and realized that she could have been totally or partially blind. 'I am Nabaneeta. Putul is like my child.'

A group of teenage boys and girls – Anand Oraon, Rajbir, Cheena Oraon, Jharna – surrounded us. All of them had to drop out of school when the gardens closed. 'The bagan school closed. The nearest government school is at Birpara, eight kilometres away. How can we go there?' fourteen-year-old Jharna asked.

'So what do you do now?'

'Most of us break stones in the riverbed. A few who have cycles and larger families (hence more people to earn) go to Birpara,' she said, pointing to a group of girls in school uniforms.

'Why didn't they go today?' we asked.

'It's raining.'

'So? Can't you use umbrellas? It will rain all through the monsoons.'

'Didi, you don't understand. When it rains, the rivers on both sides of the estate become very dangerous. At that time, no one can go out, be it for work, study or to the doctor. Often, we have been forced to miss our exams,' Jharna explained. It was then that the magnitude of their problem hit us; a problem we had seen earlier in the forest-fringe villages in Bilaspur, Chattisgarh.[12]

We looked back at the bright young faces in front of us. Surprisingly they held no complaint, no fear, no anger. Tridib Pal, an accompanying social worker said that thirty of these 'dropouts' had formed a Village Rescue and Rehabilitation Society. 'We have found a new cause. We will rescue girls from trafficking, issue flood warnings, take people to hospitals, sound red alerts for elephant attacks. After all, these are our people and we have to help ourselves to improve our lives.' We looked at the fifteen-year-old girl in a white sari with a red border who was speaking. 'I am Rupali. The Matri Sangh Jan Kalyan Ashram and Birpara Welfare Association are training us.' We felt our eyes grow moist. This time it was hope which choked the throat. Rupali and her friends had dispelled the pall of gloom that had descended on us since yesterday.

Suddenly there was commotion. 'Please hurry. The water level is rising. We have to leave immediately,' said a police officer who came running. The anguish and despair of the plantation workers took on new meaning as we hurriedly got into cars and left them to cope with their marooned lives.

The Ramjhora Tea Estate was the last garden on our agenda. By the time we got there, it was 2 p.m. It hadn't stopped raining and yet over 300 women,

---

[12] See Chapter 7

men and children had gathered inside a huge shed. This estate had closed in August 2002. Here, nothing was left, no tea bushes had survived. The workers had to work as bigha mazdoors in other gardens or go to Bhutan to earn Rs 40 a day. Their third option was NREGA, about which there was a lot of discontent. Many complained that they were not paid for their work. Anjana Khatoon was a short Bengali woman in her thirties with a small child perched on her hip. 'If we work for forty-five days, we are told we are only entitled to wages for forty days. And for the last five or six months there has been no work,' she said. Once again we heard complaints of mauling by elephants; in the last few weeks two men had been killed and one was badly injured. The district magistrate who was present at the meeting expressed helplessness over the elephant menace. 'Every time we speak to the Forest and Wildlife Department, they say that the increase in elephant population shows the success of conservation efforts.' Compensation is paid only in cases of death. This means that the people get nothing if they are injured or if their houses are damaged.

Our visit to the tea estates of Jalpaiguri – closed as well as running – left us angry and ashamed. Angry at the plantation owners who have deprived workers of electricity, water, schools and health facilities. Angry that even today there are bigha workers who earn Rs 3 an hour and Rs 18-25 a day. And ashamed that, in twenty-first century India, people continue to be mauled to death by wild animals; that despite our rapid and consistent growth-rate starvation deaths continue; that hands skilled in plucking leaves are forced to break stones and endure slow poisoning in the dolomite mines of Bhutan because we are unable to provide them with a source of livelihood. Ashamed that we have been able to provide no government safety net to the plantation workers. Under the Plantation Labour Act, estate owners are responsible for providing health, education and other amenities to the workers. But many owners have not fulfilled these obligations and the district administration is unable to enforce compliance. 'What if they too close shop and run?' the district collector asked. So the future of the plantation workers and their children continues to droop and wilt like the over-age tea bushes they tend.

What troubled us most was the fact that plantation workers were no longer on our radar. Why else were there no anganwadi centres, schools or PHCs for them despite the high incidence of malnutrition, malaria and tuberculosis? The district collector admitted that there were one hundred recorded malaria deaths in the district last year. The actual numbers were probably higher. NGOs told us that DOTS was not working because people do not have access to healthcare and when they do manage to get the medicine, there is never enough food in their stomachs for the treatment to be effective. For first-hand verification of this, we visited the Block PHC at Chalsa.

This PHC covers a population of 2.2 lakh and is for most tea garden workers the only government health facility available to them. There are just two doctors here; no specialists. When we visited the hospital, rain-water lay in stagnant pools outside the centre while the water supply line was not working. We met a plantation worker who was suspected to be suffering from leprosy. We learnt that leprosy continues to affect a number of people here. In the same compound, we saw the subcentre. The ANM, Reva Gangopadhyay, could not answer any of our questions about the population she was supposed to cover, the common ailments people suffer from or the level of malnutrition in her area.

When we were planning our trip to Jalpaiguri, we were warned about the anger among the people. 'The Naxals are gaining ground.' On the first day of our visit, there was a bandh called by a local organization asking for a state of Greater Kamatapur for the Rajbanshi. Having seen the condition of the estate workers, we could understand why this was happening. People told us with great anguish that when the estates closed and they were dying of starvation, no one came to their rescue except some organizations like the Bharatiya Swayam Sewak Sangh. 'Where was the government?' they asked.

Returning to the Bagdogra airport, we thought about the similarity between the tea and the tide countries. As in the Sundarbans, the tranquil beauty of the tea country is mesmerizing. Here too, the gently undulating terrain clothed in different shades of green, the blue mountains covered by swirling mists, and innumerable rivulets snaking across the tea estates create an illusion of serenity. But it is only an illusion. Within both these fringes of West Bengal, this calm hides the discontent brewing among wildlife as well as humans. Animals have lost their territory and are on a rampage. Humans have lost their amenities; many their livelihoods. They too, are filled with anger. Even the vegetation seems to have risen in silent mutiny, and the tea bushes are dying.

On the return flight, we remembered a song from the film *Rahi*, made in the fifties by K.A. Abbas under his banner Naya Sansar. The film was about tea workers:

> *Ek kali aur do patiyan*
> *Janey hamri sab batiyan*
>
> One bud, two leaves
> Know all there is to know about us.

The condition of these tea plantation workers is intimately known only by the sprigs of the tea bushes. The condition of the dwellers of the islands is known only by the tides. We who plan their lives remain unknowing. The poet Mir Taqi Mir said it all in a couplet:

> *Patta patta boota boota haal hamara jaane hai*
> *Jaane na jaane gul hi na jaane baagh to sara jaane hai*
>
> Every leaf, every tree knows my condition
> The entire garden knows, only the rose is unknowing.

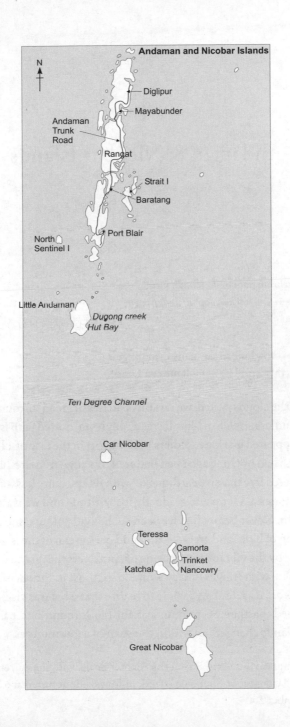

Andaman and Nicobar Islands

N

Diglipur

Mayabunder

Andaman
Trunk
Road

Rangat

Strait I

Baratang

Port Blair

North
Sentinel I

Little Andaman

Dugong creek
Hut Bay

Ten Degree Channel

Car Nicobar

Teressa

Camorta
Trinket
Nancowry

Katchal

Great Nicobar

4

Andaman & Nicobar Islands

Koi mehram nahi milta jahaan mein
Mujhe kehna hai kuch apni zubaan mein

— ALTAF HUSSAIN HALI

I have something to say in my own tongue
But in this world no confidante can I find!

As the clouds parted, we saw tiny patches of green surrounded by an endless stretch of blue. It was a rough sea, dotted with islands that appeared like lone soldiers holding fort in the face of all adversity, soldiers who had not long ago been battered by a fifteen-metre-high wall of water, triggered by a massive earthquake[1] with its epicentre less than 170 km away in Indonesia. Our plane gradually lost altitude and we watched with bated breath. Never before had we seen such vivid colours, such a perfect composition of blues and greens – the staid dark green of the island forests surrounded by the vibrant aquamarine of coral reefs that gradually yielded to a deep blue with fringes of lacy white foam. Lost in the sheer beauty of the sight before us, it took us a while to realize that what was visible was the newly formed coastline. Six months ago, the life, lore and landmass of these Emerald Islands changed, all within the span of a few minutes.

---

[1] The earthquake measured 8.9 on the Richter Scale, with the epicentre 42 km north of Bazunazerah, Simuelue Island, Indonesia. It occurred at 6.28 a.m. on 26 December 2004.

At around 6.30 a.m. on 26 December 2004, tourists and natives of the islands were fast asleep, tired after the Christmas celebrations. Suddenly, the earth shook, and their world came crashing down, quite literally. Three huge tidal waves, travelling at a speed of approximately 700 kmph hit the islands. Bleary eyed people were terror-struck as they watched entire villages being swept away by the raging waters. According to official estimates, 3,513 people were dead, 10,000 houses completely damaged, and Rs 321 crores worth of agricultural crop lost. Unofficial estimates put the death toll at over 7,000. The landmass tipped, some areas, particularly in Northern Andaman, went up by four to six feet; others in Nicobar went down. The sea swallowed over 4,451 hectares of agricultural land besides beaches, villages and forests. The archipelago suffered losses to the tune of Rs 3,836.56 crores, and over 50,000 people were affected. On the morning of 22 June 2005, when we reached the islands, the devastation unleashed by the tidal waves was still visible. Field after field of paddy lay submerged; thousands of coconut trees had been uprooted and scattered all over the coastline. Lush, once vibrant, mangroves had turned into a burnt brown mess inundated by angry young waves.

We began our visit with a two-hour session with the officials, wading through a mountain of statistics that briefed us about the impact of the tsunami and the progress of relief activities.

Located 1,200 km from mainland India, the Andaman & Nicobar archipelago consists of 572 islands, islets and rocks, covering an area of 8,249 square km. Of these, just thirty-eight are inhabited. The population of the island as per the 2001 census was 3.56 lakh; less than 28,000 belong to the indigenous tribes, some of which have inhabited the island for 60,000 years. The rest are settlers, brought in at different times, and encroachers. Situated in the sliver between the Burma and Sunda tectonic plates, and sandwiched between a choppy Andaman Sea and the Indian Ocean, these islands are in an extremely vulnerable position. The first recorded tsunami here was on 31 December 1881; the next on 26 June 1941. The one in 2004 was the third tsunami to wreak havoc on this quiet island paradise.

Officials assured us that work on temporary shelters was almost over – 9,565 units had been constructed in fifty-eight locations – and all the people had moved out of the camps into their newly constructed shelters. Now livelihood was the top priority. 'We are providing the locals with materials and forty days' wages to build the shelters. Already, over six lakh man-days of work have been generated. This year alone, we have the potential to provide over thirty-four lakh man-days. We have also distributed Rs 52.25 crores as ex-gratia to the affected families.' These facts and figures were given to us by Janak Digal, the new relief commissioner.

By the time we set out to review the field realities, it was well past noon. During the tsunami, Port Blair, which is sheltered by many smaller islands, had escaped much damage. Surrounding low-lying areas like Sippighat, Junglighat and Chouldhari were submerged. Six months after the disaster, they were still inundated with sea water during high tide, making them uninhabitable. People from these areas, most of whom were Tamil and Bengali settlers, were staying at temporary shelters in other places. Birchgunj, located on the outskirts of Port Blair, was one such site, with 162 shelters. A series of tin houses on either side of a kutchcha lane made up the temporary residence of people who once lived in Sippighat and Junglighat. The sun's rays reflected off the shiny tin roofs.

'Don't these shelters get hot?' we asked, shielding our eyes.

'They do, but what choice did we have? We required 7.5 lakh bamboos to construct the walls for ten thousand intermediate shelters. But the ships could only carry seven thousand bamboos at a time. Had we waited, we would have never finished building these shelters before the monsoon. But we have provided fans in all the homes,' explained Naresh Kumar, Secretary of the Public Works Department (PWD) in the Union Territory. By this time, a group of people had surrounded us. 'Yes, we have fans, but electricity supply is erratic. During the day these shelters are scorching.' We turned towards the voice and saw a tall, sturdy Bengali woman wearing a yellow nightdress. Jet-black hair tied back in a tight bun and a big bindi of bright red kumkum sitting prominently on her forehead, she was the spitting image of a middle-class Bengali housewife. Her gold bangles, chain and earrings spoke of better times. 'Madhulata Baidya. Please come and see my house.'

Her home was a tin box – three metres by five metres, the standard size of all intermediate shelters, irrespective of the family size. Inside, steel utensils were neatly stacked on a rack that hung from the tin walls. There was no separate kitchen. On another wall, a small mirror had been attached over a shelf to serve as a dressing table. Next to it, on the wall, a clock ticked away. Clotheslines criss-crossed the room. On the floor were sleeping mats. It was hot in the room. The ceiling fan was stationary. Power cut. Amina, Madhulata's nineteen-year-old daughter had passed her Class 12 exam. Clad in a printed white nightie, she was drying her waist-length black hair in the sun. 'Suddenly, life has changed. Our daily routines have changed. Water was always scarce here but at the shelter it is priceless. We get it just once in two days, and for half an hour. Water-borne diseases are common, and we have no doctor. We have nothing to look forward to. I wish the government would provide counsellors for us students,' she sighed.

Walking around the temporary shelters and talking to the occupants, we realized that a lot more needed to be done to ensure basic amenities. Some efforts were underway. An anganwadi centre had been opened and the children looked healthy. NGOs like Oxfam were at work and had promised to provide medical aid and livelihood training. We met a woman who had been trained as a mason. P. Kamma used to live in Junglighat before the tsunami. Now she lives in one of the tin houses. Unlike other homes in the area, hers has a cement floor. 'I made it,' she informed us proudly.

Before returning to Port Blair, we went to see what the sea had done. As the car travelled towards Chouldhari, all along the fifteen-kilometre stretch from Port Blair, we saw ravaged fields and abandoned houses. We knew this to have been a prosperous area, with luxuriant crops standing ready for harvest. Now the crops were gone and the inhabitants were forced to move all the way to the other side of the island. The road from Gharacharma to Chouldhari, on which we were driving, had been lifted up after the tsunami and bunds constructed at the cost of Rs 1 crore per kilometre! This was to stop the ingress of sea water into the fields during high tide. But these waters were untameable. We passed field after field clogged with saline water. In some of these fields where the water had been drained, the administration was planning to apply gypsum to reclaim land for paddy plantation. This was surprising. Before coming to Port Blair, we had read the report of the M.S. Swaminathan Foundation, which promoted organic farming on the islands. It had cautioned against the use of gypsum.

Walking in the Marina Park in Port Blair that evening, we saw how the sea had risen and how turbulent the waters were. A restless ocean; this was not how it had looked in the past. At Haddo Wharf, we were told that the water had risen one-and-a-half metres since the tsunami. There was imminent danger with the high tide due the next month. Rumour, they said, works overtime in the islands these days. The word going around was that the land would be submerged on 23 July 2005.

The next morning we woke up early. We were travelling to the Nicobar District, a group of twenty-two islands, of which twelve are inhabited. Being much closer to the epicentre of the quake, the Nicobar Islands suffered the maximum devastation in India. In the Andaman group, damage was generally confined to the rising of land and destruction of a few houses along the coast; here, entire islands had been destroyed, smashed to pieces by a merciless sea. As these islands are the home of 30,000 Nicobarese (declared scheduled tribe), entry is restricted. The Nicobarese are believed to be of Indo-Mongoloid stock, with their language rooted in the Austro-Asiatic family. They are the largest surviving indigenous tribe on the archipelago today; their numbers have increased dramatically from just 6,000 in 1883. As the Nicobar Islands lie on an important trade route, the Nicobarese have been controlled by different groups of people including the French, Portuguese, Dane, British and Japanese. Through all this, they have retained much of their traditional lifestyle.

The rough and rowdy Ten Degree Channel separates the Andaman group of islands from Nicobar. By ship, it takes sixteen hours to reach Carnic, the northernmost inhabited island, but we were on a Dornier aircraft, with a team of six colleagues from the Tsunami Relief Project of the Planning Commission.

The view from the Dornier was even more breathtaking than from the flight the previous morning. The entire world seemed an endless expanse of blue of different shades, shades no artist's palette could create. Where did the water end and the sky begin? It was difficult, nay, impossible, to say. Perhaps it is in places like this that words like 'eternity,' 'harmony,' 'continuum' take on new meanings. Against the constant drone of the Dornier, it was difficult to say or hear anything. There were people around us and yet we felt as if an invisible wrap had been thrown over us. It was a private world, without boundaries. In the lines of Iqbal,

'Tu hai muheet e bekaran mein ek zara si aabju'
You are the boundless ocean, I, an infinitesimal drop.

All too soon we were shaken out of our reverie by the captain. 'Look down,' he said, pointing. There, below us, extremely vulnerable, stood the saucer-shaped island of Car Nicobar. The northernmost island of the Nicobar group, Carnic or Pu in the local language, covers an area of just 127 square km. Yet more than 50 per cent of the population of the Nicobar District is settled here. The 2001 census showed a population of 21,000, of which 17,000 were Nicobarese tribals. The island was ringed by a tiny strip of golden yellow sand. Even from the aircraft, the bruises suffered by it were clearly visible.

Our aircraft stopped at the Carnic Air Force Base. It is said that when Jawaharlal Nehru, the first prime minister of India, visited this island, Edward Kutchal, a tribal leader, donated two hundred acres of land to the government. In return, he took Nehru's coat. It was on this land that the air force base was built.[2] This had once been a lively place, filled with the banter of officers. Approximately five hundred families had lived here, many in sea-facing bungalows. Everything had been reduced to rubble, flattened by the tsunami. At this base, 120 people lost their lives, including fifty-two children. Shaken by the tragedy, the government declared Car Nicobar as a non-family posting.

At the base, we met Wing Cdr Nitin Sathe. He told us that the flat island offered little protection from the killer waves and much of the infrastructure had been swept away. Yet, miraculously, the hangar survived, making it possible to bring in relief supplies. Ten portable cabins and some temporary shelters had been put up there. Wing Cdr Sathe repeated something we had already heard the previous day – the tin shelters were too hot and uncomfortable for the locals who were used to staying in large bamboo houses on a machan (raised platform). We would hear this often during the trip. 'You have to understand that the way of life is different here. The Nicobarese, especially those living here, are simple people with strong family

---

[2] http://news.indiainfo.com/2003/01/20/20vajsettle.html, accessed on January 4, 2009.

and community structures called tuhet. All the members of an extended family (or tuhet) live together in a big round hut. How can you expect them to live in these tiny single-unit tin structures? Such a move will damage the very fabric of their society – damage that would be worse than the tsunami,' Sathe explained. Already the socio-cultural ties were under strain because the island had lost many of its elders; unofficial estimates say that over 2,000 people had died here. As we walked towards the cars that would take us around the island, Wing Cdr Sathe said quietly: 'Madam, the government recently distributed compensation money. A tribal came to the base with a thousand-rupee note for a bottle of water. When the change was returned to him, he just looked at it and walked away, saying, "What use are these to me?" It is this simplicity of the tribals that is now being exploited by some.'

As the car cautiously moved on dirt tracks around the island – the forty-kilometre ring road that circled Carnic had mostly been swept away – we saw that debris was being cleared and segregated. But given the scale of the devastation, the task was far from over. New manifestations of the cataclysm were surfacing every day. New stretches of land and roads sank. Stagnant pools of water in this malaria-prone region posed the threat of a dangerous epidemic, and yet, to the administration's credit, no outbreak of disease had been reported anywhere. We saw a natural wall of sand which had come up on the beach, this was the golden ring which we had viewed from the Dornier. It had become the island's only protection against the sea, especially during high tide.

We were travelling to the village of Tamaloo accompanied by Vivek Kumar Porwal, a young Indian Administrative Service (IAS) officer from the Madhya Pradesh cadre who had recently been appointed district collector (DC) of Nicobar. Looking out of the car window, we saw pile after pile of debris, skeletons of what were once shops, government buildings, air force quarters and schools stood like ghosts against the backdrop of deep blue. The island's only movie theatre looked like a house of cards that had gone down in the wind. As we walked among the crumpled buildings, we felt tears well up. Half-buried in the sand were the memories of happy families, pages from a school notebook, a broken doll, the mangled remains of a toy car. A fridge was hanging on the branch of a tree, a wooden railing was lying intact in a mess of twisted metal. Broken houses, broken people, and broken dreams; would lives ever be rebuilt around here?

Tamaloo was home to 1,576 people. Inside a newly built bamboo shelter, which was the community hall, a small meeting had been organized for us. We were surprised to see that only women had turned up. Usually, the opposite happened. 'What happened to the men?' we asked. 'They are at work; they are daily wagers,' explained Thomas Philip, one of three men who were present. He was captain of the village of Mus, and secretary of the Tribal Council, the traditionally elected body that looks after the Nicobarese people. Under the Nicobarese system, the tuhet heads elect a village captain. The captains from all the villages come together to form the council. It is this council that arbitrates disputes, decides what developmental works should be carried out for the island and how much land should be given to whom.

Philip expressed his unhappiness with the relief and rehabilitation work. 'Drinking water is scarce, and water for bathing or washing a luxury. Look at the roads. You must have felt the jolts. But at least here we are connected. In villages like Sawaii, Titop and Aarong, people normally have to walk four-five kilometres to reach the hospital or to visit family.' The district collector gave a dismal nod. 'Every day, a new piece of land or road sinks. We are trying to raise the level of roads. We have also identified twenty-six sites for wells and five sites for check-dams. But you have to understand that because of subduction and inflow of salt water, most water sources in the island have been contaminated.' We looked at the people sitting around. The children appeared healthy, immunization had been carried out. Yet, every day was a struggle, and the strain was written all over their faces. They wanted basic amenities, which the administration could not immediately provide.

The next stop was the village of Small Lapathy. We saw a PWD signboard which displayed the number of household units at the shelter site (268) and the quantities of CGI sheets (8,340), etc., that had been distributed. Biju Verghese, the Assistant Engineer, PWD, in the camp, said that the basic problem in Carnic was the absence of stones. People were forced to use coral and limestone for roads and these did not have any binding properties. Ireena Mark, the tribal captain of the village, was the only woman on the Tribal Council. She took us to her house, a beautiful airy structure on stilts, made of wood and bamboo mats with CGI roofing. Underneath the bamboo-matted floor, firewood was stacked and a few animals were tied to the wooden posts. Inside the house, pink curtains at every door and window were neatly tied together. Checked table-cloths covered the newly constructed wooden desks. A white fan and a few kerosene lamps hung from the ceiling. 'We get power for just three hours every evening,' Ireena told us. On one bamboo-matted wall hung a large portrait of Jesus Christ; 98 per cent of the Nicobarese are Christians. It was Vedappan Solomon, a Tamilian convert and the first Government Agent of Car Nicobar, who brought Christianity to the islands in 1896. He, along with his pupil John Richardson, a Nicobarese Bishop, was responsible for the spread of Christianity and education on the island.[3] The remaining two per cent of the Nicobarese are Muslims and animists. For many on the island, it was their faith that had saved them that fateful morning.

Robert Henry was a sixty-seven-year-old tribal captain. 'I remember as a child hearing Rev. John Richardson say, "Let us remember that our Church has been built on elevated ground. If anything happens, we can run here". When I saw a thirty-foot wall of water surging towards us, I told my family to run to the church, and we ran. Everyone in my village was safe except one old man. The wall of water was huge and the sound was like a giant airplane. It was so ferocious that it tore the coffins out of the church graveyard.' Post-tsunami, the Nicobarese once again are deriving solace from their church.

Ireena told us that it had taken seven people six months to build her house, where sixteen members of her family lived. This was the ideal Carnic home. We noticed that most temporary shelters in Carnic were built on some kind of machan (raised platform) of wood, cement or bricks salvaged from the debris. Here houses were not just rows of corrugated iron sheets. People had shown remarkable innovation in the use of debris and other materials. This was perhaps why they were unwilling to find alternative sites for permanent shelters. 'Convert our intermediate shelters to permanent dwellings,' they said. Bishop Christopher Paul, chief of the Tribal Council

---

[3] http://www.andaman.org/NICOBAR/book/history/Britain/Hist-Britain. htm. Accessed on 7 January 2009. Also in Dhingra, Kiran, *Andaman and Nicobar Islands in the 20ᵗʰ Century: A Gazetteer*, p.51.

of Car Nicobar, added his bit: 'It saves time, effort and money. Just give us some wood and cement to make our kind of houses'. By now, the afternoon was waning. Officers told us it was time to leave Carnic. Choppers could not fly after dark and we had other islands to visit. So, once again, we found ourselves on a broken trail that led to the air force base. On the way, we saw some people working on a patch of land. Small green shoots were sprouting everywhere, signifying a fresh start.

On reaching the air force base, we were told that all of us could not go on the next leg of the journey, namely, to the Central Nicobar Islands, also known as the Nancowry group. They were perhaps the least accessible and worst-affected islands of the archipelago. To get to them we had to switch to the Pawan Hans helicopter, which could not accommodate the entire team, so four members had to stay behind in Carnic.

Near Katchal Island, the green of the emerald waters was replaced by a murky sea. As we flew over it, tin roofs flashed amidst the thick forests. A few submerged huts stood in the middle of the sea; these had once been the site of bustling villages. The sea had swallowed over 1,500 hectares of land in this island which has a total area of 174 square km. Thirty-four out of the island's thirty-five census villages had been affected, and nine out of its eleven schools washed away. Out of the 5,312 (2001 census) people living here, 1,551 were dead or missing, all of them tribals. The non-tribals, who, pre-tsunami, accounted for half the island's population, were mostly Sri Lankan Tamils working on rubber plantations which were located at a height, away from the sea. All of them escaped.

From the Katchal helipad, we took a kutchcha trail to the Japan Tikri Shelter Camp[4] that housed people from four villages. Officials told us that this muddy, potholed trail running through the forest became unusable every time there was a heavy shower. Pre-tsunami, most of the habitation in the Nicobar Islands had been along the coast. These lands had now been submerged or devastated and the coastal roads destroyed. The post-tsunami shelters had been built away from the coast, on higher ground, wherever it

---

[4] It is said that when the Japanese gained control of Katchal during World War II, they tortured the tribals at a place near Mildera. This place began to be known as Japan Tikri.

was available. The existing shelter sites were, in most cases, forests, which had to be cleared. So there were no connecting roads.

At Japan Tikri, we were greeted by a drunken tribal captain, Michael Yok. Once a prosperous plantation owner, Yok lost his only daughter and son-in-law in the tsunami and, like many people on the islands, turned to alcohol for solace. Alcoholism, we learnt, had become a major problem on these islands. People paid as much as Rs 1,800 to get illicit liquor.

Here, too, people had gathered to talk to us. They sat under a huge tin roof – women and children on mats in front and men on chairs at the back. The first to speak was Meena Kumari, a short woman in her twenties, clad in a simple green salwar suit, with neatly plaited thick black hair. A resident of West Bay, she lost six members of her family to the tsunami waves. She and her husband survived as they had gone for Christmas to Mildera, the only village unaffected by the tsunami. Meena's story resonates the stories of most households on this ravaged island, which has lost a whole generation – its elderly. With eight out of the nine tribal council members dead, people are left without a leader. Meena told us that she runs a makeshift school for children. 'But there are no textbooks or notebooks. There is no school building. I teach students from Classes 1 to 5 together under a tree or in a shed, if it rains,' she told us matter-of-factly. Her students were sitting in a neat row beside her. Three-year-old Jennifer, clad in a crisp white school uniform, white socks, and shoes, was one of them. She stood before us wearing a green hair-band, a shy smile on her lips. The smile promptly disappeared when we inadvertently mentioned her mother. Jennifer's mother had died in the tsunami. While she was too young to comprehend the magnitude of the disaster that hit her people, she missed seeing her mother.

'How long will we continue to rely on free rations?' We turned to see the speaker, a thin woman with shoulder-length hair, in a wrap-around skirt and purple shirt. Valina, was the tribal captain from Ibol Kappanga Shelter. 'People are still living in fear. They are afraid to venture into the sea for fishing. If we survive the monsoons, then maybe some would start fishing. We are yet to recover from the psychological trauma unleashed by the wave,' she informed us in a soft voice.

After this meeting, we walked around the Japan Tikri Camp. We passed the beautiful bamboo-and-leaf house of the captain, it was easy to see why he did not want to move from here. Suddenly we saw a brightly decorated shed. Inside, a white banner welcomed everyone to the wedding of Herbert and Christie. A smart Nicobari youth dressed in a bright pink shirt stood next to a young woman wearing a sequinned peach coloured top. On her head she wore a peach-and-white tiara. Eyes moist, face tear-streaked, Christie was one of the saddest brides we had ever seen. Villagers told us that both the bride and the groom had lost their parents. Perhaps Christie was thinking of the mother and father who would have blessed her, had the tsunami not snatched them away. From this wedding overcast by tragedy, we returned heavy hearted to the helipad.

On the fifteen-minute helicopter journey to Kamorta, the headquarters of the Nancowry group, we flew over Trinket, a narrow, long, flat island that had once been home to some 500 Nicobarese. When the tsunami struck, the raging sea hacked it into three pieces. One-fifth of the island's population perished. The rest floated to safety and are housed at the Vikasnagar Shelter site in Kamorta. Trinket is now uninhabited, and estimates say that it will be a few decades before people can once again call it home.

Kamorta is at a height and shielded by Nancowry, Trinket and Katchal. So it escaped much damage. However, till the time of our visit, the approach to the Kamorta jetty and the surrounding shops was flooded twice every day, during high tide. When the sea receded, residents and shopkeepers had to deal with the pile of debris – broken bottles, plastics, pieces of wood, etc. – the waters brought with every high tide.

By the time we reached the guest house at Kamorta, it was evening. Heavy rains were lashing the islands. Yet over half-a-dozen tribal captains from different villages and islands across the Nancowry group had braved the downpour to come and apprise us of their problems. Among them was Ayesha Majid, the great-granddaughter of the legendary Rani Ishlon of Nancowry. Ishlon was the wife of the tehsildar of Nancowry, and became its first chief. She has a special place in British Naval history for single-handedly scaring away a German battleship during World War I. It is said that when the battleship, *Emden*, approached her island, she raised the Union Jack. The Germans thought that a British battery was hiding in the jungles, ready to attack them, and retreated.[5] A grateful British government bestowed the title of Rani (queen) on Ishlon and her heirs. Succession in the Nancowry group of islands is through the eldest daughter. So Ishlon was succeeded by her daughter, Laxmi, who married a Muslim trader, Ilias Malim (also known as Ilias Yacoob).[6] At the time of the tsunami, Ayesha's mother, seventy-two-year-old Rani Fatima Yusuf was the chief of Nancowry. Dressed in a simple sarong and black scarf, Ayesha, Fatima's eldest daughter and heir apparent, had come to the meeting with her brother, Rashid Yusuf. Together, they raised the issue of the Sixth Schedule and illegal settlers. District collector Porwal who had accompanied us, admitted that though outsiders need a licence from the Lieutenant-Governor to run businesses on the island, they find ways of skirting the law. Most had entered into an understanding with the tribals and ran shops in their names. The next day, when we surveyed the jetty, we found that all shops in that area were indeed run by Tamils and Bengalis. A shopkeeper rued that, post-tsunami, he was being forced to work as a labourer, unloading ships, etc. 'The government did not offer compensation to illegal settlers. I have lost everything. I can't reopen my shop because the premises get flooded during high tide. I want to return to the mainland but my wife is a Nicobari and is unwilling to go back,' he said.

Rashid and Ayesha, however, had little sympathy for these outsiders. They blamed them for opening liquor shops on the island. 'Half of the ex-gratia is spent on alcohol now,' said Ayesha. Next to speak was Portifer, the captain of Trinket, and head of the Nicobari Youth Association (NYA). 'Transportation is a major problem. We do not have roads like Carnic or Campbell Bay. Earlier, our people used to travel by country boats but now they are afraid to venture into the sea. In any case, most boats have been damaged. In many places, fresh sand deposits make navigation difficult,' he explained.

The next morning, we took a ferry to the village of Champin on Nancowry Island. This is the village of the legendary Ranis. The forty-two

---

[5] Dhingra, op cit., p. 51.

[6] http://www.andaman.org/NICOBAR/book/history/Britain/Hist-Britain.htm#penal. Accessed on 17 January 2009.

member Yusuf family had lived in three buildings that were called Rani Ghar here. Ayesha accompanied us. Broken slabs were all that was left of the jetty at Champin. Sandy foundations and a few broken walls were the only remainders of what were once prosperous buildings in a lively village. The debris had not been cleared. Broken and bedraggled coconut palms, uprooted plants and barren branches of a few lone trees that had managed to withstand the fury of the water, littered the area. The new settlement had been built at a height. The area from the jetty to where the ascent began became submerged during high tide. Steps or even a kutchcha road leading to the intermediate shelters was yet to be constructed. It was a slippery climb. Guided by Shiba, an ANM, we made it to the first house. It was an extended hut built on a machan, with a tin roof. There were no walls. Tarpaulin sheets and bedsheets were being used to keep out the rain. Huddled inside this makeshift home was a family with two small children. They did not want to talk about 26 December. 'Madam, it is too painful.'

Safed Balu was another small island that had to be evacuated after the tsunami. Families from here, and from the village of Bada Enaka (in Kamorta) were housed at the Bada Enaka campsite in Kamorta. Tang Kumar, a small man seated on a plastic chair inside a tin shelter, was the captain of Safed Balu. He told us his story. 'It was the morning after Christmas. I was bringing my wife, Rosaline, and three small children to Bada Enaka on my donghi (local boat). Suddenly, the tsunami wave struck. I recall screaming, waving my arms and calling for help. But who was to hear? Somehow I managed to half-swim, half-float to the village of Bada Enaka. But Rosaline and the kids were nowhere to be found. Numb with shock and fatigue, I managed to get to the naval base in Kamorta. The officials then evacuated our island.' There was silence in the room. Raindrops falling on the CGI roof made the only sound. Then Tang Kumar looked straight at us. In a voice quivering with emotion, he demanded a house of concrete in place of the traditional timber construction. 'I have lost everything but my people. Now I have to ensure their safety.' Others inside the hut concurred. Their fear was understandable. Their wooden houses had been swept away. Concrete, they felt, would offer better protection. We tried to explain to them that the tsunami experience of Tamil Nadu had proved otherwise, but no one was listening.

Just as the rain stopped, something amazing began outside. A volleyball match! Strapping young boys from Chhota Enaka with their names emblazoned on green-and-yellow t-shirts were playing the Bada Enaka team. The latter sported t-shirts that had been donated by the Nehru Yuvak Kendra. As the green-and-yellow flags of the two villages fluttered against an azure sky, the teams took position. 'One, two, three!' The referee standing on an inverted tar drum blew the whistle and the match began. The muscular Nicobarese boys jumped, dodged and ran to hit the ball, while the devastated islands of Trinket and Safed Balu observed the game from across a stretch of blue. The spirit of youth against this backdrop of desolation brought tears and hope. Thomas, Deepak, Azer, Imran … these young men were offering a way of dealing with the trauma we had encountered in Carnic, Katchal and Nancowry.

This Nicobari resilience, which we first encountered at Bada Enaka, resurfaced many times during the trip. That afternoon, while walking on the Kamorta jetty, we saw a group of young men squatting next to hundreds of cycles that had been off-loaded from a relief ship. They were from the island of Chowra. A small, flat island with an area of barely 8.2 square km, Chowra had to be evacuated post-tsunami. In a daring rescue operation that lasted over ninety-six hours, the island's 1,300 residents were taken to camps in Teressa Island. Even though they had been starving for five days – the waters had destroyed every structure and tree on their island – they were reluctant to move elsewhere. Traditionally, the people of Chowra have been held in great respect by the Nicobarese. They made excellent boats and earthen pots and were said to practise magic. The boys were initially reluctant to talk. 'Only our captain speaks for us,' they informed us curtly. But, after a little prodding, they spoke about their lost homes. They were longing to return to their island. 'The shelters that we live in now are just not home. Give us our tools and let us go back to our island. We'll look after our trees, build our boats and houses and start life afresh.' Their confidence and determination to rebuild what was theirs reminded us of Tolkein's *Lord of the Rings*:

From the ashes a fire shall be woken,
A light from the shadows shall spring;

Renewed shall be blade that was broken:
The crownless again shall be king.

∽

25 January 2006. It was seven months since we returned from the Emerald Islands, seven months since we witnessed the overwhelming sadness of the survivors, seven months since we encountered hope in Kamorta. Had that hope reached the other people of the islands? Had it eased their pain, allayed their fears? It was time to find out. It was time to see if thirteen months after being battered by the tsunami, life in the archipelago had moved on.

On landing in Port Blair, we were once again presented with official statistics. This time, they revolved around the permanent shelters. The relief commissioner, Chetan Sanghi, was a bright, young man. He informed us that the wishes of both the Carnic tribals and the people of Nancowry had been fulfilled. Two designs had been finalized for permanent shelters, a steel structure with CGI roofing and timber walls for the non-tribals and people of Nancowry, and a bamboo structure on stilts for the people of Carnic. Recognizing the effort put in by the NGOs in tsunami relief and rehabilitation, Sanghi explained that 40 per cent of the permanent shelters would be constructed by them.

The next day was 26 January. Blue sky and turquoise-and-green sea across the Netaji Stadium created the perfect backdrop for the Republic Day Parade. The loudspeaker recounted the tales of courage of doctors, the armed forces, officials and ordinary people who had saved many lives. As the Republic Day programme drew to a close, we prepared to board a vehicle ferry from the Phoenix Bay jetty to reach Bambooflat. On the way, we crossed the famous Chatham Saw Mill. Established in 1883, it is one of the oldest and largest mills of Asia.

In Bambooflat, 167 families had been affected by the tsunami. These were people whose houses and shops were located along the jetty. All along the way to the intermediate shelter camp on the island, we saw signboards saying 'World Vision' and 'Salvation Army'. The shelter camp, yet another row of tin structures, was managed by a committee of shelter residents. We were pleasantly surprised to see water trickling down the roofs and being collected in tanks. Under the guidance of these two NGOs, residents had started rain-water harvesting. Nearby, little children were playing in a small playground, another gift from the NGOs. Of the 872 people housed here, 132 were illegal migrants who, before the tsunami, had run petty shops in Carnic and Nancowry. Rajan Acharya used to have a gold shop in Carnic. He was now a member of the shelter management committee in Bambooflat. 'All businesses in Carnic were run by non-tribals. One hundred and three such families have moved to this camp, but eighteen are still in Carnic. They, too, need permanent shelters.' Local shopkeepers voiced their need for bank loans and a market. The district collector, Andamans, said that space for a shopping centre had been allotted. But there was a problem. After the tsunami, shops on one side of the culvert were still running while those on the other side had been forced to close down since they get filled up with water during high tide. The people who ran these shops were not ready to move to the new space because they feared that shops around the jetty would take away all their business.

Jayanthi was a tall, slim, Tamil girl in a pink sari. Before the tsunami, she lived in Katchal. Then her world changed. She was widowed and left without any support. She told us that there were five other women like her – Budhan, Shivagami, N. Satya, Balli and Tilagam – who had not received any money from the Prime Minister's Relief Fund. 'All six of us have lost our husbands to the wave. We have children and no source of living. We don't even know how to sew petticoats,' she said, eyes brimming with tears of helplessness.

As we were leaving the shelter camp, a woman in her thirties, a Zilla Parishad member, drew us aside. 'I can't say this in front of everyone. Before the tsunami, many illegal migrants had taken shops on rent along the culvert. Many of these families have now been allotted intermediate shelter and will soon get permanent shelter. This is not fair, giving land, already scarce in these islands, to illegal migrants. It would also create a precedent; illegal migrants, unaffected by the tsunami, will try to get some land by pretending to be victims,' she warned.

On the way back, we passed remains of the shops that had been washed away along the culvert. Most were broken and seemed beyond repair. Some still had battered signs swaying forlornly in the wind. The height of the road between the culvert and the shops had been raised to prevent water from entering the shops during high tide. As we drove on the badly damaged road along the shoreline, we saw again the scenes that we had witnessed seven months ago – broken trees, broken houses, wrecked lives.

The next day, we decided to go to Little Andamans. With a population of almost 18,000 spread across 732 square km of land, this island is furthest south of the Andaman cluster. It lies at the tip of the Ten Degree Channel and was badly ravaged by the tsunami waves. Once again, we boarded the Pawan Hans and flew over tiny islands, one after another. We began to tick them off on the map: Chidiya Tapu, Rutland Island, and two heavily forested islands encircled by pools of clear turquoise water. The corals underneath the waters were clearly visible. These two tapus (islands) were joined by a narrow strip of land; their shape resembled a giant dog bone in the waters. The captain said these were Cinque Islands, famous for their coral reefs. The strip of land was a sandbar, which had vanished after the tsunami. Then, one morning, a few months earlier, it rose from the sea. As we flew over the Andaman archipelago, we wondered how nature could lacerate something so magnificent? We were reminded of Dominique Francon from Ayn Rand's *Fountainhead*, who believed in destroying what she cherished most because she did not want to leave it among people who didn't value it, who would tear it apart, bit by bit. And this is what we have done to nature. We have been gradually destroying these islands and its original inhabitants. Once a thickly forested area, Little Andaman was cleared to make way for coconut and red palm oil plantations. Settlers from Kerala, West Bengal and Tamil Nadu were brought in to tend to these plantations. Post-tsunami, they were settled in Hut Bay and Netaji Nagar while 300 Nicobarese families were sent to nearby Harminder Bay. The chopper headed towards Hut Bay.

From the landing pad we went straight to the Nanjappa Nagar Intermediate Shelter Camp. Of the 600 shelters here, 350 had been built by an NGO called SEEDS (Sustainable Environment and Ecological Development Society). After the tsunami, five intermediate shelter camps housing 7,500 settlers had been built on the island. According to the State Disaster Management Authority, 100 hectares of land (at one hectare per twenty settler families) would be needed to construct permanent shelters for the affected families in Hut Bay. In Harminder Bay, twenty-five hectares would be needed.

At the Nanjappa Nagar Camp, we sat inside a cool chaupal (traditional village gathering place) constructed by SEEDS. Residents of the camp came forward with their demands and complaints. Here, we once again heard the settlers' side of the story. A.C. Ravi, a zilla parishad member for the Hut Bay and Netaji Nagar panchayats, complained that, post-tsunami, 310 non-tribal families had fled to the mainland in fear. When they returned, they did not get any shelters. The primary concern of the settlers was the design for permanent shelters. Some favoured the use of local material because they feared that they would be unable to repair the aerocon structure. Others did not consider the bamboo structure proposed by SEEDS sturdy enough. Everyone present at the meeting said that owners should be given money and allowed to build their own houses.

Before leaving Hut Bay, we visited two permanent shelter model homes. The first was the eco-friendly bamboo home being proposed by SEEDS. The structure, at a cost of Rs 5.7 lakh per unit, was airy and spacious. It had three small rooms plus kitchen and bathroom. The second was the National Buildings Construction Corporation Limited (NBCC) structure which cost Rs 6.6 lakh per unit. It had two rooms but the toilet was outside. It was neither airy nor spacious. None of the two models had provision for rain-water harvesting. Yet, given a choice, we knew which one we would prefer to call home.

The chopper now headed towards Dugong Creek, a thickly forested area on the north-east coast of the island which is home to ninety-four of the world's oldest surviving inhabitants, the Onge. Recent studies by the Centre for Cellular and Molecular Biology, Hyderabad, reveal that the Onge, along with three other Negrito tribes – the Jarawa, the Great Andamanese and the Sentinelese – moved out of Africa more than 60,000 years ago and were among the first settlers in south-east Asia. Since then, they have lived in splendid isolation from the rest of humanity. This makes them one of the oldest and most isolated communities in the world – the last of the First People. The tsunami had triggered fears about the survival of these aboriginal peoples as well as of the Shompen, a hunter–gatherer tribe of Indo-Mongoloid origin that inhabits the forests and coasts of Great Nicobar. Yet, miraculously, no autochthon was swept away. Their age-old harmonious relationship with Mother Nature had alerted them to her foul mood. So, when the earth rumbled, the water started receding, and the birds flew away, they sensed that danger was imminent. They fled to safer areas. Their habitations were ripped apart by the tidal fury but they were safe.

We had heard about these tribes and their dwindling numbers from anthropologists in Delhi and in Port Blair. We had read that at least three of them – the Jarawa, the Sentinelese and the Shompen – were still hunter–gatherer communities who lived inside dense forests and had little contact with the outside world. The Great Andamanese and the Onge had, however, paid a heavy price for their brush with civilization.

The Onge, who share characteristics with the Jarawa and the Sentinelese, had negligible contact with the 'civilized' world until the arrival of the British. In the 1870s, the British began a dual policy of friendliness and ferocity. Between coaxing the Onge with gifts, including the highly addictive tobacco, and scaring them with firearms, they managed to establish 'friendly' relations with the tribe. By the 1890s, they had established control over the islands but after the initial skirmishes, the Onge were left undisturbed. Till the 1950s, they had remained the sole inhabitants of the island that we were flying over. In a bid to further protect them, in 1957, the entire Little Andaman Island was declared a Tribal Reserve. Within less than a decade, however, the outside world began to covet its resources. A plan was drawn up to clear 40 per cent of the islands' forests in order to accommodate 12,000 settler families who would start red palm oil and timber plantations. Though the plan was never fully implemented, large sections of the Reserve were denotified and the Onge were squeezed out of some of their preferred habitations like Hut Bay, which we had just left.

Pressing our faces against the thick glass of the chopper window, we could see below us neat rows of trees signalling the plantations that had spelled the steady decline of the Onge. The lush tropical forests we had seen all over the archipelago were missing here. Contact with the outside world had brought new diseases and addictions. The Onge began to die. A tribe which numbered 672 at the beginning of the twentieth century today has less than 100 members. The settler population on this island went up from a few hundreds in 1960s to over 17,500 in 2001. The final blow for the autochthons came in 1980, when they were bundled, divided and settled in two sites – Dugong Creek and South Bay. Post-tsunami, they were evacuated from South Bay and all of them were moved to Dugong Creek.

As the chopper began its descent on a small, sand covered strip in Dugong Creek, we craned our necks to get a better look. At the helipad, clutching flowers and leaves picked from nearby bushes, stood a group of Onge – children and adults. We were seeing, for the very first time, the descendents of one of the world's oldest communities.

We took in their appearance slowly. Their hair was like curled jute – brown and coarse – with the scalp showing between the curls, what anthropologists call the 'peppercorn' variety. They were small in stature, the tallest among them barely reached our shoulders; their eyes were like two huge orbs of white with a shiny black centre. In front of the reception party were Onge children, their white school uniforms stark against their shiny black skins. The men were struggling with their shirt and trouser buttons. Their discomfort was apparent in the way their clothes hung on them. The officials said that they had worn these terylene clothes especially for us. As we shook hands with the Onge males (only the men and boys had gathered around the helipad), we noticed that their teeth were yellow and decayed. This, we learnt, was legacy of the Adam Jan Jati Vikas Samiti's benevolence. The AJJVS is the nodal agency for the 'welfare' of primitive tribes in the Andaman & Nicobar Islands. After confining the Onge to the Reserve areas, they had started doling out free rations. Along with rice, dal, oil and biscuits, adult Onge were offered 250 gm of tobacco as a welfare measure![7]

A short man in a loose peach shirt with rolled-up sleeves came forward with folded hands. It was impossible to tell his age. We later learnt that he was fifty years old. 'Namaste. Mein Onge chief Tambolai hoon,' he said. (Greetings. I am Tambolai, the Chief of the Onge). We had expected an indigenous greeting. Hindi words sounded strange on the tongue of an Onge Chief! We followed Tambolai and the others on the path leading to their dwellings. Soon, we came to a small school building which consisted of one large room with several desks. Behind them sat a few Onge women

---

[7] *Tribal Trauma: the Andaman Story, The Hindu,* June , 1999; Available at http://www.ashanet.org/library/articles/hindu060699.html; accessed last on 17 September 2011

and several children. At the front was a big blackboard with some Hindi alphabet written on it. By now, many of the men who had come to greet us at the helipad had seated themselves on the empty benches in the back. The schoolteacher informed us that in this school, husband and wife, father and son, mother and daughter, all studied together in one class. There was no fixed syllabus; only Hindi was compulsory.

'The Onge are good at football. They are also great singers,' the teacher said.

We turned our attention to a young couple sitting at the front. 'What's your name, your age?'

'I am Vicky. This is my wife. Age ...' He looked bewildered.

'He's 23,' the teacher said.

'Your teacher tells us you sing,' we went on. 'Please sing an Onge song for us.'

Once again, Vicky's brow creased in confusion. 'Onge? I don't know any Onge song.' 'Then what do you sing?'

'Yaadon ki baarat nikli hain aaj dil ke dwaare...' He sang the evergreen Hindi film song in a lilting voice.

But we were longing to hear an Onge melody, something we could cherish and take back. 'Does no one know any Onge song?'

Suddenly, an older man, seemingly ageless, stood up. He looked at us, wide-eyed with incredulity. 'Aapko hamara gaana sunna hain?' (You want to hear our song?)

We nodded eagerly. He looked towards some of the older men in the room and suddenly five of them stood before us. As pure African music engulfed us, we realized what the Onge were losing – their music, their culture and, with it, their vitality. This was a tribe which, until a couple of decades ago, was known to be fearless and proud. Was this what daily lessons in Hindi and English alphabet had done to them?

Once the song was over, the younger men introduced themselves—Totu, Chota Nala, Jain! 'Why Jain?' we asked. 'The Onge often name their children after the doctors who deliver them or after the spot of their birth,' an official explained, adding, 'Child mortality here is very high. Only three out of the chief's ten children have survived. The rest ate some poisonous plants in the forest or died from the lack of medical aid.' This was clearly a case of loss of traditional knowledge.

As we left the school and walked towards the Onge houses, we met a short, middle-aged woman. Shanti Teressa, an ANM, has been working with the Onge since 1980 when they were first settled in Dugong Creek. She explained why the tribe could soon disappear. 'An average family has five kids. At the moment, the tribe has only thirteen women in the child-bearing age group. The threat of extinction for the Onge is very real because of their peculiar custom. An Onge man or woman who loses his or her spouse can choose any boy or girl as partner. The latter does not have the right to refuse. As a result of this, fifteen-year-old girls have been married to seventy-year-old men. Despite being in the child-bearing age, they are unable to conceive. Recently, even Tambolai married a much younger girl.'

Shanti told us more about the medical profile of the tribe. No trace of anaemia was found among the Onge but skin infections like eczema and scabies were rampant, primarily due to the introduction of clothes. Originally, the Onge, like the other Andaman tribes, did not wear clothes. But AAJVS and other contacts brought with them notions of shame and obscenity. Though the Onge started covering themselves up, they never learnt how to wash and clean their clothes. Dental problems showed up. Besides tobacco, a few years ago the Onge were introduced to paan. They now collect betel leaves from the jungle, grind shells to make chuna and savour their paans.

We asked the ANM about midday meals at the school.

'Yes. But none was prepared today,' she said.

'Why?' we asked.

'VIP visits here mean a lot of activity. So, our cook, Borai, refused to sit in the kitchen and stir his pot of khichdi.' She shrugged.

'Khichdi? We thought they are used to meat; they are hunters and fisherfolk, aren't they?'

'Yes. They used to collect tubers and honey; they ate wild boar and turtles. But then the government started free rations – rice, wheat and dal. Now, they eat our food. Look, they have even started growing sweet potatoes,' she said, pointing to the tubers growing nearby. Meanwhile, a man in a grey t-shirt was pushed forward. He was Borai, the cook.

'Why didn't you cook today?'

'Getting the kids to clean and dress up is not easy. I spent the whole morning trying to catch them,' he explained with a broad smile.

We reached a group of neatly laid-out houses on stilts. They were made of wood with asbestos roofs, covered in orange, blue and brown paint. 'Is this your house?' we asked Tambolai. He shook his head and kept walking. We noticed that the houses were empty. We asked the accompanying officials. 'The PWD built these houses for the Onge. Traditionally, Onge houses are built on the ground; a raised cane or bamboo platform serves as the family bed,' explained Das, an AAJVS official. 'Some experts thought that if houses were built on stilts, the Onge would not have to construct beds. They wanted to make life easy for them. But you know what the Onge did? They built beds on top of the raised platforms. When the tsunami struck, they fled to higher ground. Now they live in their traditional houses but are unwilling to give these up.'

By now, we had reached the clearing where the newly constructed Onge houses stood. They were small structures made of leaves and bark, with no gates or partitions; just an elevated platform covered by a slanting roof, exposing the entire house to public view. The roof was supported by slanting bamboo poles on which clothes were hung. Smoke rose gently from below the machan-like home. The flesh of a wild boar was spread over it for smoking the meat. All around, there were plastic cans of different colours and sizes. Compared to the PWD-built CGI structures, these houses appeared squalid. Yet the Onge seemed much more at ease here. Inside the first hut, we met a forty-five year old Onge man married to a sixty year old woman. Among the Onge, marriages are fixed soon after birth. When the man wants to get married, he just holds the hand of his promised bride and takes her home. He then seeks the blessings of his kinsmen and a small feast is organized. According to Onge tradition, the new bride sits on the lap of all the older men in the family!

At the clearing were the Onge women. Dressed in skirts, nighties, kaftans and even salwar suits, they quietly gathered around us. Their eyes held no light, no welcome. 'Do you know Hindi?' we asked. A shrug was our answer. Later, we read a piece by anthropologist Viswajit Pandya which said that the Onge women understand Hindi just as well as the men but they seldom use it to speak to outsiders. It is their way of showing contempt for a society that they feel has ruined them. We asked the women about their ancestors, their original home, their families; downcast eyes and silence was the only answer. Finally, Chota Nala, so named because he was born next to a small stream of water, explained that no one knew their history. The oldest Onge man, who knew their traditions and folklore, had died a few months back. With him was gone historical memory.

While the Onge did not share any folklore with us, they did tell us about their rites of passage. A doctor posted here who was part of our company told us that the tribal practices followed at birth were the best. Traditionally, when a woman was giving birth, her husband went to the coast and collected some medicinal herbs. He then built a fire and heated them. The woman was made to squat over the leaves and the vapours made her bleeding stop. These days, Onge woman deliver in hospitals at Hut Bay or Port Blair. The Onge cover the faces of their dead with hands, fold their knees and tie them with pieces of bark. Earlier, they would bury the dead in his/her house below his/her own bed. The house was then abandoned for some time. After the PWD built permanent houses for them, the Onge could no longer follow this practice. So now the dead are buried in front of the house, under a small leaf-and-bamboo roof. The members of the bereaved family cake themselves with red mud and go into mourning for forty to forty-five days.

While the men were talking, the women, some cradling infants, lined up. A carton containing parcels wrapped in coloured paper suddenly appeared. The Secretary, Tribal Welfare Department, said, 'Every time an official visits the settlement, we distribute small items of daily use as gifts. Nothing much; we just have bed sheets here.'

We stared at him. 'Do they even want these sheets?'

The secretary looked embarrassed. 'This is the norm. Madam, look at them. They are expecting something.'

Through the day, we had been witnessing how we had gradually destroyed a self-sufficient and resourceful tribe. As we walked back to the chopper, we spoke to Das. He agreed. 'Traditionally, the Onge made lovely baskets and jewellery from leaves. Now they use old plastic cans. They are fast losing their skills because they do not need to make the effort any more. We have made them so dole-dependent that they have lost self-respect. All they do is to collect a few coconuts which they exchange for rations.'

'Do they hunt for betel leaves?' we asked.

'That, and alcohol. The Onge are gradually turning to alcohol. Poachers have used their addiction to lure them into a barter system where they trade precious commodities like ambergris, turtle eggs, wild boar and honey for alcohol and tobacco.'

(Two-and-half years after our visit to the Onge settlement, we got a frantic phone call from Port Blair. Illicit liquor had resulted in the death of eight Onge and the hospitalization of fifteen; a big loss for a vanishing tribe.)

As we were walking back to the chopper, Tambolai stopped us. 'Everything lost in the tsunami. No one can fish. Need donghis (country boats). Give us three-four boats, we will manage. Only fibreglass is okay.'

'How did you manage earlier?'

'Logs of wood.'

'Why not make the boats now? Don't you have enough raw materials?'

'Oh, we have plenty of wood but it is very hard work. Takes too much time.'

'How much?'

'Ten days.'

We boarded the helicopter. What we had heard was an indictment of our entire tribal policy. The Onge, once self-sufficient and self-reliant, have lost their lands, their forests and, with it, their independence and skill. Shorn of vitality, they have stopped building boats; instead they act as menial labour for the settlers and wait for VIP visits so that they can receive 'gifts'.

Was it just the Onge or had all the tribes gone this way? Back in Port Blair, we decided to find out. We spoke to Sameer Acharya, a middle-aged Bengali with deep-set eyes and rimmed glasses. He ran an NGO by the name of Society for Andaman and Nicobar Ecology (SANE). Sameer had devoted most of his life to campaign for the cause of the tribes of Andaman. For long, he was our reference point for the islands. When a Belgian photographer smuggled himself into the forests, stayed with the Jarawa and splashed photographs of naked men, women and children on his website, when the Onge were hospitalized, when Nicobarese tribals were being robbed of their land, when tsunami rehabilitation work came to a halt, it was always Sameer who telephoned us. For most of us in Delhi and elsewhere who love the islands, Sameer was our eyes and ears. That evening, we sat with him once again. Cradling his cup of tea, face grim, Sameer listened carefully. 'Are you shocked? Wait till you have seen the Great Andamanese. They are beyond salvage. The Shompen and Jarawa, too, are going the Onge way. Only the Sentinelese are smart. They destroy us before we can destroy them,' he said with a half-smile.

The Sentinelese, who inhabit the North Sentinel Islands, are without doubt the most isolated community in the world. We know almost nothing about them – their origins, language, or even their exact numbers. Estimates vary between 100 and 300. For thousands of years now, they have lived on their tiny island without any kind of contact with the outside world. Time and again, the various administrations – whatever their colour or nationality – have labelled them hostile. Whoever ventures into their territory, whether poachers or government officials, whoever tries to establish 'friendly' contact with them or reaches their shores is greeted with a storm of deadly arrows. They are much like the Jarawa used to be before the contact began.

'If these tribes have to survive in our world, hostility is the key. You have seen what friendship has done to the Onge. The Sentinelese are believed to belong to the Onge–Jarawa family, too. At some point, they either got stuck in or moved to the North Sentinel Islands. The treacherous seas and coral reefs surrounding the island ensured that they were cut off from the outside world. And they live happily as a consequence.' Sameer spoke with bitterness. 'The government has, of course, made every effort to rope them in. Since 1967, contact parties laden with gifts, have been sent to the island on "friendly" missions. Some say the Sentinelese have become less aggressive and more open to gifts since the 1990s, but they have never shown any inclination to interact with outsiders, let alone allow them to stay, explore, or exploit. This alone has guaranteed their safety.'

'The Shompen are a different story. A nomadic tribe of hunter–gatherers, they live in small bands of twenty-five to thirty people in the tropical evergreen forests of Great Nicobar.' The term 'Shompen' is a modified version of 'Sumhalf,' meaning 'interior forest people' in the Nicobari language. It is believed that the Shompen, who came from Sumatra over 10,000 years ago, are the oldest inhabitants of Nicobar. Till 1969, the Great Nicobar Islands were the exclusive domain of the Shompen and the Nicobarese. Then the government began to settle ex-servicemen on the island. As the number of settlers on the island increased and roads were built, the Shompen began to abandon some of their traditional housing colonies. Food sources in their areas depleted. Bands of Shompen who came into frequent contact with the outside world experienced high morbidity and mortality. Diseases like dysentery and influenza wiped out scores. Malaria, hitherto unknown, began to afflict them. By 2001,[8] the number of Shompen had dwindled to 300. This, however, is at best an estimate, because the Shompen are an extremely reclusive tribe. 'Unfortunately, you can't see what we have done to them, but you must see what has happened to the Great Andamanese; that might well become the fate of the Jarawa. Don't trust what I say, see for yourself,' Sameer suggested.

So, a couple of months later, we found ourselves heading for the Andaman Islands with a specific purpose – to visit the people whose forefathers had been among the first occupants of our subcontinent. We were looking for two tribes: the Great Andamanese and the Jarawa. Before this trip, we had done some reading about the bloody and painful history of their contact with the outside world. After the 1857 uprising, when the British began to establish a penal colony in the Andamans, they met with stiff resistance from the Negrito groups. At the time, between 5000–8000 Great Andamanese belonging to 10 distinct groups[9] occupied North and Middle Andamans. The Jarawa lived in South Andamans, to the north of Port Blair. The Great Andamanese tribes fiercely resisted British incursions into their territory and suffered heavy casualties in the process. Madhushree Mukherjee, in her book, *The Land of the Naked People*, describes the brutal capture and slaughter of these tribes by the British. We read her terrifying descriptions of the extent to which they went in their quest for knowledge, power and

---

[8] Estimates vary. Some people claim that there are just 150 Shompen left.

[9] 'Great Andamanese' actually refers to ten Negrito tribes: Cari, Kora, Bo, Jeru, Kede, Kol, Juwoi, Pucikwar, Bale and Ben.

supremacy. After years of bloodshed, the Great Andamanese offered the British peace. In return, they were introduced to addictive substances like opium, tobacco and alcohol. Contact with the outside world brought diseases and, by the beginning of the twentieth century, their population had dwindled to 625. Once the British had gained control over the Great Andamanese, they used them to establish contacts with the other tribal groups – the Onge, the Jarawa, and even the Shompen.

Port Blair. Adi Basera is a single-storeyed yellow-coloured guest house next to the Raj Bhavan. This is where the tribals – Onge, Shompen and Great Andamanese – stay when they come to the city. We were informed that some Great Andamanese from Strait Island were staying here. On reaching Adi Basera, we saw a shirtless, muscular, well-built man lounging by a tree. He said he had moved to Port Blair because he had found a job with the police. Sitting next to him on a cheap red plastic chair was a frail woman wearing a printed green night-gown. Her name was Lico. She had come to Port Blair with her family to get treatment for her heart disease. She was very thin and emaciated. Her five children were busy playing. Of these, two had obviously a mixed lineage. Lico explained this. 'I left my Great Andamanese husband to marry a settler. When he ran away, I returned with the two children I had with him to my first husband.' In the verandah, we saw a man wearing a bright red shirt and a dhoti, taking care of the children. His lips were badly bruised. This was Golat, Lico's husband. Like the Onge men, he too, was dark-complexioned, with shiny skin and peppercorn hair, but black not brown. From Lico, we learnt more. The bruise marks were from drunken brawls. Alcoholism is a major problem among Great Andamanese men, and is one of the factors driving the tribe towards extinction. Due to their greater contact with the outside world compared with the other primitive tribal groups, Great Andamanese women were able to attend school. They do not want to marry men from their tribe who do nothing but drink. They prefer settlers but many like Lico are abandoned.

If the visit to Dugong Creek was disturbing, this one was shattering. A trip to Strait Island had now become essential. Tucked in the Diligent Strait between Baratang Island and Ritchie's Archipelago[10], Strait is a small island, barely six square km in area. By 1961, the number of Great Andamanese had dwindled to nineteen. Wasted in body and spirit; the remaining members of this tribe once regarded as fierce were scattered across North Andamans and Port Blair. To protect them, the Andaman administration brought them together and, in 1969, resettled them on Strait Island. After treating them for various addictions (mostly opium), and other chronic ailments, it was assumed that, if provided a stable resource base, they would revert to their former hunting–gathering–fishing mode of existence. This did not happen. Today, there are fifty-one surviving Great Andamanese (only from the Bo and Jeru tribes; the other tribes have disappeared.) but very few among them are pure-blooded. Unlike the other tribal groups on the island, Great Andamanese mingle freely and inter-marry with outsiders.

It took us a little over four hours to reach Strait Island. Getting off the boat, we could see a few houses spread out on the island. We were taken to a single-storey building which had once been a police station. Now it was a community hall with a few chairs and two television sets. Students of Classes 1 to 8 were taught here. The room was painted blue and had a few charts hanging on the wall. On a small blackboard the poem, 'Veer tum badhe chalo...' had been scrawled in Hindi. A few kids were sitting inside the room. One of them, Bulba, had settler features, like any Tamil child. All these children were studying at the Vivekananda School in Port Blair. They had come home for the holidays. Unlike the Onge, the Andamanese children and adults wore clothes with ease.

On hearing of our arrival, some adults began to trickle in. Nao Junior was forty-nine years old. He wore a bright blue-and-orange t-shirt. There was no electricity. Like everyone else in the room, his face was glistening with sweat. 'We get electricity only from 5 p.m. to 11 p.m. but when a VIP visits, there is more supply. Today must be an exception,' he joked. He told us that he was from the Mayabunder area. His father, Bo, had been employed with the bush police that had the task of guarding the Andaman Trunk Road from Jarawa attacks. 'We used to live in the Police Lines. I studied in Port Blair till

---

[10] Named after John Ritchie, hydrographer of the East India Company, who visited these islands on board the vessel *Diligent* in the late eighteenth century.

Class 5. Then, in 1969, we came here. Ten years later, I started working as a ward-boy,' he said, speaking in Hindi. He claimed that he had recognized the signs of the tsunami hours before the wave hit the island. 'But no one listened to me. They thought it was just idle talk from an old rooster. Look what happened. We were all swept into the sea. Thank God, it was a small wave, else none of us would have survived.'

A few women had come into the room. Boro was an elderly lady, one of the three oldest Andamanese women alive. She was dressed in a bright orange blouse and a green printed sarong. Seated in a plastic chair, she told us that she was Nao Junior's mother-in-law. Her husband had died long ago. She belonged to the Ora flock of Great Andamanese, and had lived near Diglipur. 'That was a long time ago. Now I have to speak the Jeru language. That is the only language people here know,' she said. In slightly slurred speech, she went on to explain the causes for the extinction of her tribe. 'Most of us here are related to each other and, in our tribe, consanguineous marriages are not allowed. So we have little choice but to marry outside. But that is against the current laws. There is one Andamanese couple who is unable to live together because the husband is a non-Andamanese. So he is not allowed here or even at Adi Basera.'

A man spoke up. 'I am Meo. When my wife fell ill, I fetched my sister-in-law to care for her. But as she was a non-tribal, she had to be sent back immediately,' he complained. Another man spoke from the back of the room. 'The boys drink and come home. At times, they get alcohol from the police people. It is scary.' We looked at the people surrounding us – dull, worn out, weather-beaten faces. Not one of them went hunting these days. Most had some sort of menial job with the Andaman government, but they seldom did any work. Unlike the older generation, these people had no knowledge of their culture. At the same time, they had no hope of interacting with mainstream society, on an equal footing. That evening when we returned from Strait Island we recounted our observations to Sameer.

'There is little hope for these aboriginals who have entered civilization's warm embrace. Having seen this, we are not sure we have the courage to visit the Jarawa,' we said.

'But it is imperative that you do so,' he said. 'The Jarawa still have a chance. You have to see why we need to leave them alone.'

In the Great Andamanese language, 'Jarawa' means 'the other people'. Traditionally, there existed an enmity between these two groups. So, the early part of the twentieth century saw the Jarawa being hunted by British search parties led by the Great Andamanese. But this fierce tribe was not to be conquered. They just pushed upwards and occupied the forests of Middle and North Andamans. They had mastered the art of survival. Today, the Jarawa are among the few classic communities of foragers left in the world. They live in the 1,028 square km of the dense evergreen forests which have been reserved for them. As late as 1997, they were 'hostile' towards outsiders who made incursions into their territory. The jungles of Middle and South Andaman have been witness to many fierce fights between the 'Ang' (the Jarawa name for themselves) and the 'Eenen' ('outsider' in the Jarawa language), be they the British, poachers, labourers or villagers. Despite attacks from the 'developed' and 'civilized' world, the Jarawa have held on to their territory and to their traditional lifestyle. Their numbers, however, have dwindled significantly. Only 365 Jarawa are left today.[11] Unlike the Great Andamanese, this community has never mingled with or married non-autochthons or even autochthons from other tribes.

In a bid to engage with the Jarawa, contact missions were regularly sent, carrying bananas, coconuts, etc., to the Jarawa areas. Since 1974, some semblance of 'friendly' contact was established but it was limited to government officials carrying bundles of new and alien foodstuff and other materials. Then, in 1997, a young Jarawa boy called Enmei was found lying injured in the forest. He was treated at a hospital in Kadamtala and sent back to the forest. This, according to many, was a turning point in the Jarawa relationship with the outside world. The Jarawa started visiting neighbouring villages and jetties in small groups in broad daylight. Like the other tribes, they also started contracting new diseases.

---

[11] At the time of our visit, the AAJVS workers and anthropologists had estimated that there were 306 Jawara. However, the latest report of the AAJVS concluded that there were 365 Jarawa; 192 male and 173 female. Source: http://www.telegraphindia.com/1101017/jsp/nation/story_13066500.jsp; Last accessed on 16 September 2011.

The Jarawa have attracted more attention than all the other indigenous tribes of the Andamans primarily because their fate has become inextricably linked with the Andaman Trunk Road (ATR). The ATR is a swathe of concrete that tears through the evergreen forests that are the Jarawa home. This 333-km road connects the 1.5 lakh people who live in North and Middle Andamans to Port Blair. It has been mired in controversy ever since a proposal to build it was mooted in the 1950s.[12] The settlers insist it is their lifeline, others regard it as the 'kiss of death' for the Jarawa. In the year 2000, Shekhar Singh, from the Indian Institute of Public Administration, was asked by the Supreme Court to look at forestry and allied matters on the Islands. In his report to the apex Court in 2002, Singh suggested that the portions of the ATR that pass through the Jarawa Reserve should be closed. The Court, in its 7 May 2002 order, accepted his suggestions. Anthropologists and environmentalists were vindicated. They saw hope for the Jarawa. They would be protected from alcohol, opium, and from exploitation by poachers and villagers. But the Andaman administration insisted that closing the ATR was not an option. Instead, it started a convoy system to ensure that vehicles passing through the Jarawa Reserve did not engage with the Jarawa.

Every time the issue of the ATR was raised in administrative circles in Delhi and Port Blair, we asked why, in an island territory, a road was considered to be of such importance? Wasn't travel between and around islands all about traversing the high seas on sturdy boats? No doubt the Andaman Sea was choppy, but wasn't the life of an islander all about conquering the sea? Weren't islanders supposed to be men and women of hardy constitutions who lived and swore by the sea? 'But the Andamans are

---

[12] Construction of the ATR only means that the different segments of the road were linked together. It does not mean that 333 km of road was laid. Portions of the road already existed on the various islands. These intra-island roads were connected to build an inter-island road link. Work was started in 1958 but after the construction and alignment of 87 km, it was suspended on the orders of the then Prime Minister, Mrs Indira Gandhi. She feared that the road might harm the aboriginals. The Bhopinder Singh Committee was formed to look into the matter and after its report, work recommenced in 1983. In 1999, the road was finally completed.

different' was the response we got each time we questioned the islanders' obsession with the ATR. 'You have to remember that the settlers are not islanders in the true sense. The sea is not in their blood. They were brought here from the mainland. For them, the natural mode of transportation is a bicycle, a bike or a bus, not a boat. Besides, look at how rough the sea is. Can't you understand how difficult the journey would be?'

No, we could not understand. We could not understand why a generation that had been born and brought up on the islands could not think like islanders. We could not understand why they found it so difficult to adapt when adapting to one's surroundings has been the key to human survival. So we decided to experience for ourselves their difficulty. Performing the journey by sea was the only way to find out. Early the next morning, we found ourselves on the Lieutenant Governor's boat, the *Rajhans*. Admittedly, the cosy, fast and well equipped *Rajhans* provided us with much more comfort than a normal steamer would to the islander. But we saw no reason why high-speed, comfortable crafts could not be introduced for the islanders if an alternative sea route to the ATR was found. So we set out on our voyage of exploration.

When we explained our purpose to the captain of the ship, he was perplexed. The ATR in South Andamans enters the Jarawa Reserve at a place called Jirkatang. This is where the convoy starts. So, it is from here that we needed to find an alternative route. Jirkatang, however, is quite far from the coastline on either side. Further, the shoreline on the eastern side is flanked by the Mount Harriet Range and is thickly forested.

'Taking the ATR up to Jirkatang and then switching to a ferry is not an option,' the captain explained.

'There must be some way,' we insisted.

'Well, let me see.' He consulted his maps and charts. 'At this time of the year, one could possibly take the open sea route. But the monsoons here last for six–eight months, and they can be brutal. During that period, the open sea is too rough for small ships. Even the bigger ships face a lot of tossing and turning – enough to unsettle the hardiest of sailors!'

Nevertheless, he conferred with the administration to see what could be done. After almost half-an-hour of poring over the maps, a ray of hope! A little before Mile Tilek village,[13] there is a diversion that leads to Shoal Bay, the last revenue village before the land merges into the sea on the eastern coast. 'We could construct a road from Mile Tilek to the entrance of the Shoal Bay Creek and there, perhaps, a jetty could be built. But the distance would increase substantially,' he warned.

Since we were already on the boat, we decided to follow the coastline and reach Shoal Bay. We passed island after island filled with lush evergreen forests interspersed with sparser deciduous trees. Different shades of green often merged with a pale brown to create a striking canvas. We noticed that North and Middle Andamans did not suffer any direct damage from the tsunami. In a few places, however, we saw mangroves which had borne the brunt of the killer waves. These patches of burnt brown were still visible. As we reached Shoal Bay, our excitement was palpable. Perhaps we would find the answer to a complex issue, which pitted the fate of 365 voiceless Jarawa against 1.5 lakh vociferous settlers.

Our excitement was short-lived; the captain explained that if a jetty was built at the entrance of the Shoal Bay Creek, it would be washed away by the rough seas during the monsoons. 'And you can't build a jetty inside the creek because the requisite depth is not there. Besides, the Jarawa often fish along this creek which marks the boundary of their Reserve.' So, if the portion of the ATR going through the Jarawa territory was closed, people would have to board the ships from Port Blair itself.

There are two stretches of the ATR that pass through the Jarawa Reserve – approximately 58 km in South Andamans, from Jirkatang to the Middle Straits, and 13 km in Middle Andamans, from Porlobjig Camp No. 3 (twelve km from Kadamtala) to Porlobjig Camp No. 15. According to the Supreme Court directive,[14] both these stretches should have been closed by now. However, closing these two stretches would mean that

[13] According to the Supreme Court (SC) orders, the ATR should be closed from Mile Tilek onwards. The diversion is after Ferrargunj.

[14] The administration insists that the SC did not issue any directive for the closure of the ATR. It only indicated that the recommendations of the Shekhar Singh Committee be implemented. Closure of the ATR was one of the recommendations.

the 129 km stretch of the ATR from Port Blair to Nimbootala would have only limited functionality, despite the high cost of maintenance. The best possible alternative, then, would be direct ferry services between Port Blair, Kadamtala, Baratang and Rangat. After Rangat, passengers could once again take the ATR to get to Mayabunder and Diglipur (in North Andamans).

With this in mind, we entered the Middle Straits. This narrow and extremely shallow creek marks one end of the Jarawa Reserve. Lush green mangroves surround it on both sides. There's something about this creek that transports you to another world – the Jarawa world. Travelling in a motor boat through these virgin territories seems a rude intrusion. The forests here are so thick that nothing can be seen – it is almost as if they warn us to stay out, not disturb their tranquillity. Was this what the world of our ancestors looked like? This is how it must have been, the bluest of blue water, the greenest of green forests, a silence so sacred that even the leaves fall into the creek very softly. It is a world where humans exist, but in their own spheres; where your space is no longer limited to the confines of a twelve feet by twelve feet room. Suddenly, we realized what it is that has been lost – this beautiful, rejuvenating space, the space that allows you to feel, to stretch, to be. We saw why the Jarawa continue to guard these virgin spaces so steadfastly. We understood the possessiveness of the Sentinelese. A treasure so valuable would need guarding with one's life.

Gunjan: How I wished that I was a Jarawa, who was a part of this space, who traversed it with the ease of an owner, nurtured it with the care of a mother and worshipped it with the reverence of a devotee. No wonder our ancestors had no need for gods with bodies. This virgin nature inspired a faith, a reverence no other could command. I passed through the creek as a pilgrim who realized that she had just been granted brief access to the Garden of Eden. And my offering was my silence; it gradually merged with the silence of the creek, the noise from the *Rajhans* notwithstanding.

The ferry ride through the Middle Straits was so exhilarating that we could not understand how anyone would want to travel any other route. Before the ATR was built, islanders used this very same route to get to Port Blair. However, the captain's worry was real. 'Look at the depth – it's too shallow even for the *Rajhans*. How would you get any ship or big ferry here?' he asked. We looked at the tiny screen which flickered next to the controls. The depth varied between 10–12 m. Suddenly, the screen gave a warning – six metres only, and the captain exclaimed, 'We should have never come this way!' These waters are uncharted and have very little depth, making them extremely dangerous even for ferries, he explained. 'The open sea route would be a much more viable alternative between the months of November and April, i.e., before the monsoons set in.'

Despite this unnerving experience, we loved the journey. Soon, we came upon two small jetties, one on either side of the creek. This was where vehicles travelling on the ATR boarded vehicle ferries and crossed over to the island of Baratang. Next, we entered Homfray's Strait and crossed the Baratang and Kadamtala jetties. This was the second ferry crossing for vehicles travelling on the ATR. Homfray's Strait once again led us into the open sea towards the Nimbootala jetty, Rangat. The ferry ride from the beginning of Middle Straits Creek to Rangat took us 2 hrs 10 mins. The total journey time from Port Blair to Rangat by the *Rajhans* was four hours. By an ordinary boat, it would be six-seven hours, almost as long as it would take to get to Rangat using the ATR.

At Nimbootala, we got into a car and took the ATR to Mayabunder. The road lay along the rocky coastline, only a thin line of trees separating it from the waters. On the way, we saw many padauk trees. We heard that Rajiv Gandhi had been very fond of this tree. An endemic species, the wood of this tree is sturdy and long lasting. It is said that the padauk wood grows harder as the years go by.

We were surprised at how bumpy the road was. We had expected the ATR to be an extremely well-maintained road, after all it was the 'road of choice' for almost 1.5 lakh people. But it was full of potholes and broken sections, a testimony to the annual onslaught of the Andaman monsoons. This stretch of the Middle Andamans is inhabited primarily by Bengali settlers who came from East Bengal. They settled here in the 1950s, and every family was given four hectares of land. They grow paddy, moong, coconuts, arecanuts and bananas. In between, there are pockets inhabited by Malayali settlers. One such place is Betapur, a famous turtle nesting site.[15]

On the way, we stopped in a market area at a place called Billyground. We asked people on the streets what they thought of the ATR, how frequently they used it and why they refused to travel by sea. The common refrain was that 'the ATR is our lifeline, our link with Port Blair and the outside world.' The people admitted that they used the road not more than once, or maximum twice, every month. 'But you have to understand that we are not islanders. We experience travel sickness on water. Besides, few ferries ply on the sea routes. The ones that do have fixed timings,' explained Haridas, a young mechanic. Another shopkeeper recounted how a boat containing 20,000 oranges encountered bad weather and the cargo was spoilt. Some people said that closing the ATR was pointless, as the Jarawa had come out of the jungles now. They claimed that the Jarawa knew Hindi and had spoken to them in the language.

By this time, a crowd had collected around us. People were pushing and out-shouting one another. And they all had only one thing to say. 'The ATR cannot be closed.' As the crowd began to get out of control, we moved on.

Near a place called Basantipur, we saw three ten-year-old boys in school uniforms walking along the road. Arun Baria, Suresh Baria, and Ganesh Patra were settlers' children, originally from Jharkhand. They lived in the village of Kaichinala, which was six kilometres from their school. Arun told us that their school bus had not come that day so they had to walk. Their uniforms were clean, they wore socks and shoes. After chatting a little, we asked if they knew about the Jarawa. They shook their heads in denial. We probed more. Finally, Ganesh, the oldest boy said, 'Sometimes we see them. They are black and don't wear clothes.' That was all they could say about one of the most ancient and unique tribes in the world. They knew next to nothing about the original inhabitants of the Andamans who lived barely fifty kilometres away from their homes!

---

[15] http://eprints.cmfri.org.in/1055/1/Bulletin_34-20.pdf. Last accessed on 16 September 2011.

With the setting sun, we reached the Mayabunder Guest House. Here, a group of 50 Panchayati Raj representatives from Middle and North Andamans was waiting. The ATR was their overriding concern. Demands ranged from turning the ATR into a national highway and building new bridges to avoid ferry crossings, to increasing the frequency of the convoy passing through the Jarawa Reserve. No one spoke about the Jarawa until we brought up the subject. 'We are not against them. But we want the government to take them away and settle them at a distance from us. It can then provide them with all the facilities they ask for.' Nagen Halder, from the Digplipur Panchayat Samiti, had, in so many words, articulated civilization's solution for the First People. Take them and put them in an enclosure away from 'us'! Feed them, clothe them, 'civilize them'. Take from them their lands, their forests, and leave them for our use. After all, we, the civilized, know how best to use them. The very same sentiments that had been expressed at different times about the Polynesians of Hawaii, the Maoris of Australia and the Native Americans of North America! Cultural anthropologists' relentless advocacy is against this convoluted sense of 'white man's burden,' the type of naked assertions being made at Mayabunder that evening. This rejection of the tribals by the settlers was an old phenomenon, very hard to eliminate.

The drive to Austin Creek Bridge later in the evening was uplifting. It was pitch-dark by the time we reached the bridge but the salty smell in the air and the sound of the waves crashing against some of the tallest mangroves on the island told us that we were walking over the sea. We walked across the bridge and stepped inside North Andamans. The Austin Creek Bridge was built in 2003 over the Kalighat Creek, and is one of the most picturesque sights of the Andamans, with mangroves that grow up to a height of thirty metres. It connects Middle and North Andamans. Earlier, one had to travel by boat from Mayabunder to Diglipur. The journey took three hours and there was only one boat every day. With the bridge, it takes two hours.

The next day, we began our return journey to Port Blair, this time on the ATR. At Porlobjig Camp No. 15, the road entered the Jarawa Reserve. The forests here were lush, full of tall canopied garjan trees and dripping green lianas that hung like huge drapes. It is said that few Jarawa stray to this part of the Reserve. Most are confined to the stretch in South Andamans. Soon, we reached Kadamtala and boarded a vehicle ferry to cross to Baratang.

Another vehicle ferry was there to take our cars to the Middle Straits. Here, we waited for the convoy to start. A large signboard had bilingual instructions about the 'Do's and 'Don'ts' in the Jarawa Reserve. Do not take photos, do not give eatables to the Jarawa, do not stop your vehicle, do not speed ... the list was long. We wondered how all this was monitored.

Soon, the convoy started and we entered the tropical jungle that housed the Jarawa. A little way into the Reserve, the cars stopped. We were going to be taken to the natural home of the Jarawa, at a place called Punno Nullah. The AJJVS officials said that some Jarawa were camping at a chadda (communal hut) nearby. We got off the car and entered the thick forest. The roots of the trees had made a kind of horizontal ladder. Stepping carefully from one rung to the other, we followed the AJJVS guide. All around us, there was silence. We saw some discarded clothes and pieces of red wool scattered around – a sign that the Jarawa were nearby. From a distance we could hear a hammering sound. Forty paces into the tropical forest, we reached a clearing and there, before us, was the Jarawa chadda. Outside – men, women, and children – everyone was busy with something or the other. Some of them had mud-caked bodies. A few men wore shorts, most were naked. Women had strands of leaves and red wool covering their private parts. Some had faces smeared with white mud. For a long time, we stood there just looking. Their vitality was palpable. Bright, laughing, contented eyes. On one side of the clearing, a few were eating a meal; pots black with smoke were being used. Two young men were hammering steel, perhaps making weapons.

The chadda consisted of a roof of thatch and leaves supported by bamboo poles. We bent our heads to go inside. Huge globs of pig meat hung from the ceiling. Our guide explained that the poles which supported the roof had a dual purpose. They marked spaces for every family. Inside each little space, there were ornaments of red wool hanging from the poles, some bags, and small fires everywhere. The story goes that at some point in their struggle for survival, the tribes lost the art of making fire. So they preserve it and do not let it ever go out.

Even as we were observing the chadda, we heard a commotion. Huge raindrops were coming down. Looking up, we saw a group of four Jarawa men returning with yet another wild boar slung on a thick branch. It started raining heavily. 'We must head back,' the AJJVS worker warned. Suddenly, we heard singing. We looked outside and the sight before us will forever be imprinted in our minds. A young Jarawa girl was swinging herself from the branch of a tree. Head thrown back, she sang as the rain pelted her face and torso. The expression on her face as she swayed in the rain is how we will always remember the Jarawa.

We headed back towards the car, blinded by the heavy tropical downpour. Thick streams of water ran down our hair and faces. We were soaked to the bone, we could barely see anything. Yet we felt happy. Watching the sheer abandon of the Jarawa had made us feel lighter.

Soon we were out of the Reserve. After changing into dry clothes, we headed for the Primary Health Centre at Tusnabad, an hour away from Port Blair. A special ward had been constructed here in the year 2000 to treat Jarawa patients. Of the dozen or so beds, four were occupied. On each bed, along with the patient, there were two-three attendants. Their stricken faces showed a totally different Jarawa. The energy and excitement we had felt in the forest began to ebb. We saw them in ill-fitting clothes, 'cartoon-natives', so to speak, similar to the ones Syeda had seen in the native reserves of Hawaii. Their faces were vacant, eyes dull.

'Why are they here? Where did they get these clothes?' we asked the doctor.

'Two of them have a cold, one fever, and one an injury. The AJJVS brings clothes from the store as soon as they come here. Otherwise people will come to stare.'

'Doesn't this terylene material cause rash?'

'It does. Skin afflictions are common, but what choice do we have?'

'Why are they here for just a cold? Doesn't the government policy call for in-situ treatment and for hospitalization only when absolutely necessary?'

Silence.

We called for the register. The record said that all the Jarawa had been admitted the previous day or the same morning. They had been given utensils, clothes and some rations – an obvious bribe to lure them to the hospital. We felt this entire scene had been staged for us. Ulegad, a young boy, had a small cut which had been bandaged. A small three-month-old baby had been admitted for a light cough. Totova and wife Achunu were sitting next to their two-year-old son, Nichayava. He had fever. 'We suspect measles,' the doctor said. There was no need to see any more.

Before returning to Port Blair, we had one final meeting with villagers living around the Reserve. Some thirty-odd men had come to tell us of their problems with the Jarawa.

Mahadeep Majhi was the pradhan of Tusnabad Gram Panchayat. He said that they had been living here since 1949. But it was only twenty-five years ago that they encountered the 'Jarawa menace'. 'They killed a lady. They would come by the moonlight and kill animals and humans. Then ten years back, they surrendered. They came to our village and police chowki, pointing at their stomach. For two months, we fed them. Then we had to stop because of High Court orders.' We learnt that this had been done to minimize dependency, and because anthropologists and doctors were worried about the effect of new foods on the tribals' metabolic processes. Majhi believed otherwise. He said that the Jarawa were given our food in hospitals and then sent back. This created a craving among them for mainland food. So they came and begged. 'They have stopped hunting. Foreigners come for their darshan (viewing),' he laughed. Similar sentiments were voiced by other villagers. 'Keep them in the jungles.' 'Don't let them rob our food.' 'Teach them to be good citizens.' 'They come to us for supari (betel nut) and sukha (tobacco).' R.K. Bannerjee, the ex-pradhan, expressed the general disdain, 'After the Enmei incident, the Jarawa came out of the forest, with their hands held up in surrender. *Woh hamari sharan mein aaye aur humne unhe khana khilaya.* (They came asking for our protection and we fed them.) But now they steal from our fruit trees. If we protest, they threaten us. The administration also does not compensate our losses. They are willing to work, so we give them work in return for food. What's the harm?' he questioned. Oblivious to our discomfort, he continued his chatter. 'Madam ji, you should keep them away. They bring infections. What if one of them has AIDS and gives it to us?' he asked, to a roar of applause. We were aghast. If anything, it was the Jarawa who risked contracting the deadly virus from the settlers if they allowed themselves to be sexually exploited. Only recently we had heard of a group of young Jarawa girls who had broken away from the tribe and had come to live near settler villagers. It was alleged that they were being sexually exploited in return for food. But in Tusnabad no one was ready to listen.

ᴄᴏ

Gunjan: Two years later, in December 2008, I returned to the Andaman Islands incognito, as a tourist. My travel agent had earlier told me that the highlight of my trip to Baratang would be the 'adivasi darshan'. I had seen travel websites which were advertising 'Jarawa tourism' and encouraging voyeurism, so I decided to play along. We reached the Jirkatang checkpost at 5 a.m. The place was buzzing with people. There were at least twenty-five cars, packed with tourists. The entire conversation was about 'seeing' the adivasis. I heard many people asking their guides, 'Bhaiyya, kab dikhenge?' (When will we see them?) 'Why can't we take pictures?'

I asked my guide, a young Tamil, Sunil, the same question. He said that the AAJVS had spread rumours among the Jarawa that if their picture was taken, they would contract diseases. Now the Jarawa resist being photographed. 'Aisa kuch hota nahi hain, Madam. Police walon ko bhi isse problem nahi hoti hain but AAJVS ke orders hain (Nothing really happens. Even the police do not have a problem with the photographs but these are AAJVS orders.),' he explained shaking his head at the apparent 'unreasonableness' of the AAJVS diktat. Resisting an urge to explain the AAJVS' reasons, I continued my ruse as the curious tourist. I asked him how they would know if I took a photo. He said, 'Madam, if the Jarawa complain, you will be fined.' I asked him what the chances were of seeing the adivasi. 'Hamesha hi dikhte hain.' (They are always seen.)

He was right. Fifteen minutes into the Reserve, we had our first 'sighting', three Jarawa tribals – man, woman and child, on either side of the road. Our car slowed down, just like all the other cars in the convoy. I saw tourists waving frantically, trying to get the attention of the Jarawa. All along the road in the Reserve area there were abandoned cans of tar, plastic mineral water bottles, bags of chips. This time, however, the ATR was not so bumpy; many labourers were inside the Reserve, trying to repair sections of the road.

The entire conversation in Baratang was about the adivasis. Various stories circulated. My driver, Mithun, was a thin Bengali in his early thirties.

He told me who the Jarawa were. 'Madam, they are ex-convicts from Uttar Pradesh, Bihar, etc., who had been let loose by the Britishers in the forests. Due to the isolation, they lost their mental equilibrium, shed their clothes and became aggressive. They started killing people with poisoned bows and arrows. That is why we move in a convoy. It keeps us safe,' he explained. Sunil, at least, knew that the Jarawa had come from Africa hundreds of years back. 'They are junglee (wild, uncivilized). In fact, there are four other jungle tribes in Andaman and Nicobar. Some, like the Sentinelese, are dangerous. Only the Nicobarese are a little civilized, like us.'

The return convoy left Baratang at 3 p.m. It was led by a tourist bus which was three vehicles ahead of us. Yet we could not open our windows because the bus was spewing black smoke. Many of us were choking. Twenty minutes into the Reserve, the car in front of us moved to the side and stopped. The convoy kept moving. 'Wasn't that illegal?' I asked. Mithun and Sunil merely shrugged their shoulders. Ten minutes later, the convoy stopped. A dozen men and women got out to answer nature's call. Strangely enough, none of them wanted to use the bathroom at Baratang! Just before the Reserve area begins, on both sides, toilet complexes which are surprisingly clean have been built. But half an hour into the Reserve, everyone had to get out and wander into the forest. A deliberate ploy to catch a glimpse of the Jarawa, I wondered? After about ten minutes, a hassled-looking constable got out of the bus leading the convoy and began to request everyone to get into the bus. A few minutes later, we came across another Jarawa. Standing alongside the road, he was signalling for the vehicles to stop. This time, however, the convoy did not stop. The rest of the journey inside the Reserve, while extremely distressing for my lungs, was uneventful. Only Mithun was unhappy. He had to adhere to the speed limit of 40 kmph. 'Usually we don't bother with these restrictions; 60 or 70 kmph is the norm.'

As soon as we got out of the Reserve, a local constable decided to ride with us to Port Blair. A stocky, middle-aged man, with a slight pot-belly, he had been on duty at the Jarawa Reserve for a year now. I asked him what it was like to be with the Jarawa. 'Earlier it was very difficult. They troubled us. Gradually, they have started listening. But we have to constantly monitor them because they are junglees. They can attack any time. Just a few days back, some tired fishermen had landed in the forest and built a fire to cook a meal. They were hungry after working all day. Without any provocation, the Jarawa attacked and killed one of them. This is how crazy they are,' he warned us. The keeper of law and order took a very sympathetic view of poachers! He completely forgot that the fishermen were not allowed to fish up to five km of the coastal line (from the high tide line). It was part of the Jarawa Reserve. I asked him how he communicated with the Jarawa. 'Their kids understand a little Hindi now. We are trying to teach them.' Towards the end of our journey, he told me that staying at the post was tiring. 'Approximately 300 vehicles pass through the Reserve area every day. The number goes up during the tourist season. Ninety per cent of the vehicles are of tourists. The rest are government vehicles and a few buses carrying local passengers. But we have to register all of them.' To me, the administration had always said that the ATR could not be closed because it was the lifeline of the locals. Yet, it seemed that it was a joyride for the tourists – a joyride through which local operators and agents make money by putting the Jarawa on display.

Three years after our visit to the Reserve, the debate on the indigenous tribes of the Andamans is far from resolved. Should we preserve them as one of the most unique societies on earth or should they be integrated with the mainstream? Voices on both sides remain equally strong. One demands that Jarawa children be educated and allowed to compete for seats at the finest global institutions. The other pleads that they would never be able to survive this civilizational leap. Caught between these two sides, without any say in the matter, the ancient tribes of the islands continue to be victims of ad hoc policies. The Great Andamanese, who had mingled with the outside world, are still being confined to a tiny island. The Jarawa, who had stood happy and proud in their chaddas and forests, are being forced to interact with outsiders. None of them are asked what they want. No one is told what decisions are being made on his or her behalf. We returned from the Andamans with a sense of urgency and impending doom. Even as experts and administrators debate and discuss their fate in the boardrooms of Port Blair and Delhi, time is running out on the oldest surviving tribes in the world. It has run out on the Great Andamanese man who lies drunk every evening, on the Jarawa child who begs for a bag of chips, and the Onge who does not even know his own songs anymore. These groups who survived in the lap of nature for thousands of years, who braved calamities – from tsunami waves and earthquakes to various bands of colonizers – and still managed to preserve their way of life may not be able to survive us. Their struggle and anguish has been lost in the all-encompassing silence which hangs over their ancient forest abode.

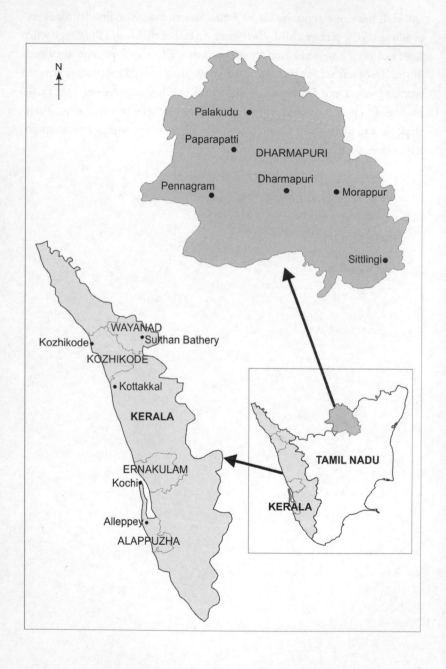

5

Kerala & Tamil Nadu

Kuch nahi to kam se kam khwab-e-sehr dekha to hai
Jis taraf dekha na tha aab tak, udhar dekha to hai

— JAN NISAR AKHTAR

Though elusive, yet we dare dream of the dawn,
We never looked there, now we look for the morn

Landing at Kochi, the country's first airport to be built in Public–Private Partnership mode, we saw the Travancore dancer and other images from Kerala Tourism flashing on the electronic display board in the arrivals lounge. Outside, there were huge hoardings towering over the large farmlands and grassy fields which lined the main road from the airport to the city. Airtel, Saudi Airlines, fashion retail and jewellery stores were featured on them. Most of the hoardings were in English, a few in Malayalam. Some models were familiar Bollywood faces. Others were Tamil superheroes and Kerala stars. These silhouettes dwarfed the tall coconut trees which stood on the roadside.

The city of Kochi or Cochin is in Ernakulam District in Kerala. With a population of 1.5 million in its extended metropolitan area, it is the state's largest urban agglomeration. It is also one of the country's oldest and most historic seaports. In 1102 AD, it became the seat of the kingdom of Cochin, and began to be called the 'Queen of the Arabian Sea'. In *The Moor's Last*

Sigh, Salman Rushdie has a lavish description of Kochi, the foremost spice-trading centre on the Arabian Sea coast since the fourteenth century. Ancient travellers and tradesmen often referred to Kochi in their writings, calling it Cocym, Cochym, Cochin, or Cochi. In 1503, the Portuguese made it the site of the first European colonial settlement in India, and it remained their capital until 1530, when they changed it to Goa. In 1947, it was the first princely state which willingly joined the Indian Union.

We, however, did not have time to explore this historic city. From the airport we headed straight towards Alleppey. Like many towns and cities across the country, Alleppey has now reverted to its original name, Alappuzha. In Malayalam, 'alla' means 'deep' and 'puzha' means 'river'. What brought us to this district famous for its criss-crossing rivulets and backwaters, were the three lakh women engaged in various coir-related activities. In 2007, Alleppey coir was registered under the GI (Geographical Indication of Goods) Act.

Though we had been looking at the village and small industries sector for a while, our knowledge about coir was perfunctory. So the Indian Coconut Committee's '*History and Home of Coconut*', published in 1954, was a good place to start. It provides an anecdotal history of coconut. Some believe that the coconut palm originated in Sri Lanka. Others are of the opinion that the coconut drifted in the sea from Polynesia and found new homes in many parts of the world. According to early Greek chronicles, it was the Greek ambassador, Megasthenes, who told the Indian king, Chandragupta Maurya about the coconut palms he had found in Sri Lanka in 300 BC. Arab writings of the eleventh century talked about the use of coir for ships' cables, fenders and rigging. Marco Polo's travelogue of the twelfth century described the uses to which coir fibre and mats were put in the vessels of the Arabs.

During the thirteenth century, there is evidence of coir yarn being used in building ships in the Persian Gulf. When the Portuguese admiral, Vasco da Gama, sailed to Kerala in the late fifteenth century, it is likely he would have seen this unusual multipurpose fibre. The first coir factory in India was established at Alleppey in 1859 by James Darragh, an American of Irish origin. Darragh enlisted the help of Henry Smail and together they established a factory under the name of 'Darragh Smail & Company'. By 1967, a little over a hundred years after the first coir factory was started,

Alleppey had 1,402 of the total 1,831 coir units in Kerala. This coastal town became the unchallenged headquarters of the coir industry. In the 1980s, however, repeated labour unrest and agitation, the absence of a strong co-operative sector, a steady decline in the export earnings, and the replacement of coir in foreign markets by 'more competent' synthetic materials undermined its existence and stability.

On its spinning side, coir is exclusively a cottage industry. On the manufacturing side of finished goods, it is partly cottage and partly factory. After the sluggishness of the past three decades, the Indian coir industry is slowly on the comeback trail. The export figures have moved up from Rs 250 crore in 1997 to Rs 605.17 crore during 2006–07. While these figures may not seem very high in terms of value, their significance lies in the fact that the coir industry directly or indirectly employs a staggering six lakh people, 80 per cent of whom are women.[1]

Though its history is inextricably interlinked to the coir story, Alappuzha has its own story, too. In the first decade of the twentieth century, the then Viceroy of India, Lord Curzon, made a visit to Alleppey. Fascinated by the lush green of the land and the abundance of water bodies, he is said to have exclaimed 'Alleppey. Ah! Venice of the East'. Thus the sobriquet found its place on the world tourism map; many have since alluded to that world famous enchantress, Venice, every time they seek to describe Alleppey and its calm but criss-crossing rivulets, the numerous bridges, and the narrow roads that border them.

Raja Kesava Das, Dewan of Travancore in the later half of the eighteenth century, is called the 'Maker of Modern Alleppey'. It was he who made Alappuzha into the premier port town of Travancore. He constructed roads and canals to improve communications, and built warehouses. Although the smallest district of Kerala (with an area of just 1,414 square km), it had the first post office and first telegraph office in the erstwhile Travancore State. Carved out of erstwhile Kottayam and Kollam (Quilon) Districts, Alleppey became a district on 17 August 1957. In February 1990, its anglicized name was changed to 'Alappuzha'. The sense that the name 'Alappuzha' conveys is

---

[1] http://www.ccriindia.org/Portal/web%20home%20page/History%20of%20 coir%20industry.pdf; Last accessed on 18 September 2011.

that of the 'land between the sea and the network of rivers flowing into it'. This reflects the district's geographical position and physical features. With a population of over 21 lakh, it is today Kerala's most densely populated district.

As the car sped towards Alleppey, we passed Ernakulam. Rows of upmarket restaurants and shops lined the road. This time, the hoardings featured Kerala girls in Delhi-style salwar kameez suits. Not a single advertisement of the white-and-gold Kairali sari, which is a must for every Malayali bride, was to be seen. As we passed the city, we looked in disbelief at what was rural Kerala – a continuum of densely packed habitations. These villages did not look like villages at all. The typical features of Indian villages – fields, hand pumps, ponds, thatched houses, stray animals – were missing. All the houses were pucca; many were painted in bright pinks, purples and oranges. It was difficult to make out where one village ended and the next began. Kerala seemed an uninterrupted urban agglomeration.

Finally, we entered the Kanjikuzhy block panchayat office which was located on the main road. Four women in silk saris with oiled and loosely plaited thick black hair greeted us. A young woman came forward and introduced herself as Jalaja Chandran, block pradhan. The red bindi on her forehead was thinly lined with white sandalwood. 'Kanjikuzhy Block covers five villages and one town and has a population of 1.61 lakh people. Our block has 2,000 SHGs (Self–Help Groups) which have a turnover of Rs 2 crore per month.' Jalaja spoke with quiet confidence. 'Men work on the manufacturing side of the coir industry, and earn between Rs 100-150 every day. Women are the primary workers – cultivators and yarn spinners; they earn between Rs 40–60 a day.' We listened intently to this forceful young woman. Women panchayat heads are no longer an uncommon sight in India. Yet, be it the salwar-wearing sarpanch of Punjab and Haryana or the ghoonghat-clad (veiled) sarpanch of villages across Bihar, Uttar Pradesh and Rajasthan, often the woman is little more than a token. The plains of northern India are full of 'MPs' and 'SPs'—mukhiya patis and sarpanch patis – who run the show with élan. In the past we had met many a woman sarpanch who did not express a single opinion. Every question directed at them was fielded by the husband or the son. Jalaja was different. Not only did she know her panchayat well, she carried her charge with confidence. For us, she epitomized the usefulness of women's leadership in the primary sector. In the years which followed, we invited her to Delhi twice to show off the work of women-led panchayat samitis.

That night, Thomas Isaac, Member of the Legislative Assembly (MLA) from this area, later to become the finance minister of Kerala, joined us for a simple meal at the guest house. Hearing of our experiences, he smiled. 'Would you believe how backward this area was? At one time, Kanjikuzhy had become famine-affected. Malnutrition levels were high, illiteracy was rampant as was unemployment. Its sandy soils did not allow much cultivation. Then we decided to pursue education. Simultaneously, people started vegetable gardens and coir work. Prosperity followed. Look at us now. We are the best panchayat in the state.' He went on to explain the success of Kerala's Panchayati Raj system. Beginning in 1997, the state began extensive training for panchayat members. 'Every year, surveys were carried out, needs assessed, sorted and prioritized. Thereafter, project proposals were prepared and discussed.' From him, we learnt other things about the state. Forty per cent of Kerala families rely on remittances from the Gulf; people have enough money to spend. Hence the excessive displays of flamboyant consumer advertisements.

The next morning, Jalaja took us to the new building of the food processing centre, established by the Kanjikuzhy panchayat. Sparkling floors, neat, clean kitchens, women wearing gloves and aprons – everything about the centre was orderly. On the stone kitchen counter, neat rows of bottles contained pickles made from bitter gourd, mango, ginger, garlic, lime, amla and asparagus. It was a hygienic, appetizing and affordable array. 'We make twenty kg of jams and squashes every day. Our women work from 10 a.m. to 5 p.m. and earn Rs 50 per day,' Jalaja explained.

Accompanied by the other panchayat women – seven of Kanjikuzhy's seventeen panchayat members are women – we moved to the village panchayat office. The famous Kudumbashree SHG programme[2] was

---

[2] Kudumbashree, literally meaning prosperity of the family, was launched by the Government of Kerala in 1998 as a community network that would work in tandem with local self governments for povery eradication and empowerment of women. Today it has 37 lakh members and covers over 50 per cent of the households in the state.

running here. We saw women making umbrellas, chappals and bags. A two-fold umbrella sold for Rs 95 and a three-fold one for Rs 125! Women were bent over rows of sewing machines in small shops. The panchayat's own computer centre had four desktops. The women panchayat members spoke to us about their day-to-day work. Like Jalaja, they too were well versed about the PRIs. They ensured that most of the panchayat funds went into water supply, sanitation, agriculture, small industries, women and children. They ran the schools, the anganwadis and health centres. Local committees to supervise the anganwadis were active. For children's midday meals, pulses, groundnuts, rice and occasionally eggs were locally procured. If children participated in sports, they got special food to ensure proper nourishment. 'By the end of this year, every house in our village will have a latrine. We also have 90 per cent electrification,' Jalaja said. We were impressed by what we saw. There was no trace left of the poverty-ridden, educationally backward place which had been described by Thomas Isaac the previous night.

It was dark by the time we reached the Coir Research Institute (CRI). The 'History of Coconut' had provided us fascinating insights into the fruit; now we were to learn about the nature and processing of the fibre. A normal coconut yields eighty gm of fibre and 160 gm of pith. The original colour of coir is a dull brown. It is removed from the coconut shells and placed in the backwaters for six–seven months. That is how long it takes to acquire its golden brown colour. This process is called 'retting'. The research institute has developed a process for controlled 'retting' within seventy-two hours by using a bacterial cocktail. To colour the coir, natural substances such as tea, coffee, cinnamon, onions and flowers are used. 'We have also devised a loom which enables women to enter the coir-weaving sector which had thus far been a 'male only' domain. This loom is called Anugraha and costs Rs 5,000,' explained the director of the institute. We learnt that, with the Anugraha loom, workers could earn up to Rs 120 per day as against the current Rs 45 per day. 'Coir is also used as manure,' he continued. We looked at the potted plants he was holding. 'We apply mushroom to raw coir pith and make manure. All these plants have been grown using the coir manure. The institute produces one lakh metric tonnes of composting annually with an export value of Rs 30 crore.' As we were talking about the multiple uses of this fibre, we entered the courtyard which was a beautifully laid-out garden. 'Look carefully,' our guide said, 'there is no soil here. These gardens have been laid on concrete using coir pith as a thick base.'

The next morning, we moved to the other side of Alappuzha – its famed backwaters. Our houseboat was called *Punnamada Kayal*. Unlike the ornate walnut wood houseboats lined up on Dal Lake in Kashmir, the houseboats of Alleppey are made of bamboo, and shaped like huts. They have a simple décor, clean and comfortable interiors that are in tune with the rivulets that meander about the lush habitations. Our breakfast was on the deck; steaming idli and dosa. Just as the sun did a lazy stretch and prepared to begin its day, we observed life buzzing along the banks on both sides. Lord Curzon had compared these backwaters to Venice but we did not see much in common between the two. Venice is a city unlike any other in the world, a place where one uses boats instead of vehicles for commuting; yet its beauty is in the elaborate and finely carved palazzos that stand on both sides of the canal, the water lapping gently at their steps; its romance is in the history, the intrigue, the gondola ride and the Rialto Bridge. Alleppey is different. There are no palatial mansions here, no Casanova, no serenading gondoliers. Along these backwaters are muddy by-lanes, small huts and houses, little country boats with fishermen in langots (loincloths), struggling with their nets, looking for 'kari meen' (pearl spot). This is no fairy-tale universe. For the skinny, sunburnt fishermen, one kilo of fish means Rs 200–300. It is this that keeps them going.

Our boat moved majestically over the waters, trampling thousands of tiny waves generated by smaller boats which passed by. The waters were a deep green, reflecting the palm and coconut trees. In these backwaters, boat races are held every year. There are a total of 230 houseboats, with rents which vary between Rs 4,000 to Rs 12,000 per night. 'That is the Kumarakom Bird Sanctuary, where the former prime minister, Mr Atal Behari Vajpayee, came every year to relax and write poetry,' someone said, pointing to a land formation in the distance.

After a relaxing trip on the backwaters, we moved to the city of Kozhikode (formerly Calicut) in north Kerala. It was at Kappad in Kozhikode District that Vasco da Gama first landed in May 1498. And it was here that we decided to go different ways. A firm believer in the Indian systems of medicine, Syeda was getting herself admitted in an Ayurvedic hospital to literally test the waters. The eternal wanderer, Gunjan, was heading to Wayanad, the poorest and perhaps the most beautiful district of Kerala.

∽

Syeda: Kottakkal, Kerala. Over the years, I had often heard about the Ayurvedic treatment at Kottakkal in Malappuram District of Kerala. Several years ago, in Kozhikode, I had visited their branch dispensary. After the free consultation, they gave well-reasoned advice but did not push their treatment or medicines. At the time, I could not visit their main hospital – the Arya Vaidya Sala. Now, I decided that it was time to conduct an experiment on myself. I expected a busy routine – a regimen of massages, prolonged yoga, mud baths, meditation. So I apportioned one week to this experiment.

Kottakkal is a small village that has become world-famous for the Arya Vaidya Sala established in 1902 by a legendary Ayurvedic doctor, P.S. Varier. Dr Varier (1869–1944) had studied Ayurveda under a great *Ashtavaidya,* Brahmasri Kuttanchery Vasudevan. He had also acquired sound allopathic knowledge from Dewan Bahadur Verghese, renowned physician and surgeon. The Vaidya Sala was originally established for the manufacture and supply of medicines. This was done in strict accordance with authentic texts, while insisting on purity and quality. Today, it has become a hospital with four buildings in one campus as well as branches all over Kerala and other parts of the country. It has herbal gardens in many parts of Kerala where medicinal plants are grown.

It took a couple of hours from Kozhikode to reach Malappuram District. On the way, I picked up two friends who had decided to come along for what they called 'rejuvenation therapy' from Karripur Airport.

The sight that greeted me on arrival was nothing like I had imagined. I always find Kerala a feast for the eyes. My eyes were accustomed to backwaters, houseboats, trees growing out of the water, banana and coconut groves and meadows, all against the silver grey of the Arabian Sea. What I saw here were neat blocks of buildings clustered around a narrow, open courtyard. It did not resemble the Kerala tourism images splashed on huge hoardings all the way from Kochi. I saw my friends look surprised and somewhat disappointed. We realized that this was no glamorous enclave for the so-called rejuvenation therapy. Kottakkal was a hospital – a regular, functioning hospital.

The hospital attendants showed me to my room. It was sparsely furnished; bare floor, bed, table, no lamp, naked walls. I was finally and totally alone with myself. I recalled the lines of Yeats: 'An aged man is but a paltry thing/ A tattered coat upon a stick'. I thought of my body as ageing, a decrepit frame that had to be put in order within these spartan surroundings, as also my clogged mind, a container overflowing with dispensable facts. The thought of facing my self for seven solitary days and nights was daunting.

My treatment began with a small pooja (prayer ceremony), an essential part of the healing. The treatment itself was a combination of shirodhara, body massage and a herbal poultice for the joints. Shirodhara is the steady trickle of oil through a hole in an earthen pot held over the head for one whole hour. The body massage is a process whereby six persons work on one, first, with bare hands, then with pieces of cloth dipped in warm oil and applied over the pain spots. The poultice is a warm paste of herbs and ingredients mixed in milk and applied to a strip of cloth which is placed over pain spots. It struck me that every part of the treatment required the human touch; it gave the body great comfort. Even if it was momentarily painful, its end result was comfort and relief. It also struck me that modern medicine has very little room for the human touch.

I discovered that the three hospital blocks were full to capacity with people from seventeen countries. With very few exceptions, most had come with families; everyone was encouraged to bring a companion. The rooms were equipped with small kitchens, and stoves were made available on request. Wives had accompanied husbands for treatment and vice versa. Young men were there with elderly mothers; mothers with sick children, people in wheelchairs, and people in walkers; women, men and children suffering from severe and medium-level handicaps. That one heals better in the presence of one's loved ones is becoming a well-accepted theory all over the world.

Several patients were from West Asia. Elderly Arab women patients were there, fully veiled. When I said 'Salaam' to them, they replied from behind their veils. In the lifts, I heard Arabic spoken; young couples from the Gulf talked animatedly while wheeling their elderly parents for the daily treatment routine.

I spent my seven days observing the people who had collected at Kottakkal in quest of health. In the Vaidya Sala, health was the only mantra. But there were no quick solutions. Healing had to do with the food one ate, the water one drank, the long periods when one sat back without being intensely preoccupied with anything but idle thoughts. I had to let myself flow with the rhythm of the place and rid my mind of its daily clutter. I did something I never did in Delhi. On a tiny screen, I watched two excellent Malayalam films minus dubbing and subtitles; my sensibilities were sharpened, so I really did not need language. The two friends I had picked from the airport returned home after a day's treatment because they did not find the 'rejuvenation therapy' they were looking for, which is advertised as Kerala's USP. It was not to be found in places like Kottakkal, which are only interested in holistic health.

Today, I feel stronger and more confirmed in my faith in the efficacy of our indigenous systems of medicine – a science we call 'alternative' and sometimes think of as quackery. It is time to take a deep and serious look at our traditional systems of health; or will we only do it when the Western world says they are good for us?

Gunjan: Wayanad, Kerala. A few hours from Kozhikode driving though the hills, I saw a Kerala very different from what I had experienced in the last few days. Gone was the urban cityscape, cake-icing constructions; even the main road was uneven.

I had first heard about Wayanad from a group of women from the closed coffee and tea plantations of the district. They had come to meet us at the Planning Commission. They were led by a woman in her late forties. Clad in a simple, starched cotton sari, P.B. Panamma introduced herself as the secretary of the Glenleven Estate Union. She told us that the plantation owners did not adhere to the law so it finally caught up with them. Estates were closed and the workers were locked out. The SDM intervened and asked the management to either reopen the estates or let workers pluck and sell tea leaves. 'But when we went to get the leaves, a NBW (non-bailable warrant) was issued against us and cases of theft were registered,' said Sakina, a woman in a black sari who worked for the Fringford Estate. 'Arrears of the last eighteen–twenty years have not been paid to workers,' she added. The women told us that in Idukki District, 30,000 families were struggling for a living. In Trivandrum itself seven estates had been closed. 'Owners are giving estates to the banks and starting other businesses. Ninety per cent of workers are women. Already three starvation deaths have been reported in Trivandrum,' Panamma told us. On this visit, however, I was not going to these closed estates. Instead, I was planning to meet the tribal groups that inhabited this district to see how differently a prosperous and well-performing state treated its tribal people.

Located in the north-east of Kerala, Wayanad was formed on 1 November 1980 as the twelfth district, carved out of Kozhikode and Kannur.[3] It has three taluks. Vythiri, Mananthavady and Sulthan Bathery. The name 'Wayanad' is a compound of vayal (paddy field) and naad (land), hence 'Land of Paddy Fields'. It is located in the majestic Western Ghats. Adivasis form 36 per cent of the population; the main groups are the Paniya, Kuruma, Adiyar, Kurichya, Oorali, Kadan and Kattunaikkan. Being extremely fertile, the district also has a large settler population from many parts of Kerala. A small Jain community consisting of Gowders from Karnataka have built beautiful temples all over the district. A fourth each of the population of Wayanad is Christian and Muslim, and the rest is Hindu.

My first stop was in the dusty town of Sulthan Bathery. Here, I met V.B. Baby, an activist, dressed in a white dhoti and shirt. He told me of a land agitation two years earlier, after which a thousand families got the land they were struggling for. 'The Paniya (worker) tribe works as seasonal agricultural labour for three–four months; then they become migrant workers in Coorg, Karnataka. Men get a wage of Rs 100 per day and women Rs 50–60. The Kattunaikkan are a Primitive Tribal Group.' Kattunaikkan,

---

[3] In 1956, when the state of Kerala came into being, Wayanad was part of Cannanore (now Kannur). A year later, South Wayanad was added to Kozhikode and North Wayanad remained with Cannanore. The present Wayanad District is an amalgam of both Wayanads.

the name sounded familiar. Suddenly I remembered why. 'Aren't they the tribe that makes the fabled tree-houses? Do they actually live in them?' I asked.

Baby's reply was matter of fact. 'I'm afraid there is no romanticism. In the forest, tree-houses are built by tribals during the summer in order to stay safe from attacks by wild elephants.'

The write-ups I had come across had always made these tree-houses seem exotic. They had made them out to be the closest thing to Enid Blyton's famous Faraway Tree. 'The tourist write-ups don't talk about issues of survival. Hence the glamour attached to the tree-houses. One can't actually live in them. You'll see why soon enough.'

With that, we headed for the Muthanga Sanctuary. Here, sixteen km away in a rain forest of the Nilgiri Biosphere Reserve, live the Kattunaikkan. As we entered the forest area, I strained my neck to look for the tree-houses. Finally, I saw a couple of them and realized the truth behind Baby's words. The much-touted tree-houses looked more like observation posts. A rickety ladder led up to a small thatched structure admist the foliage. Definitely not habitable! A few women walked past, dark and thin.

'What is your name?'

Silence.

'Are you a Kattunaikkan?'

Silence.

'Is there a village nearby?'

One woman pointed towards a mud path running through the vegetation.

'Why won't they speak to us? Is it the language?' I asked Baby.

An accompanying officer immediately sought to intervene. In the local language he explained, 'Look, she has come from the government to find out about your problems so that something can be done.'

My motives thus explained, I tried once again.

'Are you aware of any government schemes? Have any reached your village?'

After a few minutes of silence, one woman looked at me. Her eyes seemed vacant. She spoke for a few minutes in a monotone and then suddenly fell silent. I looked towards the official expectantly. He looked uncomfortable and didn't say a word. I turned towards my friend, Senthil, a young Tamil engineer from Coimbatore who had accompanied me on the trip. He looked upset. 'She says, "What use are your schemes and policies when I have to watch my children die every day?"'

Gradually, the story unfolded. I learnt that in the forest village outside which we stood, in two years, seven children had died of starvation. The young, malnourished mothers here do not even have milk to feed the children. 'During the months of September and October, when the forests bear no fruits and there is no work, we have a very difficult time,' explained Babu, a local resident from the adjoining village of Nolpura who had barged into our car to guide us.

Gram Panchayat Nolpura covers 290 tribal colonies, which is 40 per cent of the population. Of the sixteen panchayat members, eight are tribals but none are Kattunaikkan. 'This tribe is very poor and backward. They are not educated, they have no work. They stay in forests where medical aid is unavailable. They depend on God and traditional medicine. The IMR (Infant Mortality Rate) and MMR (Maternal Mortality Rate) are very high but we seldom get to know because they don't take a pregnant woman to the hospital for delivery and they don't report deaths. Women don't visit PHCs and ANMs don't visit their villages. Here, too, sickle cell anaemia is very common,' Babu continued.

By this time, I had reached the village which consisted of a few kutchcha houses. A middle-aged, bare-chested man in a white dhoti, Mahar Kutty, told me about life in these forest habitations; scarce food, no electricity and the ever-present danger of animal attack. 'If we die due to attack by wild animals, our family will get Rs 25,000; that's all our life is worth. Fifteen people from our colony have been killed by animals. Our children don't go to school, they have no future. The closest school is three km away and only up to Class 4. The upper primary school is at a distance of eight km; with the danger of wild elephants, we can't send the children.' The pain that was evident in the faces of the women we had met outside was reflected in his words.

Mahar continued: 'We have written to both the chief minister and the Forest Department for jobs, but there is nothing for us.' By now, a few other people had gathered around us. They nodded in agreement. These tribals were not asking for dole or sympathy. They were a proud people. They wanted work; they wanted land to till. Was this not their right?

Cheriakuli, a wiry, thin, dark woman with sharp features clutched the hand of her small son. 'Earlier, I worked as agricultural labour for Rs 65 a day; the men got Rs 110. Somehow, we managed. Now I get no work. Our men have to go to neighbouring states hoping to find work,' she said.

'Where do you go when you fall ill?' I asked.

Shreedharan, one of the local leaders, said, 'The nearest PHC is ten km away, in Kuruma. The doctor is seldom found there. To get there we have to pass through forests. It's not easy. At the sub-centre, there are no medicines. So we rely on traditional medicine. In the last two years, two women in our village have died during childbirth.'

Cheriakuli spoke again. 'To take them to hospital we need transportation, a jeep or some jugaad (improvised vehicle). How do we get it? Money is paid to us after the delivery but we need money in hand to be able to reach the hospital.'

The litany of woes that engulfed me was in sharp contrast to the calm of the tropical rain forest in which I stood. And once again these forests seemed to swallow up every whimper of hunger, every cry of pain and every scream of frustration. To the outside world, Kerala is a model state – one that leads in nearly all human development indices. Indeed, much has been done right in this state. Jalaja and Kanjikuzhy are living examples of why most people look up to Kerala. And yet, even in this progressive state, with the highest literacy rate in the country, the marginalized continue to remain on the margins. Their condition is no better than their counterparts in the rest of the country, their agony no less. Within a few kilometres of each other, two worlds co-exist – one, a highly urban, consumerist and progressive world that is on display for all. The other, a deprived world that remains hidden within the forest. Will the two ever meet?

It was August 2010, our sixth year in the Planning Commission, six years of hope and hopelessness; six years of non-stop travel to seen and unseen places; six years of assessing the needs of people and evaluating the performance of various government schemes. And our quest was not yet over. This time, we found ourselves on the highway from Bangalore to Dharmapuri to visit an anomaly – the worst-performing district of one of the best performing states, Tamil Nadu.[4]

Created in 1965, Dharmapuri is known for its poor human development indices – rampant female infanticide, frequent droughts, child marriage, illiteracy. It was in the forests of this district that the notorious sandalwood smuggler, Veerappan, was finally shot dead in October 2004 by the Special Task Force. In the 1970s, five out of the eight blocks in the district were Naxal strongholds. A decade later, the armed rebellion was brought under control, but even today an undercurrent of uncertainty haunts the district administration. The fear of the erstwhile followers of Charu Mazumdar and his comrades becoming active once again is not unfounded.

These problems notwithstanding, Dharmapuri today is a district filled with hope that stems from the dedication of a group of government functionaries headed by an outstanding collector, P. Amudha. A young woman with short curly hair and a determined stride, Amudha told us about her district even as we travelled through it. From her, we learnt that the Vaniyars, who are classified as Most Backward Class (MBC), account for 55 per cent of the eighteen lakh people in the district (12.5 lakh as per the 2001 Census). One-fifth of the population is scheduled caste and five per cent, scheduled tribe. At Rs 18,000 per annum (2006 figures), the per capita income of Dharmapuri is higher than that of Kanyakumari, which is among the best performing districts in the state. Yet, deep-rooted gender-based discrimination and illiteracy along with persistent alcoholism have earned the district much notoriety. The district earns approximately Rs 28 crore per month as revenue from sale of alcohol – the highest in the state! 'This distinction we can definitely do without,' Amudha told us emphatically. There is little entrepreneurship, and 70 per cent of the population is dependent on agriculture and allied activities. The district has one-third of the land under mango cultivation in the state, and accounts for half of its mango yield. The prevalence of child marriage, explained Amudha, is largely the result of migration. 'Many from the district work at construction

---

[4] State Human Development Report, 2008.

sites in Bangalore, earning up to Rs 250 per day as against the Rs 75 or 100 they would make in Dharmapuri. They are reluctant to leave young girls behind and hence marry them off early.' Interestingly, in 1989, Dharmapuri became the first district in Tamil Nadu to form self-help groups. The first woman IPS (Indian Police Service) officer in Tamil Nadu, G. Thilakavathi, also came from here.

We had been so engrossed in learning about the district that it took us a while to realize that the cars had stopped. We were in a school compound. 'Deenapatti Village, Mukano Panchayat,' the driver informed us. We stepped out and noticed an anganwadi centre in one corner of the compound. It was a two-room stone structure. Given the human development indices of the district, we were expecting a scene much like what we had seen in states of northern and eastern India. We were however surprised to find that this neat and orderly centre was no different from the anganwadis we had visited in Coimbatore and other places in Tamil Nadu. The walls were adorned with educational charts. A dozen children were sitting on the floor with aluminium utensils. Some were playing with toys. The store room had grains, eggs, utensils and a huge water-storage tank. 'But there has been no water supply for the last six months,' a middle-aged woman told us. Lakshmi, the anganwadi worker, filled registers, taught the children, and also prepared the meal as the centre had been without a helper for over a year. Even as she spoke to us, she was watching the eggs that were boiling in a large pot just outside the anganwadi. This was the children's food for the day. Lakshmi told us that the Village Health Nurse (the ANM is known as VHN in Tamil Nadu) visited the anganwadi twice every month. At the behest of the district collector, she brought from her store a packet of salt and a small bottle filled with liquid. 'This is the iodine-testing kit provided by UNICEF (United Nations Children's Fund),' she explained, as she took out a pinch of salt and laid it on a white sheet. She added two drops of the liquid to the salt. 'This salt contains adequate iodine,' she explained. 'That is why it has turned purple. The liquid contains starch and citric acid and is used for checking the presence of iodine.' Given the prevalence of goitre in the area, Amudha had tied up with UNICEF to ensure that all anganwadis in her district not just received these kits but also put them to use.

After spending a few more moments with the anganwadi worker and going through the registers, we proceeded to the school. Unlike at the anganwadi centre, we found a functioning toilet in the school premises. 'But there is no running water. We get water from a tank outside,' the teacher explained. There were two teachers for forty-five children in Classes 1 to 5. The children sat on mats and studied together in one big room which was dotted with educational charts. Learning aids were scattered around. In one corner of the room stood a huge colour TV set. Surprised, we turned to Amudha. 'All schools in Tamil Nadu are provided with a television set and mats under Sarva Shiksha Abhiyan,' she explained. Next door, in a dingy smoke-filled shed, the midday meal was being prepared. The cook told us that he received 43.5 paise per child per day for food. We were unsure about the quality and quantity of the meals even as we got into the car once again.

The PHC, Morappur, where we stopped next was twenty-five years old, had five doctors, and catered to a population of 36,000 over a twenty-km radius. None of the doctors were specialists. An anaesthesiologist and gynaecologist were hired from the medical college at Dharmapuri in case of emergencies. Five years earlier, the PHC was upgraded to the status of a thirty-bed CHC, and for the last three years it had been winning the best PHC award. We found the premises clean; an ambulance stood in the driveway next to well-trimmed gardens. These gardens had been laid from the untied funds under the NRHM. A reverse osmosis (RO) system and a condom-dispensing machine had also been installed. Dr Jeevanandan, the medical officer in charge, told us that the CHC had a link ART (Anti-Retroviral Therapy) centre as there were over a hundred HIV-positive cases in the area. 'Given the fact that we are on the highway and have a large migrant population, we are a red district as far as HIV is concerned.' Next to the condom-dispensing machine, there was another vending machine. This one was for sanitary pads. At the behest of the collector, Dharmapuri has become one of the first districts in the country to make sanitary pads easily accessible to girls and women. For Rs 2, they can get a hygienic pad. The pad-dispensing machine has been installed not just at health centres across the district but even in schools. The district has also introduced immediate birth and death registration at PHCs. As we moved towards the labour room, we were amazed to hear strains of music. 'While conducting deliveries we play music. It is good for the nerves and helps women cope,' the doctor explained. After the delivery or after tubectomy operations, women are kept under observation at the hospital for two days. Six meals are provided which are prepared by an SHG. As we moved from one ward to the next, each one clean and well kept, we realized why private nursing homes in the area had closed down. The Morappur PHC was among the few government-run health centres in the country that respected the dignity of patients and strove to provide them with every possible comfort.

It was with renewed hope that we proceeded towards Sittilingi, our final destination for the day. Eighty-five kilometres or four hours from the town of Dharmapuri, Sittilingi, literally meaning 'the place where Siddha worshipped the lingam' is a tribal area on the south-eastern tip of the district. Hidden among the hills here is another success story – the story of a doctor couple from Alleppey District of Kerala who have trained locals as barefoot doctors. On our way we crossed a mountain topped with a small temple. 'This is Theerthamalai, a major pilgrimage site,' Amudha informed us. 'According to mythology, Lord Rama sat here doing penance for forty-five days and every day Hanuman brought water for him. One day, Hanuman got delayed so Lord Shiva told Rama to fire an arrow; "wherever it lands, a perennial spring will come up". This is where the spring burst forth,' she explained.

The Tribal Health Initiative (THI) Centre at Sittilingi is housed in a few single-storey well-designed bamboo, cane and mud buildings spread across a quiet and clean campus. In 1993, Regi George, an anaesthesiologist, and Lalitha George, a gynaecologist, visited this tribal area. He was a Kerala Christian, she from the Hindu royal family of Kochi. They wanted to work in rural India and were travelling to find the right spot. What they saw in Sittilingi shocked them. Mostly a tribal area, Sittilingi was so remote that during the monsoons it was completely cut off. People had no access to healthcare. Their traditional practices like keeping the woman and child out in the cold at the back of the house for a week after childbirth resulted in high maternal and child mortality. As the child survival rate was low, family size was normally six or seven. The Georges had found the place they were looking for. 'We encroached on some land and built a mud-and-thatch hut with the help of the tribals. For three years we ran a hospital from there.

We managed to provide some care but, by and large, the problems persisted as the impact of our work did not change the retrograde practices being followed,' explained fifty-year-old Lalitha, clad in a simple salwar kameez. So they started mapping the households in the village.

In 1995, they asked the villagers to select some elderly women who could be trained to provide healthcare at the local level. Twenty-five women were selected from twenty-one hamlets. Every two weeks, these women would visit the centre for two days to learn the basics of health, hygiene, disease management, etc., and to update the data about births, deaths, etc., in their villages. These women became the healthcare providers and change agents in their tribal hamlets. At the time of our visit, there were twenty-three health auxiliaries in the forty to seventy age-group who received Rs 700 per month as a stipend and worked for two–three hours daily. Most were illiterate but, after training, they were able to explain the basics of health, hygiene, etc. As they were elderly, and from the community, people listened to them. We met some of these women, wrapped in cotton saris, standing outside the health centre. Among them was a younger woman, Rajamma. She had joined the doctor couple when they first came to Sittilingi. 'I was sixteen years old and had dropped out of Class 8,' Rajamma recalled. 'I started as wage labour when the centre was being built but went on to learn nursing and assisting in deliveries. Now I work as a nurse. I have even assisted in minor surgeries,' she said, her voice confident despite her uncertain smile. Rajamma told us that initially there was resistance from the community but the Georges along with their small group of trained women gradually won them over.

Today, the twenty-four-bed THI hospital at Sittilingi with its neonatal ward, operation theatre (OT) and special TB Unit covers over 10,000 families spread across twenty km. Around 200 births take place at the institution every year. OPD is held thrice a week and the daily attendance is 150–160 patients. In the OT, lit by a single bulb and equipped with a World War II air and ether anaesthesia kit, non-blood surgeries are carried out. The user fee for tribals is Rs 20 and for non-tribals, Rs 30. In-patients pay whatever they can afford. The results of the THI are, we learnt, astounding. The IMR has reduced from 150 per 1,000 live births to twenty. Consequently, family size has come down to four or five. There has been no maternal death in eight consecutive years. 'Over time, we realized that just providing healthcare isn't enough. We did a padayatra (foot march) in our villages to ask people what they wanted. Farming was their main occupation so we introduced organic cultivation. A co-operative of 200 farmers was formed. They grow organic turmeric, cotton, sugarcane and millets. Women make ragi papad and biscuits, and sell them under the brand name Svad,' Regi informed us.

Once, during a field-visit, Lalitha discovered the Lambada embroidery done by the women. The art was dying and only two women in the community still knew how to embroider. The Georges encouraged them and offered to sell their work. The two women trained others and, today, the Sittilingis create beautiful organic and handwoven skirts, tops, bags, etc., under the brand name Porgai, meaning pride. These sell really well at exhibitions in metros. 'Last year, we sold products worth Rs 3 lakh,' Lalitha told us.

In their efforts to transform the community in Sittilingi, the Georges are aided by a few friends. Dressed in shorts and sporting a small beard, Krishna was one such person. An architect by profession, he designed the Sittilingi hospital using local materials – the result was not an antiseptic, impersonal building but a house of health where patients feel at ease. After the building was done, Krishna did not leave. Instead, he started training fourteen- to eighteen-year-olds to become entrepreneurs. 'The dropout rate after Class 8 was high as children went to work at the knitwear units in Tirupur. So we introduced a one-year academic and technical training course for such boys. I have taught them plumbing, electric works, etc. We have now trained a total of twenty-five students,' Krishna told us.

Encouraged by the success of their endeavours, the Georges are now setting up another project in the Kalrayan Hills, situated at the junction of Dharmapuri, Salem and Villipuram Districts. Of the twenty-six villages to be covered, twenty have no form of transportation and six have just one bus a day. As we spoke to the earnest and dedicated doctors, we understood the difficulty of replicating and upscaling these models. In a country where doctors are willing to pay huge amounts of money to escape rural postings, finding practitioners who are willing to stay in tribal hamlets and treat the people is difficult. There are exceptions—the Georges or the Jan Swasthya

Sahyog of Ganiyari or the Bangs of Gadchiroli.[5] But these are few and far between. At the time of our visit, the THI hospital had just one in-patient. The rest had been discharged as the Georges were planning to go on a one-month holiday and finding doctors to take over in their absence was tough. This is the danger that hangs over such well-meaning initiatives; the challenge is to ensure that they are able to carry on even in the absence of their founding members. A daunting task but surely the Georges with their simplicity and single-minded devotion would be able to inspire medical graduates to fulfil their Hippocratic oath. It was with this hope that we left Sittilingi to begin our return journey.

A few kilometres away was the ten-bed tribal PHC at Kotapatti. Run by a doctor couple from Salem, it was a remarkably neat facility. It had the ubiquitous television set that had been bought with NRHM flexi-funds; as always it was turned off. Over the next couple of days we were to discover that most health centres had used the funds under NRHM to buy TV sets (for Information Education Communication, i.e., IEC purposes), paint and maintain walls, and install an RO system for drinking water. The money was also used to purchase emergency medicines and buy equipment like ultrasound machines and electronic weighing scales. Yet, despite all the funds and the infrastructure, no surgeries were carried out at Kotapatti. Only about thirty deliveries took place every month. At the time of our visit, there were around six to eight in-patients at the PHC. All expectant women had in their possession cards with their photographs and ANC (antenatal care) history. This, we discovered, was an innovation carried out at the PHC through the NRHM flexi-funds. A World Bank pilot project was also underway. 'Tribal mothers are brought in three days prior to the expected date of delivery and kept at the centre for ten days. The mother, along with one attendant, is provided food through SHGs,' the medical officer informed us. We asked the patients about the quantity and quality of food. They seemed satisfied.

By now, the day was worn out and so were we. But our spirits were high. Perhaps it was hope that kept the tiredness at bay. That night we slept peacefully. For once, it was a trip that allowed us sound sleep; other journeys

---

5 See Chapter 7

had been fraught with sleepless nights when we were haunted by blank faces and pleading eyes.

The next day we went to the western edge of the district. The Hogenakkal Falls, literally meaning 'smoking rock' are just that – fine sprays rising like smoke amidst rocky cliffs; it is one of the more picturesque places in the world. Sandwiched between Karnataka and Tamil Nadu, the falls were until recently not accessible to the public due to Veerappan's presence in the surrounding jungles. Since the end of that story, it has become a popular tourist spot; visitors come from all over the country to stand under the raging water. But as it was a weekday, most people we saw were locals eagerly lining up to get massages done or to enjoy crazy rides along the Kaveri (Cauvery) river in large round wicker baskets called coracles. We, too, could not resist the temptation. As we rode the waters separating the two states, we saw loincloth-clad fisherfolk, sitting on the rocks, dangling their lines. A few waved their big 'catch' before our admiring eyes. The poet Iqbal's Farsi lines on the Kaveri wafted through the mind:

> Rud e Kaveri yake narmak khiram
> Khasta i shayad ke az sair e dawam
> Dar kohistan umrha naleeda i
> Rahe khud ra ba mizha kaveeda i

> Flow softly, O River Kaveri!
> Wearied by your long and arduous journey
> In the cavernous mountains
> your tear-entangled eyelashes
> have burrowed paths

Amudha, who had accompanied us on the ride, told us that, apart from its scenic beauty, the Hogenakkal Falls are vital to the district because of the water supply project that is expected to be completed by 2012. This will supply Kaveri water to Krishnagiri and Pennagram blocks of this drought-prone district. One full hour of boat ride was a journey right out of Sindbad the Sailor's chronicles. We moved next to stand beneath the torrential Hogenakkal Falls; the force of the water was a taste of death and eternity in one swoop.

The Kasturba Gandhi Balika Vidyalaya, located in Paparapatti Block, was our next stop. One hundred girls from Classes 6 to 8, most of them children of migrant labourers, stayed here. The Vidyalaya, run by an NGO under the SSA, was housed in a white, two-storey building with a neat garden. The place was filled with the chatter of young girls clad in neat uniforms. Each classroom had a blackboard, desks and chairs. Trunks containing the girls' things were neatly lined up against the wall. We asked a few of them to read from their books. A bright-looking girl with her hair neatly oiled and braided stood up.

'My name is Usha,' she said. Then she began reading from her English textbook. Her pronunciation was good. Next, we asked a couple of girls to write some maths tables on the blackboard. Once again, they were able to do so without any difficulty. In the courtyard, a girl was playing the synthesizer. 'Besides the regular curriculum, we teach our children tailoring, computers, yoga, dance, music or karate. They can choose the activities they are interested in,' a teacher told us. She showed us passbooks for the girls. 'Every month, Rs 50 is placed in a fixed deposit in the girls' name. So, at the end of three years, when the girls leave, they get Rs 1,800.'

The school received Rs 750 per month for food for every child, enough to provide them with four meals, including milk. In addition to this, they also got Rs 50 per month for toiletries, Rs 750 for medical bills and Rs 50 as a stipend. Water was provided through an RO system. In the corner of one classroom, we saw a sanitary napkin vending machine much like the ones we had seen in the hospital on our first day. 'This machine is in all girls' schools in the district,' Amudha said. 'The napkins are made by the girls themselves,' a teacher added. 'Look there,' she pointed towards an adjoining room with a few tailoring machines. Three or four girls were busy cutting wads of cotton and wrapping them in cloth. Two girls sat at the machines and were stitching up these wads. 'It takes five minutes to make a napkin. We put the prepared napkins in the machine and students can get it for Rs 2,' explained a slim girl with neatly braided hair into which was tucked a string of jasmine. On her forehead was a small black bindi. 'I am Semnandini, from Class 6. I live in the nearby village. Do visit my home,' she invited us eagerly.

'What do you want to do when you grow older?'

'I want to become a doctor,' she replied in a shy voice, her eyes brimming with hope.

'Wow! All the best.'

'Where are the napkins disposed?' we asked Amudha. She took us outside the classroom to what looked like a huge boiler. 'A vending machine normally costs Rs 14,000 and an incinerator, Rs 25,000. So I designed this boiler. It costs Rs 5,000 and is just as effective for disposal. We have started this sanitation project in PPP mode. The cost of the napkin is Re 1 and we sell it for Rs 2,' she explained. Once again, we were struck by the creativity of this administrator.

As we headed back to Dharmapuri town, we saw many women working by the roadside. 'NREGS work,' Amudha said. We stopped our cars. Immediately, the women gathered around us. There were some 140 people at the work site, only five of them men. Many of the women were elderly. Some appeared to be in their seventies and eighties. We asked Amudha about it. 'Yes, 95 per cent of the NREGS workers in the district are women and many of them are senior. The men migrate to Bangalore or Tirupur for work; these women are left behind and take up NREGS activities,' she explained. Mariamma was in her seventies. Her card showed that she had worked for seventeen days that year. On an average, she made Rs 95 per day. 'Earlier, we used to get Rs 35 if we worked as agricultural labour and the quarries paid up to Rs 65. NREGA has proved to be a boon,' she said. 'But what will I do after the hundred days are up?' she asked. This sentiment was echoed by many women in this drought-prone district. We looked around the work site and found that there was no shed or crèche. 'We leave the little ones with our neighbours,' a young woman in her twenties dressed in a bright polyester sari said.

'What about drinking water?'

'We bring that from home.'

'Where is the shed under which you can rest?'

'Oh, there was one earlier but it was destroyed in the rain a few days back. Now there is nothing. The sun here is very harsh, Madam.'

'That is true. In fact, during summers this is a major problem. It is brutal to make elderly women do hard physical work in summer, with temperatures of 40–45° C. So they begin very early in the morning,' Amudha said, seconding the opinion of the worker. 'Let me show you something else,' she said suddenly. Turning to one of the senior workers, she asked, 'Did you send the SMS today?'

'Yes, Madam,' he answered.

'Show me the phone.' Taking his phone she turned to us. We looked on as she went into the 'sent messages' folder. She opened an SMS and showed it to us. It said: '140 present. August 5'.

'We have used technology to help us monitor the performance of our schemes. At every NREGS site, the supervisor has a mobile phone. Every morning, he reports how many people are working on the site and the time the work started. The same technology is used with schools. They tell us the number of teachers and students present,' Amudha explained. This data is compiled and surprise checks are carried out. 'We even published helpline numbers in local newspapers asking people to report if teachers were absent or if there were problems at the NREGS site,' she added. Defaulters or people giving wrong information if caught were severely punished, even expelled. This has added an element of fear and made the staff more regular. 'We are planning to introduce this system for our anganwadis as well,' Amudha said.

On the way back to Dharmapuri town, we processed all that we had learnt that day. The use of the SMS for monitoring attendance was a novel idea and yet, given the reach of mobile technology, easily doable. Once again, we discovered that the solution to one of our most intractable problems – missing teachers, anganwadi workers and supervisors – was, in fact, fairly simple. All it requires is innovation and dedication on the part of the administrators.

Over the next few days, we asked to see the mobile phones at every NREGS site and school that we visited. We found that the SMSs were always there in the 'sent items' folder. Back in Dharmapuri, Amudha showed us how the information was compiled and tracked on the computer. 'This way, we are able to keep an eye on the poorly performing centres and we pay them a quick visit to get them back on their toes,' she explained. After this brief interlude, we headed to the meeting room. The medical officers from all the PHCs and CHCs in the district had come together for their monthly maternal and child death audit, and meeting with the district collector. One by one, cases were read out. In every case, the family of the deceased was summoned, along with the village health nurse, the attending doctors and the medical officer in charge.

'What time did you bring the patient in?'

'What happened?'

'Did the doctors attend to her?'

'What treatment was given?'

The questions enabled the whole scenario to be recreated and, finally, having heard it all, the verdict was given. The aim of the audit, we learnt, was to establish if the medical staff was attending to the needs of the people and to establish if there were any cases of infanticide. A few years earlier, we had heard of maternal and child death audits in Udaipur District in Rajasthan. This was, however, the first time that we had witnessed an audit. In the subsequent meeting with PHC doctors, an important point came up. 'NRHM has helped us create better infrastructure and so the attendance at hospitals has gone up dramatically. Yet the money allocated for drug procurement remains the same. How do we supply medicines to the additional patients who have come in?' one doctor asked. Listening to him, we once again realized how important these visits were. We could design schemes in Delhi in the most consultative manner and yet, until we visited the field and talked to the practitioners, we would never be able to understand these operational difficulties.

The next morning, we set off towards Pennagram Block. This was the constituency from where Veerappan's widow, Muthulakshmi, had filed her nomination for the Assembly polls in 2006. (She lost.) Located just sixteen km from Hogenakkal, Pennagram is the most backward block of the district. The human development indices here are abysmal, and alcoholism rampant. Though the narrow road leading to the block was relatively free of potholes, the area was neither scenic nor bustling with life and activity. Was this the effect of the scorching sun or was nature simply turning away? We could only wonder. Hot, sweaty and tired after two days of non-stop travel, we stopped at a few anganwadis, health centres and schools along the road. We expected the worst and yet, to our immense relief, we found the government infrastructure here much better than in other parts of the country. Most schools and anganwadis had drinking water and toilets; meals were being cooked and few complained about the quality or quantity of food. Teachers and anganwadi workers were present. Amudha's unique SMS monitoring service had a lot to do with it. In the schools that we visited, we were delighted to find that the children could perform calculations and recite mathematics tables. Reading English textbooks and understanding them was, however, a problem.

The PHCs and health centres were milling with people. We met many women who had come for a tubectomy procedure. Most were in their early twenties and already had three–four children. We did not find a single woman who had only female children and was undergoing a tubectomy; this, despite the rich cash incentive offered by the state government. The preference for a male child was evident. After travelling across the country and seeing many health centres which were semi-functional or non-functional, the visit to Dharmapuri was a relief. The health centres here were functional, and doctors were present. Though we had come across some complaints of high-handedness by the medical staff, and had witnessed the lack of specialists, the situation was still much better compared to the rest of the country – or so we thought. Our euphoria in this regard was, however, short lived. As we travelled along the main road towards Palakudu, the northernmost block of the district, we stopped at the Paparapatti PHC. This PHC is just sixteen km from Dharmapuri town along the main road. At 5 p.m., it was deserted. Not a soul – doctor, nurse or even pharmacist – was present. Only a few construction workers walked around. There were two huge colour TV sets in the lobby. Both were switched off. The four-bed delivery room was empty, and the sheets covering the beds had old bloodstains on them. The vaccine storage case was broken, and no information on the Rogi Kalyan Samiti (Patient Welfare Committee) was displayed.

After about fifteen minutes of asking around, one of the construction workers finally called the doctor. He was a man of average build. He claimed that he had been at work at the back of the hospital.

'Funny, we went all around but did not see you.'

The doctor did not answer.

'What work is being done here?'

'Madam, the OT has been demolished and a new OT and post-operative ward are being built.'

'Where is the in-patient register?'

After shuffling through a few drawers he produced a register. It showed that women were being discharged less than twenty-four hours after delivery.

'Aren't you supposed to keep them for two days?'

'They don't want to stay here,' the doctor insisted.

We wondered why, of all the health centres in the district, only in this one the women were reluctant to stay back. No deliveries or admissions had happened in the last two days.

'We referred cases to the General hospital. Also, the ambulance does not have fuel and the driver has gone to Eriyur for spraying work.' The doctor gave us a string of excuses but we were not listening any more. Our bubble had been burst. Once again, it was clear that, irrespective of the nature of our schemes and the funds flow, the final result and service delivery is dependent entirely on the service provider. We realized this was the reason why in the entire district the only place where we had seen a host of private nursing homes was in the town of Paparapatti. Thoughtfully, we returned to the car.

'Madam, are you sure you would like to go to Palakudu?' the driver asked, apprehension lacing his tone.

'Of course, why do you ask?'

'It is dark. This area has a major problem with alcoholism. Drunks come on to the road and create a ruckus,' he said.

'Never mind. Let us see for ourselves. That is the only block that we haven't covered, so we will go,' we decided.

So our car travelled along the dark roads towards Palakudu. The roads which had thus far been good became bumpy on this leg of the journey. Surprisingly, they had also come alive with groups of men staggering about; fortunately, no one attempted to stop us. Perhaps it was the red light flashing on our car which kept them at bay. But the anxiety of our driver was palpable. We decided to visit the nearest PHC and turn back. We stopped to ask a few people and were directed to the Belrampatti PHC. By the time we arrived, it was 7.40 p.m., and pitch-dark.

We entered a large compound towards the back of which stood a single-storey building. It was too dark to make out much more. Inside, however, we were pleasantly surprised to see a spick and span hospital. Once again, a TV set, albeit switched off, stood in the lobby. A group of women were present in the hospital. Two were in nurses' uniforms.

'Where is the medical officer (MO)?' we asked.

A young Malayali woman in her early thirties dressed in a starched white nurse's uniform stepped forward. 'I am Radi, the staff nurse. For the last four months, we have had no doctor posted here,' she said.

'So this PHC is not functional?' we asked.

'No, no, Madam. We are open,' Radi said.

Nurse Chamundi, meanwhile, brought out the register and showed it to us. Approximately 150 OPD patients visit the PHC daily. This is more than the attendance at other health centres. We eyed the records with some suspicion but decided to look around the hospital. The in-patient ward was being swept by an elderly woman, Amravadi. A young woman was lying in the bed with a small child. Just as we asked the woman her name, the electricity went off. Another staff nurse, Anuradha, came rushing to us with a candle.

'Don't you have power back up?'

'No, Madam. We were supposed to get it but as there is no MO, we cannot get the funds,' Anuradha explained.

'Then what do you do?'

'We use candles. Last night, we conducted this delivery by candlelight.'

We looked in amazement at the nurse and the patient. The young woman who had given birth last night looked healthy, as did her baby. 'How are you?' we asked her.

'I am very well. Although I was scared when the electricity went off last night, the sisters were so good that I feel perfectly safe now,' she smiled. Her mother-in-law was quick to add: 'When we came, we were worried. The pains had started and it was pitch-dark. We thought they would turn us away and the nearest CHC is at least an hour away. You would have already noticed the condition of the roads. But not only did the sisters conduct the delivery, they stayed with us all night. They even arranged for food. God bless them.'

In the flickering candlelight, we looked at the seven women surrounding us. Three of them were hospital cleaners – Amravadi, Madhamma and

Kavita. Three were nurses, and one was a pharmacist, Padmini. Together, this team had battled against all odds and saved two lives. We decided to let the patient rest. One nurse and cleaner stayed back in the ward with the candle to offer the family support.

In the lobby we turned towards Padmini. 'Does this happen often?'

'Yes, Ma'am. Electricity frequently goes off.'

'Weren't you scared conducting a delivery by candlelight? Things could have gone wrong.'

'What alternative did we have? The woman could not have made it to the other health centre. In any case, we do around twenty-two deliveries every month, so we are used to it,' Radi explained.

Then she added hesitantly, 'Madam, if you don't mind, can we tell you something?'

'Of course, please do.'

'This area is known for alcoholism. We are just women here. There is not even a compound wall. Whenever there is an in-patient, we all stay together in the hospital for security reasons. Oftentimes, we are here for forty hours at a stretch. Else we use the doctor's cottage next door. But we are scared. We do not belong here. The money is barely enough to rent homes. If we could get a guard or the compound wall could be built …' she asked tentatively.

We were speechless. We had just seen the state of alcoholism in the area. The registers had also shown that patients stayed nights at the hospital. We had assumed that these women were locals and hence dedicated to help their own villagers. But this was not the case. Not one of them was even from the district. Yet, they had chosen to stay on and provide much needed service to the people despite all the exigencies. Unlike the private efforts of the Bangs of Gadchiroli or the Georges of Sittilingi, which received some recognition, no one outside the villages they serve has even heard of these brave women. Here, they work day and night, sometimes using their own money to buy emergency supplies until they are reimbursed by the BDO (Block Development Officer). We wanted to applaud them, place them on a roll of honour. This book is hopefully one definitive step in that direction. We felt tears well up in our eyes. After expressing our great appreciation to them, we left the hospital. On the way back from Belrampatti to Dharmapuri, we asked the driver to stop so we could talk to the people walking by. Our driver was not happy; he said it was late and too risky. But we stopped and asked people about the PHC; we wanted to be sure that what we had seen was the also the general feeling of the people of the area. Everyone we spoke to was full of praise for the seven women we had just met.

In Delhi and other big cities, we hold events to recognize heroes and agents of change. This makes headline news, and sometimes individuals get cash awards which they often use to support their cause. The general feeling is that such heroes and heroines are outside the realm of the government. But what we saw in Belrampatti was another story. Hidden in all the nooks and corners of the country, we have seen women and men from within the government infrastructure who prove otherwise. Some are in uniform, some are not. Some are cleaners, some teachers, anganwadi workers and ANMs. They work quietly and often do more for people than some others who make the headlines. This book is our modest effort to recognize these hidden heroes, these invisible ambassadors of change and peace. Admittedly, many of our journeys left us despondent. But this visit to one of the worse-performing districts of a well-performing state rekindled hope. We came back with the feeling that things are bound to change. Just like the Alleppey District of Kerala, Dharmapuri is shedding its old label and will soon be counted as a success story. This will happen because it has women who care, women who innovate, and women who seek to make a difference.

Lines from Iqbal come to mind:

Yehi aayeen e qudrat hai yehi asloob e fitrat hai
Jo hai raah e amal mein gaamzan mehboob e fitrat hai

This is the law of nature, this is the decree of life
Whoever strides the path of action is beloved of Nature

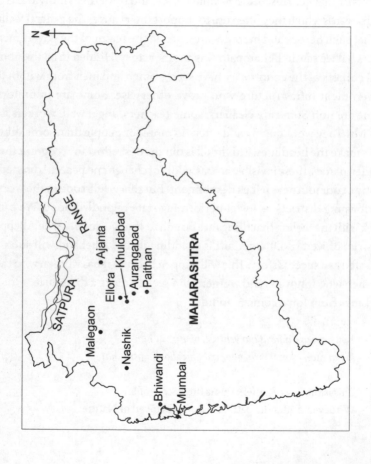

6

Maharashtra

Likhte rahe junun ki hikayaat-e-khoon chikaan
Hui chund usme huuth humare qalam huye

— GHALIB

Kept writing the blood drenched tale of my madness,
Despite the severing of my hands.

Innumerable flies buzzed over garbage heaps in the narrow lanes. Powerlooms clanged in regular rhythm. Small dwellings lined the slush-filled lane we were in. We covered our noses and mouths with our dupattas. The stench was unbearable. To our left, pigs wallowed in a pool of stagnant black water. A skinny little boy stood before us. Vacant eyes, inert body, he made no move to ward off the flies circling his head. His faded black t-shirt caught our eye. Three simple words were embossed on the worn-out shirt which hung on his bony body. Today, we can see the words as clearly as we did on that sultry Friday evening. It was October 2006.

Early that morning, we had got off at the Nashik railway station and got into the waiting Maharashtra government car. Our destination was Malegaon – a town located 280 km north-east of Mumbai and 110 km from Nashik. Situated at the confluence of the rivers Girna and Mausam, in the old days Malegaon used to be a small railway junction known as 'Maliwadi' (Hamlet of Gardens). In 1740, a local jagirdar (landlord) started building a fort and brought Muslim workers and artisans here. After the 1857 uprising, thousands of Muslim families of the Momin (weaver) community fleeing British repression relocated here. The famine of 1862 saw the arrival of weavers from the Varanasi region. Political upheavals of the 1940s and the Razakar Movement[1] brought Muslims from Hyderabad. Over the years, as the country was struck with one disaster after another – some natural, others man-made like intermittent communal riots – the number of Muslim migrants in Malegaon swelled. Today, three-fourths of its 7.5 lakh inhabitants are Muslim. This change in demography has been neither seamless nor peaceful. Communal clashes have been frequent; the worst being in October 2001, when the army had to be called out to restore peace. Yet Malegaon continues to be the oasis which Muslims facing persecution elsewhere seek. In 2002, following the Gujarat communal carnage, truckloads of Muslim families moved here. The iconic face of the Gujarat riots was a tailor called Qutubuddin Ansari, captured on camera while pleading for mercy before a rampaging mob. This man, whose face was to haunt the entire nation for years to come, was from Malegaon.

As the car sped towards Malegaon, we were struck by the relative prosperity of the countryside. We had heard about the region's industrial development including its sugar factories, a HAL (Hindustan Aeronautics Ltd) production unit and the National Currency Note Press. We saw wineries dotting the roadside. Villages which were visible from the road had pucca houses. Fields were lush with fresh harvest – tomatoes, grapes, jowar, vegetables and sugarcane. Landholdings were large and water supply seemed adequate. Heaps of tomatoes and onions lay rotting on either side of the road. In the village markets, tomatoes were selling for Rs 2 per kg, onions for Rs 5 and grapes for Rs 10. This was indeed the verdant and vibrant vegetable basket of Maharashtra.

We passed groups of children. Teenage girls in school uniforms were chattering as they made their way to school. In the distance were the magnificent Satpura mountain ranges. Across them lay the Dangs district

---

[1] The Razakar Movement was headed by Ittehadul Muslimeen to help the Nizam of Hyderabad to become independent and secure dominion status for his state. The government of India launched police action on the Razakars and many were forced to leave the state.

of Gujarat where Syeda remembered going a few years ago at a time when tribal Christians had been targeted by mobs, all in the name of forcible conversion.

After a little while, as we crossed a tiny village by the name of Pimpal, the road became uneven. 'Four-laning of the Mumbai–Bhulia highway is underway,' the driver explained in an apologetic tone. We noticed that the prosperity evident earlier was beginning to wane. Suddenly, minarets and domes of all shapes and sizes rose out of the dusty horizon. The road collapsed into a series of pot-holes, and was lined with tottering scrap-metal shops, all bearing names like Jijamata, Aaditya, Jogeshwari, Mamta, etc. Grim lines of factories were visible on either side. The sense of well-being we had experienced earlier disappeared. Even before we read the signs, we knew we had arrived in Malegaon.

The drive through town to the Circuit House revealed utter neglect on the part of the local municipal authorities. But Sheikh Rashid, second-time MLA, who was waiting for us in the verandah of the Circuit House, assured us that every effort was being made to provide the best for his constituency. Malegaon, he explained, was poised for development; all it needed was a special Rs 50 crore package for infrastructure. 'A civil hospital was announced here after communal riots broke out in 2001. But the municipal corporation, which was ruled by the opposition party, refused to sanction land. Now, since we have returned to power, the bhoomi pooja (foundation-laying ceremony) will be held in ten days' time,' he assured us. (The ten days became two months, with the foundation stone being laid finally in December 2006.)

Passing one slum after another – Hakimnagar, Karimnagar, Saman Habib Compound – we, along with a few officials, reached the Ali Akbar Hospital, which specializes in women and child care. Along the way, we saw innumerable workshops and houses fronted by open drains. No trees and parks were to be seen anywhere. Huge piles of debris and garbage were heaped all over through which pigs roamed freely. The municipal commissioner told us that over 65 per cent of the town's population lived in slums.

In a hospital room, doctors and a few (groups of volunteers) were waiting for us. 'The poor have nowhere to go in case of an emergency,' said Dr Zakia

Bano. 'Only private hospitals have emergency services, which no one can afford. And by the time patients reach Nashik or Bulia, it is too late. After the bomb blasts, we had no choice but to take victims to private hospitals.'

Next to her sat a middle-aged man dressed in a starched white lab coat. This was Dr Imdad Ali, senior physician. 'Out of a thousand people, at least twenty suffer from tuberculosis; many drop out of the DOTS treatment. We regularly see outbreaks of epidemics – dengue in 2005, chikungunya in 2006. Yet there is not a single bed available in any government health centre for people suffering from communicable diseases.' Looking out of the window, we saw swarms of flies and mosquitoes. It was no surprise when Dr Zakia confessed that she was herself just recovering from chikungunya.

A young man in light blue jeans, Khursheed Ahmed Ansari, spoke next. 'There are nearly 1.25 lakh powerlooms in Malegaon. Almost the entire population depends on them. Most units operate from homes, and all family members are exposed to their dust and noise. The din causes hearing loss. A recent survey among primary school children has shown that 33 per cent were hearing impaired.' Suddenly we understood why the MLA, Shaikh Rashid, had been speaking to us at the top of his voice. When we had asked him to lower his pitch, he had said simply, 'Madam, this has become a habit; most people in Malegaon are hard of hearing.'

Poor lighting and fibre dust, we learnt, caused eye problems such as glaucoma and cataract. Among children, Vitamin-A deficiency, and the consequent night-blindness, was common. Dr Farhan, a surgeon, said that the incidence of disability among the people was as high as six per cent. This was primarily due to orthopaedic problems caused by working on the looms – problems which are never properly treated and become permanent with time.

A slim girl sitting in the back identified herself as Dr Bhavsa. 'It is not that there are no ANMs. They do operate in the town, but the area is too big and there is no place where they can examine the women.' Dr Fatima Ansari, who was stationed at the Golden Nagar Health Post (one of the nine health posts in the city), said that women did not come for early registration of pregnancy. 'Most patients come in their eighth or ninth month. By this time, they are extremely anaemic. They don't take anti-tetanus injections or folic acid tablets.' The average family size, we learnt, was eight–ten; there are always small children at home who cannot be left alone. The women therefore never find time to come for health check-ups. Both the mother and child continue to be malnourished.

As we sat in that tiny hospital loom listening to the doctors, we asked for suggestions.'What would help you most?' An elderly doctor with a French beard, Dr Aftab, spoke up. 'Religion can help. Many see it as the underlying cause of this town's ailments. I see it as a solution,' he said. 'For years, due to obscurantism and misinformation, people were not having their children vaccinated. In 2005, there was a diphtheria outbreak. Once again, the community refused to cooperate. Just when we were ready to give up in despair, a government official enlisted the help of maulvis (religious scholars). The results were amazing. In those city wards where they spoke in favour of vaccination, the coverage jumped from 40 per cent to 86 per cent in just two years,' he explained. The other doctors agreed and narrated similar examples.

'But unless the drinking water problem in the city is solved, all these efforts will come to naught,' Dr Bhavsa rued. We learnt that only 42 per cent of households in Malegaon have access to potable water – that too, on alternate days for twenty minutes. 'At every water tap, there is a long queue. Women stand for hours to fill their buckets,' complained Dr Bhavsa. We turned to the municipal commissioner for an answer.

'Madam, there is a Rs 450 crore water filter plant installed in Malegaon. In a couple of months, work on water pipelines should be completed. By April next year, not just Malegaon but even neighbouring villages will have water supply.' His assurances were refuted by Sushobha Barve, a prominent activist, who had accompanied us from Mumbai and has been working for peace and harmony in Malegaon for the last six years. She said: 'These words have a familiar ring. In 2004, the commissioner had spoken the exact same words.'

Next, we headed towards Hamidia Mosque. A month earlier, on 8 September 2006, three blasts had taken place around this mosque. Thirty-seven people died, and 125 were seriously injured. As soon as we entered the mosque, we were surrounded by people of all ages, including many teenagers. Their nervousness was palpable. We noticed that they were looking at us with suspicion as if saying, 'Now what?'

For many months, even years, the youth of Malegaon had been closely watched; their every action scrutinized. They were branded 'anti-social,' 'bomb experts', even 'killers', and associated with groups like SIMI, LeT and words like RDX[2]. Their town was branded 'terror town'. Their loyalties were suspected, their patriotism challenged at every step. Even when their own town was attacked, instead of receiving sympathy, they were looked upon with scepticism. This attitude, along with the recent blast investigations, has left them shaken and disillusioned. For years, they had very little by way of amenities or state support; now even their looms are beginning to fall silent. Behind the hurt and anger in their hooded eyes, we detected fear and vulnerability.

The explosions had taken place in the qabristan (cemetery) adjacent to the mosque during Friday prayers. It had also happened to be the Islamic festival of Shab-e-Barat, so a huge crowd had congregated. Just as they finished their Juma (Friday) prayers, the explosives went off. There was panic all around. In a desperate bid to escape, everyone rushed to the narrow gates. Many namazis (worshippers) were trampled in the ensuing stampede. The crowd which surrounded us pointed out the craters in the walls where the bombs had gone off. Men rolled up their sleeves and their trousers to show us shrapnel wounds. At last, they had got a chance to speak to the government. Voices came from all directions.

'We were attacked, and look what the government did. They picked up and tortured our children.'

'Two Unani doctors from Malegaon have been arrested.'

'Have you heard of anyone who will bomb his own house?'

'This is a saazish, a conspiracy.'

(Almost two years later, the anti-terrorism squad of Maharashtra arrested five people affiliated to the Hindu Jagran Manch, including Sadhvi Pragya Thakur, under suspicion for their role in the Malegaon and Modasa blasts. The case is under trial.)

By the time we left the mosque, it was close to iftaar (meal that breaks the Ramzan fast); the streets were bustling with people and vendors were

---

[2] RDX stands for Research Department Explosive – an explosive nitroamine considered to be among the most powerful military high explosives.

selling food. Next door was one of Malegaon's many slums – the Saman Habib Compound. It was here that we saw the skinny twelve-year-old boy. His black t-shirt was emblazoned with the words 'The Lost Boys' across the chest. Three words which summed up the vulnerability of the youth of this town. Three words which could become the epithet for an entire generation. Three words which filled our hearts with a sense of foreboding.

'What is your name?'

A look of fear flitted across the face that had thus far been expressionless. We drew him near and smiled at him. By now, a few children, possibly the boy's playmates, had gathered around us. Gradually, he relaxed. Then in a shy voice he answered: 'Saddam.'

'Do you go to school?'

The head went down and we heard a barely perceptible, 'No'.

'Why not?'

'I am learning to work the looms.'

'What about your friends?' we asked, pointing to the other children.

'They also work.'

An older boy, possibly fifteen years old, spoke up. 'I help Abba with the looms but I also go to school.'

'Shabash (well done). What is your name?'

'Altaf. I study in Class 10.'

We looked around and asked, 'Who else goes to school?'

A few hands went up.

'So who can tell us the name of India's president?'

Silence.

'Who was our first prime minister?'

No answer again.

We turned towards Altaf.

'What is the capital of Assam?'

Altaf bowed his head.

The deprivation we had seen everywhere throughout the day, and the enormity of the task ahead us was too daunting. We desperately wanted to spot a good practice, a glimmer of hope in this small town. It appeared unexpectedly at a police station in front of which our car stopped.

'Why are we here?' we asked Aleem Faizee, a young reporter who had taken us there. 'This is one ray of hope,' he said, pointing to a small board just outside the police station. It read 'Mahila Shikayat Samadhan Kendra' or 'Women's Complaint Bureau'. We stepped inside the small, one-room building. Four women were sitting around a wooden table with a prominently placed telephone. One of them was Irfana Hamdani, a young advocate who was a volunteer at this centre. 'This centre,' she explained, 'is a women's initiative to combat all forms of violence.' We learnt that, after the Malegaon riots of 2001, women from both communities had come together to issue a call for peace which begins with fighting violence inside the homes. They had become partners with the Maharashtra police, and the Shikayat Kendra was established inside the Malegaon police station. At the time of our visit, it had been operational for three years. 'Some of us are housewives; others are lawyers, teachers and doctors. We all give our time on a weekly basis. On an average, we get five to six hundred cases every year, 90 per cent from the lower-income groups. We have already solved some 700 cases of violence,' explained Irfana Hamdani.

The subdivisional magistrate (SDM) Rajesh Pradhan agreed that this community effort had reduced the cases of violence under section 498A of the criminal procedure code. Dr Rekha Rao, a cheerful woman in her mid-forties, was a college teacher. She said that polygamy and triple talaaq (signalling divorce) were among the principal causes behind domestic violence in Muslim bastis. 'But whenever we go there and discuss triple talaaq, polygamy or sterilization, the men accuse us of being anti-Islam.' Asma Shaikh, her colleague, agreed. 'I wish we could have some police protection on these occasions.' We left the kendra after posing for photographs with the women and police. We were filled with admiration for these women who counselled people on family planning, illiteracy, polygamy, hygiene and livelihood, sometimes at the risk of social boycott. Malegaon like other medium size towns has its share of good and bad.

By this time, it was already late evening but we had one more stop – the Powerloom Service Centre run by the Ministry of Textiles, Government of India. Throughout the day we had been assailed by the sound of looms from the dark and dingy workshops along the road. Even the streets reverberated with the sound. The influx of Ansaris and Julahas had changed more than

PHOTOGRAPHS BY GUNJAN VEDA

Making arrows for Meghalaya's favourite sport–archery.
Nongkynrih village, Meghalaya

Jili Das, the dedicated anganwadi worker who cycled three km from
Suktagiri AWC to tell us that women and children in her village had
received no supplementary nutrition, deworming capsules or iron
and folic acid tablets for almost two years. Darrang district, Assam

Morung belonging to the Phom tribe at the Heritage Complex, Kisama, Nagaland

Celebrating twenty-five years of Watsu Mungdang at Mokokchung, Nagaland

Like in other states in the north-east, many women in Nagaland are adept at weaving on the loin loom

Scenes from everyday life in the tide country. A tourist boat (above) and fisherfolk at work (below). Sunderbans, West Bengal

Behind the quiet beauty of the tide country hides a constant struggle for survival. Sunderbans, West Bengal

One of the many shrines of Bon Bibi and Shah Jongli that dot the Sunderbans landscape. Also seen is Dukhey, the little boy who, according to legend, was rescued by Bon Bibi

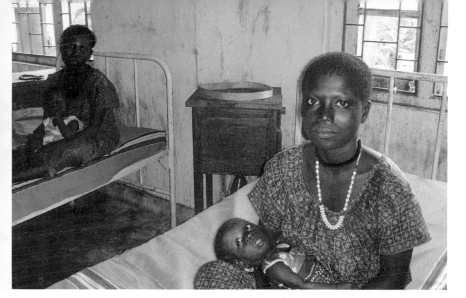

Jarawa at the Tusnabad PHC. Despite government policy promoting in-situ treatment they continue to be hospitalized for minor ailments. Andaman and Nicobar Islands

Aerial view of the havoc wreaked by the tsunami at Greater Nicobar. Large swathes of land were swallowed by the sea and entire mangrove forests destroyed

An Onge family at their post-tsunami habitation at Dugong Creek, Little Andaman

Great Andamanese at Strait Island. Boro Sr. (lady in orange blouse) was the last Khora speaking Great Andamanese. She died in November 2009

Onge children inside their schoolroom at Dugong Creek, Little Andaman. The cook said that no mid-day meal was prepared as the cooking time was spent in forcing the children to wear clothes

With Jalaja Chandran (extreme right) the woman panchayat president who changed the face of Kanjikuzhy village, Alappuzha, Kerala

NREGS site at Dharmapuri district, Tamil Nadu

Pre-school education at an anganwadi centre in Deenapatti
village, Dharmapuri district, Tamil Nadu

The Death of a Craft: There are only five people left in
Aurangabad who know how to weave the 600-year-
old Himroo. Aurangabad, Maharashtra

The only anganwadi centre in the country where we saw children wash their hands before eating. Kagzhipura, Maharashtra

Bringing Health to the Hinterlands: The Jan Swasthya Sahyog team at Ganiyari, Chhattisgarh

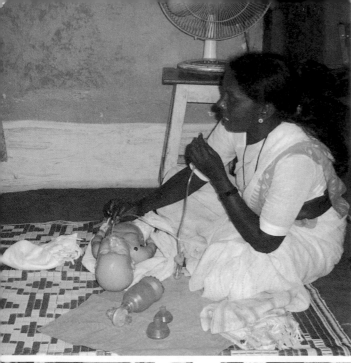

Anjana Uikey, a village health worker trained at SEARCH Gadchiroli, demonstrates the use of ambu-bag and mucous extractor in the treatment of asphyxiated babies. Bodhali village, Maharashtra

Battered and bruised sex workers at Shivdaspur mohalla, Varanasi

Maimun Nisa with her eighteen-month-old son, Imran. Due to abject poverty Maimun has been able to feed him only saabudane ka pani (gruel of tapioca) since birth. Daniyalpur, Varanasi

Syeda with Ustad Bismillah Khan at his ancestral home in Varanasi

Children working the looms. Bazardiha, Varanasi

One and a half years after the Kashmir earthquake, classes were still being held under the trees. Jabla Village, Kashmir

A Ladakhi stove at Spituk Monastery, Leh

The Brogpa in their traditional attire. Darchik, Ladakh

Dancing with the Brogpa at Darchik, Ladakh

Villagers carry fodder. Silmo Village, en route to Batalik, Ladakh

Caught in the Flow: Waiting for the flood water
to abate at Kelwara, Baran, Rajasthan

Carpet weaving at Jodhpur, Rajasthan

Crafting stories in terracotta. Molela, Rajasthan

Two months after the flood in the dunes, people continued to live under plastic sheets in makeshift camps in Kawas, Barmer, Rajasthan

Half-cooked chapattis left uncovered and some watery dal constitute the mid-day meal at the Primary School (Urdu Medium), Nehrunagar basti. Burhanpur, Madhya Pradesh

just the demography of this town. They had brought to the town a new source of livelihood. From a farming village, Malegaon turned into a centre for handloom weaving. When electricity was introduced, powerlooms took over. The migrant workers were too poor to buy new powerlooms. So they bought machines which had been discarded in Surat in the 1930s. The Surat looms needed repair, if not replacement, but the new owners had no means to do so. They continued with the old technology and, today, the town produces one crore metres of cloth on 1.25 lakh looms every day. At one time, the entire town produced only cotton cloth; now less than 35 per cent of the looms are used for cotton. Due to the hike in the price of cotton yarn, they are making cheap synthetic cloth. But productivity is low, and the average monthly income is Rs 1,200–1,500.

At the Powerloom Service Centre, the general neglect was evident. We looked towards the ceiling and suddenly the health hazards enumerated by the doctors at the Ali Akbar Hospital were there, right before our eyes. The beams of the building were coated with thick white fluff, dust which had congealed in dense forms along them. We could imagine the fluff-infested lungs of the powerloom workers and their family members who lived and worked in this lethal environment. We felt a sympathetic constriction in our own lungs.

The workers who had collected in the centre voiced their feelings: 'Malegaon is neglected because it is a Muslim majority area'. 'No one in this town has availed the housing-cum-workshop scheme meant for small weavers.' 'Although 1.25 lakh out of nineteen lakh powerlooms in the country are in Malegaon, not a single ordinary weaver has benefited from the government schemes.' 'In the last five years, the Weavers' Service Centre has managed to get only ten loans sanctioned.' The litany of complaints continued. The officers of the textile commissioner were quick to say that the Malegaon weavers were to be blamed for not submitting proposals.

Nimba Kadam, chairman of the Malegaon Powerloom Association said: 'Looms in Malegaon are hand-me-downs from the Surat mills, and can only produce low quality cloth. We get Rs 4 for every metre of cloth that we produce. If only we had new machines, we would produce cloth worth Rs 50 per metre! The Malegaon weaver cannot even dream of the shuttleless loom, which costs Rs 2 lakh!'

It was dark when we left the centre. On the roadside, we saw a sign: *'Office of Jamiat ul Ulema.'* On an impulse, we stopped and went inside. The room was full of maulvis and young madrassa students, many of them Saddam's age. They spoke sadly of the suspicion and growing polarization between the Hindu and Muslim communities. Haji Dastur Ali, an elderly maulana with a gumcha (rough cloth) wrapped around his head, spoke about the disintegration of the bond between the two communities. 'It is afsosnaak (a matter of sorrow), Madam. The lives of the two communities were (and still are) deeply intertwined by the necessities of trade; the suppliers of yarn are largely Hindus, the weavers, mostly Muslim.' Their resentment was fuelled by other factors as well. They spoke about the stepmotherly treatment given to Malegaon vis-à-vis other powerloom centres such as Ichalkarangi. Dastur Ali explained: 'The rate of taxation in Malegaon is the highest in the state. The Maharashtra government gives 40 per cent subsidy to industries in areas like Ichalkarangi but Malegaon gets nothing. The entire town survives on powerlooms, so we need electricity. But we have power cuts for six–eight hours every day, at times, more. As a result, we lose fifteen lakh metres of cloth every day; that comes to a loss of almost one crore rupees! Why? Madam, why can't we be made a separate district? As it is, we pay the taxes and all the funds go to Nashik.'

The 2006 Sachar Committee Report (on the social, economic and educational status of the Muslim community in India) has quantified the developmental divide between the two communities. Malegaon exemplifies this divide. People here have seen little progress in the last few decades. Their living conditions in fact have plummeted far below the neighbouring districts. Sub-optimal production and old, inefficient looms mean the death knell for workers. Even after the bomb blasts, the cry of the people of Malegaon was not so much for compensation but for development. The youth need work, inspiration and hope. They need security to be able to dream, and state support to fulfil these dreams. They are the 'Lost Boys', a lost generation. We, as policymakers, whether at the state or the Centre, need to listen hard to the cry of the people of Malegaon.

∽

Bhiwandi is nearer Mumbai than Malegaon, fifty kms to the north-east, in Thane District. The city, along with Navi Mumbai, is considered part of the Greater Mumbai metropolitan agglomeration. With the largest number of powerlooms in the country, Bhiwandi has been called the 'Manchester of India'. In the early twentieth century, it was a small town of Konkani Muslims and Maharashtrians who engaged in agriculture, fishing and handlooms. Handlooms were replaced by powerlooms in 1930s, and Bhiwandi became a hub of the textile industry. The decline of Mumbai's textile mills spurred the growth of the powerloom here to meet the demand for grey fabric. In Bhiwandi, forty lakh people directly or indirectly depend on powerlooms. There are eight to ten looms inside a single house. Almost 60 to 70 per cent of the town's population is Muslim.

This too, is a town of migrant workers—from Orissa, Bihar, Uttar Pradesh and Andhra Pradesh. Ninety per cent of the looms are obsolete. There are 5.5 lakh looms, eight lakh workers and thirty processing units. Weavers get Rs 15–20 per metre which retails at Rs 40. Middlemen create an artificial yarn scarcity. Daily production value is to the tune of Rs 90–100 crore. Every workshop we visited complained about the lack of electricity. The newly privatized city power supply has been given to a company called Torrent Power. People thronged to us with complaints. 'The metres are faulty.' 'Huge bills are slapped on us.' 'There is no redress. The people at Torrent don't even listen to our complaints.' 'Power cuts have worsened.' We noted their complaints in detail, especially since they pertained to public–private partnership in infrastructure.

Next, we headed towards Shantinagar, a basti on a hill inside the reserve forest zone. People have been living here since they were settled by the order of Prime Minister Indira Gandhi in the 1970s. Now they have received eviction notices. The unrest is growing. On the road winding up to the basti, we stopped to speak to an old man standing by the road.

'Your name?'

'Mohammad Muslim.'

'Where are you from?'

'Sultanpur. But I have worked here for forty years now.'

'Where do you work?'

'I don't know the name of my karkhana (factory). But I work there for nine hours every day for a wage of Rs 100. I send money home every month.'

'Where do you live?'

'Here. I pay Rs 700 rent. We are twenty people in one room. Since we are shift workers, we take turns to sleep. There is a six-hour power cut every day. For our treatment we have to depend on private doctors.'

Next to Mohammad, we found fifteen-year-old Zakir. He used to go to school, but was thrown out because he had failed his exam. He did not mind because going to school meant at least a half-hour walk one way. 'I studied until Class 2 but now I run a paan shop.'

Shantinagar has a population of two lakh people but there is not a single public or private toilet. Twenty-five-year-old Sikander said that the area has no sarkari dawakhana (government health centre). 'There are only jhola doctors (quacks). We depend on them. But, Didi, sometimes they give wrong medicines and people die.'

We climbed on top of the hill for a fuller view of Shantinagar. The sight before us was quite desolate. There was garbage everywhere being trampled on and strewn by stray animals. The two lakh people who live in these sub-human conditions are in dread of eviction notices. We were reminded of Mirza Ghalib's poignant lines, which seemed to sum up the situation of the residents of Shantinagar:

> *Dair nahin haram nahin dar nahin aastaan nahin*
> *Baithey hain rehguzar pe ham koi hamein uthaye kyun?*

> No temple, no mosque, no door, no walls
> We who sit on roadsides, why bother us?

Just 112 km south-east of Malegaon lies the historic city of Aurangabad. But it was not powerlooms which took us to this four-hundred-year-old city located in the heart of Maharashtra. It was what Prime Minister Manmohan Singh called the country's national shame: child malnutrition. In the Planning Commission we had been grappling with the problem from day one. We allocated thousands of crores of rupees to the Integrated Child Development Services programme every year, but the national health surveys showed very little improvement in various parameters of malnutrition. India's children continued to be among the most malnourished in the world. We held national and international consultations. During discussions with experts and nutritionists, one name constantly came up, that of Dr Ramani and his Rajmata Jijau Mother & Child Mission in Aurangabad. So this was where our quest took us in May 2007.

We had read about Aurangabad in history books but the place had never gripped our imaginations as much as it did after we watched in Delhi the eponymous play *Aurangzeb*, performed by a theatrical group called NATWA. The history we had read had shown the Mughal emperor Aurangzeb as a tyrant and bigot. For the first time, in this play, we saw a side of the king that had been hidden behind the mask thrown by centuries of one-dimensional history writing. It was a moving experience. So here we were in Aurangabad, the last great Mughal's final resting place.

Aurangabad was founded in 1610 AD on the site of a village called Khirki by Malik Ambar, prime minister of Nizam Shah of Ahmadnagar. His son named it Fatehnagar. With the capture of Daulatabad by the Mughals, the Nizam Shahi dominions including Fatehnagar became part of the Mughal Empire. Prince Aurangzeb's first viceroyalty of the Dakhan (Deccan) began here in 1636 and continued up to 1644. He was appointed viceroy for the second time in 1652 on his return from the campaign of Kandahar. He entered Fort Daulatabad and proceeded to Fatehnagar, naming it Aurangabad after himself. He lived here for four years and it was here that his son Akbar was born. It was here that he buried his wife, Rabia Al Durrani, remembered as Dilras Banu Begum. Aurangabad is also the burial place of Aurangzeb's favourite concubine, Zainabadi, a woman of rare artistic talent. She is recalled by none other than Maulana Abul Kalam Azad in his classic epistolary collection, *Ghubar e Khatir*. When he became emperor, Aurangzeb came back to this city and in 1692 ordered a magnificent palace called Qila Ark to be erected, which now lies in ruins. He died in 1707 and left behind an unusual will. It is hard for his biographers to conjecture why a Mughal emperor would order that his mortal remains be buried in Aurangabad rather than be taken to Delhi. Was it Dilras Banu

Begum, Zainabadi, or his love for the Dakhan which made him desire that his grave be built here? We will never know. What we do know is that his janaza (dead body) was carried to Rauza (Khuldabad), and he was buried near the tomb of the great Sufi, Shaikh Burhanuddin.

Aurangabad, with fifty-two gates, has earned the nickname 'City of Gates'. A famous landmark here is Bibi ka Maqbara, the mausoleum Aurangzeb built for his wife. On the evening of our arrival, we first went there. Called the Taj of the Deccan, this maqbara was built on the pattern of the Taj Mahal. It stands splendid within a spacious and formally planned Mughal garden with ponds, fountains, water channels, pathways and pavilions. Next to it stands the Aurangzebi Jama Masjid. The Alamgiri Mahal (Aurangzeb's palace) has monuments which have been greatly altered by later occupants, our guide told us.

Having indulged ourselves with a slice of history, early the next morning, we set out for the Jijau Mission Office. Officers had told us that the prevalence of Grade 2 malnutrition in their area of work had come down from 11.45 per cent in December 2004 to 2.33 per cent in February 2006. Similarly the number of children with Grade 3 and 4 malnutrition had reduced from 1,251 to 507 during the same period. We were excited at the findings – this could be one good practice that could be replicated. We asked Dr Ramani's team to tell us about their method and its outcomes.

A young girl in a printed salwar suit spoke first. 'What we have done is a little innovation here and there. Like anganwadi centres across the country, we use de-worming capsules, but here we train the mothers to check the child's stools the next day. We ask them to use protein-rich soya beans in cooking. Joint monthly meetings are held by the health and anganwadi workers. District-level malnutrition mapping has been carried out and kitchen gardens are encouraged. The tie-up with NGOs and the private sector such as ICICI Bank and Hindustan Lever Ltd to form the "Bhavishya Alliance" has also helped.'

Another innovation, relatively expensive, has been the use of simputers. Dr Ramani explained that matriculate women from mahila mandals (women's organizations) in municipal areas are given hand-held machines – simputers. 'They are taught to feed all data into this. For pregnant women they track haemoglobin, blood pressure, immunization, weight, and

Vitamin-A deficiency. These women also persuade the expectant mothers to visit health centres.' We learnt that one hundred simputers at Rs 16,000 each had been distributed in the city. The women who operate them are called link-community-workers, and for four hours of daily work they earn a monthly salary of Rs 1,700.

What we heard at the centre sounded promising but travelling across the country week after week, and witnessing the disarray in which the best conceptualized programmes lay, had made us doubt most of the 'reports from the field'. We wanted to see for ourselves the functioning of this method at the ground level. Our first stop was at the Abadimandi AWC. The anganwadi worker was a middle-aged woman, Charushila. She told us that she was a matriculate and had been at the centre since 1990. The wall inside the spacious room was covered with posters; children's attendance was neatly recorded on a blackboard. In a corner was a mirror, combs, games and a first-aid kit. It was 10 a.m. Some fifty children in uniforms were getting ready for their meal. The sweet aroma of meetha bhaat (sweetened rice) filled the room. We saw a group of thirty to thirty-five women standing near the container of steaming rice. 'They are mothers of children under three years of age. They have come to collect cooked food,' Charushila explained.

'Who prepares the meal?' we asked.

'We do.' The speaker was a woman in the traditional nauwari (nine-yard) Maharashtrian sari with a large bindi. 'I am Vinita Ghorpade, head of the SHG that supplies food. There are ten women in our group. We take turns to cook food in our homes. For each child we get Rs 1.98,' she explained.

The next AWC on our list was in Kaghzipura. This area came by its name because it was the first to produce handmade paper after the technology was introduced during Mughal times. It was on paper produced in Kaghzipura that the Holy Quran was printed. Seeing quite a few people in burqas and namaz caps, we gathered that it was a Muslim-dominated area. This neighbourhood was definitely poorer than our last stop, Abadimandi. The average family size here was ten; most parents of the children enrolled at the AWCs were labourers and masons with monthly family incomes of Rs 4,000-5,000. Yet it was in this poor, backward Kaghzipura that we, for the first time, saw an ICDS centre where children were provided with two meals in a day, first at 10 a.m. and then at 11.30 a.m. Safia was in charge of the Bhojan SHG (Food Self-Help Group) while Shakila, a young woman wearing a hijab, was employed by the SHG as cook. 'We buy rations once a month and cook food on firewood outside,' Shakila explained. Each woman of the group made Rs 400 per month.

The anganwadi itself was inside the compound of the Indus School for Child Labour, meant for kids from nearby brick kilns. Children were sitting inside on durries. The walls of the centre were once again filled with posters. Among them was a faded Urdu poster. Yet no one at the centre, including the AWW, could read Urdu. Just as we were leaving the centre, a pleasant sight greeted us. It was 11.30 a.m., time for the second meal of the day. The AWW announced that it was mealtime. We watched in astonishment as all the children ran outside and formed a neat queue. One by one, they stepped forward and the AWW and Shakila would pour water on their hands. Then they would raise their hands above their heads and shake them to air-dry. For years, we had been worried about the poor hygiene at ICDS centres. 'How difficult is it to teach children to wash their hands before meals and after using the toilets?' we would ask the AWC staff. But at none of the seventy ICDS centres we had visited had we seen children or even AWWs wash their hands before handling food. That one moment when we saw the children wave and air-dry their hands made our day! We left the centre with a lighter step.

No visit to Aurangabad can be complete without a trip to the famous Ajanta and Ellora caves. In the punishing forty-two degree heat, we entered the cool canopy of the Ellora caves, having travelled thirty km north-west of the city. Here, spread across an expanse of two km, are thirty-four rock-cut temples and monasteries hewn from the volcanic balsamic formation known as the Deccan Trap. Twelve of the caves are of Mahayana Buddhist origin (550–750 AD), seventeen are Hindu caves (600–875 AD) carved during the reign of the Rastrakuta kings, and five caves are dedicated to the Jain faith (800–1000 AD). As we walked through the caves, we marvelled at the architectural genius of our ancestors. Every sculpture, every crevice, had a story to tell. We tried to imagine the artisans who sculpted these edifices, sweat dripping down their emaciated bodies as they chipped away at the hardened lava rock, creating art that lives and inspires us even today.

About eighty km from Ellora lie the Buddhist caves of Ajanta. Nestling in the tranquil lap of the Sahyadri hills, these thirty rock-cut caves date back to the second century BC. Unlike the caves of Ellora, they do not lie on the trade route and hence sank into oblivion till they were discovered by British archaeological surveyors in 1819. The landscape here is more lush. The caves have been carved out of a ravine, at the bottom of which flows the river Wagura. The interiors of the caves are decorated with carvings and paintings depicting the life and incarnations of Gautama Buddha. Though many of these paintings have faded, their beauty is still beyond compare. In the dim light of the caves, their colours continue to glow and enthral visitors.

By then, the afternoon sun was at its peak. The heat forced us to take a break so we drove to the government guest house in Khuldabad. It is said that Khuldabad was named after Aurangzeb, who was called 'Khuldmakaan'. The word is derived from khuld, meaning 'paradise' and makaan, meaning 'living'; hence 'one who lives in paradise', the posthumous title of the pious king. The Khuldabad guest house itself is a beautiful old building with a splendid view of the Ellora caves. Its magnificent old colonial style furniture could have been the pride of any museum. Its high-ceilinged rooms were relics of the Raj. In the cellar, some exquisite old pieces of pottery and utensils were turning to dust. We felt a great sense of loss. We also felt helpless; even if we wrote to the state on our return would anyone care to preserve this priceless relic?

Khuldabad is where the Khuldmakaan lies. We stopped to recite the Fatiha (prayer, the opening sura of the Quran) at Aurangzeb's tomb. Its spareness is an eloquent testament to his staunch faith and spartan lifestyle. It is a simple mud grave under the open sky covered by just a white cotton cloth as canopy. It is said that the emperor desired that his grave be constructed only with the amount (Rs 14.12), which he had earned from sewing caps. The rest of his saving, Rs 350, which was earned from writing Quranic verses, was willed to charity. In the nineteenth century, the Nizam of Hyderabad added a white marble wall around the tomb. It is the simplest Mughal tomb we had ever seen.

A halt at the village of Babhulgaon on our return from the caves and Khuldabad gave us a glimpse into rural Aurangabad. The village has a population of 722. A roomful of people was waiting for us, including seven panchayat members headed by Sarpanch Raju Dhinge. The issue under discussion was health. 'The CHC is twenty km away, at Sillod. Women spend Rs 300 on transport to go there for deliveries.' 'There is no private doctor or even AYUSH practitioner here.' On an impulse, we asked to drive straight to the CHC, Sillod. We wanted to see what kind of treatment a woman would get if she was somehow able to reach in time for her delivery. Outside the hospital, pasted on the wall, was a list of duty doctors. We learnt that the hospital covered a population of two lakh, and received one fifty OPD cases every day. But this fifty-bed hospital had no gynaecologist, physician or anaesthesiologist, because of which no major surgery could be conducted here. At the time of our visit, there were ten in-patients, of which six were tubectomy cases. Most of the beds were empty. Something suddenly caught our attention. In a cot inside the 'Delivery Room' there was a newborn child. From what we could make out, the child, a baby boy, was going blue from birth asphyxia. The doctor and nurse were busy attending to us. Not one of the hospital's twelve nurses or seven medical officers was looking after the baby. 'Please go to the child,' we shouted, and the doctor went scurrying away. Distraught, we turned to a colleague, Dr N.K. Sethi, who had accompanied us; he had gone inside to look at the baby. He said quietly, 'Madam, there is very little chance of the child surviving.' We blinked away our tears. That evening, we asked him to call the hospital to see if the child was alive. He never gave us an answer.

The next morning, we took the fifty-km road from Aurangabad to Paithan. Aurangabad has always been a silk and cotton textile production centre. In the old days, a fine blend of silk with locally grown cotton was developed here and became famous as Himroo. The other classic was Paithani silk from the nearby taluka town of Paithan where we were currently headed. Till 1960, Aurangabad languished as a city, remaining industrially backward. In 1960 the region of Marathwada merged with Maharashtra. This was when the industrial development of the Marathwada region began through designated backward area benefits. Today, Aurangabad has become home to well-known brands such as Videocon, Garware, Skoda Auto, Wockhardt, Ajanta Pharma, Johnson & Johnson, Siemens, Lupin, Goodyear and Bajaj. The Indian government has approved a number of SEZs (Special Economic Zone) here, like Bajaj (automobiles), Wockhardt (pharmaceuticals),

Hindalco (aluminium), Videocon and Siemens. The road was lined on both sides with signs of these industrial houses. This was the corridor through which we entered ancient Pratisthan (Paithan), the capital of the Satvahana dynasty from the second century BC to the third century AD. We thought of these industries as the 'temples of a new civilization' who were conveying us to the old civilization.

Before reaching the town of Paithan, our vehicles turned into a mango orchard in a place called Birkin, which is a mango and pomegranate exporting area. Here we savoured the most sumptuous Kesar mangoes. About 30–35 per cent of this variety of mango, categorized as Grades 1 and 2, are saved for exports. We sat on charpoys on the uneven mud floor of the farm. The cultivator-owners told us that, traditionally, they had grown sugarcane; now they were shifting to mango cultivation because the same quantity of water could grow one acre of sugarcane or two-three acres of mango. In 1996, the Kesar variety was introduced in this very area. Jalna–Aurangabad–Beed is the export zone for this variety. Each kilo sells for Rs 35–40 and the farmer earns Rs 50,000 per acre per season. After the mango season, they grow sweet lime, cotton, lemon and chikoo (sapota). 'Didi, we need processing for the leftover mangoes,' was the common refrain. 'And a mango park at Aurangabad for better marketing. Cold storage facilities are currently only available in Jalna. Farmers have to send their fruits there or to Nashik and Mumbai. We need cold storage in Aurangabad. During the harvesting season, we hire labour at Rs 60–100 per day. Fifteen of our orchards have got phytosanitary certificates to enable export to European markets,' Karan Sanghi, a farmer in a starched dhoti and pagri (turban), said, speaking on behalf of the assembled farmers.

Once we reached Paithan, we went to the large retail store which had been kept open for us despite the lateness of the hour. Splendid Paithani saris were on display. Made with heavy gold zari thread from Surat and silk thread from Bangalore, it takes anywhere between two months to two years to make a single sari. Next to the showroom was a weaving centre with 150 weavers. We met sixty-year-old Sainath and his son Chintamani. They told us that in addition to what we saw there another thirty–forty weavers worked in the village. They earn between Rs 3,000–3,500 per month. A weaver gets Rs 11,000 for a sari that sells for Rs 40,000 and may take over six months to complete. Most weavers were men; women helped with yarn work. 'Some of us have been weaving for 300 generations. The Paithani weave itself is over 2,000 years old,' said Sainath with a toothless smile.

By the time we returned to the city, it was late into the night. But it was our only chance to look at the 600-year-old Himroo craft. As children, we had heard of Mashru and Himroo fabrics made of cotton and silk but with the lustre of satin. We had never asked where they originated. It was that night that we learnt that the Himroo was originally known as kamkhwab. Syeda recollected the word from her childhood. In her grandmother's stories, the princesses of paristan (fairyland) used to dress in flowing garments of kamkhwab. The word literally translates to 'little dream'.

Mohammad Tughlaq introduced the craft to Aurangabad when he shifted his capital from Delhi to Daulatabad. At the time, it was the members of the royal family and the nobility who used the fabric. We found ourselves in a shop with a few looms. This was one of the last repositories of this dying craft. At one of the looms sat an ageing weaver with a white cap and a grey beard. His name was Mohammad. 'I learnt Himroo weaving as a child. I used to sit on a plank and manage the threads. That is how I picked up the skill. It takes twenty days to weave a shawl that sells for Rs 2,500. We earn Rs 100 per day. There are only five people left in Aurangabad who know the original Himroo.' Mohammad's sons are cycle mechanics. He told us that, 300 years after the art of Himroo came to the city, the jacquard weave was introduced. The shawl, which took twenty days earlier, could be woven in four days with this technique using a mechanical loom. Its product was more reasonably priced.

Abbas Khan, who learnt how to use the jacquard at a factory as a child, said he had no sons to pass on the knowledge. 'I had shifted to powerlooms in 1952. For thirty years I worked on the machines but this handloom weave, it has a charm of its own. In 1982 I came back to Aurangabad and went back to Himroo. My eyes are not as good as before, but I still weave.' Majid Pawar, an elderly man in a white kurta–pyjama, has been weaving for forty years. He is one of the five people who know the original Himroo handweaving. 'In 1968 I started using the jacquard. We have been in this business for three generations but my son is a B.Com graduate. After me, there is no one.'

Our journey through Maharashtra was complete. It gave us a perspective that we had never imagined possible. All the pieces seemed to fit together. For us, the state brought to mind lines from the Urdu poet Raghupati Sahay (Firaaq Gorakhpuri) about the making of Hindustan:

Sar zameen e Hind par aqawam e alam ke Firaaq
Karvaan aatey gaye Hindostan banta gaya

People from distant lands to Hind's soil, O Firaaq
In caravans arrived and Hindustan was built

Malegaon, Bhiwandi and Aurangabad are microcosms of Firaaq's aqwam e alam, 'peoples of the worlds'. Several hundred years ago, Muslims from the north settled in these areas and mingled with the local Hindus. Mutual interdependence developed and trade, livelihoods and societies began to evolve. People began to weave 'little dreams', the kamkhwab or Himroo, in the lanes of Aurangabad. In Malegaon and Bhiwandi, they began to produce cloth for the rest of the country. Yet, over time, they became a 'lost people', identified with terror and suspected at every step. They have become restless and wary; their life seems to have stagnated just like the pools of water in the slums of Sanam Habib and Shantinagar. What they desire is not compensation but development, not grudging acceptance but compassion and understanding. They are standing on the edge of the precipice; one wrong move by us can push them over and an entire generation will be lost forever.

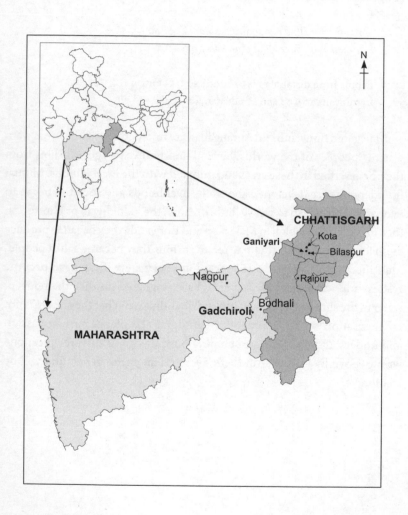

7

Gadchiroli & Ganiyari

Phula phula ruhi-e- yurab chaman meri umeedon ka
Jigar ka khoon de de kur, ye butey mein ne paale hain.

– IQBAL

My meadows of hope, O God, let them bloom,
With my heart's blood, have I nurtured and groomed

A sunny afternoon; long camera shot of the mud floor of an inner room. An old woman massaging a tiny body placed face down on her bare legs. The floor on which she is sitting with outstretched legs, precariously balancing the squealing child, is a hair's breadth away from the child's dangling arm. Focus on the woman's feet; cracked heels filled with dirt. 'This is one of the many reasons behind the high neonatal mortality in our country,' a voice rose above the video film, *Nanhi si Jaan* (Tiny Life). The speaker was a lean, bespectacled man with a small beard, dressed in a khadi shirt and loose trousers. 'Dr Abhay Bang,' someone said, introducing him. 'Simple techniques like keeping newborns clean, warm and away from dirt go a long way in saving their lives. Semi-literate village women from remote parts of Maharashtra have proved this,' Dr Bang continued. The film on child mortality in India ended but the image of the old woman – a grandmother or dai (midwife) – and the infant lingered.

So, in September 2006, along with a few colleagues we found ourselves on the wide and smooth stretch of highway that connects Nagpur to

Gadchiroli. Our destination was Shodhgram – a small, green campus located in this remote Naxal-affected district of Maharashtra from where the Bangs began an experiment that has halved the neonatal mortality in the area.

About one eighty km from Nagpur and 1,092 km from Mumbai, Gadchiroli is situated in the south-eastern corner of Maharashtra. It is bordered by Chandrapur District of Maharashtra in the north; Durg, Jagdalpur and Rajnandgaon Districts of Chhattisgarh in the east; and the Karimnagar and Adilabad Districts of Andhra Pradesh in the south and south-west. This entire belt is covered by the Dandakaranya forest. According to Hindu mythology, this is where Lord Rama stayed during the fourteen years of his exile. It was here that he cut off the nose of Ravana's sister, Surpanakha. Today, these forests are part of India's Naxal belt, also called the Red Corridor. It is believed that, the Naxal writ runs for 92,000 square km across central India, from Bhamragad in Gadchiroli to Abujmarh in Chhattisgarh. The forty-km area on the Maharashtra–Chhattisgarh border is regarded as a 'liberated zone' into which even the police do not venture.[1]

The term Naxal comes from Naxalbari, a small town in Darjeeling District in the north of West Bengal where, in May 1967, communist leaders who believed in Mao Zedong's philosophy launched a revolutionary movement against the ruling classes. It started when local landlords used goons to beat up Bimal Kissan, a tribal youth who went to till his fields after obtaining judicial orders. The local people retaliated and, under the leadership of Charu Mazumdar and Kanu Sanyal, their movement spread. Then, in April 1969, the Communist Party of India (Marxist–Leninist) was formed.[2] Today, the Naxal Movement has spread to almost 180 backward districts across fifteen states. These districts are predominantly tribal, where the population faces severe deprivation. The movement started out as a struggle

---

[1] http://www.flonnet.com/fl2221/stories/20051021008701600.htm

[2] http://www.ipcs.org/pdf_file/issue/848082154RP15-Kujur-Naxal.pdf; http://www.cpiml.org/pgs/30yrs/hist30.htm; http://www.hindustantimes.com/News/nm2/History-of-Naxalism/225549/Article1-6545.aspx; Accessed on 3 September 2009

for land rights and justice for these groups, and won widespread support. Over the years, however, acts of violence by Naxalites have increased, and the State has retaliated with all the force at its command. In the last few years more people have been killed in Naxal violence than in conflict areas like Kashmir and the north-east states.[3]

As with the other Naxal-hit areas Gadchiroli too has a large tribal population; 38.3 per cent according to the 2001 Census. Raj Gond, Madia Gond and Pradhan are the main tribes; others include Halba, Kawar and Kolam. Of these, the Madia Gond has been granted the status of PTGs by the government of Maharashtra.

Twenty years ago, it was in this predominantly tribal district of Vidarbha that a young doctor couple started SEARCH (Society for Education, Action and Research in Community Health). Both Abhay and Rani had been brought up in the Gandhian tradition. After getting their MBBS and Masters in Public Health degrees from The Johns Hopkins University, USA, they decided to plough back their knowledge into Indian soil. Their idea, rooted in their Gandhian principles, was simple. They wished to build an Aarogya Samaj – a society where people's health is placed in their own hands. They wanted most of all to find a viable and sustainable method to save the thousands of newborns who die even before they get a chance to live. Therefore, they started their laboratory for saving newborns amid the verdant forests, seventeen kilometres from the district headquarters. Thus was born Shodhgram, literally the 'searching village'.

The three-and-a-half-hour journey from Nagpur to Shodhgram took us through lush green fields of paddy, jowar, linseed and tuwar. The surroundings were fresh and serene, so unlike the desolate, barren Vidarbha that is flashed on TV channels. Accompanying officials explained this contrast. Nagpur, Chandrapur and Gadchiroli have traditionally never been a part of the cotton-growing belt. So the farmers of this area escaped the crisis faced by the cotton cultivators of Amravati, Yavatmal and Akola. Yet, the prosperity that the green cover conveys is misleading; it conceals considerable deprivation. Tell-tale signs of poverty are there for the

[3] http://news.rediff.com/report/2009/may/29/jk-ne-killings-halve-but-naxal-violence-doubles.htm; accesed on 3 September 2009

discerning eye to see – small size landholdings, tiny mud houses, frail women with huge headloads and the absence of industry or infrastructure. There are no railway lines even today; large parts of the district remain cut off during the monsoons. This, together with the absence of sustainable livelihoods and proximity to the Naxal areas, has afflicted Gadchiroli quite significantly. At one time, the tribals used to depend on minor forest produce, mostly bamboo and tendu patta (leaves used in the beedi industry), which they collected from the Dandakaranya forest, covering nearly 70 per cent of the total district. But now the forests have grown unyielding.

As we approached the gates of Shodhgram, we saw a few rifle-bearing men. These were security personnel, some in plain clothes, some in military greens who, we were told, were posted for our protection. Inside the gates of Shodhgram everything appeared in harmony with its natural habitat. The main road of the campus was made of neatly packed earth, not bitumen-topped. On either side of it stood simple, single-storey cottages made of mud, bamboo and bricks. They were set among trees, and named after them – peepal, mahua, saal. The campus itself was designed like a Madia Gond tribal settlement.

We were hungry after the long journey. Lunch was laid out in a cottage: vegetables, salads, rice, all locally produced in Shodhgram. Over the delicious home-cooked meal, Dr Abhay Bang told us the story of Shodhgram. Their work began at a small tendu patta godown in Gadchiroli town in 1986. First, they conducted health surveys in a hundred villages, especially among rural women. The results were disturbing and highlighted the need for immediate action.

'We always knew that the situation was bad but nothing prepared us for the results of the survey. The state of health and sanitation among women was abysmal; prevalence of anaemia and malnutrition was high. Less than five per cent of the deliveries took place in institutions. Though 56 per cent of the newborns delivered at home suffered from infant morbidity, only two per cent received medical care. Filariasis and malaria were rampant. About 80 per cent of the males in the 15–44 years age-group suffered from reproductive health problems, and 92 per cent of the women from gynaecological ailments. Fifteen per cent of the population was affected with sickle cell anaemia. Alcoholism and tobacco addiction was widespread; as many as 80 per cent of the children from Class 5 onwards consumed tobacco in some form,' explained Dr Rani Bang, a beautiful Maharashtrian woman in a simple cotton sari.

The Bangs realized the need of the moment. They began working in thirty-nine villages. Initially, they chose non-tribal villages because they wanted to establish a model which would be effective across the country. Gradually they spread to tribal hamlets and today they work in thirty-seven tribal villages of the Dhanora Tehsil of Gadchiroli. Bodhali is one such village. After lunch, we headed to this village.

Bodhali has a population of two thousand, of which 10 per cent is tribal. The houses are mud constructions; almost all have no toilets and only half have electricity. We visited the house of Anjana Uikey, the Village Health Worker (VHW) or Shishu Rakshak as they are called at Shodhgram. Inside a small room, barely six feet by eight feet, covered with posters on child and maternal health, thirty five-year-old Anjana recounted her journey over the last ten years, since she began work at SEARCH. She was a woman of medium build, with oiled and neatly braided black hair, an oval face with a big kumkum bindi, and a nice bright smile.

Anjana took out neatly filled registers and showed us how she maintained records for every woman in the village. 'Whenever a bride comes into our village, I make a note of it. Every two months, I check on all married women to find out whether they are pregnant. If they are, I register them and give them calcium, iron and folic acid tablets. I send them for antenatal check-ups, ensure that they take tetanus shots and advise them on the various aspects of pregnancy,' she explained.

'What if there is an emergency?' we asked.

'I refer them to the Primary Health Unit in the village. A lady doctor is there between 11 a.m. and 2 p.m.'

'What if the doctor is not available?'

'I try and do whatever I can,' Anjana said, pointing to a stack of neatly labelled bottles placed on a small shelf. Paracetamol, Salbutamol, Aspirin, Soda Mint. She told us that she charged 10 paise per tablet, and every transaction she made was carefully recorded in a register.

In Bodhali, as in all the other villages in the area, most deliveries take place at home. So, when a woman goes into labour, Anjana accompanies the dai to her house. These dais, too, are trained by SEARCH. Immediately after the birth takes place, Anjana takes over the baby from the dai. She washes, cleans and checks the respiration of the child. She ensures that the mother starts breastfeeding within half an hour of birth. She looks out for birth asphyxia, pneumonia and sepsis, which are universally acknowledged as the leading causes of newborn deaths. 'Didi, I have handled nine cases of asphyxia, of which seven were successful,' she said with confidence and a note of pride. Using a doll, she demonstrated how she uses the mucous extractor and the Ambu bag to save asphyxiated babies. Strapping a watch on her wrist – 'After all, timing is critical' – she began her demo. Fascinated, we watched the lines of concentration etched on her forehead. Her eyes flitted between her wristwatch and the doll's face, even as her hands continued to pump rhythmically. 'I pump the Ambu bag forty times a minute for up to fifteen minutes. By then, if the child does not revive, then I declare it a stillbirth.' Listening to her, all of us without exception felt a sense of confidence in the competence she displayed.

Afterwards, as she cleaned and replaced her life-saving equipment, Anjana told us a little more about herself. We learnt that this woman who had given many children a fresh lease of life had studied only up to Class 7. In addition to her job as a Shishu Rakshak, she worked as an agricultural labourer.

'How do you manage?' we asked.

'My family helps me in my work. I am lucky. They are very understanding. Many times, I have to stay overnight at the patient's house. My husband and children don't complain.' Anjana told us about traditional practices in the village. 'Didi, pregnant women were allowed to eat very little. It was believed that if the mother ate too much, childbirth would be difficult and the baby would be born with a big head.' So the woman got no food, and no iron and folic acid capsules. Even after delivery, the woman was not allowed to eat eggs or vegetables for two months. 'My mother-in-law hardly let me eat anything when I became pregnant. It was not until I joined SEARCH that I realized how important nutrition was. So when my third child was born, I broke the parampara (tradition). Not only did I eat well, I resumed work within a week of delivery. Today, this is what most women in the village do.'

Watching the poise and pride with which Anjana prepared her kit for her rounds, we realized that the SEARCH experiment has done much more than saving the lives of the babies. It has changed the lives of their mothers as well as of the workers themselves. We followed Anjana as she began her rounds of the village.

Her first call was at the home of twenty six-year-old Anita Ramdas Gautule, who was eight months pregnant with her second child. Anjana sat with her on the steps of their house and began her questions. 'Any swelling of feet? Night blindness? White discharge? Pus? Fever?' She neatly recorded Anita's answers on a form. Then she took out a thick manual with colourful pictures. Using it, she patiently explained nutrition and other pregnancy-related information to the woman. Then, with a small squeeze of reassurance on Anita's shoulder, she got up to leave.

Next on the list was the house of Sunita Vinod Bhandekar. A danda (stick) lay at the entrance to the house. 'To stop the entry of evil spirits,' an older woman, Sunita's mother, explained. Sunita had lost her first child to sepsis on the third day after birth. He had been delivered at her husband's village in Chandrapur and was unable to suck. For her second delivery, the anaemic and frail Sunita had come to her mother's house in Bodhali. This second baby, which weighed 2.5 kg, also had sepsis but luckily for her there was Anjana. Fourteen Gentamicin injections were administered and the baby survived. We saw the tiny wrinkled twenty-day-old glob of flesh in the mother's lap. Anjana carefully picked him up and placed him on a weighing sling. '2.8 kg. He'll survive,' she announced with a smile and Sunita's worry-creased face relaxed. We noticed that Anjana had washed her hands before and after touching the baby. 'Make sure you do the same,' she instructed Sunita who was herself a matriculate.

As we walked around the village, women and men stopped to greet Anjana with a smile and a 'Ram Ram, Didi.' 'This is my real reward. This, and these children', she said, pointing to two kids playing in the lane. One was four-year-old Meenakshi Chilange and the other, two-year-old Sourav. 'Meenakshi had sepsis and was terribly underweight but we managed to save her. Sourav had asphyxia but he revived after fifteen minutes of pumping with the Ambu bag.'

Looking at the bright faces of these children, we understood what Abhay and Rani Bang had done in this remote corner of India. Empowering ordinary village girls with training and practice to administer life-saving measures was their giant leap for child health in the midst of this wilderness. The children who were playing before us would have been dead but for the Gentamicin injections given by semi-literate village healthcare workers. Had the Shishu Rakshaks not pumped life into them with their Ambu bags, their mothers would have had to undergo multiple pregnancies while undergoing the trauma of delivering dead babies. We have often felt that 100 per cent institutional deliveries in our country is an impossible dream, even 60 per cent would take a very long time. It is only these 'ordinary women' who can help newborns bridge the thin line between life and death. They alone can reduce neonatal mortality because in most places even if the PHC has a doctor on duty, the child would never survive the journey to the centre. Birth asphyxia and sepsis cannot wait. In Bodhali what unfolded before our eyes was an eminently practical way of reducing mother and child mortality.

Anjana led us to the house of Nirmala Pandilwar, a dai who has been trained as a Trained Birth Attendant at Shodhgram. 'I have been delivering babies for eight years. I learnt it from my mother-in-law after I got married. After the training at Shodhgram, however, there have been many changes in my techniques. Earlier, we used a scythe to cut the umbilical cord; now we use a sterilized blade. We even sterilize the thread before tying the cord,' she said, quietly confident.

Walking out, we saw a frail old man with just a langot (loincloth), squatting on the path. Eighty-year-old Lahanu Mogarkar was all skin and bones. He had recently undergone cataract surgery for both his eyes. Only one had been successful. 'Baba, where do you stay?' we asked.

Eyes watering with mucous, he said his children had thrown him out. 'My wife and I stay on a half-acre plot nearby. We survive on whatever little we manage to grow on it.'

'What about pension?'

'Some time back, a sarkari babu (government official) had visited us. He took money from me saying he would ensure that the pension formalities are completed. It's been eight months, I have never seen him again.'

In the village, we saw several homeless old people. Nuclear families that have no place for elderly members are no longer a metro or middle-class phenomenon. In these remote villages in Maharashtra's backyard, rampant poverty has forced many children to leave their parents to fend for themselves.

Back in Shodhgram, we walked to the temple of Goddess Danteshwari. She is the most important goddess of the Madia Gond community. When the hospital was being built, the adivasis said to Abhay and Rani: 'There are no gods in hospitals, only doctors who play God!' They wanted a health centre where their gods would be present and would help in their cure. Thus Danteshwari Devi became the guardian of the gate of Shodhgram.

Later that evening, after a very busy OPD, we sat beside Rani who, despite her long day, was cheerful and happy to talk. We had read about her work in the area of women's health and wanted to know more. Over sips of cool lemonade, Rani told us that poor personal hygiene was a major problem. 'There were no toilets in the area. Some government agencies came forward and got a few constructed but it was of no use. No one used them because they felt it would contaminate their homes.' This, she said, has major implications for women's health. They go in groups, morning and night, to ease themselves. During the day, they control their food and water intake so that they do not need to go in between. During menstruation, the women stand on their feet all day to allow the blood to flow out. At times, they use soft mud bricks so that their clothes are not soiled. 'All this causes severe infections. Menstruating women are anyway considered unclean and made to sleep outside the village in a small hut. There they are left to fend off animals and other predators.' Changing these practices was a herculean task for the doctors. So they hit on the idea of using the tribals' own jatras (dramas around a theme) to dispel their myths. A jatra was instituted in Shodhgram in honour of Goddess Danteshwari.

Every year, representatives from forty tribal villages participate in this jatra. At the end of it, an Aarogya Sansad (health parliament) is held. Tribals speak about their ailments and the most prevalent sickness is voted on; its control is declared the year's mission. This process makes it sacrosanct; it is regarded as a command from the Goddess herself. The jatra over, villagers return to their respective homes and follow the Devi's command. Next year, the same process is repeated. Rani told us how effective these jatras have proved. 'One year, the tribals pledged to end malaria. I was amazed at how much effort they put in to not just follow our instructions but to understand why the disease spread.'

Their respect for the culture of various tribes has gained the Bangs the confidence of the people. Unlike many city doctors, the Bangs try to learn from their patients and practise their traditional remedies. 'It's amazing what you learn. One day, a woman brought a plant to my clinic. She said this was used to "silence" the husband if he beats his wife. Then she told me about tendu tree gum being used as a contraceptive. Every time I interact with these women I learn something new.' Rani has carefully documented this knowledge, which will be deposited at SEARCH's Wisdom Bank.

Early the next morning, we took part in the Shodhgram shramdaan (offering of labour). We picked up our jharus (brooms) and tokris (baskets) and began sweeping the campus. Little kids trudged around with their small buckets collecting any stray piece of plastic or paper. After breakfast, a meeting had been arranged with thirty-three village health workers. We sat in a circle and Abhay spoke simple words of a prayer. We looked at the women; most of them thirty or older, saris pinned to their shoulders, hair coiled in buns most often decorated with flowers. These women worked in the villages which had been adopted by the organization. Every two months, they visited Shodhgram for a few days of refresher training. They collected their wages, shared experiences and swapped notes. If they made mistakes, their wages were docked but if they conducted thirty successful deliveries in a row they earned a reward of Rs 200.

We looked around the room at these village women, most of whom had studied no more than Class 6 or 7. They were ordinary women who had done the extraordinary. They had reduced neonatal mortality in their villages by 56 per cent. Besides protecting newborns, they also work in the fields, cook, clean, raise children, and look after the elderly. In a remote corner of Maharashtra, these women are bringing a slow and silent revolution. Not only are they saving the lives of newborns, they are also striving for a better and healthier life for the women.

Wearing a pink sari neatly pinned on her shoulder, Manisha, from the village of Pardi, spoke first. 'When the village doctor's own child got sepsis, he asked me to treat him. Didi, we have saved babies who weighed just 800 gm. Village doctors refer cases of sepsis and pneumonia to my friends and me. Even the "jhola doctors" (quacks) are happy to have us around because they, too, are afraid of touching a newborn.'

Two older women sitting to our left were whispering to each other. Abhay said they were senior workers, Gyanwati Sheokhand and Durga Devi. 'Do you want to say something?' he asked. Hesitantly, Durga spoke of the traditional childbearing practices which they have been fighting for years. 'Till the umbilical cord falls, women are not allowed to step out of the delivery room. The placenta is placed in a pit right inside the room and women have to clean themselves and answer nature's call in the same pit. This has led to widespread infections, especially sepsis.' Then Gyanwati added: 'Immediately after birth, the baby is cleaned with rice husk. The result is severe skin inflammation. Then, to make her cry, the child is bathed with cold water. No clothes are put on her for almost a month.' While they spoke, we recalled that infant deaths due to pneumonia constituted one-fourth of the total infant deaths in the country. 'For three days after birth, the baby is only fed gur paani (jaggery water), not breast milk, due to the belief that the mother's first milk is poisoned. Didi, gur paani causes diarrhoea. This is what we are fighting.' Other women nodded. 'Most of our own babies were fed this way,' Anjana said. 'Some of them died within two days.'

After this, for a few moments no one spoke. A bright-looking, thirty-year old Chandrakala Kharvade from Dhonde Shiveni broke the silence. She said, 'But things are changing. Now we clean the child, wrap her in warm clothes and make sure she is breastfed within thirty minutes. We warn the mother and mother-in-law to clean and air-dry their hands before touching the child. Didi, today I can speak the truth. We have given 15,000 Gentamicin injections and there was not a single complication, leave alone death!'

As we listened to these women, we began to understand why they were successful in an area where other similar experiments had failed. These women belong to the village; they are the chachis (paternal aunts), mamis (maternal aunts), bahus (daughters-in-law) and betis (daughters). People have seen them since they were little or when they first entered in the villages as brides. They have observed them with newborns, saving the lives of babies. They have seen them always available in case of an emergency. These are women they can count on rather than the scarce and elusive doctors and nurses. With trust came the confidence to gradually give up age-old practices, and to follow the methods advocated by this band of dedicated young women.

This confidence, however, places a major responsibility on the Shishu Rakshaks and SEARCH follows a careful procedure for their selection. First, they lay down the minimum eligibility criteria, which are announced in the villages. When women apply, the field-workers go and speak to their families. If they are selected, would the family members help out? They talk to panchayats and village elders. Based on the collective feedback, they make the preliminary selection. The short-listed candidates are invited to Shodhgram. Through games, interactive sessions and plays, their potential, self-confidence and ability to respond under stress is examined. Then the final selection is made and the training begins. Four- to five-day workshops are followed by two months of fieldwork. Six or seven such sessions later, the Shishu Rakshaks are ready.

After meeting the Shishu Rakshaks, we walked over to the Shodhgram Hospital. It looks nothing like a hospital; it is a habitation of huts. Over 15,000 patients from ten blocks of Chandrapur and Gadchiroli receive treatment here every year. The reception area is designed as a ghotul (the centre for social and cultural events in a Gond village). Instead of wards, patients stay in individual huts with their families. They can even cook their own food. All linen, from bedsheets to towels, is made of khadi. The entire layout enables patients to relax; tribal people who generally shy away from the scary, impersonal hospitals seem at ease here. At the SEARCH hospital, surrounded by loved ones, their chances of recovery are much greater.

As our vehicles drove out of Shodhgram, we wondered whether we would ever return to this place which had given us a few precious moments of hope. It is not as if everything is perfect in Gadchiroli. Despite the long lines of patients and the success of the Bangs' hard work, women still refuse to take iron and folic acid capsules and forget to wash their hands before touching infants. The problem of filarial fever continues. While the anti-alcohol campaign of SEARCH has had some impact, tobacco addiction is a major issue. Post-delivery bleeding and infections are still common.

And, yet, there has been a 75 per cent decline in pneumonia-related child mortality, 57 per cent decline in infant- and 30 per cent in child-mortality.

The Gadchiroli experiment, as it is called, has resulted in empowering local communities, especially rural women. City doctors might question the wisdom of allowing village workers to give Gentamicin injections, Ambu bags and life-saving drugs, but the safety of these procedures in the hands of women has been proved. Already the SEARCH model for control of neonatal mortality is being replicated at different sites across the country under the Ankur and Indian Council of Medical Research (ICMR) projects. Gadchiroli has been strongly recommended in the Eleventh Five Year Plan. In a country where the majority of the childbirths continue to take place at home, this might be the one bright chance for our newborns. Are we willing to give them this chance?

Over 400 km from Gadchiroli, in yet another backward tribal district of the newly formed state of Chhattisgarh, there flickers another ray of hope, another success story waiting to be told.

It was November 2006. We were in Bilaspur, Chhattisgarh, having driven 110 km on the road from the state capital, Raipur. In Raipur we saw communal messages plastered all over the city. Anti-conversion messages by Hindutva organizations competed for space and attention with the religious messages of the Hussaini Sena. Communal polarization was expressed in wall graffiti all over. It made us uneasy. Already this newly formed state was grappling with widespread violence unleashed both by the Naxals and the state-sponsored Salwa Judum.[4] Given the prevailing atmosphere of fear and terror, it would be easy to stoke communal hatred.

---

[4] Literally, 'Peace March' in Gond language; this is an armed group of villagers against the Naxal Movement. It is supported by the state government. The Salwa Judum, which started in 2005, has been mired in controversy and the last few years have seen many reports of atrocities by its functionaries. According to NGOs like the Human Rights Watch, by 2008, over 1.5 lakh people in South Chhattisgarh had been displaced as a result of conflict between the Naxals and Salwa Judum. In July 2011, the Supreme Court declared the Salwa Judum illegal, and ordered its immediate disbanding.

By the time we reached Bilaspur it was afternoon. The administration was ill prepared to receive us. We were served food from a nearby hotel at the musty under-staffed state guest house. As we ate, we looked over the literature on Bilaspur, the second-largest city of Chhattisgarh.

Located in the eastern part of Chhattisgarh, Bilaspur is known for its unique rice quality, and its kosa silk. It is this feature which has given Chhattisgarh the name of Dhaan Ka Katora (Rice Bowl). Of the 19.98 lakh people in the district, 20 per cent belong to scheduled tribes such as the Gond, Muria, Bhumja, Baiga, Kanar, Kawar and Halba. The city itself is approximately 400 years old. It is said that the name 'Bilaspur' came from a fisherwoman called 'Bilasa'.[5]

After lunch, we set off towards the tehsil of Takhatpur. Located twenty kilometres from Bilaspur, more than half the tehsil's population comprises scheduled castes and tribes. Ten years ago, it was here, in a small dusty village called Ganiyari, that a group of doctors from the country's top medical institutions had begun their unique experiment. They were all young and determined to make a difference. In Ganiyari there was an abandoned colony of the Department of Water Resources. In the broken-down buildings of this skeletal colony, they saw the contours of a dream. So they leased it for thirty years from the state. At the time, it was still part of Madhya Pradesh State (Chhattisgarh State came into being in November 2000). Five of the buildings, which were completely unusable, were painstakingly repaired to create a space for providing healthcare to tribals. Today, thousands of adivasis and other poor villagers come here for healthcare.

It was getting dark by the time we reached the hospital campus. At the entrance, nine doctors were standing to receive us. These were graduates from the country's premier medical colleges – AIIMS (All India Institute of Medical Sciences, New Delhi) and CMC (Christian Medical College, Vellore) – all in their thirties. They had given up lucrative jobs, sparkling city lights and hefty pay packets to settle with families and school-going children in a remote tribal area in pursuit of a dream; a dream to provide quality healthcare to the poorest of the poor. One by one, introductions were made.

---

[5] http://www.bilaspur.nic.in/Glance.html ; accessed in October 2009.

Dr Yogesh Jain, who heads the group, is an MBBS, MD (Paediatrics). He was assistant professor at AIIMS, and adjudged the best postgraduate of the year (AIIMS, 1990). His chief interest is infectious diseases, and the growth and development of children. His wife, Dr Rachna Jain, MBBS, MS (Ob-Gyn), is a Graduate of Allahabad University. She is interested in developing low-cost and accessible obstetric and gynaecological services for rural areas.

Dr Anurag Bhargava is an MBBS, MD (Internal Medicine), from AIIMS. He was assistant professor at the Medical College, Karamsad, Gujarat. Before coming to Ganiyari, he worked on unsafe and irrational blood transfusions in the spread of HIV in rural Gujarat. His wife, Dr Madhavi Bhargava (MBBS) is an ENT specialist, and was judged the best graduate of her class.

Dr Raman Kataria, MBBS, is Magister Chirurgical (Paediatric Surgery) from AIIMS. He was an associate professor at the Himalayan Institute of Medical Sciences (HIMS), Dehradun. His interest is in developing surgical facilities in rural areas and innovating low-cost equipment and technologies. His wife, Dr Anju Kataria, MBBS, MD (Paediatrics) from AIIMS, was an assistant professor at HIMS, Dehradun.

Dr Biswaroop Chatterjee is an MBBS, MD (Microbiology) from the Medical College, Kolkata, and a postgraduate from AIIMS. He was associate professor of microbiology at HIMS, Dehradun. His wife, Dr Madhuri Chatterjee, MBBS, is interested in the diagnosis and control of infectious diseases.

Next to this group of young men and women stood an older man, their mentor, Dr B. R. Chatterjee, an alumnus of The Johns Hopkins University, USA, who has worked in the fields of leprosy, microbiology, epidemiology, chemotherapy and immunotherapy. He gave up his full professorship at Johns Hopkins to return to India and start work in Purulia in Bihar.

Soon after the introductions, the doctors excused themselves, 'The OPD is still on,' Dr Yogesh Jain explained. Whenever we visit health centres across the country, the opposite happens. Doctors leave pressing OPD work to give us a tour of the government facilities. Despite our protests they leave their duties and attend to us until we board our cars. The attitude of the Ganiyari team was a surprise. For this team of men and women, who abide by the

Hippocratic oath, treating patients is not just a job. It is a passion. For them, the crumbling irrigation building that they have managed to lease from the state government is the gateway to a dream. Within its decrepit walls they have built their Jan Swasthya Sahyog (JSS).

We walked to the single-storey buildings comprising the referral centre, out-patient clinic and hospital. In a glance we could see how carefully the place had been restored. The natural ambience had been retained; inexpensive materials had been used with a thoughtful eye for convenience and aesthetics. A sense of orderliness was everywhere. In the dusk we saw people lining up in the referral area. They would spend the night on the benches in order to get their turn early the next morning.

'Approximately 200–250 patients visit the OPD on every clinic day,' said the ward orderly, Ganesh, who was taking us around. 'Most of them come from tribal-dominated blocks like Kota, Lormi, Takhatpur and Gourela.' We saw clean wooden benches neatly marked with serial numbers lined against the walls of the waiting area. The place smelt of fresh leaves. Though it was night, the OPD was packed. We walked inside the large consulting room. Behind a make shift curtained area, we saw two young women doctors bent over a stretcher. Ganesh told us the woman lying unconscious was forty-five-year-old Godavari from the village of Masturi, twelve km away. She had come in a highly toxic state; a local quack had given her an unsterile injection due to which she had developed serious soft tissue infection. With every passing minute her breathing was getting fainter. The doctors, unmindful of their personal fatigue and the lateness of the hour, were attending to the dying woman and her distraught family. Outside, an old hospital van was waiting to take Godavari to a private hospital's intensive care unit. Dr Madhuri looked at us with tired eyes. 'We have done the best we can but we don't have ICU facilities here.' She placed her hand on Godavri's sweat-drenched forehead. A young nurse used scissors to cut the colourful beads tied to her now hugely swollen forearm. We got a feeling that, in Ganiyari, there was a seamless connection with people's suffering; their flatter noses and darker skins did not make their care inferior to what is given to patients at elite hospitals in metropolitan cities.

Through a dimly lit passage we crossed a courtyard to enter a fifteen-bed ward. Here, too, the same sense of orderliness prevailed. All the patients were lying under red blankets. There was a woman who had undergone a hysterectomy, a severely afflicted tuberculosis patient, a child who had had surgery of the scalp. Outside, in the verandah, a young woman was standing in the dark. 'Who is she?' we asked Ganesh. He did not reply. Dr Anurag, who was on his ward rounds, heard us ask the question. 'She is Sukhna Murmu, HIV-positive. Her husband died of AIDS. She lives with her sister's family. She cannot tell anyone, she's afraid. We admit her off and on as a TB patient.'

'What about anti-retroviral therapy?'

'We have no provision for ART … but we are trying.' The woman smiled at us and for a moment her wasted face lit up. Hesitantly we asked Dr Anurag. 'You have HIV–AIDS cases here in the hinterlands?'

'Yes,' he said simply. 'We have seen fifty-two HIV-positive cases in three years. You would be surprised to hear about the incidence of the so-called 'diseases of affluence' here. We have seen 600 diabetes patients in the last few years but the local CHC does not even have the means of checking blood sugar. Three hundred people in nearby villages suffer from rheumatoid heart disease. A simple surgery will make them fit again but there are no facilities.' He also told us that leprosy cases were once again showing up in the area but as the government's Leprosy Control Programme had been wound up, there was no treatment available.

We learnt that falciparum malaria and tuberculosis were major killers. Dr Raman was outside, speaking to the patients. 'I diagnose three to four TB cases on every clinic day. See Geeta here,' he said, pointing to a young girl. 'She is a TB patient but has refused treatment. Her two older brothers died during DOTS so she is scared.' Geeta was over five feet, and weighed less than thirty kg. Her thin body could not withstand the dose. 'Until I came here,' Raman continued, 'I did not believe that half-a-million people in this country die of tuberculosis every year. The problem is not just of delay in diagnosis. It is a problem of hunger. Most of the people here are extremely poor. They don't even have money for highly subsidized (Antyodaya) rations. Their bodies are too frail for DOTS treatment. Hence the high mortality. Our own statistics reveal that 95 per cent of TB patients belong to the schedule castes/schedule tribes or other backward castes, and seek treatment only in the final stages. We should learn from Cambodia; supply free food rations along with TB medicines in chronic hunger spots. Twenty per cent of TB patients in Chhattisgarh are positive; in Sub-Saharan Africa, 70 per cent of them are positive yet the average weight of TB patients there is ten kg higher than in rural Chhattisgarh.' As he spoke, we recalled the thousands of sacks of food grains that we had seen on the way to Ganiyari. For lack of storage space they were lying in the open, easy prey to rodents and rain. Pointing at them, our driver had said, 'I hope it doesn't rain. Last year, 20,000 tonnes of paddy just rotted.' Food was going waste even as the surrounding population succumbed to disease due to hunger!

By now, the OPD had closed for the night. Godavari had been sent to a hospital with ICU facilities accompanied by a doctor and an orderly. The remaining members of the team sat with us in their small office. They told us how they were trying to ensure maximum outreach with the little money they received from donations. They use low-cost drugs for treatment which are obtained from organizations such as Vadodara-based LOCOST. The difference in price is 200–400 per cent. The charts showing the rates for medicines are in full public view at the hospital. The OPD charge for registration and consultation is Rs 6. If the patient is very malnourished, the doctors assume that she is extremely poor and even this small fee is waived off. Medicines are provided free of charge. Thirty-seven different types of pathological, biochemical and microbiological investigations are available at rock-bottom prices, thanks to the low-cost technology developed by doctors here. The Ganiyari method for early detection of urinary tract infections costs less than Rs 2 per test, anaemia Re 1, diabetes Rs 2, pregnancy Rs 3. Low-cost mosquito repellent creams, breath counters for detection of childhood pneumonia, easy-to-read blood pressure instruments to prevent pre-eclampsia and a simple water purification method whereby cycling for fifteen minutes produces a bucket of potable water treated by ultraviolet (UV) rays, have been developed. These technologies have been designed in such a way that they can be used by semi-literate village women and school-going children. We saw some low-cost delivery kits equipped with everything mother and child may need such as gloves, large plastic sheets, soap, disinfectant, blade, gauze, sterilized threads, and cotton cloth to wrap the baby. There were thick sanitary pads for woman's use in the first twenty-four hours; all this for Rs 40. 'These kits are handed over to the pregnant woman at the time of registration. She gives them to the dai or the ANM who conducts the delivery,' Dr Rachna explained. A common disease among the tribal people is sickle cell anaemia. Detection requires complicated tests like electrophoresis which cost Rs 300 in the market. Responding to the high demand, JSS has developed a simple technology which performs the same diagnosis for a mere Rs 20.

We were amazed by what these young men and women had done. Its import was staggering. Their experiment could make healthcare affordable and accessible for millions of rural poor across the county. Their innovations needed to be replicated in remote areas and habitations. We chalked a plan to convince the health bureaucracy to examine and consider their innovations. Today, when we look back, we can say that our perseverance paid reasonable dividends. Healthcare professionals are talking about low-cost technologies and the Ganiyari Model is becoming steadily recognized. Dr Raman explained one simple intervention which had a lasting impact. 'Our most innovative strategy is the malaria detection system. Falciparum malaria is endemic to this region, and the testing facilities are too few and far. Often, doctors give the World Health Organization (WHO) prescribed four tablets of chloroquine and wait for the test results. But falciparum malaria can kill very quickly and many lives are lost in the process.' This we had seen with our own eyes moments after we entered the hospital. A weeping family stood beside a small body covered with a sheet. It was an eight-year-old boy who had died on his way to the JSS health centre. Four days before he died, he had made daily visits to the mini-PHC of his area. But no malaria test had been conducted. 'WHO has recommended a Rapid Diagnostic Test which provides results in twenty minutes but it costs Rs 100, which is too expensive. Something much cheaper had to be devised,' Dr Raman continued. So one day, the JSS team found the cheapest way. They began training neo-literate village health workers in taking blood smears. These were then labelled and neatly packed in small soap cases which were handed over to school children. When the children got on the public bus, they handed the small boxes to the bus drivers. During their journey, the drivers dropped the packets at the JSS health centre. Here, they were immediately tested and the reports sent back through the same bus drivers on their return trip. This free 'courier system' has been operating in twenty-one villages for five years and has saved many lives. Now the JSS doctors are extending this to cover TB detection.

During the interaction with the doctors, we learnt that they conduct three weekly outreach clinics to cater to people from 150 forest-fringe villages, mostly adivasis, Dalits and OBCs. In the absence of a state transportation system, people from these remote tribal villages find it very difficult to get to Ganiyari or even to the local PHC or CHC. Private bus operators are also unreliable; they operate only on profitable routes and charge expensive tickets. So the JSS's outreach clinics are the lifeline of tribal villages. Public transportation is a long-standing demand of the people, and a strong recommendation of the JSS.

The next morning we headed to one of these outreach centres. A fifty-km drive from Ganiyari on uneven dirt roads threading through the lush forest leads to the forest-fringe villages of the Achanakmaar National Park. The area is startlingly remote, a journey to nowhere. Very few villages here are connected by all-weather roads; most get cut-off during the monsoons. The doctors and helpers have to walk a few kilometres to reach their outreach clinics. It was a tough, back-breaking journey. On the way we saw a sign which read 'CHC Block Headquarters, Kota'. The building was desolate. We looked around for doctors but there were none. The operation theatre was locked. After a few minutes, we spotted a young man in a white uniform. He looked up at us, somewhat startled.

'Why is the OT locked?' we asked.
'Madam, it is for safety,' he stammered.
'To ensure that no equipment is stolen,' he continued uneasily.
'Where is the key? Open it,' we demanded.
He shifted uncomfortably on his feet. 'It is with the medical officer.'
'Call him,' we ordered the man.
'He is not here,' he said, clamping shut.
We realized that he was the only person in this desolate health centre. So we had no choice but to question him further.
'Where are the other doctors? What if there is an emergency?'
Silence.
'Where are the patients?'

Silence.

'How many beds do you have?'

'Thirty.'

'How many people does this hospital cover?'

'Two lakh people.'

'How many specialists do you have here?'

'None,' he murmured.

The state of public health in this far-flung corner of Chhattisgarh was dismal. It was a stark contrast to the crowded JSS hospital we had just left. We resumed our journey to Achanakmaar, the desolate CHC playing on our minds.

At the entrance to the sanctuary, there was an anganwadi centre and a SSA (Sarva Siksha Abhiyan) school adjacent to each other. Children were thronging the verandahs. It was 1 p.m. With one hour to go before closing time, the boys and girls had been waiting all day for the teacher and the midday meal. We were not sure if either would show up!

By this time, we were exhausted. What we had thought of as a short journey turned out to be too long. We almost said, 'No' when Dr Yogesh suggested: 'Our phoolwari is only ten minutes away. The road is no worse than what you have already seen!' The phoolwaris are crèches for children under three years of age run by the JSS in several tribal villages, he explained. The village donates the space; the panchayat gets volunteers from the community and decides the timings. Each phoolwari has ten children and runs at a cost of Rs 20,000 per year.

The Katani Phoolwari was a tiny mud hut with a thatched roof. It had three workers. One was looking after small children who were fast asleep in slings made out of cotton saris. The other two workers were watching the babies as they crawled around the neat kutchcha courtyard which served as the phoolwari space. Some children had runny noses and dirt from play but they looked healthy. Little handkerchiefs were pinned to the collars of their scruffy dresses. 'This, we think, could be the answer to our malnutrition problems. Little children need to be cared for and fed at regular intervals. Given the poverty in this region, women have to go to work. So our phoolwaris are popular,' Dr Yogesh said.

After Katani, we crossed the bed of the river Maniyari, and reached a village called Banhani. The surrounding landscape was an untrammelled natural habitat. The health centre itself was filled with women belonging to the Baiga and Gond tribes. Most of them were barely literate but the JSS had trained them as Village Health Workers (VHWs). They were sent to work in forty-five villages in the Achanakmaar area. We looked at their silver ornaments, body tattoos and dangling earrings. Oblivious of the heavy silver at their ankles, wrists and ears, they hurried to show us their small trunks neatly stacked with medicines like Perinorm, chloroquine, amoxicillin. They explained the use of breath counters for pneumonia detection, slides for malaria samples, dressing for wounds and pregnancy kits. Each trunk cost Rs 600. Sukhsarni, an old Gond woman, her body covered with silver, her sari hitched up to mid-thigh, said, 'We cover between twenty to thirty houses each and are trained for two days every month. This is the only option for our people. None of our villages have any government-run facility or any ANM. Coming all the way here is not easy for them, even though this is the most accessible village. Sometimes, a male health worker visits the villages to give injections, but that is all'.

Pulsita, a thin young girl in a salwar kurta, from the village of Jakarvanda, six km away from Banhani, has been working as a VHW for almost four years. 'Whenever people in my village fall ill and I suspect malaria, I prepare slides and send them to Ganiyari with school children.' For working four days a week, she gets paid Rs 200. If she puts in more hours, she is paid more. For the rest of the time, she finds other work. Some women said that they had found work under NREGS at a daily wage of Rs 58. 'But for three months we have received no payment,' many in the group complained. As we sat listening to them, there was a flurry of anxious activity outside. 'It is going to rain. We need to go now, otherwise we won't be able to cross the river,' Dr Yogesh explained. 'I have spent many such days and nights waiting for the waters to recede.'

We headed back to Ganiyari.

On our way to Bilaspur, we looked back at the road we had left behind. This dusty, remote, forgotten tribal region of Chhattisgarh, only a few hours from the state capital, Raipur, exemplified the words we find on public hoardings: 'It is in the vast expanse of rural India, where majority of Indians still live, that the battle against disease will be won or lost.'

Ganiyari is about dedicated professionals who work directly with people. It is about treating patients as partners in affecting their own cure; about using low-cost technologies; about mobilizing local resources like school-going children who drop and pick up malaria slides on their way to school and back. And the result of all this is healthcare for the poorest of the poor. Not only have the dedicated doctors here devised alternatives to high-priced tests and medicines, they have offered a solution to one of our most intractable problems – human resources in healthcare. They have recruited from the community whatever the community could offer. This very act requires courage and faith. After training the semi-literate women and men, the Ganiyari team have reposed trust in their ability to deliver health services. And their trust has been vindicated. Our trip to these hinterlands is our testimony.

Two years later, during our Annual Plan discussion, when we heard the chief minister of Chhattisgarh speak about the JSS, we realized that our quest could have a happy ending.

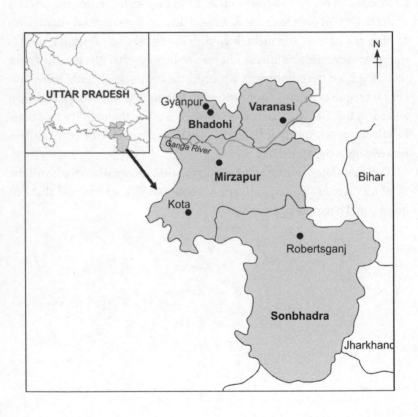

8

Uttar Pradesh

Ye haath salamat hain jab tak, is khoon mein hararat hai jab tak
Ye shaam o sahar ye shams o qamar, ye akhtar o kaukab apne hain
Ye lauh o qalam ye tabl o alam, ye maal o hasham sab apne hain.

— FAIZ AHMED FAIZ

Until these hands survive, until this blood warmly flows
These mornings evenings, these constellations these stars
This tablet and pen, these drums and banners,
this glory and splendor; all are ours

The eastern region of Uttar Pradesh is like a kaleidoscope, subsuming into its shifting tapestry every sound, sight and soul that comes within its ken. The glitter of the Benarasi sari; the soul-stirring music flowing from the shehnai of Ustad Bismillah Khan; the muscular grace of the young pandas (priests) as they perform the Ganga arti; the mellifluous azaan of Gyanvyapi Masjid mingling with the sheer abandon of the devotees chanting prayers at the Kashi Viswanath temple next door. A few kilometres away, Sarnath reverberates with Buddhist incantation; the hurried feet of boys and girls, priests and devotees shuffle through narrow alleys while tiny shops reflect the glitter of rainbow chooris (bangles). And in the midst of all this life, colour, commerce and devotion is the barely audible whimper of a hungry Musahar boy, the sleep-deprived eyes of a carpet weaver holding her wasted child, the stone face of a battered sex worker.

The four days that we spent touring Varanasi, Bhadohi and Mirzapur areas of eastern Uttar Pradesh changed us forever. We saw an abundance of cultural and creative wealth, and yet, embedded in it, we also saw decay – the same decay that was found all over, in the buildings and monuments of Varanasi. Life and death, skill and squalour, strange bedfellows! But in eastern UP, their union was complete.

Our journey began in the ancient city of Varanasi (Benaras). Mark Twain writes: 'Benaras is older than history, older than tradition, older even than legend, and looks twice as old as all of them put together!'[1] The city features in puranic literature, in the Jataka tales and in epics such as the *Mahabharata*. Benaras or Kashi, as it is also called, is described as the most sacred of all places on earth. In her book, *Benaras: A City of Light*, Diana L. Eck writes 'Kashi is the world, they say. Everything on earth that is powerful and auspicious is here, in this microcosm. All of the sacred places of India and all of her sacred waters are here. All of the Gods reside here, attracted by the brilliance of the City of Light ... Kashi is not subject to the relentless movement of the great cycles of time, the eras of universal creation and dissolution. It is the still centre which anchors the perpetual movement of time and space, without participating in the ever-turning world of samsara ... It does not bring new wonders into the scope of the vision but enables one to see what is already there.'[2] And so it was in this much celebrated city that our UP visit began.

'*Kehti thi Zainab, Biran Jaani kab tum rann se aao ge.*' The voice that sang these lines was very feeble and cracking slightly but its melody gripped our hearts. We looked straight into a pair of sparkling eyes set in a wrinkled face. We were sitting before Ustad Bismillah Khan. Earlier that morning, we had threaded our way through narrow lanes to reach his modest ancestral home in the walled city. The maestro had lived in this simple three-storey structure

[1] Mark Twain, *Following the Equator: A Journey Around the World*. Hartford, Connecticut, American Pub. Co. Viewed at http://www.literaturecollection.com/a/twain/following-equator/51/ on 24 September 2009.

[2] Diana L. Eck, *Benaras: A City of Light*, Penguin Books India, 2003, p. 24.

for ninety years. Climbing three flights of steep stairs, we reached his small terrace room. It was quite bare, with only a chair, a charpai (cot) and a fan. Clad in a baniyan (vest) and lungi (loincloth), with a small silver earring dangling from one ear, he looked happy to be in his world of music and music lovers. 'Music is the only thing that lasts in this world,' he said, urging us to eat the plateful of sweets and savouries that his family had brought up. With twinkling eyes and a big smile lighting up his thin face, he continued: 'It was 1947, the eve of India's independence. I performed before Panditji at India Gate, welcoming the dawn of a new era. And you know what?'

We drew close, hanging on to his every word. 'Two months from now, on the sixtieth anniversary of Indian independence, I have been invited to perform once again at India Gate. It is my last wish.' Then, patting our hands, he added shyly: 'You must come.' Our throats choked, we nodded. We had just been invited by the master to witness history. But it did not happen.

When we returned to Varanasi two months later, he was dying while the entire city was praying; bells at Kashi Vishwanath Mandir joined the azaan at Gyanvapi Masjid to issue a passionate appeal to death to spare this beloved ninety-year-old man, pride of the nation. Death, grim reaper, continued to gather her crop. One morning, we woke up to the distressing news – the Piper of Benaras had fallen silent. And yet, to this day, his shehnai continues to echo in the gallis (lanes) and mohallas (neighbourhoods) of this city, his home, his Benaras.

That day we sat wonderstruck, listening to his rendition of the Nauha about Zainab, Prophet Mohammad's granddaughter, wailing for her beloved brother, Husain. He had given us an extra special welcome because in the morning someone had read out to him an item that had appeared in the local newspaper. 'To stand up for the rights of the weak is the deepest pilgrimage. May Allah reward you for interceding on behalf of the girls of Shivdaspur Mohalla,' he said placing his hands on our bowed heads.

Shivdaspur Mohalla is the red-light area of this pious city, the biggest in Purvanchal (the eastern region of Uttar Pradesh). The organization which took us there was called Guria. We had known about Guria for a while, but this was the first time we saw them at work. As we entered the kutchcha courtyard of the Guria centre, we saw about thirty–forty women sitting on the floor. Chairs were brought out for us and for the few state officials who had come along. Ajeet, the founder of Guria, was a young man with an intense manner. 'Three months ago, a trafficker was shot dead in an encounter in this area and forty-nine underage girls were seized by the police. Since then the police have been hounding these women for alleged child trafficking,' he informed us.

The women nodded in agreement. Rajpa, a black dupatta covering her head, was the first to speak. 'I have been living here for the last forty years. See this,' she said, holding out her bruised arm. 'The police hit me here and asked me to leave. But where do we go? This is our home.'

Our eyes rested on an older woman in a worn-out sari, its faded white edge framing her face. She had the features of the Mughal begumaat (ladies); her name was Mumtaz, just right for that face. Clinging to her was a beautiful little boy. 'This is my grandson, Shahrukh,' Mumtaz wept, lightly patting the child. 'The police won't allow us customers. They enter our rooms and hit us with the lathis (sticks). How do I feed him? Guria has been feeding us for the last two months.' Next to her was a younger woman in a green sari with a large sindoor bindi and a swollen right eye. 'Didi, I am Sunita. I will tell my story in front of these haramis,' she said, pointing a finger at the police and other officials. 'Ten days ago, I was lying ill inside my house. At 2 p.m., a policewala called me outside. I was reluctant but he assured me that he wouldn't harm me. As soon as I went out, the blow caught my face and I fell on the road,' she said, explaining her bruised eye. One by one, the women narrated their stories; their fear was palpable. They told us that the SHO, (Station House Officer) Bipin Rai, was a habitual beater. The officer from the UP Social Welfare Department pleaded ignorance. 'Madam, this is under the Women and Child Department, not us.' The SI (sub-inspector) acknowledged the trafficker incident with visible pride. 'Madam, it is our duty to teach these misguided women,' he told us with pious deference.

'Misguided women? Do you not know that in our country prostitution is not illegal; only public soliciting is?'

'Madam, I don't know if their paisha (profession) is forbidden by law or not. I don't even need to know.'

'Have you heard about the ITPA?'[3] we asked, our anger growing.

---

[3] The Immoral Traffic (Prevention) Act, 1956.

'No, Madam, but I know that this dhanda (work) is sinful and has to be checked in the interest of keeping a saaf mahaul (clean environment). Ask the mohalla residents; they are very happy with us.'

We took one look at the men who were entrusted with upholding the law in our country but instead were busy enforcing their own code of morality. Then we turned back to the women. Between tears and curses, they exposed their backs and pulled up their petticoats to show their legs. The bruises were evident; they had been beaten black and blue. 'If you touch these women, you will have to face the consequences,' we threatened the men without raising our voices. For some minutes there was silence. For the moment the threat had worked, but how long would it hold?

We remembered the women we had met in Sonagachi, Kolkata; sex workers who refused to service their clients unless they wore condoms. They had even been able to persuade some of them to go for HIV testing. The Sonagachi women had said that in their area no underage girls were forced into the flesh trade. They had organized themselves in jatthas (bands) and regularly patrolled their locality to ensure that pimps and touts did not get hold of the girls. 'A couple of times, when we found a young girl who had been lured with false promises and sold here, we took her home ourselves.'

But these women standing before us were terrified of the cops. It was their children for whom they were most concerned. They asked us to go upstairs to see them and the work of Guria. We went up a narrow flight of stairs. In sharp contrast to the despair downstairs, the classrooms were buzzing with excitement. Cheerful kids in the six-to twelve-years age-group were busy making clay toys; they showed us Mickey Mouse, Babar the elephant, birds, gods, goddesses and even Mahatma Gandhi! But the most popular toy was a mobile phone; everyone had made one. The children were scruffy, with runny noses and unwashed faces, but were bursting with energy, thanks to Guria's hot midday meals at the cost of Rs 2 per child. From what we saw and sampled, this food was much more palatable than the ready-to-eat powder, watery dal, burnt chapatis and rotten murmure (puffed rice) given to kids in many schools and anganwadis across the country. 'We try to prepare the children for entering the school system. Our teachers initially accompany the kids to school to help them adjust,' Ajeet explained.

'Yes, there is discrimination against them,' he said in reply to our unasked question. 'But, even so, these women prefer to send their children to private schools. In government schools, the teachers are just not there.'

In the next room, over fifty small kids in the one- to four-year age-group were busy shoving and pushing each other; we entered to find complete mayhem. Some kids wanted to give us flowers; others wanted to show their dolls and yet others wanted us to take their photos. Fifteen-year-old Shaheena Bano alias Anu kept trying to shush the kids but the excitement and curiosity of the little ones was unabated. Smiling fondly, Shaheena let them have their way. 'They seldom get visitors,' she explained. 'As for me, my Ammi brought me here when I was very small. I have finished Class 8. Guria is the only home I know. I want these kids to get the same care that I have recieved. I teach them poems and tables. The little ones play with toys and then doze off.'

We looked at the bored officers who had accompanied us. Their lack of interest was evident. They had come along expecting our visit in this mohalla to be of a short duration. But we had been there for over ninety minutes! Just before we were to leave, Ajeet told us of Guria's plans. 'We are planning to build a night shelter where the children can sleep while their mothers are working. We are not going to give up. Do you know, one of our children is working for WHO?' 'Do you really mean the World Health Organization? It is hard to believe!' we exclaimed together. 'Yes,' he said, matter of fact. 'Most people think that the children of sex workers will either end up joining the trade or grinding masalas (spices) and making achar (pickles). But we are changing that perception.'

We looked again at the officials to see if they had registered what Ajeet had said. But their faces wore no expression. That evening, the superintendent of police came to pay his mandatory call. When we asked him about atrocities on the women, he denied everything. 'What atrocities? Don't listen to their bakwaas (nonsense). Those women have no shame. We have to become a little strict because we do not want such shame in our area. Other residents agree with us.' We thought, what a long haul it is before we affect police sensitization and reform.

'Of course the police will tell you that. And the neighbourhood will be happy with them because sex workers are pariahs in our society. But you can't even imagine the atrocities the police and the pimps in collusion inflict on these women.' The speaker was Rolee Singh, a young woman who with her husband, Rajiv, is part of a people's movement, Paharua. 'Not an NGO but a movement with thousands of poor residents,' she told us in the Circuit House, Varanasi, where she had come to invite us to the neighbouring town of Bhadohi.

The next morning, when we set out for a public hearing near Bhadohi in the Sant Ravi Das Nagar district, she was our guide. 'I have rescued girls whose bodies have been branded with hot irons. Pimps marry young girls and bring them into the profession. When the women get too old to work or get ill, they are often burnt to death and it is passed off as a cooking accident. No one cares. After all, what is the life of a sex worker worth?' She told us that though Vanarasi has the biggest red-light area in Purvanchal, there is just one rescue officer looking after five districts. 'Besides, there are no shelter homes for the rescued girls.'

Eighty kilometres from Varanasi, at Gyanpur village, our cars stopped. Paharua had arranged the Jan Sunwai in Shyama Prasad Mukerji Park, located in the centre of the village. Shamianas (huge tents) had been erected. Banners were strung all over announcing the public hearing. It was a sultry August morning, the kind in which the sun stings and clouds promise no relief. And yet, huge crowds were milling inside the park. The shamiana was already packed and people were still coming. The ones before us were from two communities – Musahar and Bunkar. The Musahar fall below the lowest castes in the Hindu caste hierarchy; hence they are placed outside the caste paradigm in this highly stratified state. They are called Musahar because their diet (ahar) is the maas (meat) of rats – that, and tubers; they are too poor to afford anything else. Others present at the hearing were mostly Muslims or low-caste Hindus, all bunkars who weave carpets for the domestic and export markets. Bhadohi and Mirzapur together account for over 65 per cent of India's carpet exports. Till a few years earlier, their annual turnover had been Rs 1,800 crore.[4]

---

[4] http://timesofindia.indiatimes.com/articleshow/507081.cms. Viewed September 2009.

Weaving in this area started during the Mughal period. There are many stories about how the looms became the lifeline of the locals. One interesting legend is that of Sheikh Madarullah. A master weaver of the Mughal court, he was travelling, along with other Persian carpet weavers, on the Great Deccan Road in 1790 when they were attacked by a band of robbers. The villagers of Mirzapur rescued them and in gratitude Madarullah settled down in the area and passed on his unique skill to his benefactors. Since then, the people of Bhadohi have been using their dexterous fingers to make kaleens (carpets) into which they weave their dreams. Sitting inside cramped spaces with no light or fan for ten–twelve hours every day, they create flowers, bowers, firebirds, horsemen and tigers out of their imagination. Next to them sit their small sons, fashioning the knots with small, nimble fingers. The mismatch between the weavers' sunken eyes, haggard faces and the fantasies they create filled us with sadness.

As soon as we entered the shamiana, the sunwai (hearing) began. 'My name is Kanti Devi. It was the day before Holi. There was nothing in the house to feed the children. They told me that they dreamt of a steaming degchi(bowl) of meat on the festival day. I could not bear to see them craving for food. So I went to the well and jumped in. I wanted to end my abhagi (unfortunate) life. But even that I could not do. They brought me out.' Kanti's voice broke. She was a tall woman but she appeared taller because she was nothing but a cotton sari wrapped on a frame of bones. Her skin was blackish blue; much later, when we happened to show her photograph to a dermatologist, we learnt that hers was classic case of lead poisoning. Three children clung to her legs: hollow eyes, yellow hair, pot-bellies. Their father has TB. Ussney tau khatiya pakar li hai (he has become bedridden),' Kanti drew the kids close and waited for her husband to come up on the stage.

We heard that Paharua had gone on a pad yatra (march on foot) of the entire district on the issue of starvation. For ten days its workers fanned out to villages. Information was collected and tabulated; this neat documentation was now placed before us. We looked at the sheaf of papers that contained the sad truth about life in many pockets of twenty-first century India. We read the first entry. 'Name: Krishnavati. Village: Pipargaon. Husband: Rajkumar Musahar. Children: Sunil 8, Shiv Devi 6, Anil 4, infant (male) born 19 July, died 19 July (after half hour of birth). Cause of death unknown.'

We looked up at Krishnavati, a woman with no source of income. Krishnavati, whose husband is a farm labourer earning Rs 500 per month. Krishnavati who has a BPL card but no money to buy subsidized rations. Krishnavati who owns no land and whose children are sick from remaining hungry. In short, Krishnavati, who along with her family, will die if she does not get immediate relief.

One by one, the stories spun out: Chanda Devi, Basanti Devi, Ramni Devi, Munni Devi, Meera, Gulabi Devi, Amravati Devi, Shakuntala, Bhurki, Phulvanti Devi, Dukhni, Matla Devi, Runai Devi, Jagdai, Shyamdai, Mantora, Ramvanti. The names changed; the stories of their deprivation did not. Most had no ration cards; the few who did found the ration depots empty. Most had never heard of anganwadis. In their bastis there were some badly functioning schools, but if their children went there, they were beaten up and asked to leave on account of being Musahars. Widows received no pension; old women had to beg and plead for the meagre Rs 150 old age pension. The severely handicapped ones had certificates issued by medical boards but no disability pension.

Two men also came up to depose. The first was Tulsi Ram, Village Kolahalpur, Tehsil Oarai. Ten years earlier he had woven carpets. He had to stop when he grew ill with TB. Treatment meant penury for the family. He has two sons. The older one (eighteen) is mentally handicapped; the younger (fourteen) is physically handicapped. Neither gets a disability pension. Both boys appeared on the stage with their father. Next came Bhola Nath from Village Rampur Ghat, Block Dheega. 'In my village, people take firewood from burning funeral pyres to light their choolhas (earthen stoves) at home. That is the extent of their poverty,' he said.

The final testimony came from a Ph.D student of community medicine from Jawaharlal Nehru University (New Delhi), Samar, who has been researching in the nearby district of Shankargarh. He said most bunkars suffer from fibrosis which, if untreated, is fatal. The tragedy is that these patients are wrongly diagnosed and treated for TB, which worsens the problem. He said that people who work in silica and asbestos mines also suffer from similar diseases – silicosis and asbestosis. 'The administration refuses to believe me. Ask them to conduct a survey and see for themselves. Many lives could be saved,' was his earnest plea.

The litany of grief was overpowering. We looked around for state officials. Everyone from the district administration had been invited. But only two junior officers were sitting on the stage listening to the stories of death, starvation, disease, corruption, and criminal neglect narrated before a gathering of 1,200–1,500 villagers. Each time we asked, they said, 'We will check' or 'This should not happen' or 'We won't let them die of starvation'. We had to trust their word; but we got the feeling that they were officials with no accountability for the death-drama unfolding before us.

'We want to visit a Musahar basti,' we told the officials. They looked uncomfortable and disapproving. Rolee Singh came forward and offered to take us to one. Along the way, the walls were filled with advertisements. Two subjects were most prominent: 'learn English' and 'cure male impotence'. Closer to the Musahar basti, there were some large houses belonging to landowners in the area. Behind the houses were vast tracts of barren land. Rolee told us that the land here had too much salt and was therefore uncultivable. The poor used the salty soil to wash clothes. The excess salt in the soil had destroyed the livelihood of the Kumbhars, she said. Earlier, every village had a mud khaan (mine) from where they would take out sand. Now there was no sand and no livelihood. Compared to them, the darkars or bamboo basket weavers were better off. Casteism was all pervasive, with each caste living in its separate basti.

We had read that Musahars were a tribe from the Chhotanagpur region who, at one time, used to be palanquin bearers. As we left the main road and approached the Musahar basti, we saw kids all over the place. On what should have been a busy school day, they were playing in the dirt, working in the fields, pulling carts on roads or just hanging about on the roadside. Everywhere there were signboards with names of private schools such as 'Happy Hours' and 'Jack and Jill' but these 'schools' seemed little more than signs nailed over a couple of locked rooms.

The road ended suddenly, and we found that our vehicles had veered on to a mud track. A barely readable board said 'Gohilaon'. 'But you don't need a signboard to know that you are in a Musahar basti. In UP, where the Musahars live, there are no roads,' Rolee said. The next fifteen minutes were pure torture as our vehicles manoeuvred over the kutchcha track to the village. It was a basti of tiny, decrepit, crumbling huts, home to 300

Musahars. Dogs, pigs and children were running in and out of homes. Tattered shirts or naked mud-caked bodies, runny noses, jutting bones, white skin patches, pot-bellies and wasted limbs, the Musahar kids played, oblivious of the disease and death stalking them. As soon as we got out of the car, a crowd of women with ghunghats (veils) down to their chests surrounded us. Most carried on their hips frail-looking babies.

We turned to a small woman in a green nylon sari clutching a girl who looked no older than six months. 'What's your name?'

'Geeta.'

'And your daughter's?'

'Sudha. She is one-and-a-half years old.'

We looked in disbelief at the tiny structure of skin and bones in front of us. Meanwhile, Geeta continued. 'She has been running a temperature for some time now.'

Rolee put out her hand to touch the child's forehead. She told us that she had been asking for a medical camp at the basti. 'The administration even agreed to set one up. All day, the people kept waiting, but no doctor turned up.' As we saw the drooping, sickly children standing around in the blazing sun, we asked each other how many of them would survive. They told us that the children were not allowed to enter the anganwadi centre, which was located in the Harijan basti, just half a kilometre away. The hot cooked supplementary nutrition (on which the government spends crores of rupees) was denied to them.

By now, someone had brought a charpai (cot) from a nearby house. It belonged to Chandra Devi, who was standing by our side with a punkah (fan). 'We are desperate for water,' she said. 'There are three broken hand-pumps in Gohilaon. Musahar women have to walk to Pilkhini village, three km away to fetch water. The only time we get adequate water is when it rains; but then it simply floods our homes.'

Looking at the broken thatched sheets thrown over low mud walls, the homes of the Musahars, we asked if anyone got the Indira Awaas Yojana. Rolee said quietly: 'Didi, they don't have any money; how can they contribute their share for the yojana?'

Munnilal spoke about his daughter, Ladli. 'She is twelve years old. So I took her out of school.'

'Why did you do that?'

'Siyani ho gayi hai; ab to biyah ki chinta kha rahi hai.' (She has matured now. I am worried about her marriage.) Manbhavti, the woman standing beside him, said, 'We can't expect any help from the sarkar. They promise Rs 10,000 to families at the time of marriage, however, when my Seema was married, not a paisa came. Now we are in the clutches of the bania (moneylender).'

By now, some women had lifted their ghunghats. We were shocked to see that they were actually young girls, no older than fifteen or sixteen. These girls should have been in school uniforms, not ghunghats. But they were child-mothers, carrying the malnourished babies that their underdeveloped bodies had produced.

When we reached the anganwadi at Gohilaon, no child could be seen anywhere. We saw an AWC signboard nailed over a room in the primary school. Broken window panes, layers of dust, garbage and pieces of wood were strewn on the floor. Shakuntala Devi, the anganwadi worker, was missing along with the register. The helper, Amrita Devi, told us that the register had been 'taken by Ma'am for some meeting. Ma'am hardly visits the centre but I am here every day.' She said that she hadn't distributed any food that day. 'However, I normally give them poshahaar (nutrient mix) and sattu (a mixture of powdered cereals and pulses).' The sattu, we discovered, was kept at her house. We wondered how much of it actually reached the kids.

The primary school itself was buzzing with life. Hundred-odd children of various ages were sitting on the floor outside the building. Their teacher, Dasai Prasad, was taking class. The children were studying outdoors in the harsh heat while all the classrooms were locked. Prasad explained that he had to teach all the classes; there was no room big enough to accomodate everyone together. The school, we discovered, had two shikshakarmis and a second teacher. Both shikshakarmis had gone on training and the other teacher was studying for her MSc. So Prasad has to take care of the 300 kids alone. He said that not all the children who attend school were enrolled. 'Some children from the village of Razaipur two km away come here. The hot midday meal attracts them. They are not my students but how do I turn away small kids who have walked two km to get here? Most of them run away after the midday meal.' The school had four toilets. Three were full of rubble and the fourth had no water. The doors were locked. Prasad said that the lock was there to keep the toilets clean; the kids went into the open to defecate.

Back on the National Highway, we headed east to a Kol village in the adjoining district of Mirzapur. This area had traditionally been a part of Benaras and it was only in 1830 that it had become a separate revenue jurisdiction. Today, it has a population of 16.57 lakh spread across 1,722 villages and a few towns.[5] The Kol are one of the oldest tribes in the region. In 1901, there were 27,346 Kol in Mirzapur and Robertsganj tehsils. The *Gazetteer* on Mirzapur, published in 1911, describes them as emigrants from a place called Kulati in the territories of the Bardi Raja of Rewah State. 'They name one Nanhu as their ancestor. There are legends of a kingdom in the Gangetic Valley from whence they were expelled by the Savaras or Seoris and retired into the hill country to the south.' They are related to the Mundar and the Munda of West Bengal. [6] By 1911, the Kol, who once had their own country called Kolana, had been reduced to 'hewers of wood and drawers of water'.[7] Since then, there has been very little improvement in their condition.

The district collector of Mirzapur was most reluctant to send us to the Kol area. 'It is too far, too unsafe.' His arguments were similar to the ones offered by the district collector, Varanasi, the previous night when we talked of visiting Sonbhadra District. 'It is Naxal-affected,' he cautioned. 'It is dangerous. We need to make security arrangements well in advance.' The previous night we had been too tired to argue with him. But this time we just said, 'No, we will go'. So a reluctant administration was forced to accompany us to the Kol village.

In the car we had another companion who had come all the way from Sonbhadra. He was a cheerful, burly sixty-year-old activist, Muzaffar Ali Khan, from a zamindar family of Robertsganj. In 1968 he had joined the Communist Party of India. His was a familiar face in Sonbhadra, nicknamed

---

[5] www.mirzapur.nic.in viewed in August 2009.

[6] *District Gazetteer of the United Provinces*, Vol. XXVII: Mirzapur, Brockman D. L. Drake, 1911

[7] Ibid.

'mobile information centre'; he could always be seen talking to villagers, sharing their homes and meals, documenting their problems and fighting for their rights through his NGO Jan Sewa Kendra. We had heard about his work in Delhi. When the administration stopped us from visiting his predominantly tribal and Dalit district, we requested him to accompany us on the car journey so we could talk during the drive. We were passing rows of poverty-stricken dwellings when Khan Sahib said, 'Here dupattas (stoles) serve as walls to provide privacy to families'. This poverty is above the ground, he said, smiling. Below the ground is an abundance of minerals – mica, gypsum, dolomite, coal, silica and plenty of sand. This wealth has attracted migrants from all over. In the mineral-rich blocks, the population has gone up by over 50–60 per cent in less than a decade. The adivasis have been dispossessed of their land in the name of forest or gram sabhas.

Khan Sahib spoke about displacement due to Kanha Dam, and the total absence of social infrastructure, especially in tribal belts where the population is scattered. Babni block, with twenty-four panchayats, is in the industrial belt and is inhabited by Gond, Kharwar, Boyian and Ghasian tribes. Many starvation deaths have occurred in this block. In Doodhi, the anganwadis exist only in name; they do not function. In Chopen block, many people suffer from fluorosis due to effluent discharge from factories belonging to Hindalco and Kanoria Chemicals. In places like the village of Bairkhad, children have to travel thirty km to get to the secondary school. The entire education system depends on shikshakarmis who are appointed by pradhans. There are no permanent teachers. Gram Sabhas are never held. We were to hear more about conditions in Sonbhadra from Rudrapratap Singh, an activist who came to the Circuit House later that night.

The picture was grim but every time we showed signs of gloom, Khan Sahib would regale us with one of his lighter experiences. 'Once, when I visited a forest village to document the condition of the tribals, it was very late at night. A family offered to let me sleep in their place. I shared their frugal meal – the people in this area are amongst the poorest in the country – and then it was time to sleep. Their hut was too small for all of us. So I slept inside with the goat and the family went to sleep outside. Of course, the goat wasn't too happy to get a new bedfellow so it periodically kicked me. That day, I decided never to displace anyone from his bed.'

Khan Sahib promised to arrange a visit for us to Sonbhadra. 'It is dangerous only for those in uniforms; if you go there to understand the plight of the people and to work for them, they won't let anything or anyone hurt you.' The promise could not be kept. In January 2007, Muzaffar Ali Khan passed away. In that short journey, however, he taught us more about life and courage than many others who are much more learned. We absorbed his words even as our eyes swept over the brown, dry, dead land on both sides of the road. Soon we turned towards the Kol village called Kota in Lalgunj Tehsil.

Compared to the Musahar area, the houses here were bigger and neater. Children looked cleaner and healthier, in sharp contrast to the Musahar kids. We spoke to a little girl who said her name was Arti. 'Today, I got puri, subzi and dal at school.' Beyond Arti's smiling face, we caught sight of an old, frail woman, Jagwanti.

'I am a widow,' she said. 'Sometimes I am able to get my pension of Rs 200.'

Mirzapur had been identified as a Rashtriya Grameen Rozgar Yojana (NREGS) district, so we asked the people around us if they had job cards. No one had received them.

'Where is the pradhan?' we enquired.

A stocky man with neatly oiled hair folded his hands in greeting. 'Namaste. What can I do for you?'

'Are you the pradhan?'

He smiled. 'I was the former pradhan,' he said. 'Now, my wife, Saroj has been elected.' He pointed to a ghunghat-clad woman standing a few feet behind him.

We turned to Saroj.

'How many families are there in your village?'

The veiled head bowed a little even as a masculine voice answered. And so it went for every question.

When we asked the pradhanpati to let the actual pradhan talk, he smiled indulgently. 'But, Madam, she does not know anything. She is angootha chhap (illiterate). It is I who do everything.'

On the way back to Varanasi from Mirzapur, we stopped at the Indian Institute of Carpet Technology, Bhadohi, which comes under the purview of the development commissioner of handicrafts. Here, we were met by a delegation of carpet exporters who pleaded for flexibility in labour laws.

'Ma'am, look at China. The reason they are taking over the world is because they have no labour laws. We are responsible people. We take care of our workers but how can you ask us to retain them throughout the year, even during the lean season? Our industry does not function this way,' they pleaded.

We were shocked to learn that these men who lived in huge mansions (many of which we had seen on our way to the institute) and drove in large luxury cars were allowed to use the high-tech machines and facilities of the institute at dirt-cheap rates. And yet they wanted greater exemptions and benefits! The institute, which should have been catering to the needs of the poor weavers of the area, did not even possess basic statistics about them. When we asked them to take us to the nearest bunkar basti, they were at a loss. They had to telephone around to find out where the weavers' colonies were located.

Finally, someone identified a village – Rotaha, barely half a kilometre of dirt road away from the main Bhadohi–Varanasi highway. So we set out. The first thing we saw was a building with a signboard which read 'Kulhar Child Labour School'. Beyond that was a small clearing. Our cars stopped there. As curious men, women and children surrounded us, their stories began to unfold. Of the one fifty households in Rotaha, over half are of carpet weavers. On an average, it takes three people eight days to weave a carpet. They get Rs 600 for the carpet, that, too, if the middleman is generous. 'The mazdoori (labour) rate here is Rs 40 per day for nine hours of work. But the Agent Babu always finds some flaws in our work for which he deducts 25 per cent,' Sarju, a young man, each bone jutting out his body, told us. Walking a little further we saw three ten- to twelve-year-old boys weaving a carpet in a tiny shed. There was no fan or light. The boys, Ram Kishen, Asha Ram and Lallan, were drenched in sweat. 'Even if we had fans or light bulbs, it wouldn't help because the village hardly gets electricity,' said Ram Kishen.

When we started taking pictures of the children at work, the villagers began to get edgy. 'Madam, they are only helping their parents.' After reassurances that we were not there to penalize them, they finally admitted that 50 per cent of the children between the ages of nine and fourteen worked on the looms and the Kulhar Child Labour School had no more than twenty-five children from the village on its rolls. The reason was simple – every child who helped with the weaving brought in an additional Rs 20 per day to the family kitty. We asked to see a panchayat representative. With some reluctance, a tall woman named Mukhna Devi came forward. She said that she wasn't even informed of panchayat meetings and even if she managed to find out and go to the meeting, her issues were never taken seriously.

The return journey to Varanasi threw up eerie shapes on both sides of the road. They were the outlines of villages plunged into complete darkness. Electricity, we learnt, was available only for four hours at night so that farmers could draw water for their fields. The rest of the time, power was diverted towards commercial establishments. Even Varanasi had five–eight hours of power cuts every day. We had already spent one wakeful night with the mosquitoes at the Circuit House.

In the evening, we went to the bustling heart of old Benaras. The narrow galli behind the Kashi Vishwanath temple was filled with a mass of humanity. Young girls and their old chaperones were arguing loudly with sweet sellers and chooriwallahs (bangle-sellers). Our feet hardly moved but our bodies were propelled in whichever direction the crowd was heading. Thus it was the crowd which carried us to the ghats, just in time for the arti (prayer).

The Ganga arti at the Benaras ghats is a tableau witnessed by hundreds of people of all hues and milieus. The administration had arranged seats for us. We watched mesmerized as young pandas (pundits), like ramp models in fashionably draped dhotis, performed the arti with choreographed precision to the clanging of pooja bells. Thousands of little lights sparkled across the dark waters. Clouds of incense rose everywhere. The atmosphere was overpowering. For a brief moment, everything seemed to dissolve in the overall ecstatic reaction of the crowd as it swayed to the music and chants. The scene as it played out assumed an independent life of its own.

Writing in the early nineteenth century, W.S. Caine, an English writer, explained the reason behind this milling crowd and fervent religiosity:

Benaras is the metropolis of the Hindu faith … To the pious Brahman Benaras is what Mekka [sic] is to the Musalman, Jerusalem to the Christian. The longing of his whole life is to visit this place of spotless holiness and to wash away his blackest sins in the sacred Ganges before he dies. The palaces which fringe the rivers are full of the aged relatives of their owners, come together from all parts of India, waiting with calm, patient, ecstatic happiness, the summons to *Swarga* of the angel of death, for Benaras is, indeed, the very gate of heaven.[8]

Not only is Benaras the centre of the Hindu cosmos, it is also the place where Buddha gave his first sermon (at Sarnath), and where the Jain Tirthankara Adi Parasvanath was born. Caine describes the city as the 'labyrinth of Asiatic Theology'. 'There is probably no sacred city in the world with so ancient and unbroken a record, or which even to-day exercises its sway over so many millions of devotees; dear alike to that religion which, above all others, is saturated with idolatry, and to its greatest rival which, scorning idolatry and polytheism, teaches that every individual man, by a holy life, can lift himself into and become part of the Divine,' he says. In his book *The City in History*, Lewis Mumford writes that a city is 'energy converted into culture … There are few cities in the world which have converted the energy of an entire civilization into culture, and have come to symbolize that whole civilization in microcosm'.[9] Varanasi is such a city and this is perhaps why it has inspired and produced some of the biggest names in Indian literature, poetry and music – Kabir, Tulsidas, Premchand, Pandit Ravi Shankar and Ustad Bismillah Khan. The city draws travellers from all over the world. It has sustained its own brand even in today's globalized world.

Our third day in Varanasi was spent with those people who have given this holy city yet another identity, that of a weaving hub. For decades, a handwoven Benarasi sari with its rich brocade and bright colours has been

---

[8] W.S. Caine, *Picturesque India: A Handbook for European Travellers*, London, New York: G. Routledge and Sons, 1981. Viewed at http://www.archive.org/stream/picturesqueindi00caingoog#page/n279/mode/1up in September 2009.

[9] Lewis Mumford, *The City in History*, quoted in Diana L. Eck, *Benaras: City of Light*, Routledge and Kegan Paul, 1984, p. 6.

an essential ingredient of the great North Indian wedding. Whether it is the Bollywood star or the middle-class Hindu bride, when it comes to taking the saat pheras (walking around the sacred fire seven times to solemnize a marriage), they do so, resplendent in the glittering fabric woven by the bunkars of Benaras, most of them Muslims. The six yards of silk woven in the gallis and mohallas of this holy city are special not just for the beauty of their weave but for the inter-community tana bana (warp and woof) that they embody. We were sad to see these symbols of our syncretic culture and creativity close to extinction, for people said that the weavers of Varanasi were selling their blood to feed their children.

We saw these children even before we had seen their parents. Our guide through the narrow lanes was a young bespectacled man of average height, Lenin Raghuvanshi, convenor of the Peoples' Vigilance Committee on Human Rights. For the last fourteen years he has been working for the rights of the poor of his city, especially the bunkars. His work has won him many accolades; what struck us was his simplicity and humility.

Lenin took us to see the SOS Children's Village in Varanasi. In 2003, SOS had started an outreach programme to provide non-formal education to out-of-school children of kumhars (potters)and weavers in the five to twelve-year age-group. We were taken to a small room in which a hundred of these children were seated. They looked tidy but quiet; too quiet in comparison to the grubby but cheerful children of Guria we had seen earlier. Outside the classroom the parents, who had come to collect their kids, were waiting. Most of them lived in Daniyalpur, a locality in the nearby Choubeypur Thana area. Rasheeda, a young woman in a faded green salwar kurta, was carrying her one-and-half-year-old daughter, Ruby. The child had matchstick legs. 'She has never had tika karan (immunization). Dal and rice is all I can give her. There is no money for milk.' A pretty girl in advanced pregnancy with three children clinging to her stood in a corner. Her name was Sabiha. She shyly answered our queries. 'No, I have never seen a doctor.' 'Yes, I had all my babies at home.' 'Rozgar (work)? Our family gets orders. It takes us fifteen days to make a sari for which we get Rs 500. This money is paid to us by the gaddidars (middlemen).'

Talking to these women and a few men made us understand why they were sometimes forced to take desperate measures. To feed six–seven mouths, the families before us had no more than Rs 1,200 a month. 'Come and see how we live,' they pleaded.

On an impulse we asked to be taken to Daniyalpur. At the time, we were not prepared for the sleepless nights this visit would give us; the stories that we heard in this bunkar basti, the vacant faces that stared at us have been forever etched on our minds. They have become our unfading benchmarks of deprivation among bunkars. While discussing the efficacy of our schemes or the achievements of the development commissioner, handlooms, only one face comes to mind – that of Maimun Nisa. It is her story that we want to tell.

Hers was the first house we visited in Daniyalpur. We went there simply because it was closest to where the car had stopped. It was a one-room mud-and-brick structure. A broken charpai and a run-down loom were the only furniture. A white-and-orange fabric was trussed on the loom. A frail woman sat on the floor, sewing tiny stars into the fabric. Next to her, on the floor, lying on a scrap of cloth, was a small child. As soon as we entered her home, she picked up her child and stood up.

'What's your name?'

'Maimun Nisa.' Thin face, sunken eyes, hollow cheeks, a frayed light pink dupatta covered her head. Her son, Imran, was tiny and had the face of an old man – shrivelled and shrunk. His feet were so thin that we wondered if he would ever be able to walk. His head seemed too big for his small frail body. We assumed he was about eight months old.

'He is eighteen months old,' she said.

'Eighteen months!' We could not believe what we had heard. 'What do you feed him?'

Eyes lowered, she mumbled, 'Sabudaane ka paani (gruel of tapioca).'

'What! And what else?'

Silence.

'Do you feed him milk?'

Again, silence.

'We have no money to buy milk and I have none in my breasts. All I have ever been able to give him is sabudaane ka paani.'

We heard a sound behind us. Turning around, we saw a tall, thin man with a balding head and a small white beard. He was crying.

'Mushtaq, her husband,' someone whispered.

'Madam, we have nothing. We get Rs 15–30 per day for weaving saris and decorating them with stars and glitter. If we ask for more, the middleman will give the work to someone else. And with it the house will go, too. You see, it belongs to the dalal (agent). As long as we work for him, we will have this roof over our heads.'

Looking around the bare room, we did not see a single pot where any grain could have been stored. The chulha (wood stove) in the corner seemed hardly used.

'Don't you get BPL and Antyodaya rations?'

'No. We don't have any cards. Getting them means giving money to the dalal babu (middlemen).'

'To earn additional money, Mushtaq used to sell bananas on the railway platform. Then they charged him with theft and even this source has gone,' Maimun Nisa added softly.

In her helpless eyes and face, we saw a mother who is forced to watch her child die every day because she is unable to feed him. Barely able to hold back our tears, we headed towards the car. We did not notice the woman who was pressing against the door holding her injured child. Only when she put out her hand did we stop. 'Madam, he has broken his head. No money for treatment.' Blinded by tears, Syeda, handed her purse to someone saying, 'Find some money and get the child treated.'

And with that we rushed into the car, not able to witness any more misery. We sat silently. Fifteen minutes later, the car stopped and we heard a tapping at the window. It was Lenin. 'This is Bhagwan Nala, a colony of scheduled caste weavers. In the last fifty years, more than half the looms here have fallen silent,' he said, looking at us warily, trying to assess if we could face another round of misery. Frankly, we did not want to but, at the same time, we could not go away without meeting the people who had been waiting for us for hours. Already, naked kids with pot-bellies and bow-legs had surrounded our car. Their parents had also come out into the gallis to see what was happening.

In the tiny hut we entered, two looms were stacked against the wall. A young man stood next to them. 'I stopped weaving four years back when the gaddidars said there was no work.' Now he worked as a mazdoor (labourer) but still could not make himself sell the looms which he loved. 'They are my only joy. Maybe one day, they will become busy again.' Sitting in a corner was his twelve-year-old niece, Sushila. She was bent over a mat rolling agarbattis (incense sticks). She told us that in five hours she made a hundred agarbattis, for which she got one rupee. 'I am a little slow because I have just learnt to roll. Others can make up to 1,000 agarbattis in a day,' she mumbled apologetically. We turned to the welfare officials who were probably visiting this basti for the first time. 'Do you have any scheme?'

'It is very sad, Madam, very sad. But this is not our responsibility. We only administer the Musahar schemes.'

The next house we went to belonged to Sarju, a bunkar with nine children, six of them daughters. He was sitting in a tiny, dark and airless room which had enough space for him, a small child and one loom. He said he was paid at piece rate. This meant that he had to use his own materials and run the risk of not being able to sell his work. But it meant more money per piece if he was able to make a sale. His daughter, Mana, was working in another small room. The half kg of agarbattis that she made per day meant an additional income of Rs 3 or 4. The family had an Antyodaya card on which they got rice and wheat. As we left the colony, Lenin handed us a piece of paper; it had details of malnourished children of Bhagwan Nala. He handed another list; this was a list of starvation deaths.

On the way to Nati Imli, a colony of powerloom weavers, we stopped at Handloom House, a shop where some beautiful specimens of Benarasi silk saris were selling for Rs 1,200 to 20,000. The kind of sari we had seen in Mushtaq's house was selling for Rs 1,500; he and Maimun Nisa only made Rs 150–200, that is, Rs 100 for the sequin work and Rs 50 to100 for weaving; that was what they got for three days' work. We were told that the Karuha Benarasi sari, the top of the line, takes one month to weave. It sells for a minimum of Rs 10,000 or 20,000 and the weaver gets Rs 1,500 per piece.

The houses at Nati Imli were double- and triple-storeyed. The road was wider and people dressed in starched white kurta pyjamas were walking about. These people are the weaver entrepreneurs, called gaddidars (people on gaddis or seats, and therefore exalted). Inside one of the roadside workshops, the workers explained that the land had been given to them free of cost by the UP government. But it is the rich middlemen who have prospered in their name. It is they who own the handlooms as well as the powerlooms while the weavers slog to earn a daily wage of Rs 40.

A tired-looking old man, Alauddin, said that he worked ten hours, sometimes more, every day and earned Rs 800 in fourteen days. His five-year-old daughter, Gulnaaz, helped him at the loom. A small bulb hung above the loom where he was working along with other weavers; there was no fan or window in the room. There was a loud clanging of powerlooms next door. The workers there said that the noise affected their hearing. Financially, they were only slightly better off than their handloom counterparts. They got Rs 50 per sari. If electricity was uninterrupted and they worked eighteen hours daily, they could weave up to two saris in one day.

Nearby, in a spacious building with a pretty garden, the gaddidars were waiting for us with an elaborate tea. Rahmatullah Ansari, president of the All-India Handloom Fabrics Marketing Co-operative Society, spoke on behalf of the group. He said that the 1985 textile policy had favoured powerlooms. Consequently, all master weavers moved to powerlooms and today they produced powerloom products at cheaper rates. All this has resulted in the unplanned growth of the powerloom sector. Ansari complained about the fluctuating prices of silk yarn and suggested that the National Handloom Development Corporation (NHDC) be made the nodal agency for procurement of silk yarn from countries like China. The import, he said, should be duty-free. This would make the finished products more cost-effective. The removal of duty on mill and powerloom yarn along with hank yarn had taken away the cost-effective edge from handlooms. Though eleven items were still reserved for the handloom sector, implementation of the rule was very lax. Handloom weavers did not even get credit.

When we got out of our meeting with the master weavers and co-operative owners, we found that our passage was blocked. A large group of weavers had surrounded our car. They said that we had listened only to the 'exploiters,' not to their subjects. They asked if they could meet us later that night at the Circuit House. We said, 'Yes, why not?' At the time, we did not know that they had no money to hire an auto-rickshaw or take a bus. After a full day's work, they walked over an hour to come to see us in the Circuit House.

We had eaten dinner and were waiting when they trooped in. It was evident that they had not eaten. Since the kitchen was closed, steaming cups of tea and biscuits were all we could offer. They appeared thankful for the refreshment. The first sentence was spoken by an old weaver, Nizamuddin. 'I have been weaving for sixty years; my life is summed up in these two lines. With your permission, may I recite?'

Bunkar umr bhar bunta raha, apna kafan na bun saka,

Nanga hi jiya, nanga hi mar gaya

The weaver kept weaving all his life, but could not weave a shroud for himself,

He was born naked and died naked.

Then the others spoke, one by one.

'Earlier, we got Rs 1,800 for a Patola, which took us five days. Now the powerlooms sell it for Rs 500. Mills in Surat sell Jacquard sari for Rs 150. Last year, some 25,000 weavers migrated with their families from Varanasi.'

'Twenty-four weavers committed suicide.'

'Over one lakh households of bunkars have food only once a day.'

'Fifty thousand families in the mohalla of Bazardiha are on the verge of starvation.'

'Conditions in Lallapura, Lohta, Unniya, Amarpur Mania, Batlodia, Lukki Ghat and Daniyalpur are no better.'

They said that, in 1950, the Silk Weaver's Housing Colony Co-operative Society, Chaukhaghat, was given land under the Jawaharlal Nehru Scheme for constructing a yarn depot and houses for weavers. This land, they said, was taken over by middlemen to build their own houses. 'If we protest, we are just thrown out of the co-operative fold and no work is given to us.'

There was more. 'A hospital meant for us weavers has now been converted into a labour office.'

And then their demands were placed on the table.

'Our products should be registered under the GI (Geographical Indication of Goods) Act and they should be mapped. For example, no one knows that military badges for national armies across the world are made in Varanasi.'

'Many powerloom owners have at least one handloom so that they can reap the benefits meant for the handloom sector. Can you do something about it?'

'These huge electricity bills and water taxes we can't pay.'

'For debt-ridden weavers who have no working capital, please give a one-time interest-free loan so they can resume work.'

'About 40 per cent of us suffer from tuberculosis; please give us a special unit in the hospital.'

'The situation with raw materials and Chinese silk is killing us. Sarkar (government) should remove the anti-dumping duty on Chinese silk yarn to tackle fluctuation in yarn prices and place it on the finished silk products from China which are the death knell for our market.'

Their complaints and demands were born of their dire need. We talked late into the night. When they were leaving, we promised that we would visit them the next day at Bazardiha, the biggest handloom cluster in Varanasi, with 1.5 lakh people, mostly Muslims. It is known to be among the most deprived areas in Varanasi; even so we had not imagined the extent of its deprivation, we were to witness.

The next morning, we walked through the streets of Bazardiha for two hours. The average daily income of a family of six to nine members here is Rs 50. There is no anganwadi in the entire locality. A single primary school is all they have, plus two madrassas. Most children begin work at the looms as soon as they are seven or eight years old, some even earlier. Each pair of hands means a little more food. We saw many such children working in dark airless rooms: Alimuddin and Wasim (both seven years old), Ramzan (ten), Atif (fourteen). Sweat glistened on their bony arms and pinched faces, while their eyes were glazed from peering in the dark to ensure that the weave was perfectly aligned. All of them said that they had to drop out of school. Their father, Mohammad Sultan, said that nine of his family members lived in this small two-room house. At one time, he had sixty running looms. Today, only two looms were left. On an average, the family made Rs 500 per sari which could take anything between ten–twelve days, sometimes even more. He said that they had not benefited by the ICICI Lombard Health Insurance Scheme launched by the government. 'Baji, I can't afford the Rs 200 premium.'

We stopped and asked many people in the bazaar; very few had Antyodaya or BPL cards. Those that had them said they do not get any rations since the public distribution system shops in the area only stock kerosene. 'They used to distribute food grains. But ever since the bifurcation of kerosene and food depots, we get no rice, no wheat. No food depots have been opened here,' said Syed Hasan Ansari. For water, people start queuing up at 3 a.m. in the garbage-strewn streets.

Standing in the stench and suffocation of Bazardiha, we realized how distant we were from the real problems of weavers. During our discussions, products often overshadow people, and skills eclipse the skilled. We are often liable to forget faces.

The next morning, before leaving Varanasi, we went to the river. The sun had not risen but the ghats were already teeming with devotees, tourists, sadhus and hawkers. Children playing, people bathing, getting their hair cut, washing clothes, praying, consulting astrologers, eating, taking pictures; young boys were convincing tourists to take a ride on their boats; seasoned hawkers were trying to entice devotees and tourists with their wares displayed on the ghats and even on boats on the river. Families were grieving over funeral pyres and offering the ashes of loved ones to the Ganges; piles of wood were everywhere. Even at 5.30 a.m., every inch of space was occupied and abuzz with activity – both of the living and the dead. The scenes that played out before our eyes seemed to bear an uncanny similarity to the Benaras described by W.S. Caine more than 125 years ago[10].

> Viewed from the river, it (Benaras) presents a panorama of palaces, temples and mosques, surmounted by domes, pinnacles and minarets, stretching three miles along the top of the bank. From these descend great flights of stone stairs, broken into wide platforms, on which are built exquisite Hindu shrines, bathing houses and preaching canopies. Long piers project into the river, on which sick people lie, carefully tended by their relatives, to get the beneficial healing of the great mother Ganges. Ghats, platforms and piers are alive with pilgrims from every part of India, in every variety of costume, and every stage of dress and undress, grouped under huge straw umbrellas, sitting at the feet of some learned mahant or preacher, gazing at

---

[10] Caine, W.S., Op cit, p. 301

holy ascetics, jostled by sacred bulls, crowding in and out of the water, drying themselves with towels, prostrate at the margin telling beads. Crows, kites, pigeons and parrots circle round the heads of this kaleidoscopic crowd. Up and down the ghats, all day long, but especially in the early morning, stream the endless course of pilgrims, ragged tramps, aged crones, horrible beggars, hawkers, Brahmin priests, sacred bulls and cows, Hindu preachers, wealthy rajas (kings) or bankers in gay palanquins, fakirs, pariah dogs, and scoffing globetrotters from Europe and America.

As the boatman took us across a peaceful yet busy Ganga, it seemed as if time had stood still. This eternal, static quality is a distinguishing characteristic of Benaras. As Diana Eck notes[11],

> There is another important difference between Benaras and its contemporaries; its present life reaches back to the sixth century BC in a continuous tradition. If we could imagine the silent Acropolis and the Agora of Athens still alive with the intellectual, cultural, and ritual traditions of classical Greece, we might glimpse the remarkable tenacity of the life of Kashi. Today Peking, Athens and Jerusalem are moved by a very different ethos from that which moved them in ancient times, but Kashi is not.

It is said that the Ganges has the power to cleanse all sins, to expel all sorrows. It is for this relief, this salvation, that people come to Varanasi. This is a city that has lived through the ages not only because of its rich political history or its architectural wonders but also because of the emotion that it evokes. On our last morning in Varanasi, we, too, found our way to the river, hoping that it would drive away the despair that we had felt in the last few days. That it would help us find a life of dignity for the bunkars, the Musahars, the sex workers. Kashi they say is enlightenment... Our visit to Benaras had definitely enlightened us; it had taught us about deprivation and misery, sorrow and poverty, like we had never known. We resolved to carry this light to our work as planners, with the determination that it would dispel the darkness that shrouds eastern Uttar Pradesh.

---

[11] Eck, Diana, Op cit, p. 5

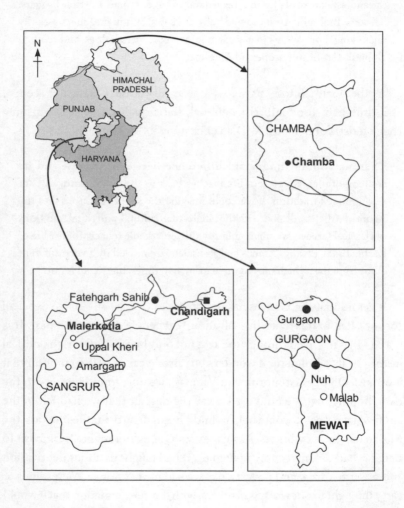

9

Himachal, Punjab & Haryana

Ye chiragh jaise lamhe kuhin raigan na jaaen
Koi khwab dekh dalo, koi inquilaah laao

– RAHI

May these flame like moments not go to waste
Witness a dream, usher in a revolution.

I t was June 2006. The helicopter from Shimla to Chamba[1] flew over an endless expanse. Himachal looked huge – thousands of terraced mountains among bottle-green deodars. In the distance, like presiding deities, were the snow-capped Himalayas. Hundreds of roads criss-crossed the mountain slopes, their hairpin bends concealed behind huge rocks. Nature appeared at once majestic and gentle, quite unlike the harsh terrain of the Karakoram ranges of Ladakh we had recently seen.[2]

---

[1] Chamba is one of the twelve districts of the hill state of Himachal Pradesh. Situated between 32° 11′ 30″N and 33° 13′ 6″N and 75°49 E and 77° 3′ 30″E, with an estimated area of 6,528 square km, it is a remote mountainous district bordering the Ladakh region of Jammu & Kashmir. It is believed that the district and its headquarters are named after Princess Champa, the beloved daughter of King Sahilla Varman. In 800 AD, this illustrious ruler subjugated the warring chieftains of this area and founded the town of Chamba.

[2] See Chapter 11

Soon, we landed in a sylvan valley through which ran the effusive River Raavi. A cavalcade of cars with senior officials like the deputy commissioner was waiting to take us on a tour of the district. Our programme for the day was to visit two panchayats: Paliyur and Sahoo. As our cars cautiously negotiated the winding and well-maintained mountain roads, we tried to soak in the sights and sounds of this remote part of Himachal Pradesh.

'Look at the mountains,' the deputy commissioner, a young IAS officer by the name of Pushpendra Rajput, urged. Nestling here and there on the mountain slopes were people's homes; a few such dwellings formed a 'village'. There they were, in splendid isolation, unconnected by road. 'It is literally an uphill task to provide facilities in every habitation,' he said.

Out of the car windows we saw smartly dressed young children confidently trudging along the roads in neatly pressed school uniforms. 'Most of them have to walk for half an hour, or more to get to school,' he informed us. 'What happens when a woman has difficult labour or requires a caesarean?' we asked. 'Her family, usually her husband or brother, carries her on his back to the nearest hospital; at times, they use a charpai (cot).' We remembered our meeting with the chief minister of the state, Veerbhadra Singh, in Shimla the previous day. He had told us of his determination to build motorable roads connecting every panchayat to the district headquarters by 2008. 'Tomorrow, when you go to Chamba, you will see for yourselves why roads are so important for the people of my state.' The problem of Himachal's hilly terrain was obvious and we saw how difficult his task was. Here, the very logistics of road building were challenging. There were some panchayats in Chamba with as many as fifty-five villages! Paliyur, with a population of just 3,500, was one of them.

Soon, our cars stopped. As we rolled down our windows, an officer came running up. 'Paliyur Panchayat is not connected with a motorable road. You will have to walk from here,' he said with an apologetic smile. 'But, before that, we can have lunch at the Sahoo Forest Rest House. We have arranged a Chamyali meal for you.' This came from a salwar-clad Himachali man who we discovered was the pradhan of Sahoo. 'We did not know if you would like our rustic food but we took the risk,' he added with a shy smile.

We were hungry. The table was laden with neatly covered dishes. As the lids came off one by one, we could not help comparing Chamba cuisine with the Kashmiri wazwan. For the Kashmiris as well as the Chamyalis, this classic meal is a must at weddings and festivals, regardless of the socio-economic status of the host. In both cases, there is a set order in which dishes are served and a manner in which it is arranged. We were first served rice, followed by the ordinary, humble rajma. Nothing special, one would say. But not so the rajma in Chamba! Here, it is a delicacy known by the name madra. 'We boil the rajma and throw away the water,' the pradhan explained even as he heaped spoonfuls of madra on my plate. 'Then we boil equal quantities of milk and ghee. When the milk almost disappears in the ghee, we add the rajma and spices.' Next in line was moong daal made with freshly plucked herbs and pure spring water. A large dish of chicken (desi, not broiler) was placed before us, tender meat cooked with fresh spices like saunf and sonth. In two small bowls there were two chutneys, one green and one red. This was Chamba chugh, made by mixing freshly plucked green and red chillies in the juice of the pahari lemon. The highlight of the meal, however, was a dish of guchhi or black mushrooms, priced at a formidable Rs 8,000 per kg. They are nature's special bounty to mountain people and their story in both Chamba and Kashmir is similar. On some rainy days, when there is a flash of lightning, these mushrooms tear through the ground and spring out on select mountain slopes. Women crouch on these slopes, waiting for the shaft of light which will lift them out of the earth. Filling their baskets and dupattas, they climb down with their precious potlis (bags).

After sampling the guchhi we moved on to meetha chawal, sweet rice cooked with almonds, raisins and cardamom. Chamyali kadhi, too, is different; instead of pakora, it has pieces of sev. (noodle-shaped savoury made of gram flour) It was followed by khatta, a perfect blend of tamarind and jaggery that delightfully teased the palate. By the time, kheer, the final course, was served, we were ready to call it quits. 'But you have to taste this,' the host, ADM (Additional District Magistrate) Chaman Lal insisted holding out a mouth freshener mixture. We took a pinch and left the table with the taste of jarees, made from saunf and sugar, fresh in our mouths.

After this sumptuous meal, known as Chamyali Dhaam, we were ready to walk to a meeting with pradhans from neighbouring areas, which had been arranged in the village of Sahoo. We decided to visit the adjoining panchayat of Paliyur. The kutchcha road took us through fields and small bastis. On the way we passed women and men of the Gujjar and Gaddi tribes. Both tribes are nomadic and grazing communities; one Muslim, the other Hindu. In Paliyur, the Gujjars are dominant, easily distinguished by their black clothes. The men wear beards, mostly dyed with henna and tie colourful safas (turbans). Women also wear black, and cover their heads. They look like Kashmiri Gujjars; they say their forefathers came from Kishtwar in Jammu & Kashmir. Due to their nomadic lifestyle, their children cannot go to regular school. So the state has attached para-teachers to some tribes; they move with the caravan, using rest halts to teach the children.

At Paliyur, there was orderliness in the panchayat functioning. Details of funding for various projects were written on a prominent chalkboard outside the samiti office. In another place, ration shop timings and the items in stock were written on a board outside the store. Also displayed was the number of people covered by 'food schemes' like Annapurna[3] and Antyodaya[4]. The Paliyur pradhan told us that the panchayat was held each month and gram sabha every three months. There was a huge turnout from the panchayat's fifty-five 'villages', some of which were not even connected with walking paths. These well-attended gram sabhas are a testimony to the robustness of the community-level institutions in the state.

We had heard stories of this robustness and of the Himachali passion for educating their children. Until a decade ago, many teachers in the state were outsiders, and people were wary of leaving their young girls under the care of 'strangers'. So the panchayats found an ingenious solution. They paid elderly village women Rs 10 per week to escort the children. Every morning, the daadi (granny) would clutch her walking stick and go from house to house collecting the girls to take them to the village school. For the next few hours,

---

[3] The Annapurna Scheme run by the Ministry of Rural Development provides 10 kg of ration per person per month to senior citizens who though eligible do not receive pension under the National Old Age Pension Scheme.

[4] The Antyodaya Anna Yojana is a central scheme that was launched in 2000 to provide wheat and rice at subsidized rates to one crore of the poorest of poor families in India. Currently, under this scheme, 2.5 crore families are entitled to get 35 kg of foodgrains every month at Rs 2 per kg for wheat and Rs 3 per kg for rice.

she would sit in a corner of the classroom, chewing jarees and keeping an eye on the teacher. This daily vigil not only provided comfort to the parents, it also gave these older women a new confidence and status.

Another distinguishing feature of the state's community institutions were the Nyaya Panchayats. In 1952, Himachal translated Gandhiji's dream of Gram Swaraj into reality by constituting nyaya panchayats under the Himachal Pradesh Panchayati Raj Act. Until 1977, these local forums for dispute resolution were manned (there were no women!) by village elders. They ensured justice in the state's scattered villages. Then, one stroke from a bureaucrat's pen changed everything. The judicial powers of the nyaya panchayat were given to the elected panchayats. As the lines between the executive and the judiciary blurred, locally offered justice and reconciliation lost credibility. Now a vibrant voluntary organization, Sutra, has started a movement for the revival of the nyaya panchayats. We had heard about this earlier from NGOs and individual panchayat members. Pahyur's panchayat brought these thoughts back to mind.

Our hope for Himachal was further strengthened by the neat and well-functioning anganwadi centre[5] we saw in Paliyur. The bright room with tables, chairs, clock and posters was in sharp contrast to many dilapidated anganwadis we had seen across the country. Here, the children were not rolling all over the cold floor of the centre; they were seated in rows and kept warm by durries (rugs). All kinds of animals and birds winked at them from the centre's painted walls. The worker, a cheerful young woman named Sreshta, used alphabet and number charts to teach. After an hour or so of reciting poems and familiarizing themselves with numbers and letters, the children sat down for a hot cooked meal. On the day of our visit, they had a cooker full of matar pulao (peas pulao). On other days they got khichdi,

---

[5] It is a centre being run in villages and towns across the country under the Integrated Child Development Scheme of the Government of India. Children under six years of age come here six days a week for supplementary nutrition. The anganwadi is supposed to provide deworming tablets, preschool education and immunization to children. Pregnant and lactating mothers receive counselling, iron and folic acid tablets, and take home rations. Currently, there are around 12.6 lakh Anganwadi Centres (commonly referred to as AWCs) providing nutrition and preschool education to around sixteen crore children in India.

dalia (oats) or channe (gram). A bright young boy caught our eye. 'My name is Arif and this is my sister, Shadma,' he said confidently. We looked up to see the smiling face of a young Gujjar woman, Arif's mother, who was introduced to us as Mir Bibi. She was sitting at the back holding her little girl. We left the centre with hope for a better future for Arif and Shadma.

We then walked along the kutchcha path back towards Sahoo, a twelve-hundred-year-old village. On the way, we stopped at its most important landmark, an ancient Shiv temple. In the centre of its courtyard, on a raised platform, was a statue of Nandi, Shiva's bull. It is said that, if you crawl beneath this statue, your wish will be fulfilled. Most of the crawlers were women, a lot of them pregnant; we decided to try our luck with our wish-lists. Crouched beneath the legendary bull, we looked at each other; we were thinking of the universality of the desire for divine intervention!

On the way to the meeting, we passed the school compound. All along the wall were blackboards displaying daily attendance whereby the villagers could see for themselves how many children and teachers were attending school.

Our meeting was at the Community Centre inside the Public Library which was constructed with shramdaan (offering of labour) and daan (donations) of the residents. In this large, bright room, there were over one fifty people including five pradhans. It was a beautiful setting, the library was set amidst trees and flowering plants. We learnt that, seven years ago, the area was a jungle, prone to flooding and landslides. Inspired by senior teacher Ratan Chand's vision, villagers turned this wilderness into a garden. The decision to plant vegetables and fruit trees resulted in an abundance of walnut and apricot trees. To preserve the environment, the villagers launched a Paryavaran Chetna Evam Grameen Vikas Kendra (Environment Awareness and Rural Development Centre). Ratan Chand, a thin man with salt-and-pepper hair and beard, told us that the people wanted to make Sahoo a model for eco-tourism. They agreed that private homes would set aside a room for tourists where they would get to live with a local family, enjoy the beauty of the mountains and eat home-cooked meals, including occasionally the Chamyali Dham. It sounded like a perfect holiday. It reminded Gunjan of the UK Government's Host Programme whereby international students at British universities are encouraged to stay with local families who introduce them to different aspects of British life. Some of her best experiences in the UK as a student came from these host visits. The quiet Sunday morning spent at the local church, the delicious tea sipped in a leisurely fashion at a Victorian-style tea-room, evenings filled with barn dancing and nights spent pub crawling – all these 'hosted' experiences made her really connect with the country and its people.

The people of Sahoo were enthused with the idea of eco-tourism for foreign visitors. 'We could teach them about our local flora and fauna; we could also share our local cures. For example, there is a plant called bichchu booti. If touched, it causes an intense itch and is a source of great discomfort for trekkers. But cook it, and it will protect your heart and control diabetes.' Many people started sharing their experiences of local cures. In the Planning Commission we were looking after the medicinal plants sector so this knowledge was very precious.

Nirmala, a thirty-year-old woman with a neat sari pinned to her shoulder, rose to speak. She said that the thirty women of her mahila mandal (women's group) give five rupees every month for bachat (savings). 'But there is much more to our movement. We first learnt to sign our names. Then we were trained to teach women to breastfeed, to register births of their children, and practise birth control to maintain a gap between children. In our area, there is 60 per cent male participation in sterilization and not more than two or three kids in the family. We also explain sexually transmitted diseases.' She then pointed to the colourful moodhas (a type of stool made by hand) placed in the corner. 'These have been made from scrap and waste materials, such as polybags which are twisted into ropes.'

'I am Urmila, from Dramand Panchayat, Sarori Village.' We were looking at the young girl who had spoken. 'I have made fifteen self help groups,' she said shyly. 'We got Rs 10,000 as a loan from the bank and began growing vegetables. Earlier, we did not even have two rupees to spend. But now we have earned our jeb kharcha (spending money).' We were overwhelmed at the quiet determination of these women and girls. That night, after we returned to the Chamba Circuit House (erstwhile Palace of Chamba rulers), we could not fall asleep thinking of pahari (mountain) woman crouching on the hillside, searching for the precious guchchi. The success stories we found were our own precious guchhis collected from this hill state. We saw these discoveries as bulbs of nascent hope which were pushing upwards out of the hilly terrain.

The next day, we visited the famous Lakshmi Narayan and Chamunda Devi temples. These temples, both of which are as old as the town itself, are closely linked to its 1000-year-old history. The former is remarkable for its exquisite stone carvings. The latter offers a breathtaking view of the Chamba Valley and of the river Raavi, which gushes by its side.

After our fill of the panoramic view, we headed towards the markets to see if we could find Chamba chappals (slippers). At one time, all over India, Chamba chappals were a brand name. That was before the market brands came in to reform our taste in footwear! And they did not need advertising campaigns for sustenance. Word of mouth ensured their popularity. Strolling through the bazaar, we saw many small footwear shops where the shoes were not only cheap but also trendy. One entire lane was lined with tiny shops selling chappals of all shapes, sizes and colours. The air was filled with the smell of leather and glue. Sitting at the back of the shop, squeezed between wooden partitions, were the artisans who can turn plain leather into beautiful art in just two hours, getting Rs 30 for every pair. The shoes that are displayed in their shops could have sold under brand names for phenomenal prices in city showrooms. And yet, the 500 families which make Chamba chappals find it difficult to survive. Even people from Chamba prefer 'foreign' branded shoes and sandals. The only takers for this sturdy and crafted pure-leather footwear are stray tourists.

The markets and museums of Chamba are a veritable treasure-house of handicrafts. Pattu (Chamba quilt), pangi thobi (goat-hair carpets which last fifty to seventy years), Chamba paintings, metal work ... the list is endless. But it is the Chamba rumaal (rumaal literally means handkerchief) which is the undisputed queen of the crafts here. It is special because it has no right or wrong side; the dorookha stitch that is used ensures that both faces look exactly the same. Women of Chamba have embroidered the rumaal for 300–400 years; it was initially used to cover trays of food and gifts at weddings and festivals. Some people trace this art to the craftspeople brought by Chamba's king, Umed Singh, in the sixteenth century. This art gradually became the forte of upper-class women, who would sit and embroider stories from the Ramayana, scenes from Raasleela, birds and animals – all on square pieces of silk or cotton. It would take between four months to one year to make a one-by-one-metre rumaal, depending on the intricacy of the design.

Today, it is a handful of women master-trainers who have kept the craft alive. We met one such woman – Shamshad Begum. 'We have to go all the way to Delhi to get the khadi cloth and the resham (silk). Imagine how our costs go up,' she complained. She told us that design intervention and product diversification across the country has led to production of reversible shirts, tops, duppattas and screens which are less intricate and hence cheaper. But quality and grandeur is the hallmark of the original Chamba rumaal. Shamshad explained that, even today, the girls who learn how to embroider Chamba rumaals practise it as an art. Looking at this pleasant middle-aged woman we realized the true meaning of India, Muslim trainer, whose students are embroidering Hindu scriptures in this rare art form! The Chamba rumaal needs to be preserved for many reasons: as an heirloom, as a form of art, and perhaps, most important of all, because it is yet another symbol of syncretism, our ganga jamuni tehzeeb (a multually participatory co-existence of Hindu and Muslim cultures). It is a bond that transcends region and religion – like the hues and motifs we had discovered at the Boondi School of Painting in Rajasthan.[6]

These bonds and cultural affinities are at their strongest in a small town in the neighbouring state of Punjab. Like Chamba, Malerkotla was once a princely riyasat (kingdom) and a part of the state of Punjab. This small town with a population of one lakh Hindus and Muslims was our next destination. Located in the Sangrur District of Punjab, it is an oasis of peace in a strife-torn land. The Muslims and the Hindus here did not grab each other's throats when bombs went off in Malegaon and Varanasi.[7] They did

---

[6] See Chapter 12

[7] Two blasts – one at the famous Sankat Mochan temple and another at the railway station – in Varanasi on 7 March 2006 killed twenty-eight people and injured 101. A series of blasts in a Muslim cemetery adjacent to a mosque in the town of Malegaon in Maharashtra on 8 September 2006 left thirty-seven people dead and 125 injured. Both these blasts which took place at religious sites escalated tensions between the Hindu and Muslim communities across the country.

not start a riot over the Dera Sacha Sauda (DSS) issue.[8] Even in 1947, when trainloads of slaughtered bodies were going from one side of the border to the other, Malerkotla did not lose its equilibrium.[9] The Muslims of this town preferred to stay here; they did not migrate to Pakistan. In fact, Muslims from other strife-torn areas ran here for temporary refuge. Later, many were safely transported across the border.

At the time of our visit to this town located in the heart of Punjab, where the Muslim minority is in majority, the DSS violence and blasts at the Mecca Masjid in Hyderabad[10] were headline news. A wave of suspicion and communal incidents had engulfed the country. Many friends tried to stop us from going there despite our assurances that Malerkotla was different; its residents have lived in harmony for many decades. As we expected, their fears were baseless. Even as Punjab and parts of adjoining Haryana were burning over the Dera incident, Malerkotla was calm.

We have often visited places in the aftermath of a conflict – Gujarat, Manipur, Malegaon – to take stock of destruction of life and property and understand what drives people to attack and kill their own; the very neighbours with whom they have lived all their lives. But this time we were

[8] The DSS is a sect based out of Sirsa, Haryana. It was founded by Beparwah Shah Mastana ji Maharaj in 1948, and describes itself as a spiritual institution. In May 2007, the states of Punjab and neighbouring Haryana witnessed widespread violence between the Sikhs and the supporters of DSS when the DSS head, Baba Gurmeet Ram Rahim Singh, appeared dressed as Guru Gobind Singh, the Tenth Guru of the Sikhs. Malerkotla, however, remained peaceful.

[9] It is estimated that 12.5 million people were displaced and up to one million killed during the violence and communal frenzy that took place at the time of Partition. Punjab State was divided between the two newly formed nations of India and Pakistan, and witnessed the maximum population transfer and violence. Trainloads of corpses moved from one side of the border to the other, yet in Malerkotla no Hindu, Sikh or Muslim was killed.

[10] On 18 May 2007, a blast took place inside the Mecca Masjid in Hyderabad where 10,000 devotees had gathered for their Friday prayers. Fourteen people were killed and over fifty injured in the blast and the violence that followed.

going to a place where neighbours protected one another. It is a place which has in fact remained so peaceful that it has never made headline news.

On the two-hour road journey from Chandigarh to Malerkotla, we followed a Sufi trail. We crossed Sirhind, the town famous for the mausoleum of Shaikh Ahmad Sirhindi, leader of the Naqshbandi School[11] of Sufism. Then we passed the princely state of Nabha and the infamous district of Fatehgarh Sahib which has the lowest rural child sex ratio in the country. We passed field after field; some had standing crops, others had been recently harvested. Punjab's prosperity was reflected in the good roads, its many vehicles, and large houses amid vibrant fields. Huge multicoloured 'footballs' were perched on all rooftops; these, we discovered later, were overhead water tanks. We passed groups of young boys hanging around. Prosperity has brought drugs and substance abuse among the youth; the fruits of one generation's toil have led to the other's undoing. Wild-growing marijuana plants, agents of this ruination, lined both sides of the road.

By the time we reached Malerkotla, it was evening. Our first stop was at the famous Gurudwara Ha Ka Nara. We had heard that in the SGPC (Shiromani Gurudwara Prabandhak Committee) office here, there was a famous painting of the Nawab of Malerkotla, Sher Mohammad Khan. According to local lore, the nawab, an ally of the Mughals in their battle against the Sikhs, heard that the viceroy of Sirhind, a close relative, had ordered the death of the two young sons of Guru Gobind Singh. The nawab was furious. 'This cannot be. Killing innocent children is against the dictates of Shari'at and Islam.' He petitioned the viceroy and Emperor Aurangzeb to stop this heinous deed. His efforts failed, and the two Sahibzadas were walled alive. The Guru, however, commended his efforts and raised his

---

[11] The Naqshbandi Order is a Sufi order of Islam that traces its spiritual lineage to Prophet Muhammad through the first Caliph, Abu Bakr. Use of the silent invocation of God (dhikr) and a strict adherence to Shari'a Law are its distinctive characteristics. Shaikh Ahmad Sirhindi is regarded as one of its leading figures. He was born in Sirhind in 971 H. (1564 AD) in a family that claimed descent from Caliph Umar. He denounced Emperor Akbar's policy of *Sulh-e-Kul* (peace to all – mixing all religions into one) and believed that anything outside the path shown by the Prophet was forbidden.

hands in prayer for the nawab, saying, 'His roots will ever remain green.' He also gifted him a talwar (sword) which, until today, is a prized possession of the House of Malerkotla. The prayer of the Guru, according to the people of Malerkotla, is the reason for the harmony among communities in this Muslim dominated town. At the gurudwara, we could not find the legendary painting but tales of the courage of the nawab were echoed by all.

On our way back to the Circuit House, we stopped at a bookstore at Sherwani Gate which was owned by Jama'at-e-Islami Hind. We went in looking for literature about this unique city. In the back office, we met a young man, Mohammed Aasaar, who had studied at the Jamia Millia Islamia University in New Delhi. He was secretary of the Jama'at. 'Most of the people here, Hindus, Muslims or Sikhs, are descendants of the original inhabitants of the town. Our mother tongue is Punjabi. We stay in mixed localities, attend each other's festivals, marriages, births and deaths. All communities are devoted to the founder of Malerkotla State, the great Sufi saint, Hazrat Sheikh Sadruddin Sadr-i-Jahan. We are sheer o shakr (mixed like milk and sugar) with each other; we have no reason to fight.' He said that, in Malerkotla, Muslims own land and are agriculturists. Most of them are from the Kamboj sect. Though their landholdings are small, they have become prosperous because of their hard work. He brought out a Gurmukhi translation of the Holy Quran – the best evidence of the language-bond between the communities.

As we moved through gallis and mohallas of Malerkotla, we saw the truth behind his words. Ghettoization or polarization was almost non-existent there. The homes and shops of people of both communities were located side by side.

The famous Dargah of Hazrat Sheikh Sadruddin Sadr-i-Jahan, Malerkotla's founder saint, is another testimony to this harmony. It is packed with people from every religion and community. We found families of Sikhs jostling with Muslim and Hindu families to kiss the dehleez (threshold) of the dargah. Sheikh Sadr-i-Jahan was originally from Afghanistan and in his later life migrated to Multan. Here, he became a disciple of Sheikh Bahauddin Suhrawardy. He came to Sangrur and married the daughter of Bahlol Lodhi of the Delhi Sultanate. As his wedding gift, he received fifty-six villages that became his jagir (landed property). In 1454, he founded the town of Maler. In 1657, his descendant, Nawab Bayazid Khan, founded Kotla. The two were later merged together to form Malerkotla.

Having witnessed the essence of Malerkotla's eclectic culture, we moved from the urban to the rural. The village of Binjoli Khurd, a thirty-minute drive from the town, has a population of 2,700, of which 60 per cent is Muslim. The sarpanch, Nusrat Bano, to whose house we were invited for tea, had been in office for four years. We were pleased to find a Muslim woman sarpanch. But each time we asked a question, the answer was supplied by her husband, Abdul Rashid, a teacher by profession. Also present that day was Rani, a panchayat member from the Gujjar community. She, too, avoided answering our questions but was voluble in her praise for the sarpanch. 'He takes great interest in the affairs of the village, especially education.'

'He?' we asked, looking at Nusrat Bano who sat demurely with her duppatta-covered head. 'She is the sarpanch!'

'You know how it is!' Rani answered sheepishly.

Abdul Rashid, a tall well-built man, seemed in control. He told us that panchayats in Punjab have no discretionary financial powers. The gram sabha met twice a year but, unlike in neighbouring Himachal, attendance here was poor; no more than a hundred people. The big issue that kept surfacing throughout our visit was the problem of drainage and sewerage. The choked, overflowing nullahs and filthy water stagnating outside houses bore testimony to this. We learnt that people suffered from diabetes, heart- and liver disease. Rural Punjab had its share of the poor; though we had not seen many kutchcha houses in the village, we learnt that the daily wage for agricultural labour was Rs 60–Rs 70.

The village has two government schools but most Muslim children go to the Islamia School in Malerkotla. 'Why?' we asked. 'Because there is no deeniyat (religious instruction) in government schools,' said Sabri, an older woman who was the secretary of a women's SHG in the area.

'Baji, please stop for one minute at my house,' Rani insisted. As we entered, we saw someone waiting for us. It was her husband, who introduced himself as 'Gulrez, ex-sarpanch'. While the women looked on, the six-foot-three-inch tall man burst into tears. 'These afsars (officers), they hate us. A few of us got into an argument about the issuing of a bus pass from Malerkotla to Patiala. I was speaking on behalf of the passengers. The officer looked at me from head to toe and said, "We don't have to listen to you. We are not servants of Pakistan". My young nephew, Yasin, applied for enlistment. He kept getting turned down until, one day, a kind officer put a hand on his shoulder and said, "Why are you wasting your time and ours? The army doesn't hire Muslims". We listened sadly to these stories of discrimination and made a mental note to bring them up in our assessment of the efficacy of our schemes in this sector. We also asked ourselves if the deep-rooted discrimination and religious bigotry would break the lasting peace of Malerkotla. Would official apathy destroy a centuries-old legacy? Would the Muslims of Malerkotla experience the frustration and alienation we had seen among people in the bastis of Malegaon, Kashmir and Mewat?

With these thoughts, and somewhat saddened, we climbed back into the vehicles which hurtled along the bumpy road from Binjoli Khurd to the village of Uppal Kheri. Almost half of the 2,200 people of this village belong to the scheduled castes; Muslims are in a minority. The anganwadi centre had a mixed group of Muslim and Dalit children, both from families of wage labourers. Jaswinder Kaur, the anganwadi worker, was a postgraduate, and her helper, Paramjeet Kaur, had studied up to Class 5. Graduates and postgraduates were working as anganwadi teachers for a meagre monthly salary of Rs 1,000.[12] We found this to be a common feature across Punjab. It was a reflection, perhaps, of the high rate of unemployment among youth. In a spacious room with fans, toys, mats, charts and a blackboard there were twenty-four children who came to the centre from 8 a.m. to 12 noon. Examining the growth register, we were alarmed at the malnutrition levels. Children were getting more malnourished; moving from grade one malnutrition to rock-bottom at grade 4 level. 'Where are these children?' we asked Jaswinder Kaur. 'They do not come here any longer. They stay home; but there is no one there to care for them. We go to their homes every month to weigh them,' she explained. We asked the District Health Officer and Senior Medical Officer about these worsening malnutrition levels but got no satisfactory answer. One said it wasn't his responsibility. 'There is no ANM here,' shrugged the other. No ANM meant more than malnutrition.

---

[12] Presently revised to Rs 1,500.

Among other things, it signified no antenatal care and iron and folic acid tablets for women and adolescent girls. This village was more like villages we had seen in eastern Uttar Pradesh.[13]

A kind-looking sari-clad woman peeped inside the centre and beckoned us. 'I am Kavita Rani, the EGS teacher.' The EGS was running in an adjacent room as part of the Sarva Shiksha Abhiyan (SSA). Kavita explained that she had twenty-seven children in this bridge school programme where children of all ages are tutored to join mainstream education. We asked how the children were enrolled and whether they got midday meals.

'Most of these children have never been to school. I have to go from house to house to collect them. No, the children don't get midday meals.'

'What are your salary and qualifications?' we asked.

'I get Rs 1,000 per month and I have completed Class 12.' Then she added: 'To help their parents, the children work as child labour. Ten-year-old Azim used to tend animals until he joined the school a few months back. This is Parveena, she also worked.' She pointed to a young girl.

We turned to see a round-faced girl with a red dupatta covering her head. She looked no older than seven years but Kavita said she was nine. Not used to being the centre of attention, Parveena answered our questions with downcast eyes. She told us that she had three other siblings. Her eldest brother worked at a cycle shop; her youngest brother Yusuf was with her. 'Abba lakdi kattey hain.' (My father cuts wood.) On her teacher's prodding, she recited a poem in Punjabi, her hands dancing to the rhythm of the verse. We looked at her for a long time. Parveena, this beautiful child, would she ever reach her full potential through this EGS School?

From Uppal Kheri we drove to the hospital at Amargarh. This thirty-bed three-storey hospital known as a PHC cum CHC covered a population of 1.45 lakh people, spread over a fifteen-kilometre radius. All five doctors here were general practitioners; no specialists were available. At midday, the hospital was almost empty. Not a single person was attending the OPD. The senior medical officer and doctors answered all our questions. 'The Dera conflict has confined people to their homes.' 'They don't come because there are no specialists here.' 'People here are superstitious; they

---

[13] See Chapter 8

252 ⟶ Beautiful Country

don't visit hospitals on Thursday.' Their daily attendance, they said, was a hundred OPD patients. It was difficult to believe the figure in view of the dismal attendance.

Suddenly, there was a commotion. Angry residents from nearby areas streamed into the empty building and surrounded us. 'Madam, don't believe what you see,' the leader of the group, who introduced himself as Kartar Singh, said. 'This cleanliness and orderliness has happened overnight to impress you. There is no doctor here after 2 p.m. None of them stay in Amargarh; no emergency facilities are available. We don't even have private nursing homes in Amargarh, just small clinics. People are forced to go to Nabha or Malerkotla.'

By this time, we were feeling exhausted. But Kartar Singh's words released a spurt of energy. We climbed three flights of stairs leading to the wards. Empty beds were covered with clean, starched white sheets. But only four out of the total thirty were occupied. Two of them had young men who had sustained injuries in a brawl the previous evening. They said no doctor had attended them for two hours after they were admitted. A twenty-five-year-old girl, Amandeep Kaur, was the sole occupant of the female ward. She had been beaten up, and had sustained head injuries. It was a medico-legal case. She had been at the hospital for twelve days. We asked why she had not been discharged or referred to a specialist. The medical officer said that he had been instructed by the local MLA to keep her in hospital; they could neither refer nor discharge her.

We had come to Malerkotla with hope and, indeed, there were many things to learn from this small town of Punjab. But a lot was also going wrong. Amargarh was one example. So we decided to inspect the Civil Hospital at Malerkotla to see if this was a consistent pattern. This time, we decided to sneak out without giving any notice to see the real face of the healthcare system. We slipped past our entourage at the peak of the afternoon heat, with the sleepy driver we found at the wheel thankfully asking no questions. The first thing that struck us about the hospital was its cleanliness despite the crowd weaving its way in and out of the main entrance. Wards were filled with people. Long queues waited outside the ultrasound unit; an operation was underway in the operation theatre. This hundred-bed hospital had surgeons; a gynaecologist, an anaesthesiologist, a paediatrician, an orthopaedic surgeon and an internist. The place was equipped to handle several operations. It was 3 p.m. when we walked into the emergency unit, where we met the SMO (Senior Medical Officer) Dr R.S. Bal. He told us how the doctors at the hospital had pooled money to carry out pest control in the emergency unit. 'We want to do it for the entire hospital now.'

This visit put us in a better frame of mind. Our final destination was the Malerkotla Palace, which sits hidden within a mini-forest of trees and bushes; a crumbling monument of bygone splendour and magnificence. Begum Munawar-un-Nisa, the third wife of Nawab Iftikhar Ali Khan, the last royal descendant of the dynasty's founder, Sheikh Sadruddin Khan Sadr-i-Jahan, presides over this ruin. Our visit was arranged by the SDM, a kind-looking Sikh officer who was on his second posting here after a gap of ten years. The palace itself is as imposing a monument as the palaces of Kapurthala or Patiala. We were ushered into the erstwhile ballroom of the nawab. On its walls were sculpted the monograms of the riyasat. In many places, the ceiling had caved in. Here, the Begum sat on a grand weather-beaten sofa. Her beautiful face was delicately lined. She wore a green ghagara with a diaphanous dupatta. She spoke softly. 'Bibi, the story is too long. Where shall I start? I came as a bride in 1948 from the royal house of Tonk (Rajasthan). Sixty years later, here I am.' She smiled and her surma (kohl) lined eyes lit up.

'Begum Sahiba, where is the painting of your husband's ancestor Nawab Sher Mohammad Khan with Guru Gobind Singh's Sahibzadas, which was supposed to be preserved at the Gurudwara?' we asked. She did not know. On the wall behind her hung an imposing oil painting of her father-in-law, Nawab Ahmed Ali Khan, famous for building the city of Ahmedgarh, along the pattern of Lyallpur (now called Faisalabad) in Pakistan. Her husband had been elected MLA from Malerkotla. He married thrice; his three wives came from the ruling houses of Rampur, Tonk and Kurwai. There were no children. After his death, his estranged first wife, Begum Sajida succeeded him to the Punjab Assembly. Our hostess, Begum Munawar-un-Nisa, had been waiting for us for the last two hours and was feeling very tired. We had arrived too late to see her album of old photographs or the famous sword that Guru Gobind Singh bestowed on her husband's ancestor. The light outside was fading just like the dynasty of Malerkotla. 'Next time, I promise,' she said. 'Begum Sahiba, the palace needs to be preserved as a heritage monument,' we gently suggested as we were leaving. She did not reply. The SDM, after taking an affectionate leave of her, told us: 'She is very apprehensive that the state will take over her property'.

It was late when we left the land of the Sufi saint Hazrat Sheikh Sadruddin Sadr-i-Jahan, where the symbol of Sikh–Muslim unity, Nawab Sher Ali Khan of Malerkotla, lies buried. We realized how important it was to listen to the voices of this town and to nurture its inherent harmony. Malerkotla should not be allowed to go the way of Malegaon. The latter, with a Muslim majority, has today become the site of communal unrest and bomb blasts. During our visit there, we had seen the anger of youth who are branded terrorists, with little hope of getting justice.[14] Malerkotla, on the contrary, is humming with work and hope. India needs to learn from this part of Punjab.

The newly created district of Mewat, located next door to the country's capital and its political epicentre, offers a stark contrast to the eclecticism and pluralism of Malerkotla. Mewat, a region once famous for its confluence of religion and cultures, has over the years become increasingly rigid.

Mewat is the land of the Meo. Originally a Rajput clan, the Meo converted to Islam in the fourteenth century. Till the 1920s, they were known for their unique blend of Hindu and Muslim customs. They proudly adopted Islam and embraced the various Sufi saints who began settling in their territory from the eleventh century onwards. (Today, the shrines of these Mashaikh, who were sheikhs or Sufi teachers, are in ruins, scattered across the Mewat countryside.) At the same time, the Meo did not let go of either their Rajput roots or their claim that they are the direct descendants of Krishna and Rama. In fact, *Pandaun Ka Kara*, the Meo rendition of the Mahabharata, traces the origins of the community to the Pandava brothers. Composed in the early eighteenth century by Meo poet Saadullah Khan, this musical retelling of the great epic begins with an eulogy to Prophet Mohammad and to the Sufi saint, Khwaja Moinuddin Chishti of Ajmer. The

---

[14] See Chapter 6

Mirasis or the Meo Muslim performers then tell the tale of the Pandavas to an audience of mostly Mewati Muslims. This multicultural ethos, however, began to wane in the 1920s when Muhammad Ilyas started his experiment with the Tablighi Jama'at.[15] It was in Mewat that he began his revivalist movement, and by the 1940s, the Meo had become more rigid in their outlook. Yet, this growing radicalism did not find it easy to sink roots in a place where for centuries people had dipped in the confluence of various religious traditions. This became evident at the time of Partition. When Mahatma Gandhi went to the village of Ghasera and appealed to the Meo to stay back in India, most villagers heeded his plea. Time, official apathy and persistent efforts by the Tablighi Jama'at have, however, taken their toll on the Meo culture. Mewat, today, offers a very different picture.

Syeda: I had first visited Mewat in 1997 as a Member of the National Commission for Women to investigate a case of honour killing. At that time, it was still part of Gurgaon District. My destination was a small village called Sudaka, where an old couple Ibrahim and Manj Bi had been tied to a charpai (cot) and left to die in the blazing heat because their son, Idris, in defiance of local custom, had married a girl (Maimun) from his own gotra (clan). The custom of jaati (caste) and gotra are among several Hindu legacies which the Mewati Muslims have retained. We brought the case to a successful ending, little realizing that patriarchy would get the better of our efforts. Six years after her marriage, when she had become the mother of two, Maimun was killed by her own brother for bringing dishonour to the family. At that time, Mewat had given me sleepless nights; a decade later, when I visited with Gunjan, I found that not much had changed. Mewat seemed to be trapped in a time warp, dating back one hundred years.

---

[15] Literally meaning the Society for Spreading Faith, the Tablighi Jama'at was founded by Muhammad Ilyas in 1926 in Mewat. Many see it as a response to growing right-wing Hindu forces. Ilyas's cry 'O Muslims! Be Muslims!' expresses the central focus of Tablighi Jama'at; their aim was to renew Muslim society by uniting them in embracing the lifestyle of Muhammad. Today, the Jama'at has become a transnational movement, with almost seventy million followers in one fifty nations.

Unlike the glitz and glitter of neighbouring Gurgaon, Mewat is in perpetual darkness; starved of every aspect of development. There are no factories, no office complexes, no residential high-rises and no corporate structures. The roads, where they do exist, are in a poor state of repair. Besides two-wheelers and bullock carts, one sees the occasional battered jeep packed with people, the ubiquitous Ambassador cars of government officials, and a few shabby, overcrowded buses. Medical facilities and schools are much fewer than required. One thing is in abundance – Gurgaon's poor sibling is distinguished by the filth which litters most of the narrow gullis and roads.

We crossed Gurgaon to the dusty town of Sohna. At 10 a.m., children of all ages – toddlers to teenage girls and boys who should have been in school – were seen along the roadside. Some were playing in the dirt, others working at shops, in the fields or carrying headloads of firewood and fodder. Small faces covered with dirt, noses runny, hair discoloured, most of them were barefoot even as they ran through narrow lanes filled with gobar (cow dung), keechar (slush) and human excreta.

Our first stop was at Maalab – a village of 9,000 people, a drive of twenty minutes from the district headquarters along the main road. A group of women and girls materialized from nowhere. 'Do you go to school?' we asked twelve-year-old Shahina. She shook her head. Twelve-year-old Mehrunissa, ten-year-old Naseema and eleven-year-old Rehana had never seen the inside of a school. We turned to the mothers. 'Why don't you send them?' Ashubi, Shahina's young grandmother stared at us for a moment and said simply 'Mahaul kharaab hai.' (The conditions are bad.) She said that girls were sent to school till Class 1 or 2 and then withdrawn. This was the case everywhere in Mewat. None of the girls we spoke to attended regular school; only a few went to madrasas. A woman pushed her way to the front. 'What is the use of educating them? Naukri karvana nahin hai hum ko!'(We don't want them to get jobs.) A young girl with a child on her hip said, 'We would educate our daughters but only if there was a girls' school close by.' We looked around to see if others agreed but they stood in silence. What they did not say was that these little girls look after younger siblings, help parents in the fields and at home. Who would do all this if they went to school?

Mahmudi, a middle-aged woman in a bright salwar suit, had put down her headload of fodder to join the group. 'What is the use of sending them to school or anganwadi? The sarpanch keeps all the rations at his house. Children are rarely given food and whatever they are given they don't eat.' Sabra, who was carrying her scrawny little grandson, Aqil, said that he didn't go to the anganwadi. 'They send our children away. Besides, it is across a busy road. How can I send him alone?' she said hugging the child to her chest.

By this time, we had reached the compound of the combined school and anganwadi. We noticed a bunch of kids near the water tap. At least, there is drinking water in this school, we thought. 'Baji,' said an old man with henna-dyed beard, 'These taps get water once in fifteen days.' He then pointed to a dirty old drum lying near the tap. 'This is filled by a tanker every day.' We looked on as children dipped a dirty glass into the drum and raised it to their lips.

The anganwadi was a collection of six centres under a single roof. One hundred and fifty women and children were milling inside a covered shed. Chaos prevailed. A thin woman held a stick which she used to 'discipline' the kids. 'Is this how you treat children?' we reprimanded her. She admitted she hit the children, 'but not with this stick. I just shake it in their face'. A few children were eating murri (puffed rice) and gur ke laddu (jaggery balls). This was their supplementary nutrition; there was no cooked food. 'Pregnant and lactating women get six laddus every week,' Akbari informed us. Her bahu (daughter-in-law), Rukhsana, was nursing her grandson, Kaif. Her one-year-old granddaughter, however, got nothing. The stick-wielding woman, Maryam Khatun, told us that since children below three could not be given laddus, they were given panjeere (a mixture made of whole wheat flour, nuts, gaund and sugar) on a weekly basis. The obvious signs of malnutrition – pot-bellies, scrawny legs, wasted limbs and yellow hair and eyes – were visible all over.

'Are they weighed?'

'No.'

'Do you ever give them deworming medicines?'

'Yes, last year. Then the supply ran out.'

'Can they recite poems?'

'Baji, how can I teach poems? I can barely hear my own voice in this din.'

It was clear that in this massive crowd of 150 children, nothing was possible other than stuffing their little stomachs with laddus and panjeere.

Outside, a group of men was waiting for us. A dark-glasses-wearing ex-sarpanch of the village with a smart henna-dyed beard spoke. 'Baji, we have a dawakhana (dispensary) but the sister visits once in ten days. Dawa bhi nahin hai (no medicines either). We have to go to private doctors or travel all the way to Alwar,' he said. Others concurred. The district officials accompanying us denied this vehemently. So we decided to visit the nearby subcentre.[16]

We got to a dilapidated building with a boarded-up door. Excreta and cow dung lay scattered between pools of stagnant water. Mosquitoes and flies were thick. There was no signboard marking the centre and not a soul around. 'This is the subcentre,' the villagers said. On the door, just above the lock, in neat handwriting was scribbled – '28. 2. 2007. *Rajender Singh going to Village Maalab for surveillance, Bhagmati going to Village Maalab for surveillance*'. All this was written in English in a place where hardly anyone could read or write. A group of village women explained, 'Doctarni to aati hain par woh yaha nahi baithti. Iss gandagi mein unki tabiyat kharab ho jaati hai.' (Nurse does come but she doesn't sit here because she falls ill due to the filth.)

The district hospital was our next stop. Al Aafiya General Hospital at Mandi Khera is a grand structure which was funded by the Sultan of Oman. It is built twenty-two km from the district headquarters, on an isolated parcel of land. The place was quite empty. In preparation for our visit, the floors had been freshly scrubbed but only six out of the fifty beds had patients. We saw empty beds in a district brimming with health problems! Even the enquiry booth was empty. 'We get eighty OPD patients in a day but

---

[16] A subcentre is the first point of contact between the primary healthcare system and the community. Typically, a sub-centre covers a population of five thousand in the plains and three thousand in the hill and tribal areas. Under the new IPHS (Indian Public Health Standards) Guidelines the staff at a subcentre has been increased from one ANM and one multipurpose health worker to two ANMs and one multipurpose health worker.

we are very short-staffed. We have managed to get two retired specialists on contract but we have no anaesthetist, no surgeon, not even enough nurses,' said a tired-looking CMO. The district had placed an order for its first ultrasound machine but the hospital did not have any operating technician. In many rooms, the electrical fittings were not working. Buzzing sounds emanated from mosquitoes and flies rather than from fans. Embarrassed doctors pointed outside the window to the surrounding fields. 'Inevitable,' they muttered.

In the gynaecology ward, there were three patients. Hafiza, a young woman from Sudaka had delivered just two days earlier. We were surprised to learn that, in this single district hospital, on an average there were only thirty deliveries every month. In January and February only eighteen babies had been delivered. And the district has an average family size of 8–10! The other two women were bleeding. Parveena had come from Firozpur Jhirka. She was three-months pregnant and extremely anaemic but had received neither tetanus shots nor IFA (iron and folic acid) tablets. Phairun from Akera village had a similar story to tell. We spoke to a few women lingering at the gate who were seven- and nine-months pregnant. They had never received any antenatal care, iron tablets or even tetanus shots. Mandi Khera was too far from the populated parts of Mewat. People had no means to get there. The district collector complained that there were only thirty-three buses plying in the entire district. 'In a place where people live close to each other, these distances are formidable; Mewat is not connected by railways either,' he informed us.

As our cars moved towards our next destination, the village of Tain, the road seemed familiar. We stopped to ask a group of elderly tehmat-clad (long loincloth also known as a lungi) men, 'Janaab yeh raasta kahan jaata hai?' (Sir, where does this road lead?)

'To Sudaka.'

Sudaka! This was the village where the Maimun Idris tragedy had played out ten years earlier! A decade later, not much had changed. Garbage dumps, ankle-deep slush and dirt roads. Naked children with mud-streaked skeletal bodies, women, faces covered with heavy dupattas, carrying water or headloads of fodder. Where was the hope in this heart of darkness, we wondered.

Six kilometres down the road, however, a sliver of hope showed up in the village of Tain. A group of women, some in bright salwars, others in neatly pleated saris, were waiting for us with garlands. 'We are from the bachat (saving) groups,' they said. A tall, thin woman, Bano, in a white salwar kameez, her face half-hidden with a dupatta, told us how she had started by saving Rs 5–10 every month. 'Gradually, I moved to Rs 50. I first took a loan and set up a shop for my son, Dildar. This I repaid and then took Rs 7,000 to set up my own shop. Profit was good, and soon I was able to borrow another Rs 25,000 for expansion. I work from morning till night at the shop but I am happy.' Shahina, her daughter-in-law who was tending the little kirana (ration) shop, dusted some stools and invited us to sit. Bano, her half-visible face looking radiant, added: 'Baji, with your blessings, we earn Rs 3,000 a month.'

Gradually, we heard other stories of women's triumph. Waheeda had started a choori (bangle) shop, Halima a chakki (grinding mill), Omvati a ration shop. The women told us how, initially, they had to cut on their 'ration paani' to save for the group. 'But now we have enough to eat.' Most of them had husbands and sons who smoked hookah all day. So their savings and shops were the sole means of support for the family. 'We will now buy buffaloes and start, what do you call it …,' Bano turned to Shahina. 'Amma, it is called Amul, Co-operative Doodh Andolan,' she said laughing. Bano turned to us and spoke words which we remember till date: 'Baji, if the women in Gujarat can do it, so can we.' Kanta, a young girl in a sari, the parting in her hair marked with bright sindoor, came forward. She was among the few literate women in a gathering of over a hundred people. 'Give us buffaloes and water, and see what we do!' she challenged us.

We left Tain with the words of Bano and Kanta echoing in our head. These women were finally breaking the shackles of tradition that had been eating into the vitals of a vibrant society. Our final stop was at the village of Ghasera. In May 2005 when Syeda had first come here, she had visited the village school where girls of all ages had been placed together in a single classroom. They were being taught the rhyme 'Twinkle, Twinkle Little Star'. Yet their eyes held no twinkle of understanding. The school had no electricity, no drinking water and no toilets. At the time, she had been assured that all this would change within a year. We had returned two years later to find that the girls' school had a building and electric poles but electricity supply was still intermittent. We saw the wires hanging out of fuse-boxes. Students pointed to the dust-covered fan hanging precariously from the ceiling. 'We have never seen it working.' Drinking water was not available. However, a few classrooms had been added. Inside one sat some forty students of Class 12, thirty-nine of them male. Among them, somewhat ill-at-ease, was the only girl, sixteen-year-old Shamshad.

Not much had changed for this school, just like not much had changed for Mewat and its twelve lakh inhabitants. Illiteracy, malnutrition, unemployment, gender discrimination, lack of sanitation and hygiene – the problems were still the same. Intense backwardness in a sea of prosperity! But our visit opened new possibilities. Our report to the deputy chairman of the Planning Commission was an important factor in the government's decision to extend NREGS (National Rural Employment Guarantee Scheme) to Mewat. This was before the scheme was universalized to cover all the six hundred districts of the country. It was but a beginning. Brick by brick, the foundation will have to be built to make Ghasera, Gandhiji's favourite Mewati village, become part of the growth trajectory on which Haryana is firmly set.

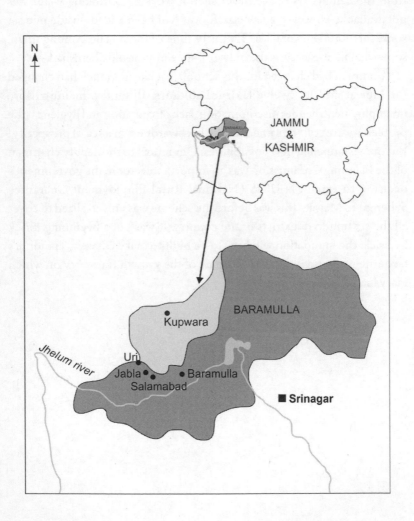

10

Kashmir

Agur firdaus bar roo e zameen ast
Humeen asto hameen asto hamoon ast'

— Jahanara

If on earth there be a heaven of bliss,
It is this, it is this, it is this

May 2007. 'Koi hamare liye kuch kyon karega, hum to doosra mulk hain na …' (Why will anyone do anything for us? We are another country after all.)

Mohammad Latif, the man who uttered these chilling words had hollow eyes and drooping shoulders. A few of us were standing in the same precincts where we had stood nineteen months ago – the village of Jabla in Kashmir. What we saw around us was neither anger nor expectation, only an overriding despondency born of the feeling that no one cared.

'Doosra mulk?' (Another country?) we repeated.

'Yes. One-and-a-half years after the earthquake, we continue to shiver in tin sheds, without water and rozgaar (work). Our children study under the open sky. No one has come to our rescue – neither the government nor NGOs. Look at Gujarat. There too, an earthquake had shattered lives. But, today, they are back on track because people cared.'

We wanted to say, 'No, that's not true, of course we care.' We wanted to argue, to convince the people who had gathered around us despite the chilly drizzle. We wanted to add: 'Kashmir and its people matter – matter a lot.' But as we went around their villages, visiting health centres, schools and makeshift homes, we understood why people were losing faith. The anguish and dejection we witnessed in the Valley left us with one haunting question – Do we really care? And today, as we think back to those words, each one rings true. As the Valley resounds with cries of 'Azadi' (freedom), and hundreds of youth fall to the bullets of the security forces, people ask, 'If we are your 'atoot ang' (indivisible part) why are you killing us?' No one has an answer, neither then nor now.

Jabla was Latif's village; it had lost everything in the massive earthquake of October 2005. 'Not a single one of the 350 houses here was left standing; village roads and water-supply pipes were broken and nineteen people were killed,' an accompanying official told us. The village is only twelve kilometres from the town of Uri but it had taken us an hour to get here because there was no road beyond the village of Salamabad. As our vehicles jumped and rattled over the mud track littered with broken stones which led to the village, we read a freshly painted sign: 'Pradhan Mantri Grameen Sadak Yojana' (Prime Minister's Rural Roads Scheme). There was however, no sign of a road.

When we reached Jabla, the villagers were waiting. 'Now you know what we face each day. We don't have Gypsy cars. No roads, no public transport, just our feet,' they said. 'But what about the Pradhan Mantri Grameen Sadak Yojana sign we saw just as we drove up?' we asked. A few people smiled – there was something about the sadness, tolerance and amusement in that smile that tugged at the heart. 'A road was sanctioned under the scheme last year but not for us. It goes somewhere else. Our only link to this road is that they have cut our trees and taken away some of our land.'

'What about compensation?'

'No, we have recieved nothing yet.'

The first thing we saw in the village was a newly painted building with a big sign: Government Unani Dispensary. A lock hung on its door. 'The doctor visits once or twice a week. For the rest, we go to Uri Hospital. There is no dawakhana (medical centre) here.' The man who spoke wore a grey salwar suit with a black jacket. 'Baji, there is no "sister" here,' a bent old woman was tugging at my shawl. 'Our women go into labour and give birth at home. They can never survive the eight-km hill journey (twelve kilometres if you go by road via Salamabad) to the Uri Hospital.' We asked her name. 'Shahnaz Begum.' Placing hands on her shoulder, we asked, 'Is there daaktri janch (doctor's examination) for the women? Is there training for dais (midwives) in your village?' She told us that the sole activity carried out here under the Government of India's National Rural Health Mission was selection of village girls as ASHAs.

Inside the village, we saw children in red uniforms sitting in a grove of almond trees. A few blackboards had been placed against the tree trunks. From a distance we could hear the teacher's voice. This was the Jabla Government Middle School. 'The village had two primary and one middle school. The earthquake destroyed all three of them. One primary school building has been constructed again – two rooms for six classes. The other is being built,' explained Mohammed Zuber. He was a college student working as a temporary teacher, rehbar-e-taleem, at the middle school with a salary of Rs 1,500 per month. His appointment would be confirmed only after completing five years of service. 'I am lucky; at least I have work. Most of the youth of our village have completed Class 10 or 12, some even graduation, and yet they have nothing.'

The middle school has 200 children. The destroyed building had six classrooms. Now, villagers have converted a community hall built after the earthquake to a school. But there isn't enough room for all. So, most classes take place in the open. On cold and rainy days, children get a holiday. During the break, we saw some children playing carrom. Carrom boards have been donated by an NGO – one of the few which has persisted in its rehabilitation work in the Valley.

Parents standing around told us that there were no midday meal, toilets, or clean drinking water at the primary school since the earthquake. This was the case all over Uri. Most people knew nothing about the Government of India's Sarva Shiksha Abhiyan. This was one of the few places where the ubiquitous SSA signboard with a boy and a girl sitting on a pencil see-saw, was missing. Just outside the village, however, a small board in front of a kiosk read 'SSA', albeit without the drawing. 'The sign is here. Perhaps the

Abhiyan will eventually reach. After all, it's a tough climb to the village,' the people laughed.

One turn on the path beyond the school brought before us the gentle, undulating valley with wisps of cloud resting on mountainsides. The tin rooftops of houses sparkled every time they caught the eye of the sun; a tributary of River Jhelum meandered through the green-yellow meadow while the snow-covered peaks watched over its course through a thin veil of rain. It was jannat (paradise) indeed; yet it was barely able to hide within its tranquillity the post-earthquake misery visible everywhere.

The village itself had become a heap of debris, broken houses and temporary sheds. The slope was steep and the small rocks scattered around by the earthquake made the walk tough. Steps were broken and planks were placed to enable people to climb. We passed a flat tin sheet resting on a mass of rubble. This was once a two-storey building. 'My house,' said Jamaluddin, standing up from his crouching position beside the wooden logs which were holding up his current roof, a plastic sheet. 'Now nine of us live in this temporary shed. There is no money to clear the debris which was once my house.'

Mazhar Husain, from Hyderabad, who has worked consistently in this area, shared some disturbing facts with us. 'Immediately after the earthquake, the Air Force conducted an aerial survey. From the choppers, they could see tin rooftops. So they assumed that the houses were still standing and reported "All is well". But what they had seen were roofs which had collapsed and were now lying on the ground; the houses underneath them were gone. It was a long time before relief reached these places!' He sighed. 'What we see from a distance, whether in Delhi or Srinagar, is often an illusion. Reality is generally buried under tin roofs, which sparkle in the sun and project a deceptive sense of well-being.'

As we moved further into the village, we noticed that, even nineteen months after the quake, people continued to live in shelters that are too hot in summer and too cold in winter. The rooms were small, cramped and dingy. There wasn't enough space to fit their beds and utensils. All the belongings were kept in the open. We saw women boiling dirty water in vessels on firewood. People complained that water from Jabla was being piped to Salamabad, but no attempt was being made to restore water supply to the village. Women were forced to walk one-and-a-half kilometres across hilly terrain every day to fetch water. Meanwhile, families were using the debris and adding new construction material to slowly rebuild their houses, one wall at a time. This mix of old and new means an unstable structure which will not be safe in an earthquake-prone area.

As we sat with the villagers, they spoke about matters close to their hearts. Akbaruddin's long white beard quivered as he spoke: 'We were given Rs 30,000 for a temporary shelter and Rs 1 lakh for a permanent house. But post-earthquake, rates of construction material and labour, Allah Allah! Earlier, we got iron at Rs 2,000 per quintal. Now it costs Rs 3,800. Similarly, a bora (bag) of cement costs Rs 270. Timber is not available. There is also the cost of transporting the material from Salamabad by headloads'. Labour costs had doubled, at times tripled, because very few Bihari labourers came to this border area due to the tough and lengthy procedure of verifying their papers.

'Currently, building a two-room structure (one room and one kitchen) with a toilet, costs Rs 2 lakh. The compensation money was so little that it was spent on consumption expenditure. Of the 350 houses in Jabla, only three have been reconstructed,' explained Mazhar, whose organization, COVA (Confederation of Voluntary Associations), is building nine permanent houses in Jabla.

At least twenty villages around Jabla have also lost everything in the quake. Yet 950 families in these villages are still to receive full compensation. A tired-looking man was pushed forward. 'Look at him. This is Abdul Kaleem. During the zalzala (earthquake), his house collapsed, crushing his little daughter to death. Yet, he received no money for rebuilding. He has five surviving children who stay under the open sky. The Aga Khan Foundation is providing him with labour, but how will he get the construction material?' asked Nasir, a young volunteer of COVA.

We were quiet; the answer came from a young gram sevak, Liaqat. 'Remove the VAT and taxation from construction material for a couple of months. Make the materials affordable and provide people with an incentive to rebuild quickly. After all, who wants to live like this?' A round of applause broke out and the villagers suddenly looked at us with hope. 'You did this in Gujarat. Why not here? Please,' Liaqat pleaded. We nodded. Their demand made sense. The discussion continued. Then the women came forward. Kumdad Begum, a widow with four sons, had lost her husband and her house in the earthquake. 'I am homeless now. Compensation money was given to my sons. They threw me out.' She looked away to hide her tears.

Rakeeba, a young widow with five children spoke, about the anganwadi. 'The worker is from Salamabad, so it rarely opens. Even when it does, it just gives a little khichdi or chana (chickpea) to children'.[1] Her seven-year-old twin children, Imtiaz and Ayaz, suffer from polio. She gets disability pension to support them. During this visit, we saw at least five polio-affected kids. The officials claimed that these were earthquake victims trying to pose as polio-affected. Our guess was that these children had been afflicted by polio before the Pulse Polio campaign started in the Valley.

Finally, we reached the anganwadi centre, which was situated in the helper's house, outside the village. It was a steep climb without a proper path. A newly painted signboard claimed that it opened from 10 a.m. to 3 p.m. every day. Inside, a dozen children, a couple of adolescent girls and half a dozen women with small babies were sitting on mats. The villagers accompanying us were surprised. 'Not just the worker and helper, but even the supervisor is here today. We have never seen this before.'

We asked for the growth registers to check the incidence of malnutrition. 'They were destroyed by the zalzala,' the helper replied.

'That was one-and-a-half years ago. Haven't you started fresh registers?'

'They are stocked at the Langma office. We haven't received them yet. But you can see the attendance and nutrition registers.'

We opened the attendance register and started the roll call. Nine children in the three-to-six-years age-group were listed. 'Rehmat.' The worker pointed to a small boy but he refused to look up. 'Shakeel.' Again, there was silence. The worker spoke a few words in Kashmiri. One of our team members, a young girl who understood Kashmiri, whispered in our ear. 'The worker just told the women to point out any child. "They are all the same. How does it matter?" So young Dawood, whose name did not figure in the register, was made to answer as Shakeel. We asked to see the

---

[1] Khichdi, we learnt, is considered the most unpalatable food in the Valley.

weighing machines. A long hunt started. Ultimately, the worker said that the machines were lost in the zalzala; we had seen what there was to see and understood the helplessness, complicity and, yes, the courage of ordinary people. We left Jabla to travel back to Srinagar with one last stop at Bandi, where we wanted to visit the sub-centre.

En route, we saw permanent houses being constructed. In Nopura village, the houses were being built by the Chennai-based NGO, Help the Child. For two rooms, one kitchen and one bathroom, their cost was Rs 1.5 lakh. Since the houses were by the roadside and closer to Salamabad, the construction material was cheaper. We spoke to a group of women who were standing at the roadside. Khaleda and Rabeena, said that their children, aged seven and eight, were afflicted by polio. They did not get any disability pension. Nahida Bano said she did not take her eighteen-month old Zohreen, to the AWC. 'What's the point? The centre only provides food to children between three to six years of age.' 'What about pregnant women, children under three, lactating mothers?' we asked. 'Nothing,' came the reply. No antenatal care, no iron and folic acid tablets and no weighing machine; this was the story of the Nopura centre.

Just below the Bandi Guest House, there was a beautiful building with a board reading 'Bandi Sub-Centre'. It had five rooms; the largest one had five beds. The place was empty but for a compounder who was sitting idly at his desk reading a magazine. 'A few people come in for dressings. I have some basic medicines here but the beds are never used since there is no ANM,' he said, his voice matter of fact.

We learnt that the centre did not have any water supply either. Curious, we asked, 'What do you do with the other rooms?'

'Oh, these! They are used for meetings when officials like you visit.'

On the return journey to Srinagar, we followed the Jhelum all the way. As one travels in the state, savouring the sights and sounds of the Valley, it becomes difficult to remember the raw hurt beneath its unblemished beauty. Yet, the khaki-clad young men with guns and rifles patrol every nook and corner, scrutinizing ordinary wayfarers; their jackboots and storm helmets were grim reminders of the pain and trauma that the ordinary Kashmiri women, men and children suffer on a daily basis.

Syeda: I was born in Kashmir. Wherever I go, I say this with great pride. At heart, I am a Kashmiri; technically I am not. The state law requires that a person should have Kashmiri parents before she can claim to belong to the soil. My parents were not Kashmiris although my father served seven years as director of education in Kashmir in the 1940s. After that, he had several stints in Kashmir during the time of Shaikh Mohammad Abdullah, Bakshi Ghulam Mohammad and G.M. Sadiq. When I became Member, Planning Commission, I was given charge of Kashmir for two years. That reason alone took me there often. My first visit was in the summer of 2004.

After landing in Srinagar, we were taken by road to District Kupwara, which is a 'militancy infested area'. Kupwara is a hilly district with 369 villages of which four are uninhabited. The literacy rate is just 59 per cent for males and 26 per cent for females. We noticed that the entire district administration, including the divisional commissioner, was following us in a long cavalcade of cars.

At Qaziabad village, Handwara Tehsil, our cars stopped in front of a sign: *'Boys Middle School, Palpura'.* As we entered the dilapidated school building, we found a verandah crammed with young girls! In this two-room school, eight classes were being held. The girls, heads covered with dupattas, were sitting on durries with open textbooks. We asked Hamida, a student of Class 7, to read the first paragraph from her English text. Neither she nor her friends, Shiraza Bano, Afroza and Jamila, were able to read a word of English. We picked up an Urdu book and opened a random page. What we found left us numb. It was a social studies lesson on tradition and culture. The page had a description of dead bodies, cremations and burning ghats. Hamida hung her head, probably in shame for failing the reading test. We wanted to hang ours for an altogether different reason.

Some mothers from nearby villages, having heard of our visit, had arrived at the school; they were full of plans for their girls. Raja Begum wanted to educate her daughter 'as long as I am able to'. Shamshada Bano complained that the school's uniform fund had been used for 'building vilding.' We certainly could not see any evidence of this building, which had deprived children of uniforms.

Outside the school, in an open ground, the gram sabha meeting was being held. The banner in Urdu read 'Qaziabad Gram Sabha'. Hundreds of men were seated in the front while the women were huddled at the back. We were promptly handed a sheaf of petitions – demands for school buildings, pensions, and complaints about distress sales of agricultural produce. Their submissions were written as qasidas (Urdu verses), in beautiful poetry.

Not far from the gram sabha, in Wudpura village, the panchayat was meeting, presided by Sarpanch Mohammed Yusuf Dar. It represented four villages: Wudpura, Takia Wudpura, Zandbadi and Khurramabad, with a total of seven members. In the meetings, which were held every Sunday, only men participated.

'Where are the women?' we asked.

The men were surprised. 'We didn't know that women should also participate. But if you say so, we will call them to our future meetings,' they promised.

On some of our enquiries, there was complete confusion. We asked: 'Where are your anganwadi centres for children under six?'

Some men said that there was one anganwadi in the village but no food for the children. Some women standing at the back shouted that there was no anganwadi in the area. Everybody said that there was no midday meal for children in schools. Then they presented their own list of demands.

'We need clean drinking water since we drink from the nullah.'

'A decent school building is very essential.'

'Our children's lives are in danger; we need a speed breaker on the national highway going past our village.'

'A bund for flood protection would be a good idea.'

The list was much longer.

A few angry women accosted us as we left the venue of the gram sabha. 'The government discriminates between children. Why is this?' It took us a few minutes to understand what they were saying. They were referring to the National Foundation for Communal Harmony, which is part of the Ministry of Home Affairs. One of its programmes is to fund education of orphans of militancy, but not of militants. 'Children are children,' cried one old woman wiping her eyes and nose with a yellow handkerchief. 'Remember, this is Kupwara. Here, a man goes to the 'other side' and disappears; for no fault of theirs, the wife and children are driven to penury. And when he is killed, you people reject his children. I ask you, when they grow up, what will they become?' We heard that the district has 4,600 children who receive nothing from the government because their fathers, who were killed, have been declared militants. We were horrified and decided to take up the issue. (This was one change we were able to effect; the Foundation now funds the education of orphans of militancy as well as of militants.)

That was in the summer of 2004. On 8 October 2005, life came to a standstill on both the Indian and Pakistani sides of Kashmir. Almost one-and-a-half years later, we found ourselves in the Kashmir Valley again. The earth heaved and retched and smashed everything it could; its massive impact respected no borders or boundaries. We rushed to Srinagar. On 10 October, we were on the Gulmarg road, heading towards Uri, one of the two worst earthquake-affected areas. Our driver, Ghulam Ahmed, a cheerful, friendly man, was observing Ramadan. As we passed through Baramulla, the phone connectivity ended. We had no means of finding out what the road condition was, and what lay ahead.

Our first stop was at Kathmulla. The car turned into the NHPC (formerly the National Hydroelectric Power Corporation) office compound. Here, the chief engineer, Khalid Umar, was waiting to take us around. He spoke of the massive damage in Uri town. 'Nearby, in Mohra village, the buildings are beyond repair. The same is true of Bandi, the sub-divisional headquarter of Uri.' Homes that had once been privy to the joys and sorrows of men and women had been reduced to a pile of rubble. The car began to slowly move on the BRO constructed road, most of which had been broken by the impact.

Passing a check-post, we saw army jawans inspecting the ID cards of Kashmiri men and women, standing in long lines before being allowed to proceed towards what was left of their houses. On both sides of the main road lay the ruins of buildings of the Pir Panjal Regiment. A huge army shopping plaza had been reduced to mounds of rubble and stone. The regiment's movie theatre, Sridhar, where the soldiers watched Bollywood films late into the evening, was gone.

Passing over the Sridhar Bridge, we entered the village of Jallu; ruined houses and shops lined both sides of the road. On reaching Salamabad village, we stopped at the Uri II campus of the NHPC. Some houses in the enclosure had turned to rubble; others had developed massive cracks. Khalid said that there were no casualties here but the bus stop and canteen were gone. The road itself had disappeared in parts. On the street, people were raising slogans: 'We want rahat (relief) we want mua'avza (compensation)'. Fresh landslides were visible all over; the mountains were graphite – soft, brittle and easily collapsible. In the distance, a holy ziarat (shrine) had collapsed. Near it, a truck stood, its bonnet crushed by a huge boulder. Someone pointed towards Kamalkot village, situated in the heart of the mountain across from where we were standing. 'Two days earlier, it was inaccessible. Forty bodies were recovered only yesterday.' A crisp wind started; signs by the roadside saying 'Medical Service Available' were flapping this way and that, giving contrary directions.

It was here that we met Mohammed Safir and Safina, with their two small children. They were walking towards the command post.

'Where are you going?' we asked.

'To Parampillon, our village, which is up in the mountains,' Safir answered. He had learnt that it was gone; all the two hundred houses were destroyed. 'My father's name is Ghulam Hasan. He was in the village,' he said, his voice choking up. 'We were in Srinagar. I am a labourer; my children go to school there.' He told us that he had seen a truck full of thirty-eight mazdoors (labourers), buried in a landslide.

With news of death at every step, moving on was becoming emotionally draining. A few words of sympathy seemed too little but it was all we could offer. Our cars drove past the villages of Dulauja and Urus, both of which had been flattened. In fact, as we drew closer to the border command post, the entire ground was flat; all the villages were gone. 'About 30,000 to 40,000 people are unaccounted for,' an accompanying official informed us. We saw trucks carrying relief materials with banners which read: 'Kashmiri Bakers and Confectioners', 'Darul Uloom Bandipore', 'Waqf Board, J&K'. Nearby, we saw women sitting by the side of the road. A sign said 'Village Kalgi'; that was all that was left of their erstwhile village. We approached a young girl who was supporting an older woman. 'My name is Saleema. This is my mother,

Gulshan Fatima. We have lost 350 homes in our village. We cannot enter our houses. We are so afraid they will crumble on our heads.' We looked around and saw that they were staying in small trekking tents which had crawl space only for one. Just as we were getting into our vehicle after a last look at the ravaged mountainside, a man with bloodshot eyes came into view. 'Aap ko kuchh mila?' (Did you find anything?) we asked hesitantly. He looked straight into our eyes and remained silent. His face has been etched in our minds since.

A visit to Lalla Ded Hospital has been a compulsory stop for us during all our trips to the Valley. Besides the fact that we looked after the health sector, the doctor who delivered Syeda, a lady called 'Dr Gabbay' (which could be an Indianized version of Gauba) was associated with the precursor of this hospital. Lalla Ded is located in the heart of Srinagar. It is named after the Vaishnav–Sufi saint, poet, philosopher, Lalla or Lalleshwari, whose vakhyas (verses) are on the lips of Kashmiri Muslims and Hindus alike, and stands next to Lal Chowk in the city centre. Lalla Ded is the most renowned women's hospital in Kashmir. In Delhi, it is still referred to as Dufferin Hospital, after the wife of a British Agent, Lord Dufferin. The first sight that greets one is milling crowds in the compound outside the hospital. Patients and their families occupy every inch of space. When we entered the reception area, we saw policemen pushing the crowd to clear the way. 'Stop it,' we shouted at one policeman, using our arms to shove him off the young man he was pushing out. The visit had begun badly.

Inside, the place was packed with people. We heard that the place had originally been a fruit mandi (market). There was a foul smell of rotting fish, probably a combination of phenyl and wet mops. Hundreds of people were outside and inside the OPD in various rooms and halls. Queues upon queues stood patiently in the sun. In the long corridor of the treatment wing, we saw women sitting on the bare floor, lined up against the walls. All of them were holding tiny infants in their lap. We bent down to touch a pair of tiny toes emerging from a shawl. 'This is Bushra,' said the woman, uncovering the pink bundle. 'My daughter Sughra is upstairs. Operation took three hours.'

We saw two dark eyes and a grubby face covered by the other end of the woman's shawl. 'Anam, her older sister,' the woman explained. 'I had nowhere to leave her.'

Grandmothers, sisters, and various other female relatives were waiting for newborn babies' immunization. Some hungry ones had begun to cry for their mothers who were recovering in the wards from various surgical procedures. The accompanying doctors said that the number of patients has increased phenomenally over the last seventeen years since the hospital was established, but no additional facilities or spaces have been provided.

'We have been waiting in line since 7 a.m.,' said a woman who identified herself as Jamila. She was standing at the head of the queue outside the OPD. Although it was past noon, her wait was not over. 'There is no dawakhana in our village.' She said that she had left Pampore after fajar prayer at 5.30 a.m. 'There is no guarantee my turn will come before the shut down time at 12.30 p m. Besides, it is only friends and relatives of doctors who get priority. Believe me, Baji, we have to bribe just to enter the hospital.'

'We have six units with around forty–fifty beds,' a harassed-looking doctor said. 'On an average, one hundred patients per unit are admitted in a day. At this time, there are 400 in-patients. Two, sometimes three, women on each bed, tucked under blood-stained sheets, are a common sight in our maternity wards.' And this is exactly what we saw. Women were packed on the bed like pairs of shoes. Some were ready to deliver, others recovering from delivery. Even in the labour rooms, women were made to double up. We saw six women sitting outside on the floor of the corridor holding their IV drips. We thought of the 200-bed multi-specialty G.B. Pant Hospital in Srinagar city. Constructed in 1992, this hospital was expected to ease the burden on Lalla Ded but had not been commissioned yet. (It has since started functioning and taken the excess load off Lalla Ded.)

Passing the Operation Theatre, we saw that it had six beds. From the hall we could see a woman giving birth, her body uncovered. An old bucket to catch the placenta was in place at the foot of the table, and male attendants freely walked around. In the room for premature and underweight babies, about a hundred children were admitted on any single day. Tiny babies with scrawny legs had birth weights as low as 1.2 kg. There were several incubators, but only two ventilators. There was no sonography or ultrasound to monitor babies before birth.

In our travels around the country, we have often witnessed crowded hospitals with severe shortage of doctors and staff; yet Lalla Ded shocked us. For 700 to 800 OPD patients, there were only ten doctors and two consultants. One nurse attended to seventy patients. Paediatricians, anaesthesiologists, and gynaecologists were scarce. The supervisors told us that they had asked their recently retired staff, some eighty-five doctors, to come back on contract but they were unwilling to return. 'Why would anyone with ambition and opportunity work for a base salary of Rs 8,000, which, including perks, adds up to a princely sum of Rs 16,000?' they said, speaking with a degree of sadness. We recalled seeing the same situation in Kupwara. There, too, the healthcare system had collapsed because of non-availability of doctors and nurses. The district had been asking for a mobile maternity unit, which is essentially just a jeep, fitted with basic maternity care. We heard that, in three months, nine or ten women had died of bleeding or of other pregnancy-related complications in Kupwara.

'I am Shaukat Ahmed from Sopore. My brother needed blood but it was not available in the hospital. We somehow managed to arrange it from outside, but there was no one to administer it. He died,' said a man, stopping us as we were getting in the car. With tear-filled eyes, Nilofer, a woman in her thirties who was standing behind Shaukat, made bold to grab our hands. 'My eighteen-year-old Naushad, she has been in labour for three days as the child is ulta (upside-down) in her uterus,' she sobbed. 'No surgery has been performed by the doctors, they are not telling me anything.' She pushed another woman before me. 'This is Shamima, my sister-in-law. Her daughter has been visiting the hospital regularly for check-ups. She was told that both she and the baby were fine. But, suddenly, after the delivery, the doctor has declared the baby dead, and the mother's condition is serious.'

Scant resources and poor management in Lalla Ded can be seen in the eyes of the distressed patients and the tired and overburdened doctors. In four years, we visited this maternity and child hospital three times, and each time we came back determined to make a difference. Two years later, things are beginning to look better. Some of Lalla Ded's burden has been taken away by the new G.B. Pant Hospital, and efforts to recruit doctors have been placed on fast track. But the sadness of that first visit, neither birdsong nor the fragrance of roses in the Srinagar State Guest House in Sonwar could dispel. We climbed to the 1,500-year-old Shankaracharya temple, hoping to find some solace but it only served to remind Syeda of her youth when this pre-breakfast climb had been easy. Now there was no breath left after the first flight. Gunjan ran to the top, wrapped in the exhilaration which only the mountain air can impart.

A shikara ride on the placid though weed-choked waters of Dal Lake presented one more heart-wrenching sight. Around us was a ring of mountains somnolent on a misty August morning. The boatman rowed past a line of richly carved wooden houseboats with bizarre names – *American Beauty, Champs-Elysées, Ivanhoe*. Sitting in the distance was a fragile-looking Char Chinar. On one bank were the Mughal gardens, Shalimar and Nishat, on the other, the gleaming dome of Hazrat Bal. The waters of the Dal, despite the burden of ever-growing internal and external pollution, were able to ease our minds and elevate our spirits.

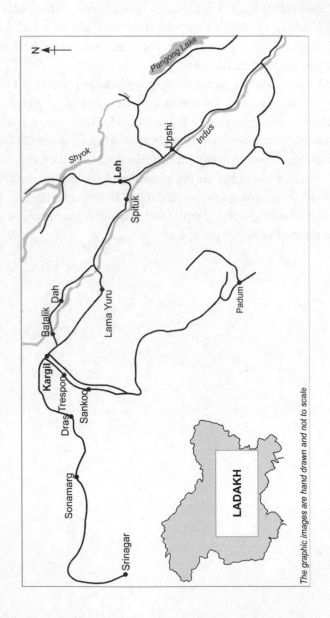

The graphic images are hand drawn and not to scale

11

Ladakh

Bulandion pe pauhachna koi kamaal nahin,
Bulandion pe theherna kamaal hota hai

— IQBAL

It is no great feat to reach the height,
Achievement is to persevere at the peak

G unjan: 6 August 2010. It was just another sultry August morning or so I thought till I switched on the news. '*Calamity: Cloudburst strikes Choglamsar*', '*Hundreds go missing in Leh Cloudburst*', '*Ladakh cut off; many feared dead in cloudburst and flash floods*'. Shocked, I dialled Syeda's number. Within half an hour, I was with her and together we scanned the TV channels and the internet. The cloudburst had occurred a little after midnight and information was just beginning to trickle in. Wordlessly we watched as images of terrible devastation flashed on the television screen. Choglamsar, the tiny, quiet settlement we had visited in Ladakh a few years earlier, was wiped out. It was in this village, where we had interacted with little children at an anganwadi centre, and seen hundreds of girls studying under a tree at the Government High School, that the cloudburst had taken place. The unprecedented rainfall – 250 cm in one hour in an area that received an average 90 mm of rainfall in an entire year – had led to flash floods and landslides. Remembering the barren and precarious mountains of Ladakh, we shuddered to think of the devastation the rain must have unleashed; the terror of the inhabitants as they must have watched the seemingly indestructible mountains turn into huge waves of earth and rock that came crashing down on them.

Almost 200 people were killed, hundreds went missing. The runway to the airport was damaged, telephone lines snapped, electric-poles uprooted, the bus stand flattened and the two highways that connected Ladakh to the rest of India washed away. Sankar, Upshi, Stok ... as we watched the debris before us, our minds went back to yet another August, five years ago, when we had begun our journey to what is undeniably one of the most inaccessible and inhospitable – despite the warmth of its people – places on this planet. Each of the names that flashed across the television screen belonged to our living reality in 2005; we had vivid recollections of the fun-loving people with whom we had spent some of the more memorable moments of our life.

19 August 2005. After spending a few days in Srinagar,[1] we decided to drive to Leh. The word 'Ladakh' is derived from the Tibetan word 'la-tags', and literally means the 'Land of Passes'. Historically, this region was made up of Skardu, Aksai Chin, Kargil, Leh, Zanskar, Lahaul and Spiti, and covered an area of 95,876 square km. The territories of Skardu and Aksai Chin are now under Pakistan and China, respectively. Currently, the area referred to as Ladakh is divided into two districts: Leh and Kargil. Most parts of Ladakh, especially the Kargil–Zanskar and Chanthang areas, are cut off from the rest of the world for almost eight months in a year. In the absence of a rail link, roads are the lifeline of this region. There are two road links to Ladakh from the Indian Territory. One goes via Zoji La ('la' means pass),[2]

---

[1] See Chapter 10

[2] The Prime Minister's Reconstruction Package provides for double-laning of this road. At present, the Zoji La is a single-lane road, and vehicles have to wait on either side for their turn. The package also promised feasibility studies for, a) construction of a tunnel to bypass the Zoji La, and b) construction of the Leh–Shimla Road via Parangla Pass.

and the other via Tanglang La (on the Manali–Leh Highway). Both these routes are extremely treacherous and open for only four to five months in the year. Since we were in Srinagar, we decided to take National Highway 1D, the 434-kilometre road that connected to Leh via the Zoji La. This route along the river Indus traces the old Srinagar–Leh–Yarkand[3] trade route, also known as the Treaty Road. Work on the highway started in 1962 as a consequence of the Sino–Indian War, and it was only in 1974 that restrictions on civilian traffic were lifted.[4]

Our first stop was seventy-five kilometres from Srinagar, at the 'Meadow of Gold', Sonamarg. Its name could not have been more apt. Rolling meadows, brush-stroked trees in all shades of green, majestic Himalayan peaks watching over the prancing polo ground ponies. Namkeen chai (salty tea) and freshly baked Kashmiri bread were brought in on walnut wood trays. As we sipped the scalding tea, its steam rose and hung in the chilly mountain air. After a heavenly half-hour, we resumed our journey towards the treacherous Zoji La. We passed by white willows, groups of Gujjars and Bakarwals trudging along with their sheep in search of pastures, huts with tin roofs, and pagoda-style masjids. Interestingly, many mosques in Kashmir have a pagoda-style roof, probably a Buddhist influence. It is said that even the famed Hazrat Bal Mosque in Srinagar originally had a pagoda which was later replaced by a dome. As we neared the pass, the road became narrower, and military convoys more frequent.

At 11,578 ft, the three-km long Zoji La is surrounded by glaciers on all sides. While there are higher passes in the region, what makes Zoji La particularly dangerous are the frequent avalanches and blizzards in the area. Some say that the name Zoji La actually means the 'path of blizzards' and that the pass offers easier access to the traveller coming from Lhasa than to those travelling from Srinagar.

Despite the almost daily maintenance, the road was bad, a legacy of the frequent storms and landslides in these young mountains of the Zanskar range. 'Madam, during the 1947 Indo–Pak war, the Pakistani troops had

---

[3] Yarkand is a county in the Xinjiang Uyghur Autonomous Region, China.

[4] Source: http://en.wikipedia.org/wiki/National_Highway_1D_(India); Last accessed on 17 September 2011

seized Zoji La, Kargil and Dras. The highway was blocked, and it seemed as if Leh would fall to the enemy. It was Gen. Thimayya who re-established Indian control over the area on 1 November 1948 and hence ensured that Leh was safe,' our driver, a middle-aged Kashmiri man who was also doubling as our guide, told us. Near the top of the pass, he slowed the car. 'Look down,' he said. The view was breathtaking. Looking into the gorges, we saw a tiny white line, a river. 'This is another route to Amarnath. And look up there, that is Baltal,' he said, pointing. Amarnath, for Syeda a montage of images from childhood came up: lakhs of pilgrims trudging along this path every year, old and young, men and women, heading to the Amarnath caves for a darshan (viewing) of the Shiv Lingam; the Muslim family of shepherds whose ancestor discovered the cave and who have been keepers of this shrine for generations; the Chhari Mubarak (auspicious walking staff), which leads the yatra every year.

Crossing Zoji La was both terrifying and wonderful. From then onwards, we followed the meanderings of River Dras. The first village we crossed in Kargil was Matayen. Next to Siberia, this was the coldest place in the world which had permanent habitation! The moment we stepped out of the vehicles, we were lashed by icy winds. The warmth of the local welcome, however, made everything worthwhile. 'Not many people come here,' said a young officer who was standing at the head of the reception line. District officials welcomed us with traditional white scarves. Then they bundled us back in our cars and led the convoy to Village Pandeas a few kilometres away. This village had a seven-member panchayat; not a single woman. Here we learnt of the phenomenal hardships of life in these cold mountains. No telephone connectivity, intermittent power supply. No water to irrigate the fields. The village is perched on a mountain above the river; irrigation is a herculean task. For four months of dead winter, the villagers are totally cut off, even from Dras.

'Next stop is Dras,' our driver announced. The place, which has recently been made into a subdivision, had become a household name during the Kargil War. A small boy standing by the road pointed to some peaks nearby. 'Tiger Hill.' We saw the peak on which scores of young men had died defending the country's frontier. It looked like an ordinary hill, its only distinguishing feature, the bloodstains on the chattans (rocks), browned from exposure to sun and freezing temperatures. 'During the war, there was intense firing in the region. This left many people, including children, traumatized. At that time, everyone from Dras had fled to Sankoo, a small town located forty-two km south of the district headquarters,' Kachu Afsandiyar, a wonderful man who was the district collector of Kargil, told us. Even today, villagers live in fear of the shelling which, they whisper, might start at any moment.

The Dras Higher Secondary School was in the compound of the Council Bhawan. All its 231 students were in the arts stream. No other options were available. We entered a room filled with students. Girls sat in front, boys at the back, rows of bright faces and sparkling eyes. Everyone, especially the girls, wanted to study further. The restrictions placed by geography and politics notwithstanding, they nurtured their little dreams. Kaneez Fatima, her face framed with a white scarf, said: 'I want a government job'. Abida Khanam, a tall, dimpled girl, wanted to become a member of the highest local body, the Ladakh Autonomous Hill Development Council (LAHDC), Kargil. 'I can do something for my people then.' There were many with similar ambitions in that single-room school.

We had expected to meet a group of angry and traumatized teenagers but this was a bunch of youngsters filled with dreams and aspirations. We were elated. But the sun was beginning to go down, and fear of the sudden cold made us reluctantly leave this vibrant group. On the way, there were thousands of apricots drying, spread on rocks along the river. Nearer to the Kargil district headquarters, the landscape changed. Leaving its green behind at Zoji La, it turned almost brown. Tiny lights in the mountains marked individual dwellings. Under a darkening sky, we followed River Dras, reaching Kargil in the late evening.

A delegation of the LAHDCK, which Abida, the young girl from Dras spoke about, was waiting in the State Guest House. The chairman, Ali Asghar Karbalai, a young man Syeda had known for many years, listed their demands. They wanted schools, especially higher secondary ones, in remote villages. 'Such a slow process of approval, Madam!' Karbalai sighed. 'Our proposals have first to be sent to the state, then to the Centre and, on sanction, the same procedure is followed in reverse.' He explained that by the time any scheme is approved, it is usually too late. 'Come September, and most of the working season is gone. The season being very short, food production is never enough. Administration stores food stock, but due to inaccessibility, distribution is difficult, especially during winter months. Besides, people cannot afford to buy rations for six months at one go from the Public Distribution System (PDS).'

For better connectivity, the 234-km Kargil–Zanskar Road had been widened till Sankoo from the district budget. Now the council wanted Rs 77 crore to complete the metalled road connecting the two areas. It would be a lifeline for Zanskar, they urged. A land-locked area, Zanskar is snowbound and cut off from the district headquarters for seven months in a year. Though it boasts of the best tourist spots and trekking routes in the country, this region is isolated and has a very scattered population. 'We need to provide them with better connectivity. Many lives are at stake,' the council members pleaded as they said their goodbyes.

We began our first morning in Kargil with a visit to the home of Kachu Sikandar Khan Sikandar, father of the district collector of Kargil, and one of the few repositories of Kargil's history and secrets. Born in 1920, this frail-looking Ladakhi welcomed us with wonderful ceremony. Arrayed before us were steaming cups of kahwa (traditional green tea from Kashmir) and juicy apricots. As we savoured the dastarkhwan (meticulously laid ceremonial dining spread) spread before us, Kachu Sikandar told us of the forefathers of his people. 'They came from the Graso family of Gilgit, and arrived before the ninth century. Earlier, this area had been under Buddhist influence, which came from Tibet. Islam came to Kargil in the fourteenth century, when Syed Ali Hamdani visited the area. Shah Mohammad Nurbakhsh, a Sufi saint, followed his path and began teaching Shiite Islam. His followers are called Nurbakhshis. They believe Hazrat Ali to be the first Imam and the supreme Wali of God,' he explained. We were spellbound by this man; then, all of a sudden, he left the room. A few minutes later, he returned with a slim, thumbed book in his hand. Flipping through the pages, he quoted: 'Ladakh Khas includes land of Sham, Rupsho, Changthang and Nobra. Porig (Kargil) includes Shanghu Shaghroo, Drass, Baltistan and Zanskar. Ladakh Khas is on River Indus and Zanskar on River Zanskar. Rupsho is around Lake Somoorere and Lake Sokar. Porig is on River Suroo. Valley Nobra is on River Shewak. In all these regions except Baltistan, Nobra is the largest, 9,200 square miles. To its north are the Karakoram mountains; in its south, Mount Kailash which separates Sind Valley from Shevak Valley.' Closing the book with great care, he presented it to us.

'This is *Qadeem Ladakh*. It will provide you with a snapshot of our land and its people. Abba wrote this many years ago,' his son, the DC, explained as we left the warmth of Kachu Sikandar's home. We were ready to begin the journey to discover the landmarks described in this book.

We charted our route; we were to go through Suroo Valley, Karpokhar and Sankoo. We decided we would stop anywhere on the way where government programmes were visible from the main road. Our first stop on the road to Suroo was an anganwadi centre at Gund Minji village. The rickety steps leading up to the room creaked under our feet and we wondered how preschoolers and pregnant women climbed up. Fatima Bano, the anganwadi worker, and Nargis Bano, her helper, greeted us. They said that the centre ran from 10 a.m. to 2 p.m., six days a week. Their menu was no different from the menu of anganwadis in Bihar and Rajasthan – khichdi, chana and halwa – items quite unfamiliar to the Ladakhi children. 'Do the children like the food?' Both women were silent. Their bowed heads told the story. Looking at the handful of children sitting inside the cold and dark room, we wondered if the alien nature of the food was the reason behind the poor attendance. 'Madam, our working season is very short, so the mothers are busy at this time. They can't bring the kids in. I have to go and fetch them myself,' Nargis complained.

The drive through Suroo Valley took us past many villages and habitations. Children were waiting for us with flowers at the Government Middle School (English medium), Gund Minji. Surprisingly, their songs of welcome were in Hindi. The school had sixty-six children but no midday meals. The principal told us that they had started the meal programme but couldn't continue since the food grains did not arrive. Once the children went home for lunch, very few came back for classes.

Our next stop, the Sankoo Higher Secondary School, taught both science and arts. Of the 502 students, only 196 were girls. In Kargil District, the enrolment of girls in schools has always been low. Girls had entered the education stream only fifteen years ago. Before that, girls' education was considered haraam (forbidden). Till 1965, Kargil was a closed society;

we learnt that even boys didn't attend school at the time. Until the 1970s, no women could be seen in the marketplace. The school, therefore, had a scholarship for girls until Class 10. For boys who travelled a distance of over five kilometres to school, there was a scholarship of Rs 100 per month.

We met Hasan and Murtuza, two bright boys who walked over two hours every day to get to school. Their love for whatever learning they could glean within their limited means thrilled us to our eyes. When they reached school, however, there were no English or Urdu teachers. 'I am helpless. Getting teachers for these two subjects is very difficult,' the principal told us. The two boys showed us their English textbooks. We were shocked to see that their lessons were not about their own land, forests and heroes but about Sherwood Forest, Robin Hood and Maid Marion!

We stopped next at the Weaving Centre at Sankoo, located in a small room on the upper floor of a crumbling structure. Eight or ten women sat on the floor. Haseena, a shy girl with glasses, told us that the room was barfeela (freezing) in winter. She and the others were being trained in pashmina weaving. 'Our monthly stipend,' she said simply, 'is Rs 100 for eight hours of work every day!' The only light in the room was from a small shaft in the roof. 'How can they work? Why is there no heater or tubelight?' we asked the officials. Lighting or heating system would be of little use, the administration clarified. 'We only get four hours of electricity in a day. Even this is purchased from Jammu and the Valley at an annual cost of Rs 1,340 crore,' they explained.

'Can't this area generate excellent electricity through solar energy?'

'It can, certainly. In fact, we get 290 days of clear sunshine. We also have the capacity to generate power using geo-thermal energy. Give us Rs 50 crore and, within eighteen months, many of our power troubles will vanish,' Kachu Asfandiyar reasoned.

We thought about the wisdom in his words as we drove towards a Leh Berry processing unit. This medicinally rich wonder fruit, Leh Berry or Seabuckthorn, is in big demand the world over. It is found in abundance in both Kargil and Ladakh. We wanted to see how its utility could be maximized for the benefit of the Ladakhi people and entrepreneurs. The factory itself was little more than a large hall with a few machines in one corner. The owner, a young salwar-clad man from Sankoo, told us that some out-of-state company had been using the Leh Berry brand name for their juices and had gained instant popularity. 'We obtained a stay order from the court. We want our own processing and packaging facilities so that we, too, can become entrepreneurs,' he said, sounding hopeful.

As we proceeded towards our final destination, the Sufi dargah at Karpokhar, we drove past many villages of the Valley: Bringy, Sarchay and Trespon. The houses were made of mud to retain the heat, and had small painted windows. We passed canals carved in the hard rocks. Prayer flags – Buddhists call them tarchuks – could be seen everywhere. Occasionally, we passed groups of students walking along the road with school bags slung across their backs, their faces red from excitement and exertion.

At Karpokhar, the cars stopped by the roadside. There was no motorable road to the shrine. As we made our way downhill through the tall grass, Asfandiyar Khan explained that 'karpo' meant 'white' and 'khar' meant 'fort'. 'It is believed that these mountains earlier housed a fort made of white quartz, hence the name. Look down, there is the dargah.'

Nestled in a green shrub forest, beside a gurgling river and tiny streams of water, and surrounded by huge brown mountains, we saw the dargah of the great teacher Syed Mir Hashim from Kashmir. Thi Namgyal, King of Suru Karchay (Kargil), on the request of his Muslim wife, Regyal or Thi Lah Khatoon, invited the teacher to educate their son, Thi Mohammad Sultan. It was due to his enlightened preaching and the vigorous efforts of the queen that the Islamic faith and teachings spread in Suru Karchay (Kargil) for the first time. Before us was a humble dargah of a humble man. The mausoleum was no more than four feet in height, so it was necessary for the visitor to bend and enter. Inside, there were no decorations, just hundreds of strips of cloth tied here and there, emblems of mannats (wishes) of the faithful. We sat there in silence. It was a rare peaceful moment, in close proximity to the gods!

Early the next morning, before starting the long journey to Leh, we visited a small private museum in a beautiful location – a hillside in Kargil town. For many years, Ijaz Husain Munshi had travelled across the region, collecting priceless manuscripts and relics that offer insights into its history and culture. From ornaments to water caskets, clothes to footwear, utensils to pictures, he painstakingly collected them all. He has converted the top floor of his traditional house into a museum where visitors can witness thousands of years of history, not just of Kargil but also Baltistan and Ladakh. As Ijaz explained the story and significance of each precious artefact, we thought of the caravans which trudged along the historic Silk Route. With proper support from the government, a Museum of the Silk Route, is what Ijaz's collection should become.

Like Sindbads of the mountains, having seen the wonders of Kargil, we moved on to our next destination, Leh. Leh, the largest district in India, can be approached through two routes, Lamayuru and Batalik. We chose the latter because we were told that on this route we would meet the Brogpa or the Dard – the less than 4,000 people who are counted among the purest Aryans left in the world. They live in five villages some 170 km from Leh and speak the Miramo language. They are, however, not the earliest inhabitants of Ladakh. The first people of the area were a Tibeto–Mongoloid group of nomads who practised the Bon (demonolatry) religion.[5] The Mon were the first immigrants into the area and got converted to Buddhism by the messengers of Emperor Ashoka in the third century BC. Fa-Hein, the first Chinese traveller to visit India via Ladakh in the fourth century AD, reported that Ladakhis followed Theravada Buddhism.[6] Today, there are some 700 Mon left in Ladakh. They are primarily flute players and musicians. The Dard or the Brogpa (literally the mountain people) came from the Hunza District of Baltistan, and it was they who introduced the Ladakhis to their national sport – polo. The Changpa, a people with Mongolian eyes and flat

---

[5] The worship of demons. It is believed that, from the time of Homer, the term 'demon' signified a benevolent being.

[6] *Ladakh: Past and Present* by Prem Singh Jina, Gyan Publishing House, Delhi, 2000, p. 11. Available online at http://books.google.co.in/books?id=zVrmBz hfhfgC&pg=PA173&lpg=PA173&dq=ethnic+groups+of++ladakh&source =bl&ots=zCdcnRUJX6&sig=i7JWbsQRLbqCfj4sBqSIlNCULV0&hl=en& ei=-FBKTfKDLIbwrQf426WqDg&sa=X&oi=book_result&ct=result&resn um=1&ved=0CBkQ6AEwAA#v=onepage&q=ethnic%20groups%20of%20 %20ladakh&f=false

Date of access: 16 January 2011. Theravada Buddhism, literally the 'teaching of the elders' is the oldest form of Buddhism, and is highly conservative. For the longest time, it was the predominant form of Buddhism in Sri Lanka and continental south-east Asia.

noses, and the Khampa, who came from the eastern Tibet province of Kham are the other ethnic groups of Ladakh.

On the way to the Brogpa villages, we passed miles and miles of good agricultural land that had been taken over by the army. The rocks we saw on top of the mountains had been weather-beaten over the centuries into the most spectacular formations; they resembled gigantic stone fortresses. Nature had created in this inhospitable terrain what no human being could dare to attempt. Passing by the same route on horseback some hundred years before our visit, a British doctor had described these mountains as 'grotesque formations like prehistoric villages or castellated fortresses, relics of some bygone civilization.'[7]

Our vehicles climbed 13,202 ft to reach the Hambotingla Pass which led to Batalik, a place that had come instantly into the spotlight because of the extensive media coverage of the Kargil war. As we turned along a bend in the road, we had our first glimpse of the mighty Indus, locally known as the Singge-Chhu (lion river).[8] It was a slightly disappointing first sight – all we saw was a muddy mass of water.

Crossing villages like Lalu and Silmo, we finally reached Darchik (meaning terraced area), this time to catch our first glimpse of the Brogpa. Men and women, beautifully attired and with exquisite features – high cheek bones, almond shaped eyes – sang, danced and played their traditional instruments for us. We had heard reports of foreigners – especially German women – trying to sneak into these villages to establish relations with Brogpa men.[9] Seeing them, we could understand why. By this time, the muddy Indus had become a raging river and it was to the roar of its waters that the Brogpa moved their bodies, while their costumes and plumes swung and glittered in the sun. They wore loose pyjamas topped with thick cloaks made

---

[7] Heinrich Harrer, *Ladakh: Gods and Mortals Behind the Himalayas*, Pinguin-Verlag, Innsbruck, 1980, p 20.

[8] Chopra P.N., *Ladakh*, S. Chand and Company, 1980, Delhi, p. 4.

[9] http://www.tribuneindia.com/2004/20041107/spectrum/main1.htm; Last accessed on 17 September 2011. A Chosen People, *The Tribune*, November 7, 2004.

of sheep's wool and tied with a cummerbund. Beaded necklaces adorned their necks. The women wore their hair in numerous braids. Both the men and women wore colourful flowers on their head – the men in their caps, and the women atop their silver ornamented headdresses called Kho. In fact, the Kho contained many other items like coins, beads and ribbons.

We were in another time dimension – Brogpa time. We climbed a steep mountain to reach Dha, one of the two Brogpa villages open to foreign tourists. All around us there were orange blooms of the Monthu Tho flowers which have become the identifying face of the Brogpa culture. When worn in the Kho, these flowers signify the marital status of a Brogpa woman. They are also considered to be an offering to the spirits. Traditionally, the Brogpa were followers of the animalistic faith, Bon chos, but over a period of time many elements of Tibetan Buddhism have been adopted.[10] Standing in Dha Village, we thought of our schemes. Had any of them reached this remote pocket? We asked a small Brogpa boy, Sorin, who was sitting outside his house. He told us that his village had a school up to Class 5, an anganwadi and a health centre. This was a marvellous attainment! On reaching the clearing where the stone houses of the Brogpa sat cheek by jowl, we were amazed to see slogans on AIDS awareness scribbled on the walls. Though they don't intermarry or mingle with outsiders – hence the racial purity – the Brogpa are aware of what is happening in the world. Tsering Tashi, a seventy-two-year-old Brogpa woman dressed in traditional attire, her grey hair in several braids, told us about her ancestors. She narrated their folklore; three brothers of the Aryan race – Dulo, Melo, Galo – left their native country Iran and settled in Gilgit. For some reason, they were thrown out of Gilgit and found their way to Leh. They first stopped at a lake to wash their hands and feet. As they removed their shoes, some seeds fell out and suddenly plants started springing up. So, they decided to settle down in this inhospitable terrain which had offered them their first water and which had been greened with the seeds from their shoes.

The river flowed with us throughout our journey to Leh and with it came stories of people who first arrived on its banks. We were driven by something

---

[10] Breton Schwarzenbach, *Brogpas*, Available at http://www.blurb.com/books/950758; last accessed on 17 September 2011

beyond our control which made us halt at several places. We got down at the roadside from which a slope led us to the river. We went in silence down to the river along the banks of which our ancestors had lived and learnt. We performed ablutions by washing our hands and feet in its freezing waters. Slipping into her shoes at one such halt, in a place called Biemma, Syeda, wondered whether her footwear could sow seeds of a new beginning, as did the shoes of the Brogpa elders...

As we entered India's only cold desert, the mountains changed face and colour. Zigzag patterns, of the type which are seen on sand beaches after the waters recede, had been traced on the rocks by an invisible hand. We sped past stone houses with wooden windows, as also many fluttering prayer flags and chortens. Chortens are white stupas under which the Buddhists bury the ashes and relics of their dead. As we got closer to Leh, the landscape became more arid; yellow and brown were the only colours the eye could see. By now, the river had vanished and we were on a vast tableland with tufts of grass and a sprinkling of tiny purple flowers. Against the softening evening light, the sky was awash with blue, clear as a mirror, and the road seemed to lead straight into its expanse. Just when the sun was sinking in its customary place on the horizon, we entered Leh, the district headquarters. We had been told that the road journey would acclimatize us but breathing in the rarefied atmosphere of this cold desert was still not easy. The state guest house was a newly constructed building in a lone location near the airport. A sense of desolation gripped us as we walked out on to the terrace to catch a glimpse of the sleeping town. A radiant moon seemed prescient in a clear sky which was filled with thousands of bright stars. Such was their brilliance that even at night, we could see the silhouettes of the snow-capped peaks that encircled us. The brown desert that we had crossed had turned an inky black.

The next morning, we went to the government S.N.M. Hospital in Leh town. It was like many other hospitals, teeming with patients who had to wait for long hours as more than forty posts for doctors and paramedics were lying vacant. In sharp contrast to this was the hospital we visited later. The serene ambience of the Centre for Tibetan Medicine (which uses traditional Amchi medicines) provided a healing touch. The fifty-bed Mahabodhi Karuna Charitable Hospital was a large, neat and clean place, abuzz with activity. Established in 1996, it is run by the Mahabodhi International Meditation Centre.

Our next destination was a pashmina-rearing farm. It was located some forty kilometres from a village called Upshi, an important junction on the treacherous Leh–Manali Highway – the alternative entry route to Ladakh. Located at a height of 15,000 ft, the farm offered a dazzling view of the Indus and the surrounding cold desert. Here we saw pashmina sheep that allow their hair to be used for weaving the most expensive shawls in the world. The livestock lives on the high mountains surrounding the area and is brought to the farm in the last week of September. We discovered that the current inhabitants of the pen had been brought down from their lofty habitat only for our benefit. Officials explained that pashmina is the fine hair which grows beneath the normal hair of the sheep to ward off the cold. During summer, the sheep shed this inner coat as it is no longer required. It is then collected and spun into the soft silky wool that the Ladakhis call 'lena' and the world calls pashmina. It is said that the King of Ladakh once presented Mirza Haider, a cousin of the Mughal emperor, Babar, with some lena. Haider got it woven into two shawls which were purchased by two Persian traders and presented to their king. The traders then went back to Ladakh and brought some more lena which they took as far as Alexandria. Thus spread the fame of the lena or the Kashmiri pashmina.[11]

On the way back to Leh, we stopped at the Stok Palace. This four-storey structure is located on the west bank of River Indus. It is a unique palace, unlike any other we had seen across the country. There is no mural, no gold leaf work, no inlay or coloured glass. The palace is sturdy and bare, like its surrounding landscape. Constructed in 1814 by Ladakh's last ruler, it is now a museum that houses a rare collection of thangkas, some of which date back to the thirteenth century. Also on display are garments, coins, religious objects and chunky silver jewellery encrusted with lapis lazuli, jade, amber and coral. The cascading landscape around the palace reflects the rare, primordial magnificence of Ladakh. It was surreal, its colours so bold and clear that the photographs we had been taking all day seemed to be artificially colour-enhanced. We were surprised to see that the land on

[11] Chopra, P.N., *Ladakh* p. 56; Heinrich Herr, *Ladakh*, pp. 84-85.

both sides of the river was a lush green. In fact, we had noticed this as we were driving from Upshi, along Leh–Manali highway. Unless one looked into the distance where the stark yellow of the sand dunes came into view, the landscape that surrounded us looked nothing like a desert. Later, we learnt that the patches of green in and around Ladakh had been increasing rapidly due to 'development' ushered in post the Sino–Indian war. This transformation of Ladakh from a nomadic to an agrarian society, this act of making the 'wilderness fertile'[12] has alarmed environmentalists and with good reason. Many believe that it was these innocuous patches of green that were responsible for the cloudburst of August 2010.[13]

The next day, we visited two schools. The Government Primary School in Sankar did not have an approach road. Like the teachers and children, we too, ambled over rocks and stones to enter the building. Here, a handful of children sat on the cold stone floor next to a broken chair. Besides this, there were no tables, chairs or even carpets.

'How do the children study during the winter when the temperature dips well below zero?'

'They don't,' said the teacher, Zubeida, a young Ladakhi girl in her late twenties.

'Why aren't these children in uniforms?'

'We have received no uniforms this year.'

'Why? Isn't this an SSA school?'

'It is but … In fact, midday meals were also stopped three years ago.' She explained all this with a weary smile.

---

[12] Heinrich Herr, Op cit., p. 45.

[13] http://economictimes.indiatimes.com/news/politics/nation/calamity-cloudburst-in-choglamsar-ladakh/articleshow/6277615.cms Economic Times; August 9, 2010. Accessed on 16 January 2011. Areas far from the sea receive rainfall when the warm moist air from the surroundings rises due to solar heat. As the height increases, this warm air cools and condenses to form clouds. As the weight of water droplets increase, it can lead to torrential rainfall if the clouds encounter cold air currents at high altitude. In Ladakh, the hot and cold currents had always been present but there was no moisture to lead to rainfall. But the greens brought in moisture, and this triggered the catastrophe of August 2010.

The condition of the Girls Higher Secondary School located in Choglamsar was worse. Located in a huge compound which it shared with the Middle School, this school had just one classroom. Inside it, 193 girls of Class 12 were crowded together. They were lucky, they at least had a roof to shelter them from the harsh sun and biting chill of this cold desert. Their juniors studying in Class 11 had to rely on an old tree for protection. At the time of our visit, it was still summer, so it was possible to hold outdoor classes. During the rainy season and the long winter, the children got holidays. 'What about toilets; these are adolescent girls,' we asked the manager. There was no answer.

We saw about one twenty girls sitting in the open under a tree reading from reference works from Tata Mcgraw Hill, books by Gomber and Gogia. Familiar names; Gunjan remembered, not so long ago, browsing through the same books. As far as textbooks went at least, the girls here were no different from their counterparts in Delhi schools, she thought. But this was not the case. Though the session had started twenty-two days ago, the students did not have any textbooks. These expensive reference books were their only texts. As a science student, Gunjan remembered that these supplementary books were not easy to follow, at least not until the fundamentals were covered. 'How are the girls faring?' she asked their Science teacher. He shook his head sadly. 'The pass percentage for Class 12 is only 22 per cent. The problem is not just the non-availability of books; getting teachers for subjects like Maths, Science and Urdu is very difficult.' The physical education teacher was being made to double as an English teacher.

Later that evening, when we sat with the leaders of the LAHDC, we wanted to take up this issue. But school buildings and textbooks were, we discovered, low on their list of priorities. 'Most of our areas are cut off from the rest of the country and even from district headquarters for six–seven months annually. Leh, our capital, has to depend on the single flight that connects it to Srinagar,' a councillor explained. We were amazed to hear that Leh District, with India's highest civilian airport, was better connected to Delhi than to its own state capital. 'Our winters are long and our people have no means of earning. But these very people have unparalleled skills. Have you seen our exquisitely carved tables, our jewellery, and our carpets? Every summer when tourists flock to Leh, we are forced to sell wares procured from other parts of the country. We have very little of our own to offer. Just provide us some training and working capital and see how our products become popular in the global market,' they said.

The next morning, as we explored the markets of Leh, we realized the truth behind these words. There had been no exaggeration; stall after stall was filled with intricately carved Ladakhi tables, most of them bearing the dragon symbol. We saw tourists buying Tibetan carpets and chunky Ladakhi jewellery adorned with lapis. The art of hand printing by the wood engraving process had been brought to Ladakh from China via Tibet in the seventeenth century, under King Nyima Namgyal.[14] We saw exquisite hand-printed scrolls and tables on display. For travellers like us, the prices seemed high. But, as a shopkeeper explained, the two-month tourist season is the only source of livelihood for most artisans. They have to live on these earnings for the whole year.

At the end of our journey, we visited the monasteries about which we had read in travel, adventure, and spiritual literature. We found them as we had imagined. Standing proudly against the azure sky of this barren brown landscape, these monasteries are not just tourist attractions but a source of hope and strength for the Ladakhis. At one time, they also served as fortresses as wars were common in Ladakh. The town of Leh itself has many Buddhist monasteries in its vicinity, each with its own special significance. Twenty kilometres from Leh, near Village Stagmo, on top of a hill is the twelve-storey monastery of Thiksey. Built 600 years ago by Palden Sangpo, this monastery is the seat of the Gelug or the Yellow Hat Sect of Buddhism in Ladakh. The youngest school of Tibetan Buddhism, Gelug, with its strong focus on monastic life, was founded by Tsongkhapa in the late fourteenth century at Ganden, Tibet. It is famous world over because of its leader, the Dalai Lama.

More than a hundred monks live at this monastery, which contains numerous stupas, statues, thangkas, wall paintings, swords, and a large pillar engraved with the Buddha's teachings. The Gompa contains ten temples, and the hill on which it stands is dotted with chapels and houses of monks.

---

[14] Chopra, op. cit., p. 28.

On entering the prayer hall, there is a fifteen-metre high statue of Maitreya Buddha (denoting compassion) painted in gold. This statue, built over a period of four years, was constructed to commemorate the visit of the Dalai Lama in 1980, and is presently the largest Buddha statue in Ladakh. Another important attraction for religious tourists is the Thiksey library, containing rare books on Buddhism. Located directly above the temple is a small narrow room where local boys are trained to become lamas. Here, we saw small Ladakhi boys sitting and reciting the Buddhist texts. Traditionally, Ladakhi families sent one son, usually the third, to become a lama. The first two sons were normally married to the same woman (Ladakh has a long history of polyandry which, according to many sociologists, was necessary to keep the population under control and keep families from splitting up the little land that was arable) and the remaining sons became makpas or khandamads, that is, they left their father's home to serve in the home of their wife.[15] However, polyandry was made illegal by the statute of 1941.

After Thiksey, we proceeded to Spituk Monastery, literally meaning 'exemplary'. Eight kilometres from Leh, this eleventh century monastery is built on a conical hill and offers a panoramic view of the town. At one time, Spituk followed the Kadampa (Red Hat) School of Buddhism but soon switched over to the Yellow Hat sect. When we reached the monastery, the lamas were performing a ritual. From the road, we could see the inner courtyard where boys eight to ten years of age, dressed in lama robes, were playing.

Life in the monasteries has always been mysterious. Some of it was revealed to us during these visits. For example, the Ladakhi stove, which resembles an intricately carved, gold painted wooden table. On top of it are placed huge pots. There are water taps directly above these pots for boiling rice and preparing other dishes. Behind this structure is a small room with an enclosure for burning wood to heat the stove. As we walked around the monastery, we revelled in the sense of orderliness and calm that enveloped it. We could not help but wonder at the ingenuity of a people who had managed to create such a life for themselves in this inhospitable, dangerous and now, increasingly unpredictable terrain. Theirs was a tough

---

[15] Ibid, p. 48 and Herr, Op.cit., p. 65

life; the criss-crossing wrinkles on their weather-beaten faces were a living testimony of their hardiness and adaptability. Yes, Darwin would be proud of them, we thought with a smile.

That was five years ago. Then, as we took in the vast expanse of green that was visible from the courtyard of Spituk, we were completely oblivious to the vengeance that nature was plotting. The murmured warnings of environmentalists notwithstanding, we were confident that the Ladakhis had reached an understanding with their surroundings and that nothing could disturb their 'perfect harmony'. Little did we imagine how soon our confidence would be shaken; how sorely the forbearance of these sturdy people would to be tested.

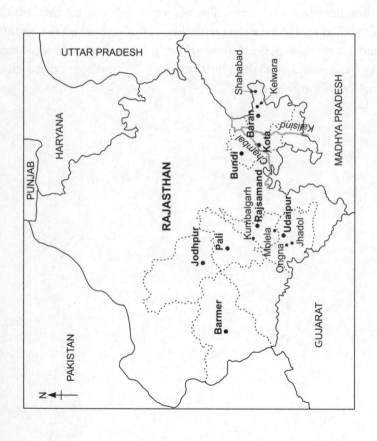

12

Rajasthan

Qana'at na kar alam e rang-o-bu puur
Chaman aur bhi aashiyan aur bhi huin
Tu shahin hai parvaaz hai kaam tera
Tere saamne aasman aur bhi hain

— IQBAL

Don't be content with this ephemeral world
There are many gardens and dwellings ahead.
You are a falcon; to soar is your creed,
There are skies beyond the existing sky.

U daipur is called the 'City of Lakes'. With over forty lakes[1] in an area less than forty square km, the name fits well. In October 2005, when we reached this five-hundred-year-old city, its lakes were brimming. After many thirsty years that had turned the lake beds into parched playgrounds for children of all ages, Udaipur had finally received good rainfall. The farmers called it excess rainfall because it had spoilt their crops. It had also submerged the motorable road that had been built to take tourists across the Pichola Lake, in the centre of which sits the splendid Lake Palace Hotel.

---

[1]   There are forty-two lakes in all.

In the sixteenth century, on the banks of the Pichola, the young Maharana Udai Singh met a saint who made him a prophecy. 'Your fortunes will change if you build a palace on this spot,' he said. The Maharana, who had recently lost Chittor to the Mughal emperor Akbar, obeyed the saint and, one by one, the palaces were built. Today, they stand proudly, narrating the tales of valour of their Rajput inhabitants, tales that continue to enthral visitors year after year. In the entire state of Rajasthan, this tribal region in the south attracts the highest number of tourists. Some call it the jhoomar (ornament) on Rajasthan's brow. And yet, over half of its twenty-five lakh people continue to live below the poverty line. Almost 63 per cent of the population is malnourished and, every day, a woman dies during childbirth.[2]

Our journey began in the verdant backyard of the district. The undulating terrain along which we travelled flaunted its newly acquired green. All along the thick (and sometimes sparse) forested hills ran row upon row of low stone walls. 'Save the forests' was written on them in white paint, and signed 'Joint Forest Management' (JFM). Our guide was the district collector, Shikhar Aggarwal, a bright young man full of ideas and plans for his district. He told us that the villagers had built stone walls to protect their forests. In return, they had received rights over minor forest produce. They also received a share of profits from the sale of major forest produce. Over a hundred 'Village Protection and Maintenance Committees' had thus been formed.

We noticed that within the stone wall enclosure, the vegetation was dense; but outside, the forests were bruised. To encourage people to manage their own forests, the administration has come up with a unique scheme. They identified sixteen best JFM villages and gave them, on priority, their choice of teachers, medical centres, dairy routes or seeds. This incentivization brought instant results. Adjoining villages began demanding JFM.

Our first stop was the village of Pai, thirty km from the city of Udaipur. Here, the Adivasi Mahila Grah Udyog Sahkari Samiti, a co-operative of 264 women, is doing mushroom and sericulture cultivation. We were received

---

[2] Malnutrition figures are provided by a Sewa Mandir publication dated September 2004.

by a tall, middle-aged woman called Anita. Folding her hands in greeting, she smiled. 'I am the president. My co-operative has been cultivating mushrooms for ten years. We place bhusa (hay) in water along with anti-fungal matter and sponge, and produce butter and oyster mushrooms for the local market.'

'Where are they sold?'

'We sell them door-to-door in Udaipur. People know us now. It's good money. Oyster mushrooms fetch Rs 40 per kg and butter Rs 70 per kg.'

Anita took us to a small, musty hut next door and proudly displayed the group's mulberry cultivation. For twenty years, under a scheme of Tribal Area Development, the co-operative has been rearing silkworms and doing mulberry cultivation. Women work for six to seven hours daily and earn Rs 80 per kg of thread which they manage to reel in two days. 'Every family earns an additional Rs 4,000–Rs 5,000 from these activities. Not only do we reel silk, we also weave saris,' said another woman whose face we could not see since it was partly hidden behind the pallu of her red-and-yellow printed sari.

From Pai, we set off for the next tehsil, Jhadol. On the road there was a sign which read 'Makra Dev Village'. Right next to it was a school, the Rajkiya Adarsh Higher Secondary School. It was 12.20 p.m., and two women were cooking chappatis and dal for the midday meal. Children of Classes 1 and 2 were seated together in front of Rani, a young para-teacher. Loud whispers started as soon as we entered. Immediately Rani shushed the children. 'What are you studying?' we asked a shy little girl in a dirty, patched-up uniform sitting at the front.

'Hindi.'

'Do you live close by?'

Silence.

'Didi, many of these students have to walk two-three km to get to school every day,'[3] said Rani, who was in an advanced stage of pregnancy.

We turned towards her. 'Is there a toilet?' we asked.

---

[3] However, the Rajasthan government has now initiated a scheme whereby tribal girls are given bicycles to enable them to get access to higher education.

She looked embarrassed and shook her head. 'A toilet had been built but it was broken. Students and teachers have to ease themselves in the field,' she said, eyes fixed on the floor.

'How do you manage?' we asked.

Rani said nothing.

'What about water? Does that hand pump work?' We pointed at a rusty looking hand pump sitting forlornly in the school courtyard.

'We use water from an open well nearby. The hand pump has very poor quality water.'

As we got back into the car, Shikhar Aggarwal explained that potable water was a problem all across the state. 'The water table is falling at an alarming rate.'[4]

Soon we reached Jhadol, the sub-divisional headquarters. Our first stop was the Community Health Centre to which eight PHCs and sixty-three sub-centres referred their serious cases. The signboard outside read '24-hour service delivery'. We saw many women arriving, dressed in bright odhnis (chadors draped over upper bodies). Sterilization was in progress. Some women who had been anaesthetized were lying semi-conscious outside the Operation Theatre, awaiting their turn. After the surgery they would receive Rs 200 and return auto rickshaw fare. But the ANMs (Auxiliary Nurse Midwives) who brought them said they didn't receive the full amount. Aruna, in a starched white sari, was one such ANM. She had brought two women to the centre. 'Didi, it is very hard to convince them,' she said, pointing to the women on the floor. 'Most women are not even willing to hear about it unless they have borne three children.' Then lowering her voice, she said, 'Two or three babies out of a hundred die within one week of delivery. How can we blame them?'

The doctors at the CHC proudly gave statistics for institutional deliveries – 45 per cent, much higher than in other parts of Rajasthan. Walking through the corridors, taking stock of the surroundings, we almost landed on the floor as we tripped over the most unexpected protrusion. 'God, what is this?' we screamed. It was a dreadful sight. At the entrance to the female

---

[4] The groundwater situation in Udaipur is, however, better than in many other areas of the state.

ward some ten-twelve bodies were lying on the floor. 'Didi, don't be scared. These women are just unconscious,' Aruna spoke. We looked again. The women were lying next to one another, their shoulders touching. Their faces were covered by their pallus (loose end of a sari or a dupatta).

'What happened? Why are they lying here?'

'Madam, these women have just been sterilized,' the Chief Medical Officer, Dr Bhanwar (name changed) informed us. 'Though fifty beds have been sanctioned, we only have fifteen. Post-operative patients have to lie on the floors.'

'What about these beds?' we asked, pointing to the vacant beds in the wards. 'Madam, they are for the women currently undergoing surgery,' a young intern said. He was quickly cut short by Dr Bhanwar, who pointed out that lying on the floor was part of the culture here. 'These women prefer it this way,' he tried to assure us.

Next door to the CHC was the Tribal Boys Hostel, Jhadol. About one hundred boys were waiting for us under the hot sun. They were students from Classes 6–12. Streams of sweat were trickling down their glum, unhappy faces. The first thing we did was to ask them to move inside the verandah. They only spoke after much prodding by us and their teachers. They said that they never watched TV or listened to the radio. The hostel had an old TV set but it hadn't functioned for over four years. There was no school library. Not even a daily newspaper to tell them what was happening outside the four walls of their school and hostel. 'Didi, I want to know what's happening in our country, in our state. But here nothing reaches us.' The speaker was a bright sixteen-year-old, Nathulal. 'Earlier, they used to take us on exposure visits once a year. We learnt so much, saw so much. Now even that has stopped.'

'Why?'

A state official came forward. 'No funds, Madam,' he said.

'What would you like to become in life?' we asked, listing possibilities one by one – doctor, engineer, journalist, computer programmer, teacher. Suddenly, barring half a dozen students, everyone raised their hands. 'So almost everyone here wants to become a teacher?' we asked. Once again, it was Nathulal who spoke. 'Madam, I wanted to become a doctor that treats animals ... what do you call them?'

'Veterinarian or vet for short.'

'Yes, I wanted to become a vet and help my people but how can I? No school in the entire tehsil offers science or even commerce. We can only become teachers.'

'Is this true?' we questioned the officers accompanying us. One of them explained apologetically: 'Madam, science is only taught in schools at the district headquarters. There are no science teachers here.'

Suddenly Gunjan remembered her own school in Noida; her indecision about which academic stream to choose, the hours of discussion spent with various teachers trying to figure out what she wanted to do in life. These bright young boys standing before us would never have that choice. They, too, wanted to do something in life but for them, the options were limited. They could either pursue the same trade as their families or become teachers in a rajkiya shiksha kendra (government school) of their area. As we got into the car, we saw that as planners we needed to create opportunities for every child in Jhadol to select his or her own career and pursue it.

The road from Jhadol to Ongna, our next stop, went on for miles through a forested hill road. On either side there were mountains, and a serene river ran along the roadside most of the way. It was a perfect trek for nature lovers. As we neared Ongna, we could see on the road ahead of us the damage caused by the monsoons. Our bones registered every bump and lurch as the car jumped from one pothole to another.

Just before entering Ongna, the cars turned left. A road sign read 'Peepal Baran'. 'This is a settlement being constructed by the state for fifty-five Kathodi families,' the forest guard sitting behind us spoke. 'Kathodi?' we had never heard of this tribe. 'The word 'kathodi', Shikhar Aggarwal said, 'is derived from kattha (catechu, an astringent), the stuff these people used to collect from the kher (Acacia catechu) trees. The Kathodi tribes migrated from Songarh and Nawapur in Maharashtra and settled in Jhadol and Kotda tehsils of Udaipur District. But as the number of kher trees declined, and collection of kattha became unviable, they were reduced to penury. Today, these people are among the poorest in the region. They make a miserable living here by weaving baskets or migrate as labour to Gujarat.'

The short ride to Peepal Baran was jarring since the one-and-a-half km stretch from the road to the settlement was unconnected by road. We were severely tossed, bounced and jostled through small streams and hill shoulders. As the vehicle hurtled towards Peepal Baran, the local policeman sitting next to the forest guard began to regale us with his version of the Kathodi story. 'Madamji, these junglees (wild people) used to eat monkeys and, until some years before, went around naked.'

'Look at those dhanis (hamlets), Madam,' the policeman said, pointing at individual houses atop hills. "They live in scattered houses across different hillocks, close to the forests and their small plots of land. After their kattha trade died, some of them moved as a tribe to villages like Ongna.'

Finally, we reached Peepal Baran. Here we saw typical sarkari (government) construction which looked like the Cellular Jail of Andamans – a series of small one-room cells adjoining each other. Each family unit was one room, no toilet and no partition. 'This is the kitchen,' someone said, waving at an empty corner. 'Toilets and bathrooms are common.' For people who have always lived far apart in their own dhanis, this cheek by jowl arrangement was probably quite alien.

From there, a narrow road led us to the Kathodi colony in Ongna village. There were 132 Kathodi families living here. At the village entrance we were given a grand welcome with dhols (drums). We were the only representatives of the Indian government that they had ever seen. The Kathodi were good musicians; some of the young men we spoke to said they wanted to start their own band. 'Could someone teach us music?' they asked. We promised to find out from the administration. Leaving our vehicles on the road, we walked through the village to where the panchayat had organized a public meeting. On the way we noticed the beautifully painted doors of their houses.

Before reaching the chaupal (traditional village gathering place), we were taken to see a maawadi. The Maawadi scheme is run by the Rajasthan government in order to reduce dropout rate, especially among tribal children. The centres run from 8.30 a.m. to 3.00 p.m. for school dropouts and children who have never been to school. Here, they sing songs, play games, learn the alphabet and get acclimatized to a classroom environment. They are provided uniforms and shoes. The children brush their teeth, comb their hair, wash their faces and their uniforms. Health checks are arranged from time to time. We were told that the state had approved one hundred such maawadis.

Inside the centre we saw games like Animal Safari and Toss the Ring placed neatly in a small cupboard. Children were being served hot breakfast which we learnt was prepared by the community women. A young girl in a bright salwar kameez was introduced as Shanta Kathodi. She was the maawadi teacher and the only Kathodi girl who has passed Class 8. Shanta looked at us and smiled shyly.

She stood before thirty uniformed children who sat on a durrie with nicely oiled and combed hair and clean faces; quite different from the grubby children we had seen all along the way at various anganwadis and schools. Shanta taught them songs and told them about sanitation for an hour every day. 'Didi, I want to study further,' she said with eyes lowered. We felt so proud of her; for us she was the star of this place! Hers was an example that needed to be shared at national and international forums. But when she lifted her eyes to look up, we were shocked at their yellowing whites. 'Since when have you been unwell?' The symptoms of jaundice were evident. 'Please ensure she gets urgent medical attention,' we asked the officials as we left the maawadi centre. At the door we met Sohan Kathodi, a thickset twenty-year-old who was president of the Kathodi Samaj Development Committee. 'Didi, when our children go to school, they are beaten up by kids from other castes and tribes. They are made to feel "neech" (inferior) so they prefer to stay home,' he said. 'There is one more thing, didi. When parents migrate for work, they are forced to take the children along. So the kids are not able to attend school. If only there was a hostel, parents would be able to leave the children behind and they would attend school.'

'Would the parents leave their children behind?' we asked.

'Of course, they would,' he said with great confidence.

At the chaupal, a meeting had been arranged by the tehsildar with the panchayat representatives and health workers who were introduced as swasthyakarmis. The swasthyakarmis are tribal women who are trained to check for tuberculosis (rampant in the region), and promote DOTS treatment. For this area, 800 adivasi women from different villages have been trained. They have learnt the use of basic medicines and method of identifying symptoms that require immediate care. A young swasthyakarmi in a bright pink lehnga was introduced as Tipu Devi from the village of Samijha. She confidently opened her little attaché case and explained the use of the antacid tablet, Digene, a contraceptive pill, Mala D, clove oil and Paracetamol. 'Didi, we also make people construct toilets and teach saaf safaiyee (good hygiene),' she said, smiling. 'In my village, many houses now have latrines.' As she spoke, she replaced the medicines neatly into her case.

The mothers who had gathered at the meeting told us that their children went everyday to anganwadis and schools. As they spoke, we heard shouting outside the tent. Everyone rushed out. A group of Kathodi women were shouting. They said their kids were often sent back hungry from the anganwadis. We asked, the anganwadi workers whether this was because of caste issues or food shortage, but they angrily denied this. They maintained that, using the pretext of their children, the women wanted rations for the whole family.

By the time we reached Udaipur, darkness was setting in. The day's travel in the heat had drained away every drop of energy. Just as we were dropping with fatigue, Udaipur worked her magic like an old enchantress. After a hot shower, tiredness forgotten, we found ourselves once again on the road; this time to Sajjangarh Fort, also known as Monsoon Palace. This fort commands a spectacular view of the city from a hill in the Sajjangarh Wildlife Sanctuary. The ruin of what was once a hunting lodge and pleasure dome, the fort overlooks the City of Lakes. By the time we reached, the last stragglers of the sun's army had fled, and the twinkling city lights were performing their daily victory ritual against a dark clear sky. The sound of the silence emanating from the surrounding forests, and the cool breeze that accompanied it, were most soothing. We left Sajjangarh with lightness in our hearts.

Two years later, we found ourselves back in the City of Lakes. 'I have to show you something before you set out for your trip,' Shikhar Aggarwal, still district collector, insisted. Our cars stopped in the M.B. Government Hospital Campus near Chetak Chowk, in the heart of Udaipur.

'Here?' we asked dubiously, as we saw the typical government hospital with paan-stain covered walls. 'This is the Pannadhai Government Janana Hospital,' the collector said, smiling. 'Let's go upstairs.'

A flight of wide stairs brought us to a different world. A smart reception area with spotless marble flooring, comfortable chairs, a glass table and a busy but smiling receptionist greeted us. It resembled a private hospital in a big city. 'This is our new initiative, our attempt to ensure healthcare for the school-going children,' the collector explained. 'For two years now, Hyderabad-based Naandi Foundation has been running a School Health Programme for the children of Hyderabad. So we in Udaipur decided to partner with them to see if we could deliver health to over 43,000 children from 222 government schools and madrassas, 24×7.'

We saw the ward. There were twelve beds, covered with clean sheets. A few were occupied. Next door was a state-of-the-art paediatric ICU with seven beds. 'This is very impressive, but the costs?' we asked the collector.

'You won't believe it. Just 50 paisa per day per child; one-fourth the amount you spend on midday meals or ICDS. This much is enough for us to run twenty-two out-patient clinics in schools where doctors sit for six hours on alternate days and identify the acute problems among children which need immediate attention. We provide free treatment, free medicines, free food for in-patients and their attendants at the hospital.' We learnt that all the children were issued identity cards with photographs under the programme and underwent regular check-ups. In case of a serious illness, they received complete care. This unit at M.B. Hospital had nine doctors, four of whom were paediatricians. In addition to that, the programme had tie-ups with several hospitals and diagnostic clinics in the city of Udaipur. 'For more difficult cases, we take the children to Ahmedabad. We have tie-ups with three super-speciality hospitals there – Sterling, Sal and Apollo.' The programme had started in Udaipur in January 2007.[5] Such was its success that the Rajasthan government extended it to Jodhpur and Bikaner. At the time of our visit, the programme was still relatively new in Udaipur. It had been operational for six months but already a few cardiac surgeries

---

[5]   The School Health Programme (SHP) has now been included as part of National Rural Health Mission (NRHM) in Rajasthan with NICE (Neonatal Intensive Care and Emergencies) Foundation – the implementing partner for the Hyderabad-based Naandi Foundation as the supporting NGO and partner.

had been carried out.[6] The success and potential of the initiative was clearly visible. We decided to make a strong pitch for it through convergence between the Ministries of Health and Education.

With hope in our hearts we set out for the second part of our journey. We had heard that the longest wall in the world, second only to the Great Wall of China, was in nearby Rajsamand. We had also been told about other heritage sites in and around Udaipur. 'They are our real treasures; if only word could go out that it is indeed Incredible India!' It was these sites that we wanted to discover. Some thirty-five km from Udaipur is Tehsil Gogunda – the second highest point in the Aravalli ranges. Here there is a small museum dedicated to the legendary Rana Pratap. It was in this little-known town that the Rana, who became famous for his defiance of the Mughal emperor Akbar, was crowned the 54th ruler of Mewar. Between Udaipur and Gogunda, work on the national highway was in progress; the trees and shrubs were layered with dust. We saw sliced up mountain sides and uprooted trees on both sides of the road. The degradation of the environment was the trade-off for this highway which would make travel easier for the tourists and locals alike. A little beyond Gogunda, we saw the ranges of the Aravallis in patches of rust and green. The road became winding as we negotiated our way through the rocky mountains dotted with barren 'sculpted' trees. Jain temple ruins were scattered all along the way. We had entered Pali District. Five kilometres into this district (which is known for its textile industry) was the 600-year-old Ranakpur temple cluster. Located ninety km from Udaipur, just off the main Jodhpur–Udaipur Highway, it is the most spectacular sight.

Built in the fifteenth century by an illiterate Shaivite architect Deepaji, the main temple of Lord Adinath has 1,444 pillars, all with different designs. This Chaturmukh (four-faced) Jain temple has eighty-four dungeons and two huge bells weighing 250 kg each. When the pujari (priest) strikes the bell, its 'Om' can be heard in villages five km away. This three-storeyed sandstone edifice with marble interiors is spread across an area of 48,000 sq feet, and is managed by the sixteenth generation of the family of Dhanna Seth who commissioned the project. Looking at the intricate designs that

---

[6] As of end 2009, the SHP Udaipur had provided medical treatment to 1.35 lakh children and carried out 167 surgeries.

adorn the walls, pillars and the highly ornate ceilings of the temples, we saw the reason why these temples draw not only pilgrims but hordes of tourists from across the world. Sixty-three years of work by the best masons, handpicked from all over the country, is clearly visible in the exquisite design motifs and sculptures. This visual feast was followed by another kind of feast. The rasora is the kitchen of this temple complex. Here we sat down for a simple Jain meal, delicious dal and vegetables beautifully served, minus onion, garlic or tubers. Everything, even the sweets, had been prepared in the rasora.

From Ranakpur we set out on the sixty-five km journey to Kumbhalgarh, along a single-lane road. Often, we saw farmers driving their bulls around the Persian wheel to irrigate their fields. On one such occasion, we got down to watch the bulls ambling along as the water came up in tiny buckets and flowed in channels to the fields.

As we entered Kumbhalgarh, the sun had almost set. We tried to catch a glimpse of the Wall and the Kumbhalgarh Fort but all we saw were the contours of the mountains. The fort, we later learnt, was built so that it could not be seen until you reached the carriageway leading to its gate. This was to ensure its security and give guards time to repel invaders. As the road turned, there it was, the majestic structure built by Maharana Kumbha. The setting sun had thrown a red-tinted swathe across the thirty-six km wall which fronted the fort. The width of the wall was enough to take four horses abreast. The fort stood on top of the hill and overlooked the 610 square km Kumbhalgarh Wildlife Sanctuary. It appeared invincible; in its entire life, it had been breached only once, that too, not by an armed attack. The enemy breached its security by poisoning its water and thereby forcing its inhabitants to surrender.

Gradually, the lights came on. With thousands of specks appearing in the pitch-darkness surrounding us, the stars above seemed to pale. We were standing in the jharokha (overhanging balcony) of one of the many temples inside this fifteenth century fortress. Looking up through the curtain of a light drizzle, we saw an ethereal sight. Sitting on the peak, dressed in full royal attire and glittering with accessories, stood the two main structures of the Kumbhalgarh Fort; palaces of Maharana Kumbha and Rani Udai Singh. 'And if you turn a little to your right, you will see a group of the most unique Jain temples,' someone said. We turned around to witness the rarest example of temple architecture; it seemed to float in the darkened forest like a lit up ship. We tried to imagine what this magnificent fortress would look like during the Kumbhalgarh festival which is held over three days in December every year. Against the backdrop of palaces and the wall, India's top artists and dancers perform. The festival is a tourist event but it is offered as a tribute to Maharana Kumbha who was himself an accomplished veena player, writer, and dancer.

The next morning, the Kumbhalgarh Fort had a completely changed garb. The stone structure had taken on a rugged look against the azure sky. A flight of steps took us atop the second longest wall in the world. From here as far as the eye could see, across 24 square km of wilderness, there were crumbling yet beautiful monuments and structures. Most of them were Jain and Shaivite temples. Others were baoris (stepwells), rest houses and gates. There were no trails leading to these monuments. Each seemed to be waiting to be 'discovered' by an archaeologist or an adventure tourist. The only trail which existed was the steep climb that led to the palaces of Maharana Kumbha and Maharani Udai Singh. These palaces were unique in their simplicity. It was here that Panna Dai had faithfully smuggled and hidden the young infant Udai Singh to save his life. When he grew up he founded the city of Udaipur. The palaces offered a view which starts at the mountains and wildlife sanctuary, and, on a clear day, extends up to the desert region of Marwar. The administration told us that they planned to open a Maharana Kumbha and Udai Singh Museum here. They were also planning to hold performances and stalls all year round featuring local artists and artisans.

Kumbhalgarh has other attractions as well. For animal- and adventure-lovers, there is a less frequented wildlife sanctuary spread across Rajsamand, Pali and Udaipur. Apart from animal sightings and jeep safaris, there are a few trekking routes in and around the area. But there is no tourist infrastructure; the town has only four hotels, with a total of one hundred beds. Being a sanctuary, there is no scope for building, though some entrepreneurs have started innovative projects like fancy tents on raised platforms. We visited Dera, one such camp hotel.

That afternoon we discussed with local officials the accommodation problem and how to realize Kumbhalgarh's tourist potential. Bhanwar Singh, a local tourist guide, hesitantly shared his idea. 'I know the perfect spot', he said. 'It's a small village, just seven km away. Khelwara. It is a picturesque spot which could be developed for village tourism. Travellers could stay there and experience the lifestyle of Mewar, its food, and culture. They could then go to the famous Charbhujaji temples just forty km away.' The tourist circuit was right there, waiting for someone to join the dots. We told them that we would make a strong case for it with the state government as soon as we got back.

Our journey continued. We moved from Kumbhalgarh to Nathdwara, passing en route the lovely Rajsamand Lake.

Nathdwara is a temple town; thousands of pilgrims come here every day to seek the blessings of Srinathji. The temple is dedicated to a childhood avatar of Lord Krishna. Every day 600 kg of ghee and 600 kg of vegetables are used to make prasad (offerings to God), which is then sold to devotees from all over the world; most of them come from Gujarat. Srinathji opens six times every day for short durations. During afternoons, darshan (viewing) is allowed for only fifteen minutes. When we entered, it was overflowing with devotees of all ages and backgrounds, each clambering past the other to get one glimpse of the Lord. Despite the jostling and elbowing by the crowds, we were very moved by the devotion we saw everywhere.

The town of Nathdwara is famous both for its intricate silver minakari (enamelling) and fake Bollywood jewellery. The latter is used primarily in films and beauty parlours. 'Our jewellery is used to deck the bride for the camera. It is made for wedding albums and wedding videos,' explained an obliging Sarvesh Modi, whose jewellery workshop was located above his small showroom. The technique of cutting lead into small pieces, polishing it and neatly laying it across metal frames to resemble period jewellery was developed in Maharashtra. 'There is great demand for such items. We used to get the pieces from Maharashtra and finish them here. So we decided to make the pieces ourselves. We now get the designs direct from Mumbai and other places. The pasting is done at home by women in and around Nathdwara,' said Mukesh, a young salesman with gelled hair dressed in a bright printed shirt. Business is good and each of the forty families engaged in the trade makes a monthly profit of Rs 5,000–Rs 10,000. 'This is the famous sat-lara (seven strand necklace) Aishwarya Rai wore in the movie *Jodhaa Akbar*; now it is in high demand for wedding functions,' Mukesh said, carefully lifting a glittering red-and gold-ornament from its case. 'And this is the necklace from Deepika Padukone's last dance sequence in *Om Shanti Om*.' Mukesh held the necklace to his chest and flailed his arms in a dance movement. 'Madamji, dreams of Bollywood, crafted in Nathdwara!'

We next visited the sunars (goldsmith). There are twenty sunar families in the city who engage in silver minakari. After straining their eyes for long hours, they create intricate patterns on silver with pink, black, aquamarine green colours. The patterns and colours used on the silver bangles, earrings and ittardanis (containers for perfume) reminded us of Persian miniature art. But when we asked the craftsmen they said they had not heard much about Persia. For twenty days of hard work they make about Rs 3,000. They create beauty while living in poor, unsanitary, cramped houses and surroundings.

Our next stop was Molela, a small village sixteen km from Nathdwara, known for its terracotta work. Forty families in this village excavate clay from lake beds and mix it with horse and donkey excreta to create images which are embedded in terracotta panels. They tell stories of village life and the world of deities. Mohanlal Kumbhar was one such terracotta artist. His house cum-workshop had panels in all hues and sizes. Traditionally, the terracotta artists used to make panels only about the life of gods and goddesses. These had a local market, and were used by most households in the nearby villages. 'Now we have started depicting our festivals and culture through these panels. They are greatly admired by tourists,' said Mohanlal. We watched as one of his artisans began creating a panel telling a story. Sitting on his haunches on the mud floor, the kumbhar (potter) rolled out the clay mixture and began to create figures with his fingers. He told us that it took him one day to make one intricate panel. This would then be baked to get the required texture and colour. We noticed that the work itself was good but it lacked finish. If the artisans could be trained to give their work the proper finish, and find means to arrange a display, Molela could become a part of the Udaipur–Ranakpur–Kumbhalgarh–Nathdwara–Udaipur tourist circuit and its artists could find their market at their doorstep.

The final stop on the tourist circuit which we were thinking about would be Haldighati, forty km from Udaipur. This was the site of the famous battle of 1576 between Rana Pratap of Mewar and Raja Man Singh of Amber, who was sipah salar (army general) of Akbar. Haldighati has a museum of weapons with paintings of the famous battlefield and a 'Sound and Light' show which offers the history of the Ranas and glimpses of the battle.

We returned to Udaipur, full of ideas about tourism and sustainable livelihoods which could reduce the ubiquitous malnutrition and poverty levels. The officers we had met offered to draft a proposal for the tour circuit and ask for central government assistance. It has been three years; the proposal is yet to come.

Our next destination lay to the west of Udaipur, the contiguous districts of Kota, Bundi and Baran. Travelling around Kota, it is difficult to believe that one is in Rajasthan. There are no lakes in this area but the lush green fields, criss-crossing rivulets and undulating terrain of the region are in sharp contrast to the stereotypical images of the 'desert' state: hot unrelenting sun beating down on an endless stretch of sand. This primarily urban division[7] is just four hours from Delhi by the Rajdhani Express. In mid-July, when we reached Kota, its annual affair with the monsoons had just begun. Incessant rains and waterlogged streets under a darkening sky welcomed us to this city known to most Indians for the superior coaching classes that it offers. Every year, thousands of students come here, take up paying-guest accommodation and attend coaching classes. Hundreds of signs all over the city announce the tutorial bonanza; low fees, spectacular success rates in all entrance examinations!

Kota is located in the opium-producing Hadoti belt of Rajasthan. Till some time ago, the people of Kota and its neighbouring districts used to proudly say that they were just opium producers, not consumers![8] The last

---

[7]   The Kota Division located in south-eastern Rajasthan comprises six districts – Kota, Bundi, Baran, Jhalawar, Karauli and Sawai Madhopur.

[8]   The Divisional Commissioner, Kota, told us that the government had allotted 7,000–8,000 pattas (land ownership documents) for opium production. People

few years, however, have seen more and more youth taking to smack. We were invited to flag off an anti-tobacco and anti-drugs rally. It was pouring all the way to Umedh Club, which was the venue for the flag off. We were almost certain that the event would be a no-show. To our surprise, we saw over 200 students from local schools standing in the rain with their umbrellas, chanting slogans in perfect cadence. The rain had drenched everything but their spirits.

Next we planned to go to the historic town of Bundi. Named after a Meena tribal chieftain Bunda, this area was inhabited by tribes such as the Bhil and the Meena. In 1193 AD, when Prithvi Raj Chauhan was defeated by Sultan Mohammed Ghauri, the Chauhan nobility such as the Hada Rajputs moved towards the Chambal valley and overpowered local tribes to establish the kingdom of Hadoti. Later, two branches of Hadas formed the separate states of Kota and Bundi on either side of the river Chambal. Though the area and importance of Bundi State diminished over the years, it continued to remain independent, if only nominally, during the British Raj.

The rains had turned the Kota–Bundi highway to a country road filled with potholes and pools of water. Anxious officers warned us that the climb inside Bundi's famous citadel was treacherous, absolutely unadvisable during the rain. But we did not heed their warning and decided to go. We had been in the car for almost an hour when a wondrous sight appeared to the left. Perched on a hill, the Taragarh Fort was like a castle rising from a dream. A sonnet of the poet John Keats came to mind: 'Then felt I like some watcher of the skies/When a new planet swims into his ken'.

Our wonderment at seeing Taragarh was the same as Keats felt when he watched the shooting star. The cars stopped. The fort stood at the end of a steep and slippery climb. Just outside the huge gate, Mugdha Sharma, the district collector, was waiting. She helped us on the treacherous climb and took us to see the masterpieces of art that adorned the walls and ceilings of Garh ki Paras, the local name for Taragarh. 'We no longer find such workmanship. Our painters have switched to the Kishengarh school

---

were supposed to turn in their entire produce to the government at Rs 1,200 per kg. However, in the open market, they can earn up to Rs 1 lakh per kg and Rs 6 lakh per kg for morphine. So there is a lot of smuggling.

of painting. The delicate mix of blue and green, the confluence of Persian and Hindu art, the straight lines and fine bone structures which were the hallmark of the Bundi School have disappeared,' she said sadly.

What once brought international fame to this town is now lost. The exquisite seventeenth century lapis lazuli and gold work that adorned the walls of the palace and the ivory inlaid doors is today a sad reminder of the neglect and apathy that has beset Taragarh. The Belgian mirrors which hang on the walls are broken and distorted. Precious stones have been gouged out of the palace walls, and the paintings in the courtyards are faded or defaced. Lighting inside the fort is poor, no guards are stationed and international tourists, so careful in their own countries, are seen trailing their fingers along the walls, touching every precious relic. One exception to this neglect is the small garden inside the palace, which the Archaeological Survey of India (ASI) maintains with manicured precision. The remainder of the fort, private property of the Raja Sahib of Bundi, is not open to the public.

This run-down abode of Raja of Bundi, with its exquisite workmanship and multiple views of the city, could be developed much better. It is the only remaining repository of the Bundi school of painting, which can be beautifully displayed in its original setting.

The bronze-coloured walls of Taragarh Fort, sundry hunting lodges and palaces like the Sukh Sagar Niwas on Jaitsagar Lake where Rudyard Kipling found inspiration for his classic novel, *Kim*; the fifty stepwells including the forty-six-metre deep Raniji ki Baori with its intricate carvings, romanticize what is essentially a dilapidated town. In the evening light, the small houses nestled at the foothills of the Aravallis; whitewashed with lime mixed with neel (indigo), appear porcelain blue. We asked why Bundi (unlike Udaipur) does not attract thousands of tourists. 'Despite the many wondrous sights in this historic town there is no supporting infrastructure' said Mugdha. 'Tourists are forced to limit their visit to a day and return for the night to Kota.' The town was a mess; haphazard, littered and dirty; in the entire area there was no drainage. We learnt that one-and-a-half metres below the surface there was solid rock. Thus it was very difficult to dig and lay drainage pipes. During monsoons, there was consistent waterlogging. The road turned into dirty black streams and puddles. The problem in Bundi was exacerbated because the town, like many others, was never meant for the one lakh people who live here today.

From Bundi, all the way to our next destination, Kaithun, there was a persistent drizzle. Kaithun is a weavers' town. Two-thirds of the people living here are Bunkars (weavers), most of them Muslims. They sit in their tiny homes in overcrowded, dirty localities, with their feet hanging in pit-looms creating the most exquisite Kota Doria saris. As with the minakari artisans of Nathdwara, here, too, beauty is born out of penury and squalour!

The tiny kutchcha road which we took into the village was edged with filth. Pigs, black with dirt, loitered in the lanes, while barefoot, half-clad children played in the same dirt. We were ushered inside a small hut. Shahana, the young woman at the loom, covered her head with a printed dupatta when we walked in. She was creating a soft shade of pink doria and edging it with delicate gold. Her feet were stuck inside a pit beneath the loom. The room had very little light and the space was just enough for the loom. Kulsum, her mother-in-law, who stood in the doorway, answered all our questions. 'Baji, my bahu (daughter-in-law) is a heera (diamond). She cooks and finishes all the household work in the morning. Then she sits at the loom and is there from 11 a.m. to 4 p.m. every day.' Shahana herself spoke very little. The only thing she said was that earlier the government used to buy their work at local rates but now that had stopped. So the weavers (almost 90 per cent of them are women) are forced to sell their products dirt-cheap. We saw their stock – the saris were beautiful. When we enquired about their prices, we were shocked at the pittance for which they were sold.

Back on the street, there were lots of children playing. None of them would, we realized, opt for the profession of their parents. Abject poverty is drawing them away from their traditional occupation. They see on their walls certificates which their parents' excellent workmanship had won. But they see nothing by way of a sustained livelihood. Cheap powerloom imitations have edged out the handloom artisans. Though Kota Doria has now been registered under the Geological Indication Act[9] to make sure

---

[9] Later, the Divisional Commissioner, J.C. Mohanty, clarified that the Kota Doria Saris have been registered under the GI Act by an organization called the

that only the Kota Doria Hadoti community can make these saris, the weavers are yet to reap the benefits of this registration.

In Kaithun, we learnt that the plight of the 150 weaver families from Mangrol, a small town next door, was even worse. The same story: no markets, abject poverty, inability to compete with 'do number ki Kota' (fakes) being mass-produced on the power loom. One of the officers accompanying us offered his explanation: 'Madamji, what can we do? There is just no demand for these saris.'

In five years, we had heard this expression often, especially in official Delhi circles. 'The fate of our weavers is sealed because today's generation does not believe in wearing saris. There is nothing practical about a sari, etc., etc. ...' But how could one believe that the sari was impractical and hence a thing of the past? Syeda's entire odyssey through India was performed comfortably in the traditional six yards of cloth.

The officer continued his explanation, 'We have tried to get the weavers to diversify. Design experts have been brought in from home and abroad. But these weavers, they are too traditional. We had received a large order for curtain linen, but they were reluctant to venture into new territory. So we could not service the order.' Even as the officer complained, we could understand the fear that must have seized weavers like Shahana and Kulsum. Suppose they altered their looms and started making curtain linen. Then what? What would they do after the order was complete? What if there was no new order? Could they afford the risk? What would they do if as a consequence their kitchens remained empty?

The next day, we moved towards Baran District, accompanied by J.C. Mohanty, divisional commissioner in charge of Kota, Bundi, Baran and Jhalawar. We were heading to the Kishenganj and Shahabad tehsils, to the Sahariya areas. The Sahariya are the only PTG in Rajasthan and are recognized as one of the first inhabitants of the state. The name 'Sahariya' comes from the Arabic word 'Sehera' meaning 'wilderness.' It is believed that the term was coined by the Muslim rulers of the area when they came across

---

Hadoti Bunkar Sangathan with the help of Manjri Joshi. This organization has membership from weavers across the region.

the tribes residing in the jungles.[10] Today, there are about 76,000 Sahariya spread across the Shahabad and Kishenganj tehsils of Baran District. Dravidian in origin, they have over the years given up their tribal religion and become practising Hindus. The Sahariya collect forest produce and work as agricultural labour. They also live in abject poverty and are ridden by continuous debt and malnutrition. In 2003, the reports of starvation deaths among them made national headlines.

Soon, we crossed the raging Kalisindh and Parvati rivers. Both these tributaries of the river Chambal wreak havoc in the district every monsoon. Mohanty, told us that, till a few years ago during the monsoon, Baran was cut off from the rest of the state, such was the fury of these two rivers. Only after it was made a separate district in 1991 and the Kalisindh bridge constructed, did the area become accessible. Suddenly it struck us why this district was called Baran; the Persian word for a rain-bearing cloud is abr-e-baran. The skies of Baran are filled with such clouds. The name Baran was just right for this district; we found that no one from the area knew about this etymology.

Kalisindh Bridge is the longest bridge in Rajasthan. Once we reached the other side of the bridge, a new kind of landscape began to unfold. In stark contrast to the greens of Kota, this was a barren and rugged territory, a bright parched and rocky scrubland. We sped past hamlet after hamlet with small kutchcha huts; women's colourful ghagras (traditional skirts) were patches of colour amidst rubbish strewn all over. Many children of school-going age, clothed in dirty rags, were loitering in the streets. 'These are mostly Kherva, Gadiya Lohar or Sahariya children,' an accompanying officer informed us.

By the roadside, we saw a small cluster of ramshackle houses. We stopped and so did the long row of cars behind us. Immediately a group of children and adults appeared and surrounded the vehicles. Someone said this was a Kherva hamlet just outside Pinjna Village. The Kherva people are extremely poor tribals. Unlike the Sahariya, they have not been declared a scheduled tribe. The houses we saw were built of mud and leaves. Gradually, many women gathered around us. 'We can't send our children to the village

---

[10] http://baran.nic.in/sahariya.htm; accessed on 27 July 2009.

school. We are asked to pay a fee of Rs 30.' The mothers and children all appeared undernourished.

'Do you get wheat at Rs 2 per kg?' we asked.

'No.' We looked at the accompanying officials for an answer. After a short silence, someone spoke up. 'Only people with BPL or Antyodaya cards are entitled to such subsidized rations.'

'Do you have cards?' we asked two ghoonghat-wearing (veiled) women, Kanti and Shanti, sisters-in-law. They were both pregnant. They said no. They also said there was no anganwadi in their gaon (hamlet) of 250 people; the nearest one was in the village which was more than one kilometre away. 'It gives only murmure (puffed rice) to children and pregnant women once a week. So we have stopped sending our children there.'

Most of the Kherva children who were standing around us had pot-bellies and dirty little faces. We insisted that they be immediately admitted to the village school. The children were herded together in one of the accompanying jeeps and we moved on the road in a large convoy. The closest school consisted of a dilapidated structure and a small courtyard in which the classes were being held. We learnt that for 350 kids there were just two classrooms; so when it rained, classes were cancelled. There was no toilet. The children said they went home or to the fields to relieve themselves. There were no regular teachers, only shikshakarmis (educational workers). We asked a few students to read aloud. Surprisingly, they were able to read from the text and even recite poems. Just then, the lunch bell rang. We watched the kids bringing steel plates and spoons and sitting in neat rows around the courtyard. Akshaya Patra, an NGO which provided midday meals, served the kids aloo ki sabzi (potato curry) and poori from steaming containers. This organization provides free meals to over one million school children in seven states including Karnataka, Uttar Pradesh and parts of Rajasthan. At the time of our visit, it was providing meals in twenty-four villages in the area. In the two months since they had been working here, they had seen rampant casteism. Children from the upper castes refused to eat meals cooked by lower-caste women.

Next door to the school was the anganwadi. We decided to walk over. A terrible stench from a rotting carcass hung in the air. No one, neither the people nor the panchayat had bothered to remove the dead animal. The anganwadi was a tiny two-room building on a high plinth; we did not see any children or mothers. The helper, Kasturi Devi, a sad-looking woman, told us that the centre was used as a storehouse from which 125 gm of murmure per child per day was distributed every Thursday. 'But, didi, the children don't like murmure,' she said, gesturing towards the next room. We saw sacks of rotting murmure piled up under a leaking roof. Who could blame the kids?

From here we headed towards the Sahariya region. From the car window we saw beautiful designs painted on the doors of houses along the road. The sign read 'Village Gajreta'. We asked the driver to stop near a door which was beautifully painted with birds, flowers and creepers. A host of officials came along behind us, admiring, perhaps for the first time, this lovely form of darwaza (door) art. 'My wife made this,' said an old man in a dhoti(loincloth) whose name was Bhogilal. 'All women in the village make such phad paintings.' He invited us inside. We found ourselves in a small courtyard. He placed a cot for us to sit on. We noticed that it was beautifully woven with baan (jute rope) in lively colours. 'My wife,' he repeated. 'She has gone to work in the field but you must have tea.' As we sipped tea, we spoke to him about thousands of villages in this division where unknown local artists may be creating many such vibrant pieces of art.

Mohanty looked at the crowd and called out to a smartly dressed young boy. 'What is your name?'

'Sir, I am Naresh Mehta, student, Class 10.'

'Get the villagers together and let them produce cots. Once you have fifty cots ready, come and see me. I want to see you become a successful cot manufacturer. Naresh will be the first entrepreneur of Gajreta!'

There was a chorus of approval from the crowd.

Finally, we reached the Sahariya territory. We learnt that the Sahariya usually live in forest enclosures called CIG (Common Interest Group). The scheme under which they operate is the Sahariya Vikas Jan Van Shakti Yojana. The cars turned at a sign which read 'Vivekananda CIG'. We were at Shahapura in Shahabad Block. Two women with red bandanas stood at a gate, waving red flags. 'Yeh hamare closure ka jhanda hai (this is the flag of our [en]closure),' they said, welcoming us with smiles. Following the neat stone-lined path, we came to a clearing with a hut in the centre. A small group of women and men were waiting for us. 'For our plantations we dig trenches. In three years' time, every family here will earn Rs 10,000 per year from Jatropha alone,' the forest conservator explained. Janaki Sahariya, a fifty-year-old pradhan, described how the people had fenced off their enclosures. 'We dug trenches and sowed Jatropha, neem, Aloe vera and hamata grass. We were given mazdoori (wages) of Rs 65 per day for making the enclosure; three-fourths of the wage was in the form of wheat at Rs 4 a kg.'

Kanti Bai Sahariya, in a dhoti and red scarf, explained other features of the CIG. 'We sell fruits and flowers of the forest to make a living. One head-load of grass sells for Rs 10. Five of our people guard the enclosure every day by rotation to protect the forest from encroachers. But the Forest Department has provision for only thirty-five people to patrol the over 1.5 lakh hectares of forestland in Kishenganj and Shahabad, that too, without any vehicle!'

Hamroo Sahariya, who did not know his age, spoke next. 'Didi, when I fell ill I had to go all the way to Kelwara and pay Rs 900 in medical fees.' Kunti and Sarju, (like many youth here, we were told) complained of stomach ailments. 'Bad drinking water is making us sick.'

Bahadur, a smiling Class 3 student, came forward. He counted up to twenty and recited the Hindi alphabet. 'Didi, let me show you something,' he said grabbing our hands and ushering us inside a tent which had been pitched in the corner. Everyone followed us. Inside, we saw a unique lighting system developed to electrify their guard post. Two fused batteries were immersed in a glass packed with cow dung and a small amount of salt. This was connected with a wire to a small bulb. The young Sahariya innovator Shivnath told us: 'If you give me twenty-five fused batteries, I will generate enough power to play a CD!'

In the wilderness of Baran, we saw how the Sahariya were trying to carve out a future. Everyone asked for work, not dole. Now that the hundred days of work for construction of enclosures had run out, they had nothing to do. 'The Jatropha and other crops will take a couple of seasons to come up. What will we do until then?' Janaki Sahariya's question asked for a policy to fill the livelihood gap.

As we left the enclosure, it began raining heavily and there were tiny streams and rivulets forming all over the roads. Like a faithful companion, not once did the rain leave our side. Sheets of water were pouring as we headed for a nearby village, Bainta, where we were going to visit another tribal maawadi.

At this maawadi, there were thirty Sahariya children of different ages. The walls of the small classroom were pasted with educational charts and aids. Their teacher, Nandlal Sahariya, had passed Class 12 from an ashram school-cum-chhatrawas (hostel). Grubby faces in faded uniforms were trussed up in little ties. The children chanted the alphabet and sang the national anthem. Bainta Village held out hope for a better future. Something good was happening here.

The next stop, Shahabad, was at a short distance from Bainta. There we saw the magnificent Shahi Mosque, built during the reign of Aurangzeb. Our first sight of it was through the rain. We were told that this masjid was the inspiration for the Jama Masjid in Delhi. The huge gumbad (dome) and tall minarets set against the azure sky were a magnificent sight. The grandeur of Rajasthan's biggest mosque with its pure white facade was a moving sight. Further on, we could see the Shahabad Fort perched on top of a hill. Built in 1577 AD by the Chauhan ruler Vanshi Dhandhel Rajput Mukutmani Dev, the chronicles say that the fort once had eighteen cannons, one of which was nineteen feet long. The amber-coloured ramparts of Shahabad Fort rising from the green brush reflected human genius and fine workmanship. The fluffy white clouds floating above transformed it to a surreal sight.

It was growing dark when we began our journey back to Kota to catch the night train to Delhi. The weather was turning nastier by the hour. The road on which our vehicles had run earlier that day, had disappeared at many places.[11] The tiny streams which we had seen playing on its tarred surface had become strong lehars (waves) that were dangerous to cross.

Our cars stopped at a place called Samaraniya. The bridge over the nullah (stream), which had been damaged a few days earlier, had been difficult to

---

[11] The Road from Bundi to Kelva Thana in Baran has been declared as National Highway 76. The National Highways Authority of India (NHAI) is undertaking a Rs 72-crore project to make it a four-lane highway. Two bridges will also be built to ensure accessibility to this area during monsoons.

cross even in the morning. Now with the waters flowing well above it, it was unapproachable. Cars, buses and trucks were haphazardly lining up on either side of the small bridge. No one could see where the bridge was located in the roaring waters. A police posse tried to locate the broken stretch of the bridge. They formed a human chain along the boundary of the bridge and the broken stretch to estimate how much of the bridge was still standing. Our drivers shook their heads helplessly. One of them suggested that we board the Rajasthan Roadways bus which was lined up in front of us. 'It's steadier,' he said. So we boarded the bus. Gradually, it edged forward. Halfway on the bridge, at the broken part, the bus gave a huge lurch and then with great difficulty heaved itself across. The first hurdle had been surmounted.

Just as we were about to get off the bus, a harried Mohanty appeared at the window. 'There's three feet of water at Gharawali. The only way is to travel by bus.' So we stayed inside the bus and crossed Gharawali and a few other big streams before reaching Kelwara. What we saw here made our heart sink. This was no small stream, but a huge mass of raging water. There was no question of the bus or any vehicle crossing over. Suddenly there was panic all around. 'Please call the state plane,' we requested. But they shook their heads. Phone lines in Samaraniya had been dead for four days. 'In any case, the plane is at Jodhpur and landing is not possible after dark.'

In the darkness we could hear the commotion. People were scurrying back and forth from trucks lined up on either side of the furious stream. Everyone was guessing when the water would abate. A boy on a tractor assured us that the water would begin to recede in one hour and then he would take us across. After the hour was up, we asked. He said that though the water had ebbed a little, it was still impossible, even for the tractor. By now it was 6.30 p.m. The boy who had promised to take us across said he would do so as soon as the stone markers on the bridge become visible. 'That would indicate the water depth is at three feet; I will be able to make out the road. Not now …' he said, shaking his head.

Here we were, stuck on the banks of a raging river, with no hope of crossing over. Nature was giving us a taste of the annual trauma suffered by the local people. Phone lines dead, people stuck in markets or in their fields. The only thing to do was wait for the water to recede. Baran thus lived up to its name; the 'Baranis' suffer this condition at least once every year.

A little while later, torches and headlights were switched on at both ends of the bridge in an attempt to assess the level of water. Finally, the boy decided to try. The overriding fear was that the force of the water may might sweep the tractor downstream, so fifteen policemen and villagers clambered onto the tractor to make it steady. With a couple of floodlights to guide it, the tractor began its slow and arduous journey. After ten long minutes, it made it across to the other side. The crowd shouted with relief. The tractor's return journey was quicker but the verdict: still too dangerous; wait for another half-hour.

The minutes went by agonizingly slowly. Everyone said that crossing by truck was safest; at least it wouldn't overturn. Zayed Khan from Kalesingha offered to take us. Climbing onto a huge loader truck is no easy task, especially when one is wearing a sari. A Gypsy was brought as a footstool, next to the truck. From its bonnet we scrambled onto the truck. At the stroke of nine, we were ready to take on the waters, which were gradually losing volume and energy. Within ten minutes Khan had taken us across safely. We arrived in Kota just in time for the train.

'Sehra mein bhi kabhi sailaab aata hai? Tabahi ka woh manzar humne dekha hai.' (Have you ever heard of flood in the dunes? We have seen the devastation it unleashes.)

In August 2006, fate played a cruel trick on the people of western Rajasthan; people who live in scattered habitations across large tracts of barren, sandy desert land; people who have learnt to survive in the face of all adversity. The merciless sun beating down relentlessly on their heads and homes hasn't cowed them down. The enervating heat of the desert, its sheer desolation has not sapped their energy or broken their spirit. Instead, they have learnt to make the best of their circumstances. The waste available to them – rags, stems of desert plants, camel hair, goat hair, camel bones and even sheep horns – is used to create vibrant, colourful handicrafts and intricate patterns which adorn homes not just in India, but across the globe. Indeed, the people of Rajasthan have done Darwin proud; they have made themselves fit enough to survive in this inhospitable, almost hostile terrain.

Then, suddenly, in the course of a single night, all this changed. For some unknown reason, nature wreaked a strange vengeance on them. People who always prayed for a few showers of rain to water their bajra (millets) and moong (lentils) were suddenly greeted with torrential rains. They, who had hardly seen rain were crushed under a fifteen–twenty foot wall of water. Mounds of sand caved into small lakes and streams. Houses, bajra fields, cattle, roads, all were swept away. On television screens, viewers saw men, women and children clinging to rooftops of houses, mosques, temples, wildly waving at rescue helicopters, their faces filled with terror. Reports of inadequate relief and fear of impending epidemic poured from all quarters. So, in October 2006, we found ourselves heading towards the barren sand hills of Barmer to see what nature had done to a tough and resourceful people, and to assess what needed to be done to restore their battered lives.

The landscape grew more and more arid as we approached Barmer. As far as the eye could see, there was endless sand. The only dots visible were camels, cacti and sheep. On the way, we noticed how scattered the habitations were. In the midst of the desert we would see a small patch of bajra and a solitary hut. No electricity, no telephone. We learnt that the men of these dhanis migrate for work to Gujarat and Maharashtra for six to eight months every year. The women, children and seniors are left behind to wage a lonely struggle in the harsh weather.

On the way to Barmer, we passed the textile-dyeing town of Balotra. Our convoy was heading towards the village of Kawas, still under six feet of water. Before the flood, 500 families had land in this village.[12] Kawas is located in a depression or low-lying land. It is here that the water gushed from the Jaisalmer side, breaking anicut after anicut, flowing and flooding. It was 3 a.m. when the kutchcha houses filled with sleeping families collapsed. People who had pucca houses were terrified and locked themselves inside. They had never witnessed such a phenomenon. Over fifty lives were lost.

---

[12] When we visited Kawas, it was under six–eight feet of water. By November 2006 draining efforts had begun to show results and water levels had come down substantially. However, there was still 350 mcft of water in Kawas and almost 50 mcft of silt.

In Kawas, our first sight was water being carried through pipes to a long row of train wagons. Some of the standing water was being drained out in this way. Filling up seventy-two wagons with 25,000 litres of water was taking a long time. But it was not making much difference to the water level, we were told.[13]

Along the road we saw a series of army-tents. Some were little more than plastic sheets tied together. The railway line along the roadside was under four feet of water.[14] Only the tops of trees and roofs of submerged houses were visible. Scattered here and there were smashed bodies of cars which had been retrieved from the water. Ghostly walls of what was once a prosperous gypsum factory were half submerged, telling a tale of devastation and destruction.

Belaram, an old man with a dusty pagri (turban), said there were thirteen members in his household. 'Although we were stuck in the water for over twelve hours, luckily all of us survived.' He asked us to enter the plastic sheet enclosure which was the four walls and roof of his new 'home'. Antri, Belaram's daughter-in-law, was lying inside, delirious with fever. Fever and diarrhoea were common in the camp. We learnt that a doctor was now stationed here round the clock. We noticed many children coughing; some of them had open sores on their legs and arms. Even two months after the flood, the terrible smell of dead animals hung around the campsite.

The people said they had received relief material and tents five–seven days after the flood. At the time of our visit, they were cooking with the rations distributed by NGOs. Water tankers visited the camp regularly. All of them had their own stories about death and survival; how a family of four had died in the waters; how a woman fell to her death because she was unable to cling on to the rope lowered by the rescue helicopter.

---

[13] A *Hindustan Times* report dated 22 October 2006 stated that this had been discontinued as it was proving to be a very expensive method of draining water. Instead, the pipelines laid for the trains were being used to drain water directly to nearby fields. According to Divisional Commissioner, Barmer, the farmers had agreed to sow a rabi (winter) crop and so they wanted this additional water.

[14] As on 20 November 2006, it was under 1–1.5 feet of water, according to Divisional Commissioner, Barmer.

What bothered them most was that they had nothing to occupy their time. Kawas, due to its gypsum deposits, had been a relatively prosperous village. The workers employed at gypsum factories had earned Rs 200 per day. Young boys and girls were in school. Many people worked at various jobs in the state bus transport corporation, at railway counters or had their own shops. 'Didi, we want to work,' Ghotelala, who was the doctor's local assistant, spoke for the many boys who had collected around us. 'But we want to stay here. Don't send us away from home. Just drain out the water.'

The officials spoke of a fifty-km channel that could be dug to connect their village to Loni River, so that the water could be drained out at that end. Such a channel would take at least six months of non-stop work by at least fifty engineers. It would also be extremely expensive since the ground is largely gypsum and granite which is difficult to cut and cannot absorb water. Ironically, gypsum which was once a source of livelihood here, was, in a way responsible for taking lives. The land just could not absorb any water and, as a result, everyone and everything was submerged.

Other areas were luckier. The Chortan sub-division of Barmer, where some of the best handlooms and handicrafts come from, had received the highest rainfall but due to its sandy soil, the water had been absorbed into the ground. Sheo, Baytoo and Barmer had been badly affected because of the granite. Worst off was Kawas, located along the course of the Rohili River. The river used to end at Kawas, therefore the gradient of the land naturally sloped in that direction. The divisional commissioner told us that though the administration had tried to warn the villagers when the anicuts began to break, they had laughed off the warning because floods in the dunes were unheard of. The only time Kawas had seen water was in 1990, and that too, about knee-deep. The average annual rainfall in the area for the last ten years had been 277 mm; in the year of the flood, it was a massive 631 mm. It had shattered roads, including a one-and-a-quarter km stretch of national highway between Bakhra and Nimla. This we saw as we moved from Kawas to Bhimra. We could see along the way where land had been sliced off, trees uprooted, and houses flattened. Small remnants of what were once roads were all that remained. The road to Barmer itself was little more than a track built as a temporary access since the national highway had suffered heavy damage. Someone pointed out the spot where a bus had beencaught in the swirling waters, killing eleven people.

By the time we reached the Circuit House, Barmer, it was late. Just as we were getting ready to sleep, we heard desert music and soulful singing. We went outside and saw a small group of Langas, desert bards, who had come there to sing and welcome us. The Langas are Muslims who have been traditional singers of the dunes. The group, made up of six men and a small boy, was seated on the grass outside our room. It was a full moon night. Typically, after a scorching day, the desert evening had turned cool. For the moment, the songs of the Langas made us forget the disease, despair and devastation which we had seen throughout the day. They had a spirit in their music which remained undaunted. We had seen that spirit at work all day among the survivors of the flood.

Sharfuddin, the tall and lanky lead singer said: 'We have performed all over the world, yet we do not earn enough to feed our children. Since the flood, they have stopped going to school. The waters swept away our houses and whatever little possessions we had. Our musical instruments, sindhi sarangi, kamacha, Raavan-hatha, khadtaal, mar chanag, algoza, all have gone with the water.'

Haji Rahim Khan Chhipa, the elderly mentor of the group, summed up in one line the situation of the 2,500 Langa families: 'Kalakar kya hai? Manch ka Badshah, raaste ka faqir' (What is an artist? King of the stage, beggar of the street). We felt our eyes grow moist even as the music flowed.

The next morning, as we were leaving Barmer behind, we thought of the enormity of the task for us planners, both at the centre and in the states. To ensure that health and education are made accessible to the people living in these remote scattered dhanis. To empower the ghoonghat-clad women to speak out for themselves and their little daughters. To change mindsets which condone silent killing of female foetuses. To provide artisans, artists and musicians from the remotest places a life of dignity.

Barmer imparted the lesson of being prepared for the most unexpected of disasters. This calamity of flood in the dunes bent and shook even the hardiest and most resilient people. Watching television footage of the disaster from Delhi, one could not grasp the suffering of the people of this arid and inhospitable land. Their fear, uncertainty and anguish revealed itself only when we sat with the men and women on the burning sand under plastic sheets and army tents which are their current homes! For policy makers, these visits are a must. It is here that we see women die during childbirth, and many infants fight a losing battle. Life here is a daily struggle for survival. We planners have to go into the eye of the storm to discover its true destruction potential. As the poet said:

'Kinaron se mujhe ai nakhuda, tum dur hi rakhna
Wahan le kar chalo toofan jahaan se utthney wala hai'

O boatman, keep me away from the shores,
Take me to the sea where the storm is brewing

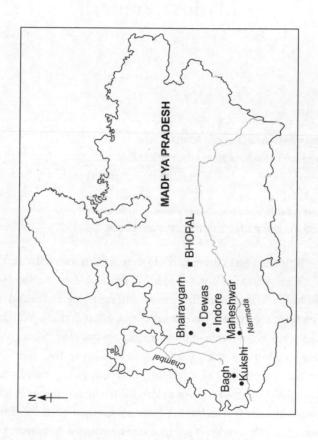

13

Madhya Pradesh

Tera sarmaya teri aas yehi haath to hain
Aur kuch bhi to nahi paas, yehi haath to hain

             – FAIZ

Your wealth, your hope, only these, your hands
Nothing else sustains, only these your hands

A little less than a thousand kilometres from the hustle and bustle of Varanasi, in the heart of Madhya Pradesh, lies another handloom hub – Maheshwar. Early one April morning, we found ourselves in this historic town, just two hours' drive from Indore. Walking along the banks of the river Narmada, we saw the crystal clean water. Wave after wave rose to greet the ghats (stone steps leading to the river) in a well-orchestrated symphony. Located along one side, rising majestically was a row of temples. Hundreds of stone steps led to the monuments which rose like sentinels above the river bank. What struck us most was the simplicity of the architecture. There was no gold, no silver, no tinsel. Miniature paintings, inlay work, Belgian mirrors, marble – the expensive ornaments adorning royal palaces and temples across the country were conspicuous by their absence. As far as the eye could see, it was just grey stone. And these stones were privy to the story of a woman, a young queen who charted a new life for the people of Maheshwar.

Ahilyabai was a simple girl from a town called Beed in Maharashtra. During one of his tours, the ruler of the Holkar state, Maharaja Malharao, spotted her at a Teej festival. Something about her youthful bearing struck the sagacious ruler, and he chose her to be the bride of his young son, Khonde Rao. She came as a child bride to Maheshwar in 1753. Some years later, Khonde Rao Holkar suddenly died, and Ahilya prepared, as was the custom, to ascend her husband's funeral pyre and become sati. But Malharao stopped her. 'You must live, my child. Maheshwar needs you,' he said. Thus, Ahilyabai Holkar became regent for her young son, and ruled from 1765 to 1795.

Gradually, the young queen began to get acquainted with the life of her people. After her morning prayers she would sit on the ramparts of her palace so she could meet her praja (people) and listen to their problems. The more she heard, the more determined she became that no one in her riyasat (kingdom) would be denied a decent livelihood. But how was this to be achieved? What could she do to ensure that her people had a source of income not just for a season or a year but forever? At that time, 167 km from Maheshwar was a town called Burhanpur, known for its rich tradition of handloom weaving. It was from here, and from the town next door, Mandu, that Ahilya brought skilled weavers. She made them set up looms in her riyasat to teach the art of weaving to the women and men of Maheshwar. Her people acquired the skill fast enough but what they needed now were beautiful patterns that would win the hearts of consumers for all time to come. Ahilya mulled over this morning and evening as she watched the Narmada flow beneath her palace, blue and clear, creating thousands of patterns with its waves. Narmada or Rehwa, as the river is known locally, is regarded as the 'Mother' because its fertile banks feed people throughout the year. It was from Rehwa and from her own deep faith that Ahilya finally drew inspiration.

The patterns created by the boisterous waves of the Rehwa were first etched on the stone steps and on the walls of her palace. Then Ahilya began to construct temples along the banks of the river. And on their pillars, walls, chhatris (domed pavilions), doors and jharokhas (overhanging balconies) were engraved stone flowers, animals, birds, waves (the Narmada lehar) and many other intricate designs. Neat horizontal lines ran in borders, and a unique design palette was created. Morning ablutions and worship at these temples took on a new meaning. People came to pray and returned with a unique benediction – a design for their looms from the temple carvings. These they replicated with great devotion and finesse in their weaves. Till today, one has only to pick up a Maheshwari sari and the designs woven on the pallu or the border can be found etched on some stone slab partially immersed in the mighty Narmada, narrating the story of this visionary queen.

We saw Ahilyabai's palace, her personal mandir (temple), and her gaddi (throne). There was a mark of simplicity in all her footprints. As we stood at the spot from where she must have viewed the flowing river, we learnt that there came a time when only twenty-five looms were left in the bustling handloom town of Maheshwar. Powerlooms produced cloth cheaper and faster. As the demand for handloom declined, the skills of the Maheshwari weavers had no takers. Slowly, the din of the looms began to fade; in the ensuing silence, misery and penury engulfed the people. Skilled weavers were forced to take up wage labour or migrate. As despondency grew, the Holkar family once again stepped in to save the people of their erstwhile riyasat and to keep alive the tradition of their dynamic ancestor. Richard and Sally Holkar created the Rehwa Society. While retaining traditional designs, this society introduced new concepts. They changed the customary nauwari (nine yard) sari to six yards. Sophisticated designs were introduced and exhibited all across the country. Orders began to pour in. A new brand for the Maheshwari weave was created under the banner of Rehwa. And, today, there are 1,500–1,700 looms in Maheshwar.

The weaving centre of the Rehwa Society is next to Ahilyabai's palace, just above the ghats. The centre opens into a beautiful tree-covered courtyard where several women work at the looms. This is one of the best instances we saw of Corporate Social Responsibility (CSR) during our travels. Over 60 per cent of the 120 workers at the society are women. Their children attend the crèche and the school run by the society in a large building next door. Meals and uniforms are provided. There is an adjoining health centre with doctors and visiting specialists for Rehwa weavers and their families. Every employee gets a two-room house and two looms. Most have been around for the last fifteen–sixteen years. They work from 10 a.m. to 5 p.m. and earn Rs 100–150 per day. When they retire or perchance grow disabled, they receive a monthly pension of Rs 500 to Rs 1,000. This means that the pricetags on Rehwa saris are high; the cost of providing social security is woven into them.

By the time we left the Rehwa Weaving Centre, the outside temperature was a scorching 45°C. Yet, even as the sweltering April heat sapped our energy, our hearts were filled with hope for the sixty–five lakh handloom weavers of India. For three years, some of our most disheartening moments had been spent with handloom weavers. In Varanasi (Uttar Pradesh), in Pochampally (Andhra Pradesh), in Kaithun (Kota, Rajasthan), in Berhampur (Orissa), we had seen misery and despair on the faces of weavers and their families. But Maheshwar offered hope.

We had first heard about Maheshwar from our friend Chinmay Mishra during a visit to Indore, a year back. We shared with him our concern for the dying handlooms. He did not share our gloom; he showed us *Tantuja*, a book he has written on the handloom tradition of India. 'If you want to see the real potential of handlooms, go to Maheshwar. Three decades ago there were less than twenty-five looms left there. Weavers put up their looms and began to migrate in search of work. Then, in 1979, the scion of the royal family, Richard Holkar, and his wife, Sally, started the Rehwa Society to give life to the dying weaves of Maheshwar. Today, there are 1,750 looms in Maheshwar and they are making everything – dress materials, dupattas, furnishings.' This was why, in the summer of 2007, we found ourselves sitting among the weavers and artisans of this temple town, which is famous also for its association with the Narmada Bachao Andolan (NBA).[1]

Against the distinct hum of an old air-conditioner, the weavers narrated their stories. 'I used to make the nauwari sari and sell it in Maharashtra. Gradually, the demand fell and I was forced to shut down my loom. I left Maheshwar and went to Khandwa where I worked for five years.' The

---

[1] The Narmada Bachao Andolan or Save the Narmada Campaign is a non-violent protest led by environmentalists, adivasis and activists like Medha Patkar against the Narmada Development Project that envisaged construction of thirty large and 135 medium dams on the river Narmada. Since 1985, the movement has been highlighting the displacement and environmental degradation that the project, particularly the Sardar Sarovar Dam, will cause.

speaker was an older weaver, Mohammad Shafi. 'Then Rehwa Society came in and everything changed. Earlier, I had one loom; now I have more than a dozen. Today, there are 5,000 people weaving in Maheshwar. In 1972, we got a wage of Rs 9 per sari, now we get Rs 150; two people can make one sari a day. I buy my own material so I earn more. Others do job work,' he said with a happy smile on his face. His story was endorsed by many others. The names changed but the mood was the same: celebrating their small successes.

'But all that we have gained over the years may be lost now,' said Tejpal, a weaver in his forties. 'The old foe is back with a vengeance. Now powerlooms are masquerading as handlooms. Earlier, printers from Bagh used our Maheshwari cotton. Maheshwari Bagh saris were the most unique product to come off the loom and the printing table. Now the printers are just buying powerloom cloth. Even if powerloom owners keep a large profit margin, their material is 20 per cent cheaper. So we are left with empty looms.' Others spoke about the perennial issue of yarn. 'We get cotton yarn from Coimbatore, zari from Surat and silk from Bangalore and China. But the fluctuations in yarn prices and delay in getting supplies is killing us. Come and see our difficulties for yourself.'

We got into our cars and drove a short distance to the weavers' colonies. Shaali Mohalla had twenty houses and 150 looms. In one of the houses we met a tall man wearing a dhoti and bunyan (vest) who introduced himself as Jiten Lal. He showed us around his house which consisted of four looms cramped into a single room. His children slept underneath the looms. Working on one of these looms was a lean middle-aged man in a white vest and a cotton dhoti. 'I am Shankar Rao Patre from Nagpur. I live here; my family is back in the village. I miss them but here at least I get to do the work that I love. I earn Rs 60 to Rs 75 daily from the seth (employer or loom owner). This is more than I could have earned elsewhere. At the end of the month I send a decent money order home.'

From Shaali Mohalla we moved to Malharganj and Mominpura. The first is a basti of bunkars belonging to the scheduled castes; the second is a Muslim mohalla (colony). The first thing that one notices in Mominpura is a huge, newly constructed mosque which is in stark contrast to the squalour of the surrounding basti. We spoke to the children playing in the dirt road skirting the mosque. Some of them went to school; others worked the looms with their parents. We learnt that this was a basti of jobbers, people who didn't have their own looms but worked on the looms of the prosperous weavers of Shaali Mohalla. Teji Ram, an elderly man clad in a dhoti, eyes hidden behind a pair of thick glasses, was one such job worker. He, too, had come all the way from Nagpur. He told us that he sat behind a loom in a small, windowless room all day and made dupattas for a daily wage of Rs 150. As we walked around Mominpura, we saw a semi urban slum – dwellings, out-of-school children, scrawny pre-schoolers and filth strewn everywhere. Yet the overriding destitution and the misery which grips the people of Varanasi or Bhadohi was mercifully absent. While it is true that all the weavers of Maheshwar have not become prosperous but even the poorest here are better off than their counterparts in other places. That is what draws workers from Maharashtra and Uttar Pradesh to this small town.

Leaving Maheshwar behind us, we moved to the famous printing centres of Madhya Pradesh. There were three towns on our agenda; all of them had once been renowned centres of chhapai or hand printing in MP. But their story was not a happy one.

The towns of Bagh and Kukshi lie in the neighbouring district of Dhar. On the Maheshwar–Kukshi road, our cars bounced and rattled. The sun was blazing and the land was parched. The first town we passed was Bakaner, after which we crossed the Gambhiri River to enter Kukshi. We were told that Kukshi used to be the main centre for hand printing and that the Gambhiri river was intrinsic to its fame. After placing the first drawing impress on the fabric, the rangrez (dyers) used to bring the cloth to the river. When it was washed in these waters, the copper sulphate in the river gave the cloth its characteristic black and red colours. The exact technique was kept a close secret by the masters. Their fame grew, and after a few years they were called to Bagh to train the karigars (artisans) of that town. In an ironic twist of fate, the master having passed on his skills to the student was forgotten. Today, no one remembers Kukshi. The student has eased out the master! The red-and-black distinctive print, born in Kukshi, has now become famous all over the world as the Bagh print! Even the people of Kukshi sell their produce under the Bagh brand name. Before Independence, there were 500 families that lived in the Rangara Mohalla in Kukshi; now only four are left. In summer, when the Gambhiri dries up, these families have to take their cloth 16 kilometres away, to the river Narmada.

Having seen the master, we proceeded towards the illustrious pupil. In less than an hour, we reached the river Baghini. Bagh gets its name as well as livelihood from this river. Printers wash their cloth in the river and artisans use its mud to make khaprail (roof tiles made of mud). In Bagh, we met Ibrahim, a master craftsman who employs 250 people. In his family this skill has been passed from father to son. He started working in 1980, and now gets orders from all over the world including Fabindia in Delhi. Some of the seasoned printers of Bagh are now diversifying into chiks (blinds), jajaums (cotton spread), rugs, cushion covers and dress materials.

It was in a small store on the main market road in Bagh that we met Govind Lal Prajapati, an elderly man wearing a loose kurta–pyjama and topi. He was sitting with hunched shoulders, training tribal youth in making wood blocks – the essential material for printing. He came from Pithapur in Gujarat. 'I started making blocks with my father at the age of eleven. By eighteen, I became a master. For the last twenty years I have been supplying blocks to the printers of Bagh,' he said. His cataract-afflicted eyes seemed lost in memories. With both his eyes affected, Prajapati cannot make intricate blocks with the same ease as before but he wants to pass on his skills to the youth. This is what had brought him all the way to Bagh. 'On an average, it takes four days to make a block which sells for Rs 1600; the cost of wood is Rs 250. Good money, but it is back-breaking work,' he said with a slight smile. The striking designs and colours of the bedspreads and the Bagh print on Maheshwari cotton saris made us happily empty our purses in one single shop. Then we proceeded to the third and final printing hub – Bhairavgarh.

Situated on the banks of the river Shipra, this basti was at one time a hand printing centre renowned for its use of natural dyes. It is said that printed cloth from here was exported by the East India Company. Today, there are few visitors to this village of 6,000. The central jail of Ujjain is located here and it was in these premises that the story of printing in Bhairavgarh began, almost two centuries ago. At that time, blocks were made of potato. Gradually, wooden blocks began to be used. Printing was taken up by

Muslim artisan families of the area and the intricate Bhairavgarh booti (motif of Bhairavgarh) shot to fame.

In the 1970s, when water in the Shipra ran low, there was trouble for the dyeing community. This was explained by Mohammad Ibrahim, an elderly dyer. He said that the Bhairavgarh method of printing using natural dyes was a complicated one; it took a long time to prepare the cloth and they relied primarily on the waters from the River Shipra. 'So when the Shipra began to dry, especially during the summer, we faced great difficulty. People began to use chemical dyes and tin chloride. With that we were able to print three hundred pieces in ten days; with the earlier method we barely managed thirty,' he clarified. 'The cost of the vegetable-dyed bedsheets was almost twice the ones that used chemical dyes. The last original Bhairavgarh print we saw was done in 1976. Now I am desperate to revive it but much knowledge has already been lost.' He shook his head sadly, only to be comforted by his young son. 'Abba, we will do it.' This brought a smile to Ibrahim's face. Suddenly he went into an adjoining room and came back with a beautiful single bedsheet. 'Let me show you what the original Bhairavgarh was like. After a lot of effort, we created this bedsheet,' he said. Transfixed, we stared at what could only be described as a piece of art, an heirloom. It was then that the magnitude of our loss actually hit us – this is what has died, this is what we have not cared to save. Heavy-hearted, we left Bhairavgarh. The excitement with which we had started our textile tour of Madhya Pradesh was beginning to wane. But we kept our fingers crossed, hoping that the last stop of our journey would change our mood.

In all our wanderings around the textile centres of Madhya Pradesh, Burhanpur was a name that kept coming up. We were told that our journey would be incomplete without a visit to this once booming town. Besides this, Burhanpur held another attraction for us. It is a town imbued with the history of Mughal rule. Emperor Shah Jahan had given it the title of Dar-us-Suroor (Door of Delight). His beloved wife, Mumtaz Mahal, was originally buried here; after the Taj Mahal was completed, her remains were moved to Agra. The city with almost one fifty Mughal and Farooqi monuments, famous for its temples, masjids and gurudwaras, is just 228 km from Aurangabad. Well connected by road and rail, it only needs tourist infrastructure like lodges, hotels, public amenities to become a tourist hotspot.

By the time we neared Burhanpur, it was evening. The sky had draped itself in folds of shimmering orange and red. Against this fiery backdrop stood a weather-beaten warrior keeping vigil from its lonely station atop a verdant hill – Asirgarh Fort. A little less than twenty km from Burhanpur, this fort commands a pass through the Satpura ranges connecting northern India with the Deccan Plateau. From 1388 till 1601, it remained a stronghold of the Farooqi rulers. Later, it was visited by two of the great Mughals, Humayun and Akbar. Today, even as dense foliage hides the ravages of time and human apathy on its facade, Asirgarh continues to welcome the weary traveller to the Deccan Plateau.

The first thing that struck us on entering the historic town of Burhanpur was its crumbling city wall. Built in the late sixteenth century by Adil Shah Farooq, this three km brick-and-lime wall surrounds the old town. Today, it has been broken in many places to make way for homes, shops, bus-stands and even passageways. Garish advertisements have been pasted and painted on moss-covered bricks. Garbage lines the wall; polythene bags foreground 400 years of history. As we contemplated the humiliation heaped on this venerable chronicler – the Burhanpur wall – by generation after generation of callous locals, we recalled yet another wall. We had seen it in a place called Khiva in Uzbekistan in Central Asia. Beautifully and painstakingly preserved, tourists from all over the world flock to see its grandeur. The Burhanpur wall is no less majestic than the Ichan Qila of Khiva. But in Khiva, people have pride in their heritage and their cultural emblem has rewarded them by bringing employment and much-needed foreign exchange. The same possibility exists in Burhanpur. Here, too, people who are in dire need of alternative livelihood opportunities could benefit a lot from the restoration of this wall.

The town of Burhanpur, with a population of two lakh (2001 Census), 30 per cent of them Muslims, was once famous for its handloom industry. Then, in 1935, powerlooms were introduced. Weavers bought old machines from Surat (Gujarat) and Bhiwandi (Maharashtra) and this handloom town soon became the 'Manchester of Madhya Pradesh'. Today, over one lakh people here depend upon the 30,000-loom industry. But time has robbed this historic centre of its sheen and significance, leaving behind a lacklustre town trapped in a cluster of urban slums.

We visited two of these slums, Nehrunagar, home to 12,000 bidi rollers and powerloom mazdoors (workers) and Hameedpura, a gram panchayat of 6,000 voters who work at powerlooms. People accosted us everywhere for basic amenities. Health, education, water, sewage, roads – there was nothing for them. In Nehrunagar, a slum located inside the walled city, disabled people, who had no pension, surrounded us; we saw sick and severely malnourished children who had never been examined by a doctor. We met TB patients who said that they took medicines 'only when we have money to buy them'. With the powerloom industry in a slump, most households here rely on the Rs 25 daily wage that comes from rolling a thousand bidis in eight hours. Khairunissa, a fifty-year-old salwar-clad widow with betel-stained teeth tugged at our elbows. 'All day, I roll bidis. These are my small madadgaars (helpers).' She pointed to her grandson, Mohammad Rehan, and granddaughter, Muskan. 'With barely enough money for food, medical treatment is impossible.' Children were running around barefoot in the filth; six-year-old Shiekh Imran and ten-year-old Yasmeen were selling boiled potatoes and amrood (guavas) from a battered old basket. Yasmeen, beautiful black eyes set in a dark-complexioned face of finely chiselled features, told us that she could earn as much as Rs 20 to 30 if she sat with the basket all day. There was no time for school. 'I have never stepped inside one,' she said, her large eyes turning to us with hope. Most of the other children in this neighbourhood were enrolled at the school but they did not attend because 'teachers are always missing'.

We saw the basti's Urdu Primary School. At 11 a.m., the midday meal was being served; a flowing liquid pretending to be dal with half-baked thick cold chapatis. It had been provided by the Nagar Nigam (Municipal Corporation). The children stood with outstretched bowls and plastic tiffin boxes. Distaste and disgust was written all over their faces, but for many this was their first meal of the day. Of the four teachers at this Urdu medium school, only one knew Urdu! The rest taught in English or Hindi. Toilets, mats, benches and even textbooks were missing though the Class 6 children had to pay Rs 50 and Rs 175 as maintenance and building fee. We called the local officers who had accompanied us and told them that the prevailing situation was unacceptable. All they could give us were assurances.

Hameedpura was slightly better off. Here the people worked on rented looms (they were too poor to buy them) and used them in their homes that doubled as work sheds. We went inside one of the houses. 'This is Mohammed Ramzan, powerloom weaver,' an official informed us. Ramzan, forty-five years of age, folded his hands in a humble greeting. 'I started weaving when I was eight; I never saw a school.' His wife, Razia Bano, and three children live in a one-room house which belongs to his father-in-law. Every bit of the space in the hut was taken up by five looms; a tiny stove was squeezed between two machines. 'I pay monthly rent of Rs 400 per loom. With five-six hours of daily power cut, my monthly electricity bill is Rs 1,500. Like most weavers of this area I make low-quality cloth, mostly for kafan (shrouds for the dead).'

His Marwari seth pays him Rs 1,200–1,400 in a week. After paying rents and bills, he has Rs 2,000 left to run his household every month. He is insured under the group insurance scheme of the Ministry of Textiles but due to a flaw in the design of the scheme, only Ramzan is covered. So, if Razia gets hurt while working at the looms, she will get no compensation. This is the story of most weavers in Burhanpur where families spend days and nights in the shadow of the looms, quite literally. Here, the din of the working looms is the only lullaby a child grows up with; she sleeps content in the knowledge that as long as the noise continues, she will not go hungry.

By this time crowds were milling around us. 'Our Hameedpura Gram Panchayat has a population of over 6,000 voters but we have no health facility, not even a sub-centre,' said a young man, perhaps a wannabe pradhan, who had become the crowd's spokesman. 'They are the only source of our medical care.' He pointed to two young men in jeans who were standing in identical tin sheds which were their clinics. They had set them up, side by side, to treat this mass of humanity. We spoke a few words of praise. They looked embarrassed. 'We have to do something for these people; they have nothing.'

Their words echoed in our ears as we left Burhanpur with a welter of emotions swirling inside us. Anger tempered with pragmatism, hope with despair. In these Muslim mohallas of Madhya Pradesh which have the highest incidence of TB in the country, we had witnessed the resilience of the people. Each time we saw a bright young girl, sitting in a cramped classroom, eagerly soaking in every lesson her teacher imparted, we rejoiced. As we visited one community-run school after another, meeting dedicated teachers and workers, the clouds of despair lifted. We bowed in spirit to these people; their ability to cope, and their determination to carry on with life despite being lashed by deprivation, administrative apathy and politically contrived communal flare-ups. And yet, we could not dispel the anxiety that dogged us. Yes, our people are resilient but there are limits to human tenacity. The occasional wave of suspicion that time and again ruptures our composite existence sometimes turns into a whirlpool of intolerance. How long would it be before the links that bind communities to one another snap?

The state highways of Madhya Pradesh are filled with signs of resurgence of cultural identity in the idiom of religion – women in burqas, men in namazi topis, signboards of Saraswati Shishu Mandirs.[2] Earlier, friends in Indore had told us how in MP, 'Muslims are not allowed to buy land, open shops or build houses outside demarcated Muslim areas'. We read slogans such as 'Hindu jagey to jag jagey,' (When the Hindu wakes, the world will wake) pasted all over the Muslim mohallas in Bagh and Kukshi. As we left the state, we could not help but worry about the consequences of this growing suspicion and widening chasm between communities. That was in June of 2007.

One year later, we discovered that our apprehension was not unfounded. On 3 and 4 July 2008, when Jammu & Kashmir was in the throes of the Amarnath crisis,[3] the repercussions were felt in faraway Indore. In the

---

[2]   The Saraswati Shishu Mandirs are a group of schools run by the Rashtriya Swayamsewak Sangh (RSS). The first such school was started in Gorakhpur in Uttar Pradesh in 1952. The education style in these schools is 'Hinduized' though children receive modern education along with instruction on religious texts like the *Ramayana* and *Mahabharata*.

[3]   On 26 May 2008, the Government of India and state government of Jammu & Kashmir decided to transfer ninety-nine acres of forest land to the Shri Amarnathji Shrine Board (SASB) in the Kashmir valley. This led to widespread opposition in the Valley. The J&K government sunsequently revoked their decision but the violence spread to other parts of the country and led to polarization along religious lines.

police firing and violence instigated by political mischief-makers, seven young boys were killed. Khajrana, Indore's biggest slum and the symbol of its syncretism, suddenly made national headlines. It was a month after these killings that we reached the water-logged gallis and mohallas of this urban ghetto. This was our second visit to Khajrana.

We had first visited this place in April 2007. Khajrana is a mini- township of 50,000 people spread over twenty mohallas. This is an area of stark contrasts; palatial homes of the rich Hindus and Muslims from the Patel community stand next to hundreds of jhuggis (huts), mostly of poor Muslims. Splendour resides cheek by jowl with squalour. The only links between the two worlds are the almost non-existent roads and ubiquitous garbage. Little wonder then, that, in 2006, when there was an outbreak of chikungunya in Indore, its first victims were from Khajrana.

Rising above the squalid houses is the splendid marble dargah of a Sufi saint, Shahenshah-e-Malva Hazrat Ghazi Syed Nuruddin Iraqi. Next to it is a 130-year-old Ganesha temple, Bada Ganapati, built by Maharani Ahilyabai Holkar, where devotees from all over the country throng to pay obeisance to the longest Ganesha idol in the world.

In Khajrana Hindus and Muslims live together, but in separate enclaves. As we entered the slum, we read the signs on the shops: Ganesh Kirana, Vishnu Footwear, Mateshri Jewellers, Rajyashri Chemists, etc. Past the Ganesha and Kali temples, the names changed; Abu Altamash Traders, Shakeel Cycle Services, Sabiha Tailors. Burqa-clad women were moving around in the bazaar on the Muslim side.

'This is Ashrafi Colony,' our young guide informed us. We went inside a small room which opened on to the street. A group of women were sitting on the floor. They had formed the Rahbar Mahila Mandal, a basti sangathan which used nukkad nataks (street plays) to initiate behaviour change and create awareness. The president, a woman in her mid-thirties, introduced herself. 'I am Shakila Khan. Most men in our area, Hindu and Muslim, are daily wagers. The women are domestic workers and reza mazdoors (piece-rate workers). Our incomes are abysmally low. We get Rs 5 for every twelve hundred glass gems we glue to ornaments. Our daily earning is no more than Rs 15 or Rs 20. A family of eight has to live on an average monthly income of Rs 1,500.'

Shakila then looked at the others. 'Why are you quiet? Speak up.' A woman in a red dupatta got up. 'In our Rajiv Nagar mohalla, the anganwadi worker has not been coming for the last four months. Nearby mohallas like Mayapuri with 150 houses and Jalla with 650 houses have no anganwadi centre.'

An old woman behind me asked: 'Shall I speak?'

'This is Bisso Apa from Baba ka Bagh,' said Shakila.

'Our trouble is that the anganwadi worker has shifted the children's centre away from us,' Bisso said.

'Why did she shift the centre?' we asked.

'Because she thought our area was too congested. She wanted an open location. But there are no children in the new area where she has moved, plus it is too far away for our children.'

We turned to the accompanying officials to demand an explanation but before we could berate them Shakila spoke up. 'Baji, these problems notwithstanding, we are trying to bring about a change in the health sector. When we started, mothers were too scared to bring their babies for immunization. There was just one nurse, queues were long and often no vaccine was available. We were desperate. So we divided the lanes among ourselves. Every Rahbar member is assigned thirty houses; she has to visit these and talk to pregnant women and young mothers. We now run monthly health camps with gynaecologists and paediatricians.' The women proudly told us that, since the project had started, health problems in the area had been reduced by half. 'We have learnt to work with the government,' Bisso Apa said. They said that the state government and municipal bodies had started listening to them.

Sixteen months later, when we returned to Khajrana, it was under very different circumstances. As we looked around, we wondered how the painstaking work of the Rahbar women had coped with the politics of hate. Outwardly nothing seemed too different, the physical impact of the 3 July violence was fading with every passing day. People were going about their daily routine, continuing with the business of living. But fear and suspicion, the residual debris thrown up every time the tide of violence surges, were still embedded in people's minds, ready to surface at the slightest provocation.

After trudging in the ankle-deep slush in which the colony was mired, we reached the two-room shanty of seventeen-year-old Imran, one of the seven boys killed in Indore during the two days of violence. His family of eight is yet to come to terms with losing their eldest son and sole breadwinner. Sitting on the floor in the bare room surrounded by her children and husband, Mehrunissa, Imran's inconsolable mother, clutched his photograph and a news clipping. She wiped her tears with the edge of her dupatta as she recounted how her son was killed by cops in front of his twelve-year-old brother. 'That morning, curfew was sounded at 11 a.m. Imran was rushing home when he heard some commotion. The next moment he was dragged down by two constables and shot inside his mouth. The following day, when we took out his janaza (funeral procession) the police beat up the mourners. Even our Hindu neighbours were scared to come for afsos (condolence).' With Imran gone, there is no regular income for this household. His grandmother, a frail-looking woman with a black dupatta draped over her head told us that she does not receive any pension; she has been declared dead in official records for four years now. His young brothers and sisters have never been to school. Imran's father, Rafiq, a thin, sickly man, used to work as a driver till he met with an accident two years ago. Since then, he has been jobless. These days, he is often unwell, and so unable to pick up the odd jobs that would get the family some money. The family has used some compensation money to pay off a part of the mortgage on their house.

Following the trail of devastation caused by the communal violence, we reached Juna Risala, a locality with 1,500 houses of Hindus and Muslims. Here members of both communities share everything, even the walls of their houses. They are privy to one another's joys and sorrows. On the day of the bandh, no violence had been reported from this area. A little distance away from this neighbourhood, on Subhash Marg, is a mosque called Safed Masjid. Trouble had started there. We sat in the house of one of the victims. The room was full of people. They were still trying to understand what made three police constables fire indiscriminately at a bunch of teenage boys on the afternoon of 4 July, killing three and injuring eight. Rizwanur Rahman was killed on the spot. His smiling photograph was on the wall. The first testimony was given by Salman Ahmed. 'The day after the bandh, when Indore was under curfew, stone pelting started around the masjid.

We were a group of fifteen–sixteen teenage boys, returning after jumme ki namaaz (Friday prayers). When we heard the chaos, we stopped to see what was happening. We saw some policemen running and thought they must be going towards the trouble spot. The next moment, however, they started firing at us. I got hit on my chest and arm.' As he spoke, eighteen-year-old Salman, a final year B.Com student from Christian Eminent College, showed us his bandaged arm. He told us the names of the three constables who opened fire – Neeraj, Jiten and Yashwant. Salman's story was corroborated by nineteen-year-old Irshad, who had been hospitalized for eight days, and nineteen-year-old Gulrez, who still had a steel contraption attached to his injured arm. One by one, the rest showed their injuries or recounted the pain. Seventeen-year-old Faiz, a student of Class 12, said he hadn't attended school for over a month. His father, Ijaz-ul-Hasan, was shot in the stomach and was bedridden despite two operations.

Rizwan's parents and elderly grandmother sat in an inside room and tried to put on a brave face but broke down when they showed us the photo album of their only son. Today, their life and many other lives in Juna Risala revolve around a single question: 'Why?' 'It wasn't communal violence,' said Sabra, mother of Rizwan, sobbing. 'Our Hindu neighbours shed just as many tears as we did.'

Ghulam Ahmad Khan, an elderly kirana (ration) shop owner with henna-dyed hair, emerged as the undeniable hero of Juna Risala. He defied the vicious bullets rained on fresh targets and saved many innocent young lives. With the help of three humane police constables – Dara Singh, Awasthi and Shukla – he took the injured to hospital and tended to them even as the curfew kept their families away. Today, a slew of cases have been filed against Khan who has offered himself as a witness in this case. He told us that when he took the injured to Rajshree Hospital in Bhoi mohalla, a mob of young boys with swords and saffron headbands surrounded him. 'I don't think any of us would have survived if the Maharashtrian women of the mohalla hadn't chased the boys away. These were Hindu housewives.'

We left Rizwan's home convinced that the violence of 4 July had aimed at creating hatred among the Muslims and Hindus. Luckily, most inhabitants of Juna Risala had seen through the ploy. They recognized the miscreants by their intentions, not religion or even profession. They applauded the efforts of a few helpful policemen. But other events were vitiating the restraint which they had exhibited so far. Cases being filed against the injured as well as witnesses, insinuations linking them to banned and reviled outfits and the impunity of constables who killed innocents; all this was taking its toll. We heard murmurs. 'Is this happening because we are Muslims?' In some parts of Khajrana, violent reactions had already been reported.

We were witness to one such outburst when we entered the home of seventeen-year-old Zeeshan. It was a rented jhopdi (hut) with a plastic sheet for a ceiling, next to a tiny masjid. Nizamuddin, Zeeshan's father, with henna-dyed hair and beard, told us the story. 'I work at the masjid. Zeeshan had just passed Class 10; he would have turned eighteen on 6 December. He was learning how to repair air-conditioners.' Mohammad Hanif alias Pyare Mian, standing near him, came forward. Zeeshan had been his apprentice. 'Hum sab Hindu Muslim hamesha saath rehte they. Par dekho Sahib, kameeno ne kya kiya. Hum bhi pathan ke bachche hain. Bandook nahi hai varna deekha dete.' (We Hindus and Muslims used to live together. But look what they have done. We are also Pathans. I don't have a gun, else I would have shown them.) A woman stepped up from the back of the hut. Zeeshan's mother, Salma. 'Main ne tinka tinka karke apni zindagi banayi thi. Sab khatam ho gaya. Khoon ka badla khoon. Mere bachche ko jisne mara voh azaad ghoom rahe hain' (Bit by bit, I made my life. Everything is over now. Blood demands blood. The people who killed my child are roaming free). The anger was palpable.

Juna Risala reflected the cycle of despair unleashed by communal triggers: justice delayed – justice denied–fresh injustice – more violence – more hatred, it is a vicious cycle.

We found instances of injustice in other pockets of this state. Our quest took us from Indore to the four-lane Bombay–Agra Road which links Bhopal to Dewas. Bhaurasa is the name of the village where a small NGO Garima Abhiyan dedicated to ending manual scavenging has been working. The village still has 350 houses with dry toilets which are cleaned by Valmikis (Hindus) and Helas (Muslims). Ninety-eight per cent of these scavengers are women. Their touch 'pollutes'; untouchability is practised not only against the engaged scavengers but also against those who have quit manual scavenging!

At the village, a large group of women was waiting. They were introduced as 'former scavengers'; Garima Abhiyan has empowered them to stop hauling human waste and find a new life and livelihood. The moving spirit of the Abhiyan is a young man, Asif. In the last two years 2,000 people, most of them women, have joined his movement. They spoke to us of 'rights and dignity'. Kiran Fatrol, in a bright pink dupatta, said she had started this work with her mother-in-law soon after she was married. 'We used to get one roti a day from each of the fifty households from which we lifted maila (waste), plus old clothes and Rs 5 at the end of the month.' But when she stopped and began to work in the fields, she was still considered untouchable. 'Earlier, our kids used to get scholarships but since the schemes were for scavengers, the money stopped when we gave up maila uthana (hauling human waste). For a full day's manual work, I get Rs 30. How can I send my children to school?' she asked.

Durga had a similar story to tell. All her children had to leave school after Class 6. One of them, seventeen-year-old Jyoti, was married; now she is six months pregnant. Khursid Bi, Shobha, Munni Bi and Sulochna – their stories were the same. Not only had their kids dropped out of school, they had also become child labourers. 'Only if a state official certifies that a woman has been scavenging for one hundred days does her child become eligible for scholarship. But since the MP government enacted the Manual Scavenging Act in 1997, no officer is prepared to testify that the practice still exists. Denial means double affliction for the women and children. 'In fact, it seems as if our schemes are designed to keep people in scavenging because if a woman stops, her children are no longer eligible!' Asif explained.

Women who have tried to move out of scavenging also face other problems. There is social boycott by the village and, at times, even by their own families. When, after fifteen years, Munni left scavenging her entire family protested. The Mali and the Thakur communities (who still have dry toilets) threatened her. 'We won't allow you to collect wood, draw water and work anywhere else.'

'It was tough,' Munni said, wiping her eyes.

'There is chhoot-chhaat (untouchability) at every step. Five hundred to seven hundred of us (Valmiki and Hela women) walk two km and queue for two to four hours to get water; there are several wells in the village but we are not allowed to draw water from them. Our children are not allowed to sit with the swaran jaatis (upper castes) in school. Barbers refuse to shave our men,' said Kiran, pink dupatta draped over her head. The rest nodded in agreement.

Till date, all the eleven urban areas in Dewas have manual scavenging; twenty-four rural areas also have scavengers. In addition to scavenging, thirty other menial tasks are assigned to the scavengers, all for zero payment. Hence the upper castes are reluctant to let them go. Free labour for doing dirty work is precious!

From Bhaurasa we returned to the town of Dewas. Scavengers from nine districts, Bhind, Chhatarpur, Neemuch, Mandsaur, Ujjain, Dewas, Tikamgarh, Shajapur and Sehore had gathered in the hall of a modest roadside hotel to tell their tale of deprivation.

'My name is Lalibai. I am from the village of Daira Kheri, Mandsaur District. I was married at the age of eight and forced to start scavenging when I was twelve years old. I got skin disease from the maila dripping on my face and hands. My children were thrown out of school. Three years ago, when I stopped, the Thakurs made my husband throw me out. My entire family was beaten up. The police took no action. I was not allowed to return to my family. When my daughter was about to deliver, I took her to the ANM; she was an upper-caste nurse, who simply refused to touch her body.' The speaker was a frail-looking middle-aged woman clad in a crumpled cotton sari. She had a stoic look but her voice shook with emotion as she spoke.

'Why don't you Valmiki and Hela women apply for appointment as ASHAs, ANMs and AWWs?' we asked. The women stared at us for a moment; some smiled and looked at each other. 'Bibi, to be hired as an ASHA or ANM, people have to pay bribes. So no Hela or Valmiki woman gets appointed to these posts. Women are hired from upper castes and they refuse to service our needs no matter what the emergency.'

Other stories began to tumble out. We realized that discrimination begins at birth for both the Valmiki and the Hela. They are not allowed to enter most hotels, temples, mosques. They cannot draw water from hand pumps; children have to carry their own plates for midday meals and are not allowed to drink water from taps. Most of the time, they are not allowed to wear slippers or to sit inside vehicles. Even the Manihars (bangle sellers) refuse to place chooris (bangles) on their wrists. When they do so, it is only after they have removed their shirts to avoid soiling the garment; once they have finished with their 'untouchable' customers, they wash their hands. Before attending higher-caste women customers, they bathe and cleanse themselves of the 'pollution'.

A woman had walked up to where we were sitting. 'You are from the sarkar (government) so let me tell you about sarkari yojanas (government schemes).' She was a tall, strapping woman in a yellow salwar suit. 'I am Yashodabai, from Tikamgarh. Even if we manage to get job cards under NREGS, we are not given work. I had received a patta (ownership document) for land given by the government but it was located inside the field of an upper-caste farmer. Every time I tried to go to my property, I was beaten up. Even our own elected members cannot help us. Our Dalit woman sarpanch from Marwa Panchayat is not allowed to attend meetings or call a gram sabha. The secretary takes decisions while she cleans the filth.'

Next, a male voice spoke from the corner of the room. 'I am Dev Singh from Dr Bhimrao Sansthan in Bhind. Our condition is the same. My district still has 150 scavengers; 147 of them are women. Pattas given to us are always grabbed by the upper castes, or the land is located inside the fields of Thakurs and we do not dare enter their fields. Three men from our village, Saddupura, near Khajuraho, who dared to do so were made to sit on donkeys, garlanded with shoes and paraded around.' Suddenly the room was silent. We looked for answers at a few junior officers who were sitting quietly. They were reluctantly attending the meeting only because of our insistence. They just shrugged as if to say 'this is not our mehekma'(department)!

Jayanti Agarwal was from Chhatarpur District, which still has sixty-three manual scavengers. 'In Jaitpur village, when the Pulse Polio campaign was on, drops were handed to a Valmiki girl. She was told to administer them to babies from her community; the woman conducting the campaign was fasting and did not want to contaminate herself by touching Valmiki children.'

Some men said that villagers threaten them saying, 'either you clean or you will be thrown out'. And these threats are not empty. Asif recounted an incident. 'In Chaipuri village, a boy who quit scavenging was banished; it has now been seven months and he cannot return. The practice is so ingrained here that not just Thakurs even the police station in Dewas had a dry latrine until we (Garima Abhiyaan) raised a hue and cry.'

The atrocities being faced by the women and men before us were shocking. But, for us, perhaps the biggest shock was to learn of a Muslim community of scavengers. We had never associated such practices with Islam. As a child, Syeda had been strictly told never to demur from drinking water at the hands of the women who came to clean the toilets of the house. But in MP as in some other states, caste had become part of the Muslim ethos. The Muslim scavengers here are called Hela. There are 30,000 of them in the region. Ali Husain, a smart young man in jeans and a bright t-shirt, had come from Ujjain. 'As a child, when I went to the masjid, the maulvi sahib sent me away saying "tumhari Amma latrine saaf karti hai, tum bhaago yahan se". (Your mother cleans toilets, you run away from here.) Not only do we have separate masjids and madrasas, our Muslim brethren do not even sit with us for Roza Iftaar. When my eighteen-year-old cousin died in an accident, for three days no doctor was prepared to do a post-mortem,' he recounted matter-of-factly.

An old woman stood beside him. 'My mother,' Ali said, putting an arm around her. Raisa Bi narrated the story of her thirty-five-year-old son, Yunus. 'He has six children, and has been diagnosed with throat cancer. He has no means to support his family. Bibi, I, too, have nothing. Since I gave up scavenging, I have no income. Sometimes I think I should go back to the same work. Else how will I save my son?' she asked, wiping her eyes.

We had read Mari Thekekara's book, *Endless Filth,* which is a chilling account of the lives of manual scavengers. And now we were seeing it with our own eyes. What had so far been academic knowledge had become a graphic reality. As we got up to leave, two voices rose above the din. 'At Shahjahanpur in Sundarsi Gram Panchayat, all village waste is thrown next to the Valmiki basti.' 'In the village of Vishniya in Mandsaur District, a cremation ground has come up right next to our colony. Every time a cremation is done, we have to leave the area for three days because of the stench and the fear of disease'. This was the last faryaad (plea) we heard from the Hela and the Valmiki before we boarded our car.

As we left Madhya Pradesh, we tried to understand the asymmetries that had unfolded before us during our visits. It is a land blessed and cursed in the same breath. It is the land of the visionary ruler Ahilyabai who ensured rozi roti (daily bread) for her people through temple carvings. At the same time it is also the land which continues to deny many groups of people the basic right to a life with dignity. The good and the bad – in MP, they cohabit. As the poet Iqbal said of life so also we can say of Madhya Pradesh:

Hai alam ka surah bhi jusv e kitaab e zindagi

The chapter of sorrow is essential to the book of life.

Postscript

I t has been seven years, seven packed years since we started this journey of ours, our gard and gardish (dust and movement). We had embarked on it with one lesson in optimism that we learnt long ago:

Safar hai shart musafir nawaz bauhtere
Hazaar ha shajar e saayadaar raah mein hain

The condition is to travel; there are many who love travellers
Thousands of shade trees line the ways

We saw her many faces, beloved country.

We know in our hearts how these journeys changed our lives. Every face we saw became our personal cameo. But you, our reader, would ask us what difference these journeys made to the people we met. In other words, have we, in these seven years, been able to bring about any change for the people to whom this book is dedicated? Reading the chapters you may well ask, 'You saw, you heard their stories, you experienced their pain and deprivation, loved their resilience and equally their *jugaad*, but then what? What did you do? Did you try? Did you have a goal? How close did you get?'

We would have liked to say that yes, we changed it all. That we didn't just observe and record but actually wrought change. The weaver of Kota, the

Jarawa of Andaman, the sex-worker of Benaras; all found a life of dignity because of what we were able to do. But that is not what happened. Even as this book goes to press, we read that the weavers are still struggling to survive, the Jarawa is still the subject of voyeurism, and sex-workers are still in the trap of their trade.

No, our dream world remained just that, a dream. The hope with which we began started waning. What sustained us, however, was the feedback on our visits that trickled in; phone calls and occasional news items. Somewhere in the dhanis of Udaipur, in the chars of the Brahmaputra, the bazaars of Bagh and Kukshi some lives were made more livable because we undertook this journey. A few Kathodi children were admitted to schools, a health centre became functional, a health insurance scheme for weavers was launched, handloom and handicraft clusters were announced.

Yes, some things did change, howsoever slow and small the change. It is these changes that have made every moment of our journey worth it. Malnutrition has not shown a dramatic decrease but we were able to place the Gadchiroli experience of reducing neonatal mortality within the policy framework of the health sector. Weavers' children are still quitting their ancestral hunar (skill) for garment factories but two superstars have gone on national media to salute their talent and urge the youth to make handloom the fashion statement. Disease and deprivation is still ubiquitous in many parts of our country but communities themselves are monitoring, reporting and demanding answers.

We believe that in these seven years we carried the unheard voices and unseen faces of India to people in the highest echelons of decision making. They have listened to us. We seeded a little hope in the people with whom we came face to face in the countryside and in the gallis and mohallas of bustling cities. Today we continue to hear from them, all hours of the day and night. They have reposed some little faith in us and, through us, in the system. And hope. Hope that sustains you in the darkest of nights when you sit beside a sick child, or crouch in fear of an animal attack, or quell hunger pangs. *Voh subh kabhi yo ayegi* (sometime that dawn will break). We feel we left in them just that kernel of hope to sustain them while we continue to look for answers.

The answers have begun to emerge. The National Rural Employment Guarantee Scheme, despite its flaws, has provided assured livelihoods; Sarva Shiksha Abhiyan, still crying for quality, has seen dramatic improvement in school enrolment. Howsoever riddled with defects, the National Rural Health Mission has registered its presence in areas where no health care existed. Peoples' ingenuity is being channelized and harnessed in the thrust that has been given to innovation. And nutrition, the much neglected foster child of health, has taken centre stage. We could go on...

When we started out we were impatient. We wanted the alchemist's stone to alter the properties of the base metal and exalt it to gold. Over the years as perspectives were gained we saw that our mission will only be achieved in slow motion, a lesson that we have learnt from the poet philosopher, Jalaluddin Rumi:

> Constant, slow movement teaches us to keep working
> Like a small creek that stays clear
> that doesn't stagnate but finds a way
> through numerous details, deliberately.

And so we keep moving, keep trying, keep urging the policy makers, the media and you, our readers, to listen to these voices of the voiceless. The lesson that we have learnt from the India we experienced over five years is that change does not always require numbers: one person can impact millions of lives; all it takes is one act, one idea, one dream, one voice...

The sum total of our experience and, let's say it, our love for our land is expressed in this couplet by Faiz Ahmed Faiz:

> *Chaaha hai isi rang mein laila e watan ko*
> *Tadpa hai isi taur se dil uski lagan mein*

> In this form we have cherished our beloved watan
> In this manner has our heart yearned in its longing.

Abbreviations

AAJVS: Andaman Adim Janjati Vikas Samiti, an autonomous body to look after the welfare and development of the PTGs in A&N.

A&N: Andaman and Nicobar Islands.

AFSPA: Armed Forces Special Powers Act (1958).

ANM: Auxillary Nurse Midwife. A multi-purpose health worker for providing primary health care.

ASHA: Accredited Social Health Activist.

AWC: Anganwadi Centre. The place from where the ICDS scheme is administered.

AWH: Anganwadi Helper. Each anganwadi centre has at least one AWH to look after the children and the anganwadi premises.

AWW: Anganwadi Worker. The AWW is responsible for the functioning of the AWC and all the programmes administered through it.

BDO: Block Development Officer.

CHC: Community Health Centre acts as a referral centre for the neighbouring PHCs. Covers a population of 80,000 to 1,20,000 and is equipped with 30 beds for indoor patients, operation theatre, labour room, X-ray machine, pathological laboratory, standby generator, etc. The centre has specialists in medicine, surgery, paediatrics and gynaecology.

DC: Deputy Commissioner.

DH: District Hospital.

DM: District Magistrate.

DOTS: Directly Observed Treatment, Short course (WHO recommended tuberculosis control strategy).

FHW: Female Health Worker, also referred to as the ANM.

ICDS: Integrated Child Development Scheme. (See p. 361)

IDA: Island Development Authority, set up under the prime minister in 1986 to ensure the ecologically sound, sustainable and integrated development of the Andaman & Nicobar and the Lakshadweep group of islands.

JFM: Joint Forest Management.

JSY: Janani Suraksha Yojana. (See p. 364)

KSY: Kishori Shakti Yojana. A centrally sponsored scheme to improve the health and developmental status of adolescent girls.

MCD: Minority Concentrated District. (See p. 364)

MCH: Maternal and Child Health.

MDM: Mid Day Meal. (See p. 362)

MHW: Male Health Worker. Functionary responsible for immunization and control of communicable diseases at the sub-centre level.

NGOs: Non-Governmental Organizations

NREGS: National Rural Employment Guarantee Scheme. (See p. 363)

NRHM: National Rural health Mission. (See p. 363)

OBCs: Other Backward Castes.

PHC: Primary Health Centre acts as a referral centre for six sub-centres and covers a population of 20,000 – 30,000.

PRI: Panchayati Raj Institutions. These are tiers of local self government created below the level of the state to promote decentralized development.

PTG: Primitive Tribal Groups. They are the poorest of the poor among the STs with (i) pre-agricultural level of technology; (ii) very low level of literacy; and (iii) declining or stagnant population.

SSA: Sarva Shiksha Abhiyaan. (See p. 362)

SDM: Sub Divisional Magistrate.

SC: Scheduled Caste.

ST: Scheduled Tribe.

Notes on Select Government Schemes

1.The Integrated Child Development Services (ICDS)

The Integrated Child Development Services (ICDS) Scheme was launched in 1975 as a comprehensive programme to tackle all the needs of children under the age of six – to improve their nutritional and health status, provide non-formal pre-school education, and reduce the incidence of child malnutrition, mortality and morbidity. It stipulates that every habitation should have an anganwadi centre (AWC) that provides hot cooked meals and pre-school education to children in the three-to-six-years age group. It also mandates take-home rations for children below the age of three and for pregnant and lactating women. Regular health check-ups, immunization, referral services and nutritional and health counseling are the other services provided through ICDS. The ICDS team comprises of Anganwadi Workers (AWWs), Anganwadi Helpers (AWHs), Supervisors, Child Development Project Officers (CDPOs) and District Programme Officers (DPOs). The AWH fetches small children from their homes, cooks, serves the food, cleans the Anganwadi premises, fetches water, etc. Duties of the AWW include, but are not limited to, providing pre-school education; maintaining records of pregnant and lactating women, adolescent girls and children; providing supplementary nutrition; assisting the ANM in immunization, de-worming and administration of vitamins and iron/folic acid tablets. ANMs and ASHAs visit the centre regularly to take care of health related functionalities.

As of October 2011, the scheme covers seven crore, fifty-seven lakh children and one crore, eighty lakh pregnant and lactating women through a network of 12.4 lakh AWCs across the country. For more information visit http://wcd.nic.in/icds.htm

2. Sarva Shiksha Abhiyan (SSA)

The Sarva Shiksha Abhiyan (SSA) is Government of India's flagship programme for achievement of Universalization of Elementary Education (UEE) in a time-bound manner. It is implemented in partnership with state governments to address the needs of nineteen crore, twenty lakh children in eleven lakh habitations. The programme seeks to open new schools in those habitations which do not have schooling facilities and strengthen existing school infrastructure through provision of additional class rooms, toilets, drinking water, maintenance and school improvement grants. Existing schools with inadequate teacher strength are provided with additional teachers, while the capacity of existing teachers is strengthened through extensive training. Under the SSA, the government is committed to providing a primary school within one kilometre of every habitation.

For more information go to: http://ssa.nic.in/

3. Mid-Day Meal Scheme (MDM)

The Mid-Day Meal Scheme was launched by the Ministry of Human Resource Development on 15 August, 1995 for the benefit of students in primary schools in 2,368 blocks across the country. Subsequently it was extended to cover all students of Class I-VIII in the government and government-aided schools. Under this scheme lunch is provided free of cost to school-children on all working days. This meal is expected to not just protect children from classroom hunger and malnutrition, but to also increase school enrolment and attendance, improve socialization among children belonging to all castes, and provide employment to women. It is the largest school lunch programme in the world.

For further information, visit http://education.nic.in/elementary/ mdm/index.htm

4. National Rural Employment Guarantee Act (NREGA)

Enacted in 2005, the National Rural Employment Guarantee Act (renamed as Mahatma Gandhi National Rural Employment Guarantee Act on 2 October 2009) is expected to enhance people's livelihood on sustained basis by developing economic and social infrastructure in rural areas. Implemented from February 2, 2006 through the National Rural Employment Guarantee Scheme (NREGS), the Act initially covered 200 most backward districts of the country. Later it was extended in two phases to cover all of rural India.

The Act guarantees 100 days of rural employment to households whose adult members volunteer to do unskilled manual work. Salient features include: employment on demand within fifteen days; minimum wages; payment within fifteen days; and basic work site facilities like drinking water, shade, crèche. If employment is not provided within fifteen days, an unemployment allowance has to be paid.

The Ministry of Rural Development is responsible for monitoring NREGS which is implemented as a Centrally Sponsored Scheme on a cost-sharing basis between the Centre and the States.

5. National Rural Health Mission (NRHM)

To ensure effective healthcare, especially for the poor and vulnerable sections of the society, the National Rural Health Mission (NRHM) was launched on 12 April 2005 for a period of seven years (2005-2012) throughout the country with special focus on eighteen states, viz., Arunachal Pradesh, Assam, Bihar, Chhattisgarh, Himachal Pradesh, Jharkhand, Jammu and Kashmir, Manipur, Mizoram, Meghalaya, Madhya Pradesh, Nagaland, Orissa, Rajasthan, Sikkim, Tripura, Uttarakhand and Uttar Pradesh.

The NRHM attempts to carry out necessary architectural correction in the basic health care delivery system. It adopts a synergistic approach by relating health to nutrition, sanitation, hygiene and safe drinking water. It also aims at mainstreaming the Indian systems of medicine.

The NRHM covers all the villages through village-based Accredited Social Health Activists (ASHA) who act as a link between the health centres and the community. It stipulates that one ASHA be trained from every village or cluster of villages to advise villagers about sanitation, hygiene, contraception, and immunization, to provide primary care for diarrhoea, minor injuries, and fever, to escort patients to medical centres, etc. In 2011-2012, the government allocated Rs 17,842 crore towards NRHM.

6. Janani Suraksha Yojana (JSY):

Launched in April 2005, the Janani Suraksha Yojana (JSY) is an integral component of NRHM that seeks to reduce maternal and child mortality by incentivizing pre and post delivery check-up and care. It offers cash assistance to women for institutional deliveries, encourages breast feeding and immunization. As of 2010-11, one crore, thirteen lakh women have benefitted from the scheme.

7. The Health Insurance Scheme for Handloom Workers:

Launched by the ministry of textiles in November 2005 in partnership with ICICI General Insurance Company, this scheme extends health insurance cover to handloom weavers and other ancillary handloom workers and their families. Eighty per cent of the premium is borne by the Central Government and paid directly to ICICI; the balance is paid by the weavers and/or state governments.

8. Multi-Sectoral Development Programme

To implement the prime minister's fifteen-point programme for welfare of minorities, the Government of India identified ninety minority-concentrated districts (MCDs) with poor socio-economic and basic amenities indicators. In the Eleventh Five Year Plan a Multi-Sectoral Development Programme was launched in these districts to plug the 'development deficits'. Under the scheme, each MCD receives Rs 15 crore or more to fulfil the needs of its rural and semi-urban areas. The aim is to provide drinking water, pucca houses, toilets and electricity to every household in these districts by 2012. The scheme focuses on improving living conditions and on providing livelihood opportunities by strengthening marketing infrastructure, credit, projects for skill training, providing high value seeds and veterinary facilities. Land and water management projects like check-dams, lift irrigation projects are also being taken up.

Acknowledgements

For seven years we have lived this book. Today it is real because of a few people who have been with us at every stage of this journey: Dr Mubashir Hasan, Zakia Zaheer, Chitranjan and Sarita Veda, Bimal Dimri.

We are grateful to Dr Montek Singh Ahluwalia for suggesting six years ago that we share the India that we saw. To Khushwantji we are beholden for prodding us, especially at difficult junctures.

Special thanks to Ruth Zothanpuii, ever cheerful companion year after year, for the long days and nights she spent on the details and to Ruchira Gupta for helping us find a publisher who would do justice to our dream.

Then there were wonderful friends who stepped in, at extremely short notice, to help us with all the art – Rima Zaheer, Iffat Fatima and Jitendra Pant. To Raza Kazim our gratitude for sharing his beautiful picture which became our cover and to Manish Chopra a big thank you for his creativity and patience with the last touches on the book. And salaams to our meticulous, sensitive publishers HarperCollins who understood all our aspirations.